WISDOM OF TWO

Wisdom of Two

*The Spiritual and Literary Collaboration
of George and W. B. Yeats*

MARGARET MILLS HARPER

OXFORD
UNIVERSITY PRESS

OXFORD

UNIVERSITY PRESS

Great Clarendon Street, Oxford OX2 6DP

Oxford University Press is a department of the University of Oxford.
It furthers the University's objective of excellence in research, scholarship,
and education by publishing worldwide in

Oxford New York

Auckland Cape Town Dar es Salaam Hong Kong Karachi
Kuala Lumpur Madrid Melbourne Mexico City Nairobi
New Delhi Shanghai Taipei Toronto

With offices in

Argentina Austria Brazil Chile Czech Republic France Greece
Guatemala Hungary Italy Japan Poland Portugal Singapore
South Korea Switzerland Thailand Turkey Ukraine Vietnam

Oxford is a registered trademark of Oxford University Press
in the UK and in certain other countries

Published in the United States
by Oxford University Press Inc., New York

British Library Cataloguing in Publication Data

Data available

Library of Congress Cataloging in Publication Data

Data available

Typeset by Laserwords Private Limited, Chennai, India
Printed in Great Britain
on acid-free paper by
Biddles Ltd., King's Lynn, Norfolk

ISBN 0–19–928916–6 978–0–19–928916–5

1 3 5 7 9 10 8 6 4 2

For George Mills Harper (5 November 1914–29 January 2006)
and Mary Jane Harper

Preface

The library of W. B. and George Yeats was housed for many years at the home of their daughter, the painter Anne Yeats, in Dalkey, a quiet suburb of Dublin that is now famous for its celebrity-studded exclusivity. Books and papers lined three walls of the room, and a picture window looked into a garden lit with bright flowers and the island's continually changing sky. The collection no longer has this setting; it has been bequeathed to the National Library of Ireland. Scholars cannot learn now what I studied there, while I was ostensibly on scholarly missions but in fact, I now think, conducting research into a sense of wonder, forgetting various doubts in the presence of Anne Yeats's delight in the world and how it might be expressed. I hope that this study retains some of that wonder.

I have wondered about the woman whose handwriting dominates the automatic script from my childhood. My father and mother spent most of the years I was growing up working with the Yeatses' occult papers, composing and compiling various books and articles along the way, and I tagged along, and then gradually helped with the *Vision* papers as the mass of folders and notebooks in the house of Michael and Gráinne Yeats in Dalkey became filing cabinets full of photocopies, typed transcriptions, the dissertations of four graduate students, computer files, and finally the four volumes of a scholarly edition. My progress through high school, college, graduate school, and the years since has had as a backdrop many hours sitting in my father's study, with its own three walls of books and one of plate glass looking out at a lush patch of north Florida woods, squinting through a magnifying glass at some indecipherable word or other, copying a diagram on to a page of typing paper (or, later, into a graphics file), noticing how 'automatic' one script or even one response seemed as opposed to another, reproducing the straight lines that indicated refusal to answer a question, and matching up pages of numbered questions with pages of answers. My interest in the part played by the woman behind the initials 'GY' that appear occasionally in the margins of the automatic script may derive from the fact that I was not a Yeatsian before I was a reader of the *Vision* papers, and so was not as predisposed as I might have been to look for the poet before I looked for the main writer of the manuscripts.[1] Perhaps being a girl interested in Latin and Greek played a part in sparking my interest in a young woman with a gift for languages and antiquities, and a penchant for esoteric study. I came of age while the modernisms of my father's circle of scholarly friends were shifting, reshaped under the pressure of ideas from influences like postmodern critical theory and second-wave feminisms, and certainly that circumstance also led me to this project. I came to see GY as a figure who entered, made a place for herself, and undertook creative work, with its own strong generational markers, in the context of strong personal, social, and aesthetic myths involving her famous husband and the various worlds he occupied, but in other contexts as well. At any rate, I believe I was watching out for GY's work before I knew I was on the track of anything.

The study that follows presents some of my discoveries. Readers will find no newly published 'lost' work in these pages; GY's great work is both irredeemably collaborative and fragmentary, more drama than document, although documents abound. Correspondingly, my interest is in the process no less than the products of the Yeatses' work. That process has much to say about WBY's creative endeavours and assumptions about creativity, and also about such matters as gender, belief, and selfhood. I approach the automatic experiments as a collaboration, an analytical point of view that allows me to view the influences that the script had upon WBY's poetic voice, imagery, and favourite techniques such as dialogue, as well as deeper structures like his characteristic emphasis on opposition (within poems or volumes

---

[1] For the sake of simplicity as well as the desire to emphasize roles rather than 'real' people in this study, I have chosen to refer to the Yeatses by the initials they inevitably used in the script, GY (*née* GHL) and WBY.

as well as between one and another). I am also interested in what the collaboration has to say about Yeatsian textual revisions and topics such as performativity or the relation of 'high' literary art to popular movements like spiritualism. Like any study of genetic materials, this one expects that analysing the process of writing, from first pen stroke to post-publication revisions, can shed light on the many published works that were made out of the documents at hand, both individual texts and also thematic, rhetorical, and structural aspects of WBY's late work generally. The additional issues that esotericism brings to the table—that host of 'instructors' and the many questions they raise, philosophical as well as cultural—make this study a bit unusual, and are its justification for wandering into more uncertain territory than is common in literary study. My hope is that this project, grounded in the historical specificity of one imaginative enterprise in the early decades of the last century, will contribute to ongoing conversations about authorship, partnership, gender, creativity, spirituality, and literary modernism.

M. M. H.

Acknowledgements

The road to this book was paved with support, beginning with the encouragement, knowledge, and loving wisdom of my parents, the late George Mills and Mary Jane Harper. The Yeats family, especially the late Anne Yeats, Michael and Gráinne Yeats, and Síle Yeats, have been unfailingly generous and helpful. I owe a special debt to Ann Saddlemyer, the definitive biographer of GY, who has always been available for advice, information, patient criticism, and encouragement. Of the many scholarly friends who have offered me assistance along the way, I can name only a few. I am particularly grateful to George Bornstein, Rand Brandes, Fran Brearton, Patricia Coughlan, Elizabeth Butler Cullingford, the late Richard J. Finneran, Anne Fogarty, R. F. Foster, Michael Patrick Gillespie, Warwick Gould, David Holdeman, Walter K. and Connie Hood, Clare Hutton, Edna Longley, Lucy McDiarmid, Gillian McIntosh, Catherine Paul, James Pethica, Deepika Petraglia-Bahri, John Rickard, Louis D. Rubin, Jr., W. Ronald Schuchard, Weldon Thornton, Deirdre Toomey, Helen Vendler, George Watson, and Clair Wills. Among the many students whose work has enriched mine I thank Joanne Baste and Christopher Blake especially, as well as Sabine Müller and Josephine Yu, student assistants whose help went well beyond the call of duty. My colleagues at Georgia State University have been unfailingly helpful, reading drafts and answering questions; thanks are due especially to Gayle Austin, Janet Gabler-Hover, Randy Malamud, Marilynn Richtarik, and Calvin Thomas. Friends who have provided encouragement, criticism, and material support (sometimes in the form of spare beds and square meals) include Barbara Allen and Leonard Reich, Eugenia Colina Bolado and Ciaran Dawson, Sue Buchholz and Mary McFarland, Randy Hecht, Currie Leggoe, Donagh and Lizanne MacArtain, Julie and Michael McBride, Claire Ní Mhuirthile and Pádraig Ó Duinnín, Larry Roddam, Tom Clyde and Gillian McIntosh, Gail Vogels and David Ray, and Fionnuala Carson Williams. My sister, Ann Christian Harper, is a never failing source of support, and I owe her much. Three wonderful young people have also had a part in the life of this project, and I love them dearly: Rayvon, Grace, and George Pettis.

A number of librarians gave invaluable assistance along the way. Dr Noel Kissane and Peter Kenny at the National Library of Ireland enabled me to work with the Occult Papers of W. B. Yeats, as Mr Kenny ably created an ordered collection from an office-full of boxes. I am especially grateful to them as well as to Tom Desmond in the Manuscripts Reading Room. Thanks are due also to Dr Stephen Ennis at Woodruff Special Collections, Emory University; Kristen Nyitray and F. Jason Torres at the William Butler Yeats Microfilmed Manuscripts Collection, Special Collections Department, Frank Melville, Jr. Memorial Library, at the State University of New York at Stony Brook; and members of staff at the following collections: the British Library, the British Library Newspaper Library, the Robert Manning Strozier Library at Florida State University, the William Russell Pullen Library at Georgia State University, the Berg Collection of the New York Public Library, the Library at Queen's University Belfast, Special Collections in the Morris Library at Southern Illinois University at Carbondale, the Special Collections Department at the McFarlin Library at the University of Tulsa, the Library at University College Cork, the Library at the University of Georgia, the Walter Royal Davis Library at the University of North Carolina at Chapel Hill, and the Warburg Institute at the School of Advanced Study in the University of London.

I am most grateful to the National Endowment for the Humanities, which supported this project with a fellowship, to the College of Arts and Sciences and the English Department at Georgia State University for research and travel grants as well as time away from teaching duties, to the English Department at University College Cork for providing a home-away-from-home institution for a year, and to the Institute for Irish Studies at Queen's University Belfast, which offered me a senior visiting research fellowship at a crucial time.

I would like to thank Jacqueline Baker, Production Editor at Oxford University Press, as well as the Senior Commissioning Editor, Andrew McNeillie, and the Assistant Commissioning Editors, Elizabeth Prochaska and Tom Perridge, for their unstinting labour in turning my manuscript into this book, a messy business that they transformed into an exercise in clarity and pleasure. I am also most grateful to Jean van Altena, who copyedited the text with expert precision and grace, to Carolyn McAndrew, a patient and exacting proofreader and to Christine Rode, Production Editor, who seemed to manage the unwieldy last stages of the process effortlessly.

Quotations from poetry, prose, plays, and unpublished writings of W. B. Yeats appear with the permission of A. P. Watt. For occult manuscripts, letters, and the contents of the Yeatses' library, I consulted documents in the possession of the Yeats family along with photocopies in my parents' home and at the William Butler Yeats Microfilmed Manuscripts Collection at Stony Brook. While this book was being written, the library and occult manuscripts were donated to the National Library of Ireland. Correspondence between WBY and GY will be available in a forthcoming scholarly edition prepared by Ann Saddlemyer.

Finally, this book owes its life to Rick Stoops, my beloved partner and dearest friend.

Contents

List of Illustrations

List of Abbreviations

Au	W. B. Yeats, *Autobiographies*, ed. William H. O'Donnell and Douglas N. Archibald (New York, 1999)
AV A	W. B. Yeats, *A Vision* (1925) (London, 1926)
AV B	W. B. Yeats, *A Vision* (1937) (London, 1937)
BL	British Library
CL	*The Collected Letters of W. B. Yeats*, gen. ed. John Kelly (Oxford, 1986–)
CVA	*A Critical Edition of Yeats's* A Vision *(1925)*, ed. George Mills Harper and Walter K. Hood (London, 1978)
E&I	W. B. Yeats, *Essays and Introductions* (London, 1961)
Ex	W. B. Yeats, *Explorations* (London, 1962)
L	*The Letters of W. B. Yeats*, ed. Allan Wade (London, 1955)
'Leo'	'The Manuscript of "Leo Africanus"', in Steve L. Adams and George Mills Harper (eds.), *Yeats Annual*, i (London, 1982)
Mem	W. B. Yeats, *Memoirs*, ed. Denis Donoghue (London, 1972)
Myth	W. B. Yeats, *Mythologies* (London, 1959)
MYV	George Mills Harper, *The Making of Yeats's* A Vision, 2 vols. (London, 1987)
NLI	National Library of Ireland (Leabharlann Náisiúnta na hÉireann)
VP	*The Variorum Edition of the Poems of W. B. Yeats*, ed. Peter Allt and Russell K. Alspach (New York, 1957)
VPl	*The Variorum Edition of the Plays of W. B. Yeats*, ed. Russell K. Alspach (New York, 1966)
W	Allan Wade, *A Bibliography of the Writings of W. B. Yeats* (London, 1958)
YA	*Yeats Annual*, vols. i and ii, ed. Richard J. Finneran; vols. iii–, ed. Warwick Gould (London, 1982–)
YAACTS	*Yeats: An Annual of Critical and Textual Studies*, ed. Richard J. Finneran (various places, 1983–)
YVP	*Yeats's* Vision *Papers*, gen. ed. George Mills Harper, 4 vols. (London, 1992, 2001)

Have I a third daimon apart from medium
Each had but after marriage only one between two

Have 2 beings become one
Yes not *inseparably* one yet

Can 2 distinct beings become one being
3rd daimons yes

Ameritus, through GY, 12 September 1919

Introduction: 'She finds the words'

WBY's personal library, as anyone might expect, contains a number of items that are 'his' in two senses: books he wrote as well as those he owned. Quite a few of the books by WBY in his library are the actual property of his wife.[1] Some of her volumes are sprinkled with editorial annotations from the ongoing processes of republishing and correcting his poetry and prose, tasks that GY undertook for many years before and, more controversially, after her husband's death.[2] Her name is written in his handwriting in a number of the flyleaves, sometimes with injunctions to himself: 'George Yeats her book not to be taken by me. WB Yeats'; 'George Yeats' copy not to be given away or taken to cut up or for any other purpose by me WBY'; or 'George's copy. I am not to take it whatever the need'.[3]

---

[1] Saddlemyer quotes from a letter from Lily Yeats to Ruth Lane-Poole, written after an 'invigorating and good' luncheon with her brother and sister-in-law, including a passage that is cautionary for an eager interpreter inclined to make too much of book-plates: 'They were playing with each other like hares in the moonlight. They were really putting book-plates into books and darting at each other to see if it was really his or her book. "Darling, that book is mine", George would say. "It's mine now", W. B. said, dabbing in his plate' (Ann Saddlemyer, *Becoming George: The Life of Mrs W. B. Yeats* (Oxford: Oxford University Press, 2002), 403).

[2] For criticism of GY's editorial efforts see Richard J. Finneran, *Editing Yeats's Poems* (London: Macmillan, 1983), esp. ch. 3, and Connie Kelly Hood, 'The Remaking of *A Vision*', in *YAACTS*, i. 33–67.

[3] I am indebted to the late Anne Yeats for permission to work in WBY's library. See Edward O'Shea, *A Descriptive Catalog of W. B. Yeats's Library* (New York and London: Garland, 1985), 2398a, 2430e, and 2397, among other entries. Connie Kelly Hood interprets one inscription, in *A Vision*, as referring to WBY's 'enthusiastic gift-giving of copies of the book' (Connie Kelly Hood, 'A Search for Authority: Prolegomena to a Definitive Critical Edition of W. B. Yeats's *A Vision* (1937)' (Ph.D. diss., University of Tennessee, 1983), 57).

Is the tone of such little messages simply generous, the inscription of gift copies of work completed after his marriage, with practical reminders so that one copy in the house could be kept separate from another? Is it patronizing, a great writer half-humorously warning himself not to let his appropriation of material overwhelm the rights of his wife to her own books? Perhaps it is thoughtful, a reminder by someone who was unmarried until relatively late, unused to maintaining boundaries with another person in his domestic life, to be careful with her property. It might be a professional reminder not to let anything happen to copies being corrected for revised editions. It could be strategic, a string around the finger of an over-generous man not to give away heedlessly something that might already have been given. Or perhaps it is a response to a message from GY of which we have no trace. If the last, then further questions arise: was she commanding or requesting, hinting or being overtly judgemental, in wanting her books to remain safely her own? Her attitudes are even further from the historical gaze of interested parties than his, and his are unrecoverable.

Does such a small detail matter? Surely interpreting inscriptions in books is not a terribly important activity. These little bits of writing are a fairly insignificant field in the large estate of literary history.[4] Nevertheless, I would like to think of them as small emblems for the study that follows. GY's surname was bestowed on her by her husband, without whose fame she would have none. He has insured its survival over space and time, as the books in the library endure past the lives of their owners. Equally, though, her name written in the pages of these volumes marks them as her property. His books with her name in the flyleaves are hers, and his writing is hers as well, to the extent that his words bear traces of messages from her,

---

[4] Or perhaps not. As Roger E. Stoddard notes, 'Books no less than tools, apparel, and habitats can show signs of wear, but their markings can be far more eloquent of manufacturing processes, specific of provenance, telling of human relations, and suggestive of human thought. The book may be humankind's most complex tool, so it is potentially the most evidenciary' (Roger E. Stoddard, *Marks in Books, Illustrated and Explained* (Cambridge, Mass.: Houghton Library, Harvard University, 1985), 1).

unreadable and invisible except through the work of WBY. They are available only as mediated through his language and sensibilities. If we want to study what she may have thought and said, we need to study what he did.

I began, and this project begins, where the accounts of the strange collaboration between WBY and his bride Georgie, or George, Hyde Lees usually end.[5] The story goes something like this: in the autumn of 1917, after years of frustration in both romantic and religious questing, WBY found a good measure of fulfilment in both realms. He gave up hope of marrying either Maud Gonne McBride, the woman whom he had desired, of whom he had despaired, and about whom he had made love poetry for decades, or her daughter Iseult Gonne, the subject of a messy emotional interlude that had begun the previous year. A quick turn led WBY again to GY, a young member of his British set, who was connected through her mother with Olivia Shakespear, an old and intimate friend. GY, who had been interested when the poet had approached her several years earlier, returned the attention. The two were well matched in intelligence and strength of will, as well as artistic and spiritual inclinations, though the age difference was sharp. She was a member of a new generation: among her close friends were Shakespear's daughter Dorothy and, through her, Dorothy's husband, the urgent American, Ezra Pound.

For several years, WBY had been reactivating his search for spiritual comprehension, which had received a series of setbacks beginning with the fracturing of the Hermetic Order of the Golden Dawn early in the new century.[6] His mode was shifting, though. After renewing his serious interests in astrology, he was now gravitating toward

[5] It is unclear who chose the given name George to replace the diminutive with which she was christened: it may have been GHL herself, or possibly Ezra Pound; certainly her husband liked George (even going so far as to rhyme with it) (Saddlemyer, *Becoming George*, 5). In his informative web site, Neil Mann suggests that there may have been numerological reasons for the change (Neil Mann, *The System of W. B. Yeats's* A Vision (17 Oct. 2004); <http://www.yeatsvision.com>).

[6] See George Mills Harper, *Yeats's Golden Dawn: The Influence of the Hermetic Order of the Golden Dawn on the Life and Art of W. B. Yeats* (London: Macmillan, 1974) for a full account of the magical order, including the crisis of 1900–1.

spiritualism[7] and psychic research, and lessening his involvement with ritual magic and the fellowship of other practitioners.[8] GY, although a member of the Golden Dawn, was also pursuing other occult studies, including astrology and historical hermeticism as well as spiritualism. She was unsettled by the War and had sustained losses in her family; he was trying to break himself of the habit of falling in love, or mistaking pity for love, with Gonne women, and working also to come to terms with the Irish Rising. By 1917, she was ready to commit herself to a risky chance at happiness with a husband who seemed challenging enough to suit; he was convinced that an *annus mirabilis* was in his stars, if he could but grasp it. They both may have been right: as it happened, challenge, revelation, and a measure of happiness were both finally at hand.

After initial difficulties that threatened to destroy the new marriage along with the psychic well-being of both partners, by the end of the year all seemed thrillingly well. The turn came in the midst of a traumatic honeymoon, when WBY was physically ill and near emotional breakdown, caused in large part by the sense that he had made a potentially ruinous mistake. During the crisis, GY tried and succeeded in producing automatic writing, a type of mediumship well known in spiritualist circles, in which the writer touches a pen to a sheet of paper and empties her mind as if she were engaging in formal meditation. Inexplicably, sometimes the pen moves. This is

---

[7] Spiritualism, an energetic religious movement that claimed to be a new and scientific form of Christianity, swept the United States, Great Britain, and parts of continental Europe beginning in the mid-nineteenth century and waning early in the twentieth (with a late resurgence during and immediately after the Great War). For the sake of simplicity, its doctrines may be reduced to two: the continuance of the human personality after death (whether through one or many incarnations) and the ability of human spirits to communicate from beyond the grave through sensitive individuals in this world. See Saddlemyer, *Becoming George*, 52–4, for a brief summary of the movement, as well as a distinction made in some circles between *spiritualism* and *spiritism*, the latter more popular in continental Europe and especially Brazil.

[8] This is not to say that his interests in magic faded altogether; e.g., in a letter written to WBY in April 1917, Iseult Gonne responds encouragingly to a recent discussion, 'I am so interested in what you tell me about your order' (A. Norman Jeffares, Anna MacBride White, and Christina Bridgewater (eds.), *Letters to W. B. Yeats and Ezra Pound from Iseult Gonne: A Girl That Knew All Dante Once* (London: Palgrave, 2004), 78).

the moment of mystery, the moment that, in retrospect as well as on the immediate occasion, may provoke either ridicule or true belief. It has done both as the tale of the automatic writing has been told and retold in Yeats studies. For the Yeatses, the mysterious event caused neither full-blown belief nor dismissal. Rather, it impelled them to further investigation. The writing, and the almost obsessive inquiry, lasted for several years of almost daily work, during which messages purporting to be from disembodied communicators from realms of spirit brought thousands of bits of information, information that was questioned, trusted, distrusted, and elaborated upon. Gradually, it coalesced into a philosophic and religious 'system', which WBY eventually compiled in his strangest book, *A Vision*. The work lessened in intensity during the mid-1920s, when WBY's writing of *A Vision* seemed well in hand, and the couple settled into a companionable partnership; but they resorted to automatic writing well into the next decade, if only to check on a stray detail for the book or its revised version. GY tired of the activity before WBY; besides the ongoing occult work, she was rearing children, acting as secretary, bookkeeper, and nurse to her often ill husband, and organizing any number of household moves. Automatic writing is hard on its practitioners: that it was potentially dangerous was a commonplace in the contemporary spiritualist press. 'Much power is needed for this work,' one source explains, 'and it is drawn from the mediums themselves and not from the spirit people. I speak of physical power—not mental—and only those whose health is good, and whose body is strong, should ever attempt this work.'[9]

At first, GY wrote seemingly disconnected words and phrases, for the most part in large rounded letters sloping down sheets of

[9] The author is presumably William Morris, an authority on the value of life-affirming work, speaking through the medium May Hughes. His practical advice from beyond the grave continues: 'Those who are weak, or unfit, will find themselves much depleted after an hour of writing and will, in time, become sick and ill. Do not allow a friend from the spirit side to use you for this form of communication for more than fifteen minutes at a time, and never when the vitality is impaired by sickness, or ill health of any kind' ([May Hughes], *From Heavenly Spheres: A Book Written by Inspiration from William Morris; Poet, Socialist and Idealist Who Passed on—October 3rd, 1896* (London: Rider, n.d.), 73).

paper, a far cry from her normally neat and angular hand. On one of these sheets, a large word 'NO', a response to a question presumably spoken by her husband, is followed by a prophetic sentence: 'I give you philosophy to give you new images you ought not to use it as philosophy and it is not only given for you—.'[10] The philosophy that arrived did indeed provide WBY with images, a wealth of them, which he used in his creative work for the rest of his life. No one has yet devoted a critical study to these 'images' (and ideas), and that task is one purpose of this study. The final phrase of this early message is also important. From the outset, the philosophy was 'not only given for you', meaning that it was given for both participants: the man asking the questions and the woman writing down the answers. It was given for them together, and, later, for their children as well (although the weight of the information is about WBY's life rather than GY's, an important aspect of the pattern of this union of public writer to reticent wife). The study that follows is not particularly biographical, but it does take the position that an analysis of the automatic experiment must recognize how inextricably personal as well as abstract the Yeatses' project was. In fact, part of the genius of that project is its determined blend of daily activity and intellectual or imaginative structures. Two word-loving occultists had rushed into marriage, and they came to know each other, build their joint lives, and justify them in an oddly appropriate way: through psychomantic writing.

---

[10] The first scripts had been assumed to be lost. However, I suspect they are the ten sheets of manuscript filed amid drafts of the introduction to the 2nd edn. of *A Vision* (in which WBY misquotes the phrase 'to give you new images' in his famous version of the story) (NLI MS 36,260/4; see also *CVA* Notes 3). The Introduction recalls:

On the afternoon of October 24th 1917, four days after my marriage, my wife surprised me by attempting automatic writing. What came in disjointed sentences, in almost illegible writing, was so exciting, sometimes so profound, that I persuaded her to give an hour or two day after day to the unknown writer, and after some half-dozen such hours offered to spend what remained of life explaining and piecing together those scattered sentences. 'No,' was the answer, 'we have come to give you metaphors for poetry.' (*AV B* 8)

Beginning on 5 November 1917, the automatic sessions were carefully dated and identified as to which of the many spirit 'communicators' was speaking, as well as the precise location in physical reality. As the couple moved from the Ashdown Forest Hotel, where they spent their honeymoon, to other homes and temporary lodgings, in Ireland, England, and elsewhere, they took their esoteric work with them. The communicators came along, in all their varied glory: controls, guides, mendacious frustrators, secondary personages from other lifetimes, and behind them other spirits, daimons, and a whole complicated array of presences or essences. Reading the documents, one cannot but be impressed at the Yeatses' extraordinary diligence in sorting it all out.

As time went on, they found ways to make their work more efficient. The script almost always retains some free-flowing discourse, for the most part at the beginnings of sessions. However, as time passed, an increasingly urgent need to organize makes itself felt. The Yeatses numbered questions and answers, and worked to have the messages give them the information they needed, pressing for complete answers or suggesting topics, especially once the foundations of the system were in place and the couple were looking for details to fill in charts, lists, or ideational symmetry. After the first fortnight, they recorded questions in one book and answers in another. The questions are now in WBY's hand, suggesting a refinement that presumably saved GY from having to shift gears from one mental state to another as she took down phenomenal questions and then waited for noumenal answers. As the months passed, WBY often wrote the questions down. GY's automatic handwriting also altered. In script from early sessions, large rounded letters that are very unlike her ordinary hand underscore the alterity of the automatic state, but as the supernormal experience became increasingly integrated into the Yeatses' 'normal' lives, GY's automatic hand came to look no different from the one she used to write letters or make notes.[11] Sometimes,

---

[11] The changes in handwriting co-occur with the change in her title from 'medium' to 'interpreter'; see Ch. 2 below for more discussion of this point.

though, GY remained both automatist and scribe. She was also typist, diagrammist, and co-'codifier' as the amount of script became large enough to be unmanageable without efforts to summarize, describe, and arrange the elements of the underlying 'system' that the partners believed from very early on to underlie the individual messages.

Beginning in 1920, the various methods of reception underwent a major change, as WBY recorded in a notebook, under the heading 'New Method': 'George speaks while asleep' (*YVP*iii. 9).[12] In fact, this 'new method' involved a number of methods, all involving GY in a sleep-like state, during or after which she would speak.[13] Later, she or WBY would write down what they recalled, or they would have a conversation that elaborated on the ideas consciously. They also experimented with discussions of dreams, joint meditations, or even, 'now & then', revelations 'from vision' (*YVP*iii. 75). The communicators were by now felt to be present in the Yeatses' daily life as well as the automatic one, and messages crossed paths through waking and sleeping states. For example, a notebook entry in GY's hand, from the same spring of 1920 when the first change in method was tried, notes that the communicator would now use the couple's rereading to further his own formulations: 'There was to be a new method. We were to read over sleep accounts & Dionertes would then develop the subject' (*YVP*iii. 21). This discussion continues with an argument about whether this development would occur over many days or in one exposition ('no no no I said I would write *in*

---

[12] When referring to the *Vision* papers I most often quote directly from the published edition, but I have occasionally substituted other transcriptions from the manuscripts which better preserve the appearance of the script and notebooks. In either case, many vagaries of punctuation, spelling, and other mechanics are preserved.

[13] The state seemed like sleep in this realm but waking in the other, the Yeatses learned in one of many messages that suggest the complicated levels of consciousness as well as relationship and authority that were presumably at play. On 1 July 1920, according to an entry in GY's hand from the notebook of 'sleeps' which they were keeping, the message was cut short because, according to the control Ameritus, the 'Interpreter went to sleep. Meaning of course that *he* found her asleep, instead of merely sleeping to me, waking to him. He then explained that when she turned away from me she could no longer hear him. This was because she associated him with me. I asked if he came more through me than her. He said no' (*YVP*iii. 28).

once the entire subjective after life state', the voice insisted). These new methods, perhaps appropriately, as they increasingly blurred the lines between normal and supernormal states, were accompanied by physical signs like smells and sounds, from flowers and burnt feathers to whistles and trumpets.

By the end of the experiment, the Yeatses had spent years working devotedly to take fragmentary pieces of data and assemble them into a system to explain truths about the universe, history, and individual lives—not to mention how the mysterious communicators themselves might be explained. Despite attempts (such as the sleeps) to ease some of the burden of the automatic writing, GY was often overloaded. For her, the end of the affair was as exhausting as the beginning, though it had provided fascinating productivity and a successful creative and conjugal partnership. For her husband, the years of intense concentration on the occult system had also resulted in a number of poems, plays, and expository prose, not to mention a systematic philosophy that sustained him for the rest of his life. WBY recalled much later, in the words of a poem, his 'Gratitude to the Unknown Instructors' and their redemptive system: 'What they undertook to do/They brought to pass' (*VP* 505).

Despite the monumental status of WBY as a literary and historical figure (and because of that status, among other reasons), the part played by his mediumistic wife in some of his most important works and ideas tended for many years to be understated or misrepresented, although the publication of Saddlemyer's definitive biography is doubtless changing matters for the better.[14] It has generally been known that GY was the source for many of the ideas that occupied her husband's time and creative energy in his astonishingly productive late years, and it is also no secret that she was a woman of dauntingly independent intelligence;[15] yet she and

---

[14] Saddlemyer, *Becoming George.*

[15] Aside from the voluminous automatic script, relatively few autographs of GY have been published, but witness the letters to her friends Dorothy Shakespear and Ezra Pound (Ann Saddlemyer, 'George, Ezra, Dorothy and Friends: Twenty-Six Letters, 1918–59', in *YA* vii. 4–28), as well as the record contained in the Pound–Shakespear

her work remained occluded in Yeats studies.[16] This indistinct-
ness has long interested me. GY has tended to be overshadowed
in Yeats studies and the popular imagination by other influential
women like Maud Gonne MacBride and Lady Gregory. Many readers over the years have assigned GY biographical importance but
little literary relevance other than the oddity of having functioned
as medium in the occult revelations that she and her husband
received. In turn, the spiritual knowledge that the Yeatses believed
they gained through automatic writing and other related methods
is often acknowledged for having inspired certain poems and plays,
but tends not to be interpreted as having much critical value. Yet
the famous Irish poet and his work were both changed utterly by
a young Englishwoman with magical interests, a gift for automatism, and a quietly imposing intelligence. As Terence Brown puts
it, since the start of the script, 'Yeats's own creative work had been
increasingly dependent on a collaborative engagement with his wife's
mediumistic powers.'[17] Her work affected his, most profoundly in
the 1920s and 1930s, decades during which he produced his best
writing.

GY hid her labours from public view. In fact, especially in the
years between WBY's death in 1939 and her own in 1968 she was
one of the most powerful makers of the myth of WBY that ignores
her. She hand-picked the scholars who would write about material

correspondence: Omar Pound and A. Walton Litz (eds.), *Ezra Pound and Dorothy
Shakespear: Their Letters 1909–1914* (New York: New Directions, 1984).

  [16] This situation has been changing in the last decade or so. Besides Saddlemyer, see
Terence Brown, *The Life of W. B. Yeats: A Critical Biography* (Oxford: Blackwell, 1999);
Brenda Maddox, *George's Ghosts: A New Life of W. B. Yeats* (London: Picador–Macmillan,
1999), published in the USA as *Yeats's Ghosts: The Secret Life of W. B. Yeats* (New York:
HarperCollins, 1999); and David Pierce, *Yeats's Worlds: Ireland, England, and the Poetic
Imagination* (New Haven and London: Yale University Press, 1995). See also Bette
London, *Writing Double: Women's Literary Partnerships* (Ithaca, NY: Cornell University
Press, 1999), 179–209; and Frances Wilson, *Literary Seductions: Compulsive Writers and
Diverted Readers* (London: Faber, 1999), 219–26. My own 'The Medium as Creator:
George Yeats's Role in the Automatic Script', in *YAACTS* vi. 49–71, and 'The Message
is the Medium: Identity in the Automatic Script', in *YAACTS* ix. 35–54, also argue for
GY's importance as collaborator of the system and its assumptions.

  [17] Brown, *Life*, 261.

in her possession, and supervised what they saw with great care.[18] In particular, she kept unpublished and for the most part unseen the more than 3,600 pages of the automatic script and related documents stored in a chest in her house on Palmerston Road in the Rathmines section of Dublin.[19] These papers reveal her making of the system, the hybrid of psychological, astrological, geometric, historical, and spiritual theory that lies behind *A Vision* (1925 and 1937).[20]

She was anything but a passive medium during the proceedings, a supposedly empty vessel whose hand was guided across the page by 'controls' from the other world. Such a highly idealized figure, derived from the popularization of the spiritualist movements of the nineteenth century in North America, England, and elsewhere, was common. However, the Yeatses were too familiar with the large and varied bodies of writing about and direct experience of spiritualism, which regularly tried to counteract this stereotype, to be determined by it.[21] Their practice was at least as informed by notions of joint

[18] See Saddlemyer, *Becoming George*, ch. 21, 'Seekers and Friends', for a discussion of GY's role in the first generation of Yeats scholarship following the poet's death in 1939.

[19] Before the publication of the *Vision* papers, the most careful attempt to go through the holographs and typescripts was made by Curtis Bradford (he recounted his experience in the essay 'George Yeats: Poet's Wife', *Sewanee Review* 77, (1969)). Stacks of manilla envelopes representing attempts at sorting fell into disarray from years of handling and duplication. Before the papers were donated to the National Library of Ireland in 2000, the envelopes comprised a sort of textual-archaeological site, with strata deposited by various scholars who had studied the manuscripts inside them. Along with the handwriting of WBY and GY appeared that of Bradford, Richard Ellmann, Kathleen Raine, and George Harper, among others. See Hood, 'Search for Authority', 100–2.

[20] The 1925 edition was actually sent to subscribers on 15 Jan. 1926, although the colophon is dated 1925 (W 149).

[21] In 2005, a search under *Spiritualism* in the British Library catalogue resulted in 685 hits for books and journals printed in English before 1975. A number of these are guides to the practice, and they routinely offer advice similar to that of E. W. and M. H. Wallis, *A Guide to Mediumship, and Psychical Unfoldment* (London: Friars Printing Association, [1903]). Part 2 of the guide, 'How to Develop Mediumship', is firm on the topic of passivity, asserting that a medium should 'intelligently cooperate with, rather than render blind obedience to, the spirits':

We unhesitatingly affirm that it is not necessary that mediums should regard themselves as mere 'conduits' through which the spirits are to pour just whatever they choose. Nay, we go further, and claim that if mediumship is to be lifted above the plane of mere

adeptship, including the idea of an occult marriage. The Yeatses'
sense that they were chosen to accomplish profound spiritual work
together is echoed in a number of variants in occult tradition on
the idea of superhuman agents working with a couple or group of
human recipients, whose power would thus be greater than that
of someone working alone.[22] Their daily ritual of writing together
quickly assumed a form of its own, with unique patterns of questions
and responses, the development of intricate relationships among the
personalities of the participants (the human partners as well as their
many spirit collaborators), and increasingly subtle considerations of
the facets of their personalities and conscious or subconscious minds
that were causing the ideas and images of the system to emerge. The
system was not, in the words of the control and the guide[23] for 9
April 1919, 'pre-existant in anima mundi', that is, already formed in

sensationalism, mediums must study their own powers, and learn how to provide the
conditions requisite for their own unfoldment, so as to exercise a determining influence
over the results and share the responsibilities as well as the pleasures and spiritual benefits
accruing from the co-operative association. (p. 111)

[22] WBY stresses the importance of the magical convocation in his ill-fated essay 'Is the
Order of R.R. & A.C. to remain a Magical Order?', written to prevent the fragmentation
of the Golden Dawn in 1901 (G. M. Harper, *Yeats's Golden Dawn*, 259–68). Prominent
among the examples of an occult marriage were the fourteenth-century couple Nicholas
Flamel and his wife Pernella, whose alchemical successes had witnessed a revival of
attention, especially in France, since the eighteenth century. WBY used their story
(sometimes confusing it with the romantic legends associated with the thirteenth-century
Raymond Lully) as a symbol of the relationship he hoped for between Maud Gonne
and himself, in the Cuala Press edition of *The Green Helmet and Other Poems* (1910);
see G. M. Harper, *Yeats's Golden Dawn*, 161 n. 55. Flamel is mentioned in *The Speckled
Bird: An Autobiographical Novel, with Variant Versions*, ed. William H. O'Donnell
(London: Palgrave Macmillan, 2003), 163, and *Memoirs*, ed. Denis Donoghue (New
York: Macmillan, 1972), 49–50. Flamel is among the alchemists meriting a sketch
in Arthur Edward Waite, *Lives of Alchemystical Philosophers* (London: W. Foulsham,
[1888]), a copy of which WBY owned, although the entry for Flamel occurs among pages
that WBY never cut. See also William T. Gorski, *Yeats and Alchemy* (Albany, NY: State
University of New York Press, 1996), 122–6.

[23] The instructors were most often of these two types. Controls have more or less
human names (like Thomas or Ameritus), which often evoke various etymologies, though
they are seldom self-explanatory. These communicators are almost always male (except
for two brief visits from Epilamia, who presided over automatic script after the sleeps had
begun (*YVP*iii. 44–5)). Controls seem to wield more authority than the less articulate
guides, which, like Shakespearian fairies, have names taken from nature (the four that
regularly appear, Apple, Fish, Leaf, and Rose, also, as Saddlemyer notes, are 'notably

the collective memory of humanity, waiting for discovery. Rather, 'All the bones are *in* the world', not the astral plane. Nor is the being fully fleshed there, either. The whole is formed thus: 'we only select & our selection is subordinate to *you both*—therefore *we* are dependent on you & you influence our ability to develop & create by every small detail of your joint life' (*YVP*ii. 240, emphasis original).[24] In other words, the system is both personal and collaborative, the necessary product of what GY called in a notebook entry the 'Wisdom of Two' (*YVP*iii. 146).[25]

Two other inscriptions from WBY's library, in copies of the first edition of *A Vision*, make relevant points. The first appears on the flyleaf of a copy that is filled with corrections (by WBY, GY, the printer, and an editor) for setting sections of the 1937 revised edition that were the least changed from the first edition.[26] WBY wrote, 'This copy must not be given to any body on any excuse however plausible/W B Yeats/George Yeats.' The tone of this note sounds like further evidence of reckless generosity—WBY writing to himself or, if he doesn't stop himself in time, perhaps even depending upon the recipient of the book to catch the giver's mistake and return it, especially since it belongs not only to the magnanimous poet but also to his careful wife, who looks after his things even if he doesn't. Besides functioning as an example of a conjugal myth (once he is married, husband can be publicly open-handed because wife is privately prudent—a myth that seems to have had

reminiscent of Willy's early poetry' (*Becoming George*, 112). A notebook entry in GY's hand from 1920 defines the difference between guides and controls: 'Guides are called by such names as leaf Rose etc while spirits who have been men are given such names as Thomas Dionertes etc—' (*YVP*iii. 19).

[24] Actually, by this time the Yeatses' 'joint life' included a third person, their infant daughter Anne, as the communicators noted: 'The system is *not* preexistent—it is developed & created by us by you two or three now from a preexisting psychology.' For more on the Third Daimon, associated with Anne Yeats, see Ch. 5.

[25] See also a guide's description of the 'wisdom from 2 people' (*YVP*i. 185).

[26] For details of the complicated textual history and the role played by these copies of the first edition, see Richard J. Finneran, 'On Editing Yeats: The Text of *A Vision* (1937)', *Texas Studies in Literature and Language*, 19 (1977), esp. 121–2; Hood, 'Search for Authority', esp. 123–9; and Hood, 'Remaking', esp. 52–5.

some appeal to the Yeatses even though it was no truer than such myths usually are), the tone of 'any excuse however plausible' is the kind of smiling self-deflation which runs throughout *A Vision*, although it has not often been recognized as such.[27] Self-deference is a significant rhetorical strategy in the book behind this flyleaf, linked with the narrator/writer's sense that he is not the sole author of his philosophical text and that he does not even understand all of it. The WBY who presents *A Vision* and has a secondary role as a character in some of its bewilderingly prominent framing stories and poems is in fact several Yeatses, sliding between subject and object positions, who refer to each other in complex ways that are uncertainly and simultaneously serious and comic. Moreover, *A Vision* is two books, separated in time by some eleven years, which refer to each other in terms that are equally slippery and equally performative. A duality or multiplicity of subject makes itself felt throughout this/these work(s), in points of view, rhetoric, the relation of framing material to what is inside the frames, and within the content of the system itself (so that one gyre becomes two at the least touch, for example). This dramatic doubling and multiplying, no less integral to the book than it has been maddeningly difficult for many readers, may be analysed also in terms of the joint endeavour that was its inception and elaboration.

The inscription in GY's personal copy of the first edition of *A Vision*, with her book-plate, is my favourite. It clearly accompanies a personal gift: 'To Dobbs in memory of all tribulations when we were making this book/W.B. Yeats'.[28] The use of the private nickname and the acknowledgement of 'tribulations' distinguish this inscription from the others, but these details follow a relatively

---

[27] Hazard Adams and Steven Helmling are two notable exceptions to this general state of affairs. See Hazard Adams, *The Book of Yeats's Vision: Romantic Modernism and Antithetical Tradition* (Ann Arbor: University of Michigan Press, 1995), and Steven Helmling, *The Esoteric Comedies of Carlyle, Newman, and Yeats* (Cambridge: Cambridge University Press, 1988).

[28] A note on the brown paper dust cover of this book reads 'Copy for Printer/July 26, 1937'. It was not the copy from which the new edition was set, but, according to Finneran, it was sent to Macmillan at this late date to clarify the positioning of some diagrams. For more details, see Finneran, 'On Editing Yeats': 131 n. 17, and Hood, 'Search for Authority', 127–8.

standard format of inscriptions in the front covers or flyleaves of books given by authors to their friends or family members. Not so the last phrase, 'when we were making this book'.[29] These words are the heart of the matter, for they imply not only behind-the-scenes support but co-authorship, of a complex kind implied in a poignant message from the script itself, midway through the trouble of receiving and assimilating it. WBY asks, 'Has not all this painful process merely brought us to state of natural affection which many must reach at once? If not, what is the difference[?]' The answer stresses a meaning for the hard work: 'Bringing two unlikes necessary to us together & then making script possible—if neither had met each would have had separate partial illumination—we none.'[30] *A Vision* is too often read as 'partial illumination', but it is not only the culmination of half a lifetime of occult study and creativity on WBY's part; it also records GY's major body of work.

In what follows I consider GY's part in the 'making' of 'this book' as a unique collaboration. By 'making' I include tasks beyond what authorship usually means in literary criticism or theory, giving a nod toward the antique, William Morris–like unalienated labour that WBY no doubt intended to echo in his choice of words in the inscription, but also moving toward the ambiguities of authorship that a scholar of my generation tends to see, formed as I am by an interpretative environment changed by poststructuralism as well as technologies and media that emphasize collaborative and anonymous creation. GY's work needs to be put in intellectual contexts that will illuminate its complexities, such as textual theory that regards authority in terms of 'a social nexus, not a personal possession',

---

[29] Her personal copies of the 2nd edition were accompanied by a like acknowledgement: WBY sent her three of his six authors' copies, 'as you are part author' (letter of 29 Sept. 1937, quoted in Saddlemyer, *Becoming George*, 535).

[30] *YVP*ii. 331–2. I hope to be pardoned for relegating to a note, at this point anyway, the co-authorship of the spirits themselves. WBY was surprised at the last two words, 'we none', implying as they did that the communicators would not have known the system unless the human beings had met and taken on the task of discovering it. But so it was: his next question, 'You mean it is an actuall illumination to you?', received an affirmative reply.

in Jerome McGann's words; feminist or poststructuralist analysis that would point to its quality of what Gayatri Spivak has called the 'inaccessible blankness circumscribed by an interpretable text'; revised histories of individual authorship and copyright; rhetorical implications of anonymity and collaboration; attention to the sexual dynamics of its deep structures; and the location of the whole experiment in a time and place in which conjunctions among technology, spirituality, and the structures of perception are defining characteristics.[31]

Further, the 'making' of *A Vision* refers to the automatic and semi-automatic reception/invention of the system, as well as the use of a wealth of information, both personal and philosophical, that does not appear in the published book. Further, the Yeatses 'made' the daily drama of talk and action that accompanied and informed the automatic sessions. They engaged in delicate negotiations that changed two people entering a marriage under trying circumstances into satisfactory partners, a partnership that was essential to their mutual occult and writerly work as well as to their lives together in general. They created a family, an entity that included not only two children during the years of the automatic sessions but also a daimonic and ancestral extended group. They reworked memories and knowledge into newly understood conceptions on topics ranging from subtle readings of their own personalities to ways of understanding the conflicted larger worlds of Ireland and Europe in the war-torn early decades of the twentieth century.

Similarly, by 'book', I admit elements from both versions of *A Vision*, although I am slightly more interested in the 1925 edition, which is closer to the primary research of the automatic experiments. Interestingly, several inscribed copies are also marked with corrections, as the first edition began to be revised almost as

---

[31] The two quotations are from Jerome J. McGann, *A Critique of Modern Textual Criticism* (Chicago: University of Chicago Press, 1983), 48, and Gayatri Chakravorty Spivak, 'Can the Subaltern Speak?', in Cary Nelson and Lawrence Grossberg (eds.), *Marxism and the Interpretation of Culture* (Urbana, Ill.: University of Illinois Press, 1988), 294.

soon as it appeared in print. Thus the words inscribe an object that represents, now as in the years between January 1926 and October 1937, a dynamic and unfinished business. Nor was that business put to rest after 1937. The Papermac edition of the revised edition (first produced in 1981) still features a misleading note on the back cover mentioning that the edition 'incorporates all of Yeats's final revisions to the text'. What 'final' revisions there are were made for the most part by GY and Thomas Mark, the editor at Macmillan, to a text never completely reset. In other words, the book that students buy in college bookstores or general readers pick up still bears the ghostly imprint of GY's hand.[32]

In addition to *A Vision* I also stretch the plain meaning of the term 'book' to include the messy, necessarily unfinished book of the system, of which a fraction appears in the printed work, as well as various poetic, dramatic, and prose texts that are related to it. A personal book—I am tempted to quote WBY out of context and call it 'the book of the people', two of them, at any rate—also exists in the vast amount of material in the *Vision* papers related to the Yeatses' intimate lives. To see GY's work properly requires looking at all of these 'books', a task that requires replacing the idea of a final, public, and written document that has a recognizable individual as its author with something less fixed temporally or spatially than what is often meant.

The compromises and collaborations that are a necessary part of authorship are not news, of course, not to writers and theorists, and certainly not to scholarly editors of large projects. One of the pleasures of being a part of the editorial team producing *YVP* was the sense that it was something of a family affair from start to finish, that all of

---

[32] Having exhaustively examined manuscript and printed materials, Connie Hood describes the version of the book that is now in print (a 1962 reissue) as

a syncretic text, based partly on Mark's re-editing of Mrs. Yeats's editing of the 1956 reissue and partly on their joint editing of the Coole proofs; the 1956 reissue was itself based on Mrs. Yeats's re-editing of Yeats's editing of the 1937 edition and possibly on the editing of the Scribner edition by Mrs. Yeats, Yeats, or both; and Mrs. Yeats's re-editing of Yeats's editing of the 1937 edition was based on the editing by Mrs. Yeats and Thomas Mark of the Coole proofs: *A Vision* had become a modern palimpsest. (Hood, 'Search for Authority', 155)

us were working on texts that were also collaborative in nature. It is impossible to miss the dialogue in the automatic script; we knew that on some level the editorial project was mistitled and misattributed in using his name but not hers on the title-pages. And yet 'The Yeatses' *Vision* Papers' would hardly have been an improvement. For one thing, GY would surely not have wanted her name put forward any more than Macmillan, our press and theirs, would have urged it. It is tempting to suppose that she was responsible for vetoing WBY's drafted dedication of the second edition of the book, and to wonder how different the reception of the 1937 *A Vision* (rocky without it) might have been if his drafted, joking attribution had been allowed through the press:

> To my wife
> Who created this system which bores her, who made possible
> these pages which she will never read & who
> has accepted this dedication on the condition
> that I write nothing but verse for a year[33]

As it happened, of course, she was not too bored to work on subsequent editions, even in the difficult months just before and after WBY's death when she made corrections to the error-ridden text for two major editions of his collected works in progress at the time.

There is a further complication for any editorial or critical project involving the automatic script, of course. To assign the communications written by the hand of GY to her volitional authorship is to ignore the spirit communicators, difficult as they are to reckon with. Barthes's *morte de l'auteur* is almost too cute a phrase to describe a project whose 'authors are in eternity', to use one of WBY's favourite quotations from Blake.[34] Should they be granted any status besides that of fiction, self-delusion, or fraud? Should they be regarded as

---

[33] White vellum MS book begun 23 Nov. 1930, 178. Cited by Richard Ellmann, *Yeats: The Man and the Masks* (New York: Norton, 1978), 266; Hood, 'Search for Authority', 113; and Saddlemyer, Becoming George, 761 n. 109.

[34] William Blake, *Complete Writings*, ed. Geoffrey Keynes (Oxford: Oxford University Press, 1966), 825.

distinct from GY? or from her husband? What meaning should we assign to the fact that both partners believed that they had independent existence as well as depending on the Yeatses' joint psyches for their abilities? How does their existence sit with various social and cultural phenomena, such as conventions of authorship, technologies of representation or communication, or political ideologies, which are also present as determinants of the spirits' energies? Mainstream publishers are unlikely to allow 'authorship' to follow the pattern of numerous spiritualist publications, such as the last book 'written' by W. T. Stead, *Life Eternal*, which was dictated to his daughter Estelle W. Stead through the medium Hester Dowden in 1933, some twenty years after his death.[35] His name, not the names of either the recipient or the automatist, appears on the cover and the title-page, although the unusual circumstances of its composition are

---

[35] WBY had known Stead from his theosophical period. Stead's spiritualist centre in Wimbledon, 'Julia's Bureau', was the location of seances frequented by both WBY and GHL from as early as 1912—when WBY first 'met' the spirit of Leo Africanus, although he came to believe that he had encountered Leo in 1909 and, before that, 'fifteen or twenty years earlier', in early 1899; 'Leo', 23–4; R. F. Foster, *W. B. Yeats: A Life*, i: *The Apprentice Mage 1865–1914* (Oxford: Oxford University Press, 1997), 465. Hester Dowden (Mrs Travers Smith) was the daughter of Edward Dowden, a Trinity College professor, minor poet, and family friend of WBY. She worked with Frederick Bligh Bond on the Glastonbury Scripts and was the author of *Voices from the Void: Six Years' Experience in Automatic Communications* (London: W. Rider, 1919) and the widely read *Psychic Messages from Oscar Wilde* (London: T. Werner Laurie, 1923), the result of automatic writing. Her daughter, apparently also mediumistic, eventually married Lennox Robinson. See Nandor Fodor, *Encyclopædia of Psychic Science* (Secaucus, NJ: Citadel Press, 1966), s.v. 'Dowden, Hester' and 'Stead, William T.'; Hood, 'Search for Authority', 27–8; *MYV*i. 176–9; and *YVP*i. 2. See also London, *Writing Double*, ch. 5, for analysis of the famous *Cummins* v. *Bond* case, which granted legal authorship to automatic writers.

Geraldine Cummins was also acquainted with WBY. After his death, this famous Anglo-Irish automatic writer and author of *Unseen Adventures* (London: Rider, 1951) received a message from him by means of automatic writing, addressing the vexed question of where his remains should be permanently interred. Wondering how to convey his post-mortem message, the automatic script asks at one point, 'Do you know my friends or my wife', to which Cummins responds in her own hand, 'This woman here through whose hand you write used to know you & knows many of yr friends. But it will be difficult to speak to yr wife—'. This may well have been true, although perhaps not for the reason next stated: 'My wife is afraid of spirits and the grave I fear she would not listen to you.' I am grateful to my parents for lending me the copy of this script which was given to my father by Kathleen Raine in 1983.

explained on the dust flap and in introductory notes by both Miss Stead and Dowden. Librarians and bibliographers can be thankful that Thomas of Dorlowicz and Ameritus are not listed as authors of the *Vision* papers, not to mention Rose and Fish or the spirits and daimons who use the controls and guides as mouthpieces.

Yet simple dismissal of all these spirit collaborators in the name of scholarly or common-sense rationality is also unacceptable. I do not want to approach a complex set of actions and ideas, in settings very different from my own, from a perspective characterized by an outsider's sense of easy superiority to the commitments and practices of others.[36] GY was not a fool, nor did she suffer fools willingly, a fact to keep in mind when analysing her occult work. Indeed, one mark of her sanity, as of her husband's, might be their willingness to engage in activities that challenged them, whether or not they might be thought foolish for doing so. As Terry Castle has noted in a similar context, a supernatural event experienced collectively raises epistemological and rhetorical issues that may multiply difficulties for a sceptic bent on discrediting its objective validity. The need to explain such an experience away may well embroil scepticism in 'its own kind of folly—[a] debunking "mania", or compulsion to disprove', so that 'to disbelieve ... is to risk losing oneself in an alienating welter of evidence and counterevidence'.[37] The force of

---

[36] Such an approach would be ahistorical, in addition to being merely impertinent, running into difficulties such as those noted by Stanley Jeyaraja Tambiah with reference to Western anthropological examinations of non-Western cultures: 'The historical origins and derivation of the concepts of religion, magic and science bear relevantly on the question of using them as general analytical categories for the understanding of the modes of thought and action of non-Western societies' (*Magic, Science, Religion, and the Scope of Rationality* (Cambridge: Cambridge University Press, 1990), 4).

[37] Terry Castle, *The Female Thermometer: Eighteenth-Century Culture and the Invention of the Uncanny* (Oxford: Oxford University Press, 1995), 213. Ch. 11 of this study examines *An Adventure*, the well-known account of an apparition of Marie Antoinette seen in 1911 by Charlotte Anne Moberly and Eleanor Jourdain. *An Adventure* excited a number of energetic rebuttals. The Yeatses were fascinated by the book, which is mentioned several times in the automatic script, to the extent of corresponding with and meeting the authors while in Oxford. See *MYV*i. 78–9, 224–5; *MYV*ii. 67–8, 424 n. 29. See also Richard J. Finneran, George Mills Harper, and William M. Murphy (eds.), *Letters to W. B. Yeats*, 2 vols. (London: Macmillan, 1977), ii. 346–8. Interestingly,

such a desire to disprove should not be underestimated. Through several generations of Yeats scholarship, discussion of the Yeatses' occult experimentation still tends to begin, and often to end, at the question, Did they, or Do you, believe it?, with lines between camps drawn on the basis of the answer to the latter. The Yeatses themselves were by no means distracted by such compulsions.

Saddlemyer's detailed psychological account of what might have happened in the nightly sessions draws attention to the heterogeneous sources of what she suggests may have been self-hypnosis. Saddlemyer also points to two interesting facts: that GY herself apparently first used the critical word *fakery* in association with her first attempt at automatic writing; and that she was keenly aware that, having done so, the word would damage her reputation. As she told A. Norman Jeffares, 'the word "Fake" will go down to posterity'.[38] Interestingly, GY's use of the term occurred in the context of working with Yeats scholars (notably Virginia Moore and Richard Ellmann) who took the script seriously and were working to understand its elaborate ideas as such, hardly efforts they would have made if they thought that GY had simply made everything up. On the contrary: her honest admission added to the complexity of the affair.

both Moberly and Jourdain were disinclined to delve deeply into occult matters. Their pseudonymously published book stresses their position in the *status quo*: 'We belong to no new schools of thought; we are the daughters of English clergymen, and heartily hold and teach the faith of our fathers' ([Charlotte Anne Moberly and Eleanor Jourdain] Elizabeth Morison and Frances Lamont, *An Adventure* (Glasgow: The University Press, 1911), 101–2). They firmly renounce interest in 'excited', 'abnormal', or 'low' activities involving the supernatural:

Both of us have inherited a horror of all forms of occultism. We lose no opportunity of preaching against them as unwholesome and misleading; because they mostly deal with conditions of physical excitement, and study of the abnormal and diseased, including problems of disintegrated personality which present such close analogy to those of insanity. We have the deepest distrust in, and distaste for, stories of abnormal appearances and conditions. We find narratives of *revenants* unconvincing, and studiously avoid (as utterly lowering) all spiritualistic methods of communication with the dead. We have never had the curiosity, or the desire, to help in the investigations of psychical phenomena. (pp. 101–2)

[38] Saddlemyer, *Becoming George*, 103.

The issue was not new to the Yeatses' script, of course. It was a common theme in psychic research. In June 1911, for example, WBY mused in an address before a like-minded audience that 'Like every other student of the subject [i.e., spiritualism], I have been bewildered by the continual deceits, by the strange dream-like manifestations, by the continual fraud'. He continues:

Why, e.g., does Miss "Burton" when she is entranced commit ingenious frauds which deceive not only the sitters but Miss Burton when she is awake? . . . Why is it that when Albert de Rochas asks his sensitives to go back into past lives & tell him who they were they can sometimes describe scenery, names families even, that they have never heard of in their waking state, & yet claim to be people whose existence can be disproved? Why this mixture of reality, of messages that seem to come precisely as they say they do from the dead, with messages that but express the thoughts of the living?

He goes on to propose complex interplays between mind and reality, comparing psychic phenomena with dreaming and hypnosis. Two further comments in particular seem almost to foretell these issues as they are raised in the automatic script. First, WBY suggests, 'the dead are simply dreaming souls, souls suggestable from without or from within, when they go to séances they are constrained by us when we question them, for every question is a suggestion. It suggests an answer. And that we would only get from them the truth in our own sense of the word.' Second, 'They are all phases of the dissolution of the fixed personality.'[39]

William James also addresses the issue of fakery in 'The Last Report: The Final Impressions of a Psychical Researcher', written in 1909. James suggests bearing in mind that 'In most things human the accusation of deliberate fraud and falsehood is grossly superficial. Man's character is too sophistically mixed for the alternative of "honest or dishonest" to be a sharp one.' Later in the essay, James addresses automatic writing in particular:

[39] Remarks delivered to the Ghost Club, 7 June 1911 (BL Add. MS 52264).

I have come to see in automatic writing one example of a department of human activity as vast as it is enigmatic. Every sort of person is liable to it, or to something equivalent to it; and whoever encourages it in himself finds himself personating someone else. . . . Our subconscious region seems, as a rule, to be dominated by a crazy "will to make-believe," or by some curious external force impelling us to personation.[40]

The *Vision* documents take this observation one step further to claim not only that every person is 'liable' to such a phenomenon, but that it is in fact essential. The Mask, one of four Faculties whose interactions describe each human being, is defined as 'something put on and worn: a form created by passion' in order 'to reveal or conceal individuality', 'as a protection or revelation of the soul', or, finally, 'to unite us to ourselves', in various rephrasings, which suggest in their repetition how important the idea is (*YVP*i. 262; iii. 163; iv. 15; *AVA* 18).

From an intellectual point of view, oppositions between the material and the supernatural in wby are complicated by the arrival of the spirit communicators of the automatic script. It is just this unmanageable eruption of spirits into the Yeatses' daily life and writing, however, that makes these documents exciting. Among other things, they are indices of significant and widespread aesthetic and philosophical trouble with writing and the real. Such trouble haunts a number of modernist texts, but the Yeatses' experiment dramatizes it in especially bold ways. For example, voices here are not merely standard terms in literary critical discourse, signs of an orality or bodily immediacy imagined as lost from Western literary culture. Nor are they synecdoches only for the uncanny, that lack of fit between an imagined perceptible world and an unimaginable real so common in the modern period, and so commonly expressed through the instability of texts.[41] The communicators of the script intrude into historical and textual analysis no less than they did into

---

[40] William James, *William James on Psychical Research*, ed. Gardner Murphy and Robert O. Ballou (New York: Viking, 1960), 312, 322.

[41] See the Preface to Julian Wolfreys, *Victorian Hauntings: Spectrality, Gothic, the Uncanny and Literature* (London: Palgrave, 2002), pp. ix–xiv. Wolfreys cites

the lives of the people who summoned them. They complicate a
number of polarities, for example, of material versus spiritual worlds,
the individual will as opposed to machine-like automatism, agency as
male or female, and conscious or unconscious sources of knowledge.
They point to the inadequacy of formulations that feature such neat
oppositions. We might think of them as a third term that makes
the Yeats couple, and their joint production, possible.[42] At any
rate, my point of departure (once again, as in the matter of flyleaf
inscriptions) will be identity. This focus will allow me to take up a
number of questions which the Yeatses asked themselves and their
work asks of readers, about performance, authority, and subjectivity,
all simmering in an ontological, epistemological, and ideological
stew that is made (as are all the best stews) from local and seasonal
ingredients, picked fresh from the times and places in which they
grew.

Analysing this body of material is a more diverse business than
looking for evidence of agency or influence in a straightforward
causal model. I am not interested in separating GY's 'work' from
her husband's, a critical act which would downplay its radically
collaborative quality. Nor is my study primarily biographical or
historical, although it assumes that both the personal and the cultural
inform the matter that is its main focus. I am drawn to mysteries

---

Jean-Michel Rabaté on the systematic haunting of texts (*The Ghosts of Modernity*,
(Gainesville, Fla.: University Press of Florida, 1996), p. xvi) and Slavoj Žižek, who notes
that 'there [is] no reality without the spectre', for this reason:

reality is never directly 'itself', it presents itself only via its incomplete failed symbolization,
and spectral apparitions emerge in this very gap that forever separates reality from the
real, and on account of which reality has the character of a (symbolic) fiction: the spectre
gives body to that which escapes (the symbolically structured) reality. ('Introduction:
The Spectre of Ideology', in *idem* (ed.), *Mapping Ideology* (London: Verso, 1994), 21)

Žižek also notes that 'This gap that separates the real from reality is what opens up the
space for performative in its opposition to constative' (p. 32). That is to say, spectres do
not merely symbolize or point to something symbolizable; they attempt to conjure up
or create something that is unfixed, outside such structures. On performativity and the
script, see also the interlude on automatic performance below.

   [42] I am borrowing the formulation of Marjorie Garber, *Vice Versa: Bisexuality and the
Eroticism of Everyday Life* (New York: Simon & Schuster, 1995).

and perspectives that admit them with as much enthusiasm as I am inclined to enjoy the act of reducing them. To look for GY's work in multiple senses, and indeed to write about *A Vision* at all, is to engage in analysis that must be able to accommodate the irrational or at least the 'antithetical', as Hazard Adams calls it (borrowing WBY's term).[43] The first objects of my attention are some of the issues that surface when empirical logic is used to analyse events and commitments that run, if not counter, at least at odd angles to it. My method borrows from various theoretical and historical modes, working backward from my own place in intellectual history as well as trying to imagine what meanings these phenomena had in the Yeatses', examining cultural assumptions of their time and trying to see those of the present that are also constitutive of the meanings I find in their occult revelations. Points of divergence between my point of view and theirs are frequent. There are also some points of agreement, among which are notions of knowledge as radically subjective, the self as non-unitary, and faith as an important component of human expression.

The study is organized into five chapters and two shorter 'interludes'. The first chapter addresses the question of how to read WBY's occult work, arguing for a revised critical attitude toward the texts at hand, and so forms a sort of manual for the rest of the book. The subsequent chapters proceed by focusing on themes from anonymity to sexual desire, geometry, and multiplicity, as well as fragmentation of personality, in a structure loosely based on the identities of the major parties involved. Chapter 2 focuses on GY, the anonymous writer of the automatic script; Chapter 4 on her husband; and Chapter 5 on the other personalities whose voices fill the documents. A middle segment (Chapter 3) looks at the published results of the occult experiments, emphasizing poetry, drama, and the two versions of *A Vision* itself, to see how the Yeatses' joint work is realized in WBY's

---

[43] See Adams, *Yeats's Vision*, 12–14, in which he redefines a term he has used before; see also Hazard Adams, *Blake and Yeats: The Contrary Vision* (Ithaca, NY: Cornell University Press, 1955), esp. ch. 6, and *idem*, *The Book of Yeats's Poems* (Tallahassee, Fla.: Florida State University Press, 1990), 9–12.

literary output. The interludes ponder, first, the genre of *A Vision*, a book whose notoriety in WBY's *œuvre* has much to do with the sort of book it claims to be, and second, the cultural significance of spiritualism and concurrent scientific and technological developments, especially those involving communication, from photography to the telephone to the typewriter.

The study as a whole proposes that understanding GY's work not only advances awareness of a gifted woman, alters opinion about her famous husband, and reconstructs the social canvas of their time and place, although all these results may well accrue. I hope also to uncover ideas worthy of attention, about such issues as the relation between expression and subjectivity, knowability, the relation of the body to the concept, performativity and textuality, and the nature of a text or indeed a self in a world of multiple influences and diaphanous boundaries. Difficult though it is to extricate GY's contributions from WBY's in the collaborative automatic documents that form the main record of her intellectual and spiritual accomplishments, this study both watches for her work and assumes its intrinsic value.

One of the last notebook entries that the Yeatses made in their years of elaborating the system together contains a particularly rich explanation of the 'incredible experience', meaningful, as the documents are generally, in its attribution and symbolic resonances no less than at the surface level of information. 'When I asked how they could adapt themselves to our language and limitations', WBY recalls, 'he said it was plain I did not understand the nature of communication through Interpreter'—that is, GY, the medium who outgrew her original title. In a glorious *mélange* of writerly confusion, WBY was here dictating to his wife a message he had heard from her lips earlier, when she was 'asleep' (whatever state that may have been). GY wrote the name of Dionertes in parentheses at the start of the entry to indicate to whom 'he' refers, but did not need to indicate who was meant by the 'I' of the paragraph she was taking down as secretary. Then she enclosed in quotation marks her own-Dionertes' - WBY's exact words: ' "She finds the words, we send the wave & she as it were catches it in a box" ' (*YVP*iii. 102). The metaphors are significant. Does finding words imply invention or revelation? Are the wave energy and the box a sort of spiritual version of an electrical transformer (reminiscent of a number of nineteenth-century theories about psychic phenomena)? If the system is caught in a box, does GY play the role of scientist or stage magician by trapping it in words? Does WBY play the role of Pandora when he writes *A Vision* and opens the box in public? Does he play Aladdin when he traps inspiration in verse? (In a letter to Dorothy Wellesley, years after the script and the marriage had waned in intensity, WBY repeated the striking figure, noting that 'The correction of prose, because it has no fixed laws, is endless, a poem comes right with a click like a closing box.'[44])

Whatever meanings I may assign to these words (or the myriad others in the *Vision* documents), it is surely important that GY found them. That discovery is the starting-point for any discoveries of my own.

[44] 8 Sept. [1935] (W. B. Yeats, *Letters on Poetry from W. B. Yeats to Dorothy Wellesley*, ed. Dorothy Wellesley (London: Oxford University Press, 1940), 24).

1

'A philosophy ... created from search': Preliminary Issues

> ... all our deep desires are images of the truth.
>
> Leo Africanus, through WBY, 1915 ('Leo', 28)
>
> The image received must be of the nature of the person receiving it.
>
> Rose, through GY, 12 February 1918 (*YVP*i. 348)

I begin with WBY. In an essay written near the end of his life to introduce a collected edition of his works to be sold by subscription by Charles Scribner's Sons, the poet formulated a kind of *credo*:

> I am convinced that in two or three generations it will become generally known that the mechanical theory has no reality, that the natural and supernatural are knit together, that to escape a dangerous fanaticism we must study a new science; at that moment Europeans may find something attractive in a Christ posed against a background not of Judaism but of Druidism, not shut off in dead history, but flowing, concrete, phenomenal.
>
> I was born into this faith, have lived in it, and shall die in it; my Christ, a legitimate deduction from the Creed of St. Patrick as I think, is that Unity of Being Dante compared to a perfectly proportioned human body, Blake's 'Imagination,' what the Upanishads have named 'Self': nor is this unity distant and therefore intellectually understandable, but imminent, differing from man to man and age to age, taking upon itself pain and ugliness, 'eye of newt, and toe of frog'. (*E&I* 518)

These are strong words: WBY intended that the American audience of this never published 'Dublin' edition of his works to be sure of the importance of what he called his faith, to that *œuvre* and to his life. (One of those works, of course, was to be *A Vision,* proofs of which were waiting to be corrected as he wrote.[1]) However, his essay is less definitive about just what that faith is and on what level he expects his audience to participate in it. Over sixty years later, readers of the essay and his work generally are still in the process of coming to terms with WBY's metaphysical ideas and practices. It is not as fashionable at the start of this millennium as it probably was a generation or two ago to reject non-orthodox spiritualities: the occult, the uncanny, and the non-Western are nearly as popular in the west now as they were at the turn of the last century, when WBY was a young man or in the years surrounding the Great War. Along with such popular phenomena as Wicca, new versions of Native American spiritualities, aromatherapy, alternative healing arts, and self-help books and programmes packaging various Eastern beliefs for Western consumption, even high cultural institutions like colleges and universities are pleased to tolerate, if not genuinely respect, the non-rational in various stripes of postmodern and global thought. In literary criticism, reactions against formalist approaches that found much to criticize in WBY's fuzzy supernaturalism have also yielded sympathetic attitudes toward expressions of the esoteric. It would make sense to assume that WBY's alternative enthusiasms might attract renewed interest. And so they do, assisted by editorial projects like the publication of the first four volumes of the complete letters and the *Vision* papers, not to mention a thoroughly reconceived authorized biography.[2] None the less, though it is generally accepted that these beliefs are vital to, and inseparable from, his aesthetic productions, reading WBY in the context of his spiritual and magical life is still difficult. Ironically, of all the poses, voices, and masks that dominate

---

[1] A letter to Dorothy Wellesley mentions this fact (*L* 864).

[2] To date, the *Letters* do not cover the years with which I am most concerned, but they thoroughly document WBY's magical life through 1907.

his work—WBY the lover, the nationalist, the dramatist, the last Romantic, the modernist, the political actor of socialist or fascist leanings, the young dreamer or the wild and wicked old man—the most consistently important to him are the very personae that critics have tended to make the most marginal and capricious: WBY the theosophist, the hermeticist, the Rosicrucian adept, the spiritualist, the occult metahistorian, the seeker after Celtic or Indian mysteries.[3]

The reasons for this state of affairs are multiple, of course, and range from the relatively straightforward to the vaporously indirect. For example, relatively little was known for some time about WBY's decades of involvement with the Hermetic Order of the Golden Dawn, for the very good reason that it was a secret order. On the other hand, WBY's feelings for Maud Gonne were and are widely known, especially in a popular version that does not include occult resonances, in part because their relationship had significant political value for her, for WBY, and for others. Academic approaches to poetry in the wake of I. A. Richards's *Science and Poetry* (published in the same year as the first version of *A Vision*) tended to share Richards's enthusiasm for a science of criticism and his disinclination for WBY's 'supernatural world', and literary criticism managed for at least a generation to admire the poetry and read *A Vision* (when it did) for its elaborate symbols, but to regard the 'embarrassing' beliefs as trivial and irrelevant.[4] In an

---

[3] By this generalization I do not intend to suggest that WBY's occult interests have been slighted by all critics and scholars. Some of the studies in this area are Mary Catherine Flannery, *Yeats and Magic: The Earlier Works* (Gerrards Cross: Colin Smythe, 1977); G. M. Harper, *Yeats's Golden Dawn*; *idem* (ed.), *Yeats and the Occult* ([Toronto]: Macmillan of Canada, 1975); *MYV*; Graham Hough, *The Mystery Religion of W. B. Yeats* (Brighton: Harvester Press, 1984); Virginia Moore, *The Unicorn: William Butler Yeats' Search for Reality* (New York: Macmillan, 1954); and Kathleen Raine, *Yeats the Initiate: Essays on Certain Themes in the Writings of W. B. Yeats* (Mountrath, Ireland: Dolmen Press, 1986).

[4] Ivor Armstrong Richards, *Science and Poetry* (London: Kegan Paul, 1926). In 1938, Cleanth Brooks Jr. wrote one of few early defences of *A Vision*, which argued its hard-edged modernity (as opposed to escapist Romanticism) and also influenced later critics in regarding the system as a myth rather than a set of beliefs ('Yeats: The Poet as Myth-Maker', *Southern Review*, 4/1 (Summer 1938), 116–42; repr. Cleanth Brooks, Jr., *Modern Poetry and the Tradition* (Chapel Hill, NC: University of North Carolina

often-repeated remark, even as careful a reader as W. H. Auden could ask, 'How on earth, we wonder, could a man of Yeats's gifts take such nonsense seriously?'[5] Literary history has tended to follow intellectual history in assuming, as Janet Oppenheim has shown, that 'the agnosticism embraced by the comparatively few intellectuals who dominated the historical record' of the 'Victorian crisis of faith' was the ongoing norm; this habit of thought led to underestimation along with devaluation of various religious energies of the late nineteenth and early twentieth centuries.[6] In addition to literary history, various theories that begin with politics, from literary Celticism through nationalism, revisionism, post-coloniality, and globalization have all been of greater interest to publishers and buyers of books about an Anglo-Irish writer than material about

Press, 1939), 173–202). Other such approaches to the book are summarized in the epilogue to Adams, *Yeats's Vision*, 159–67. A number of the critics who did not discount WBY's occultism outright echo Kermode in minimizing it: in a book that began as a series of lectures for the centenary of WBY's birth, Frank Kermode notes that 'Now and again [WBY] believed some of it, but in so far as his true commitment was to poetry he recognized his fictions as heuristic and dispensable, "consciously false" ' (Frank Kermode, *The Sense of an Ending: Studies in the Theory of Fiction* (New York: Oxford University Press, 1965), 104). The tradition of denigrating WBY's 'spooks' (p. 240) but taking *A Vision* seriously endured through at least 1970, when Harold Bloom published his massive study *Yeats* (New York: Oxford University Press, 1970). The history of criticism of *A Vision* often includes pressing the book into service as a document demonstrating the lamentable loss of faith characteristic of the modern age, in the extraordinary lengths to which WBY would go for a system of belief. A. Norman Jeffares, e.g., claims that WBY found it impossible to believe and blames the times: 'it was at once his tragedy and his gain that he was born in an age when he could not believe wholeheartedly' (*W. B. Yeats: Man and Poet* (London: Routledge & Kegan Paul, 1949), 53). However, Jeffares does admit that 'The fact that he [WBY] could believe, even temporarily, in the strange system which he built up in *A Vision* is responsible for some of the positive strength of the poems he wrote after his marriage. It is essential for the interpretation of much of his later verse; for the system lurks behind many of those poems which are not acting directly as mouthpieces for his thought' (p. 192). Jeffares also notes, correctly, that 'to dismiss [WBY's] accounts of visions and communications completely is too easy a method of treating the problem, as wrong as accepting all his own assertions on their face value' (p. 204). It is worth noting that Jeffares knew GY; his more subtle interpretation of the question of belief may owe something to her.

   [5] W. H. Auden, 'Yeats as an Example', in J. Hall and M. Steinmann (eds.), *The Permanence of Yeats: Selected Criticism* (New York: Macmillan, 1950), 345.
   [6] Janet Oppenheim, *The Other World: Spiritualism and Psychical Research in England, 1850–1914* (Cambridge: Cambridge University Press, 1985), 2.

philosophical and religious traditions that are difficult and largely non-Irish.

Speculating on the reasons for the uneven success with which this aspect of WBY's work has met is largely beyond my scope, but it is important to remember that WBY's insistent engagement with the occult, presented most dramatically in the second edition of *A Vision* with its tell-all recital of the automatic experiments that resulted in the book, has been bothersome to any number of readers. Indeed, the bothersomeness is part of the book's design. WBY's published positions anticipate and in fact encourage and use the antagonistic stances of unsympathetic readers as part of his projects.[7] So did GY's more private efforts: from behind the scenes, in the 1940s and 1950s, she provided help and guidance for many of the most influential critics of her husband's work. While doing so, she also promoted, or at least did not impede, narratives that also reduced the extent to which years of work on her part were taken seriously.[8] Nevertheless, to study the spiritual work that resulted in *A Vision* always includes questioning the extent to which it is to be believed. Faith is constantly at issue, in other words. It is vital to recognize that the veils that hang around the Yeatses' years of automatic writing, complementary dreaming, compilation of material, and composition of the two versions of the book *A Vision* are as much a part of the matter as what lies behind them. The act of hiding, in other words, is as significant as what is hidden or misconstrued. To use one of the Yeatses' terms, 'frustration' is essential to success.[9]

---

[7] To date the best treatment of this issue is Helmling, *Esoteric Comedies*.

[8] Among the scholars who received her help were Allt, Alspach, Bradford, Ellmann, Jeffares, Stallworthy, and Saddlemyer. Virginia Moore, whose particular interest was in WBY's religious life, had a closer relationship with GY than most (see Saddlemyer, *Becoming George*, 626–7). Moore's book *The Unicorn*, which has always been a slightly unusual item on the shelves of Yeats criticism, becomes the more interesting when GY's particular approval is taken into account.

[9] In the introduction to the 1937 text, WBY mentions that among the communicators of the script were 'others whom they named Frustrators', who 'attempted to confuse us or waste time', although 'who these Frustrators were or why they acted so was never adequately explained' (p. 13). These deceiving spirits caused considerable trouble during

Frustration is the place to start in order to appreciate the audacity and genius of the whole unwieldy business of the *Vision* enterprise: automatic creativity resulting in a chaotic system published in two versions of a misleading and, in some sections, practically unreadable book, which has been keenly appreciated as well as dismissed out of hand by some of the most penetrating readers of the generations since.[10] I will later be concerned with how the Yeatses regarded their occult collaboration, but it is important first to interrogate how readers may do so. How are approaches to this book conditioned by various conceptual frameworks and kinds of discourse into which I and other readers translate the material we read, conceptions grounded in such notions as the impersonally and the objectively present? Where are the personal, the performative, or the spiritual located in reference to the acts of reading and interpreting WBY's magical beliefs? Such questions have long and glorious ideational contexts, from ancient hermeneutics to postmodern theory, and they occur in material circumstances from medieval bookmaking to contemporary university classrooms. I cannot of course retrace them with any degree of comprehensiveness, but I will touch briefly upon a few conditions that relate to the Yeatses' project. Then, by way of illustration and in order to examine some of WBY's rhetorical purposes that condition his readers' responses, I will return to the late essay quoted above and look at a few other examples from WBY's published prose not related to the *Vision*-related material that treat issues of faith in a supernatural world. Just as we cannot look at the *Vision* project without first interrogating our own assumptions, so we cannot approach any of WBY's occult prose without

the receiving of the script, and especially later during the period of the sleeps. WBY did not encounter frustrators for the first time in the *Vision* experiments. A stray note filed with the automatic script of Elizabeth Radcliffe shows him toying with the philosophical problem they represent: 'I ask what is the cause of the deception—"a spirit" who seems to have given every proof of goodness will deceive. . . . I am looking for some theory that will reconcile belief in spirits, in whom I believe, with evidence of deception'. See also Ch. 5 for more discussion of frustration.

[10] Hazard Adams once suggested 'exasperation' as the term to use: Hazard Adams, 'Symbolism and Yeats's *A Vision*', *Journal of Aesthetics and Art Criticism*, 22 (1964): 428.

recognizing the active manipulations of its readers' beliefs that is one of its hallmarks.

Faith

> The great world, the *background*, in all of us, is the world of our *beliefs*. This is the world of the permanencies and the immensities.
>
> William James, letter to Helen Keller, 17 December 1908[11]

A number of twentieth-century methodologies have assumed that hidden forces operate on the arts (as other disciplines), whether the schools of thought focus like materialist criticism on historical and material implications, like psychoanalytic interpretation on the unconscious, or like structuralism or semiosis on elements of received form or language. These forces operate in the contexts in which works of art exist, which for *belles lettres* include most prominently the act of reading, the constructions of authorship and readership, the various economies in which texts are made, disseminated, or destroyed, and the aspects of culture or group life that they may be changed by and which may be changed by them. Spirituality may be one of these sources of energy. It manifests itself as an excess that is inexplicable and invisible if considered in contexts that are self-conscious in material, psychological, social, structural, or linguistic terms but do not take their own belief systems into account. Obviously, the culture and logic of the analysis itself are implicated in all critical approaches. Thus psychoanalytic criticism tells of its own unconscious, materialism struggles with questions of its historicity, and structuralism builds theories of constructedness not only of texts but of language and the practice of criticism. It may take 'spiritual' criticism to come to terms with the spiritual qualities of artistic expression. If so, such criticism is well advised to take note

---

[11] Quoted in Ralph Barton Perry (ed.), *The Thought and Character of William James*, 2 vols. (Boston: Little, Brown, 1935), ii. 455.

of the spiritual, or perhaps it would be more accurate to say, the occult, the hidden and magical qualities of its own praxis.

Several philosophers and theologians make this point. Heidegger, for example, has influenced recent speculative theology more than any other philosopher (even as he has been criticized for supposedly replacing logic with mysticism), and he has done so in good part through his critique of the relationship between interpretation and metaphysics.[12] A number of theologians and philosophers, following Derrida, have noted the parallels between deconstruction and negative theology, whether they highlight the differences or the similarities between them.[13] The paths taken by Benjamin and Levinas in particular bring mystical Judaism into dialogue with æsthetics. Harold Bloom, his criticism of WBY's spirituality notwithstanding, actively

---

[12] See esp. Martin Heidegger, *Kant and the Problem of Metaphysics*, trans. James S. Churchill (Bloomington, Ind.: Indiana University Press, 1962), and *idem*, *The Principle of Reason*, trans. Reginald Lilly (Bloomington, Ind., and Indianapolis: Indiana University Press, 1991). For an informative study of the relationship between philosophy, especially deconstruction, and Christian theology, particularly metaphysics and mysticism, see Kevin Hart, *The Trespass of the Sign: Deconstruction, Theology and Philosophy* (Cambridge: Cambridge University Press, 1989). Hart asserts Heidegger's centrality to contemporary theology (p. 237), and, coincidentally, distinguishes between Derrida and Heidegger on the contradictions inherent in reason by way of Paul de Man's reading of the closing lines of WBY's poem 'Among School Children' (pp. 250–1). See also Graham Parkes (ed.), *Heidegger and Asian Thought* (Honolulu: University of Hawaii Press, 1987), for examinations that relate Heidegger to religious thought from traditions that include Vedānta, Zen, Taoism, and modern Japanese philosophy.

[13] On the resemblances between these two concepts, which Derrida first mentioned in the essay 'Différance' (in *Margins of Philosophy* (Chicago: University of Chicago Press, 1982), 1–27) and have been debated ever since, see Toby Foshay, 'Resentment and Apophasis: The Trace of the Other in Levinas, Derrida and Gans', in Philippa Berry and Andrew Wernick (eds.), *Shadow of Spirit: Postmodernism and Religion* (London: Routledge, 1992), 81–92. See also Derrida, 'How to Avoid Speaking: Denials', originally published in Sanford Budick and Wolfgang Iser (eds.), *Languages of the Unsayable: The Play of Negativity in Literature and Literary Theory* (New York: Columbia University Press, 1989), and repr. in Harold Coward and Toby Foshay (eds.), *Derrida and Negative Theology* (Albany, NY: State University of New York Press, 1992), 73–142. This collection of essays places Derrida not only in a Christian context but also in relation to Hinduism and Buddhism. See also John D. Caputo, *The Prayers and Tears of Jacques Derrida: Religion without Religion* (Bloomington, Ind.: Indiana University Press, 1997); Hart, *Trespass*; Robert Magliola, *Derrida on the Mend* (West Lafayette, Ind.: Purdue University Press, 1984); and Mark C. Taylor, *nOts* (Chicago and London: University of Chicago Press, 1993).

participates in this dialogue, to the extent of linking the study of literature specifically to the study of the cabbalah.[14] In *The Gift of Death*, Derrida clearly links the *mysterium tremendum* that is at the heart of Christian responsibility to all Western discourse, private and public, and all ethics, including the discourse and ethics of his own thinking. All philosophy participates in what Derrida calls an 'aporia of responsibility', which is to say that not only knowledge, but also a lack of knowledge, is required for any responsible action. 'If decision-making is relegated to a knowledge that it is content to follow or to develop,' he notes, 'then it is no more a responsible decision, it is the technical deployment of a cognitive apparatus, the simple mechanistic deployment of a theorem.'[15]

If I avoid the issue of faith, then, whether that is faith in spirits, magical evocations, astrological projections, or anything else, using whatever rationale I please, it could be argued that I abnegate my responsibility as a critic in a Western linguistic and cognitive tradition to pursue knowledge, if only because knowledge and its antinomy, the unknown, always coexist. To pursue the one without acknowledging the other is folly. While it is essential to embed religious convictions in the physical workings of the human mind and in the politics of various social phenomena, I suspect that it is reductive to treat the question of a supersensual world in terms that preclude its validity at the outset. If we fail to leap, in Heideggerian or Kierkegaardian fashion (to cite one theologian influenced by the philosopher), we may impede our general motility. Or, to shift the metaphor, if I assume from the start that the idea of 'ghosts in the machine' is absurd, I am relinquishing the opportunity first of all to accomplish a number of traditional academic tasks, like contextualizing the Yeatses historically and biographically with some

---

[14] Harold Bloom, *Genius* (London: Fourth Estate, 2002). For a general study of how 'Modern criticism is haunted indeed' by Jewish 'theological specters' (pp. xiii, xv), see Susan A. Handelman (ed.), *The Slayers of Moses: The Emergence of Rabbinic Interpretation in Modern Literary Theory* (Albany, NY: State University of New York Press, 1982).

[15] Jacques Derrida, *The Gift of Death*, trans. David Wills (Chicago: University of Chicago Press, 1995), 24.

degree of sympathy, or understanding internal patternings and non-patternings—that is to say, various stresses, in the poetry, drama, and prose.[16] Once the supernatural seems to have been controlled, as Faust found, or contained, as the Ghostbusters did in the 1984 Hollywood film, or observed as an outsider, as field anthropologists are well aware, it tends to exert control of its own, if only to escape from the researcher's view. Is the point of a darkened seance room only to hide the charlatanry of a table-rapping medium or also to symbolize the principle that truth contains darkness? In David Michael Levin's rendering, Heidegger remarks that 'self-concealing, concealment, *lēthē*, belongs to *alētheia*, not just as an addition, not just as a shadow to light, but rather as the heart of *alētheia*'.[17]

Thus, I take the question of faith as critical in the study that follows. However, a critique that takes faith seriously must also take care not to eliminate the wildness from the system by turning the question of faith into a question of whether something is or is not real, or by pinning down just what level of trust in an idea constitutes bona fide belief. So although I am sure it will seem to some an evasive manœuvre, it is a critical part of my purpose not to answer some of the questions that rational Western people ask in the universe, such as whether I think that the spirits that spoke through GY actually existed as such. It is especially important not to stop at this question when examining the Yeatses' spiritual practices, since they are strikingly aware of the dangers of over-explication, the relationship between essence and mask or chance and choice,

---

[16] Like Gilbert Ryle, who coined the phrase 'the ghost in the machine' to argue the absurdity of the idea of the mind existing independently of the brain, I do not want to separate the machinery of criticism from whatever ghosts criticism may raise. Unlike Ryle, who uses the phrase 'with deliberate abusiveness' to undermine the notion of an occult mental realm, I find that it usefully infers the sense that the inexplicable is meant to invade the texts and events examined in this study. See Gilbert Ryle, *The Concept of Mind* (London: Hutchinson's University Library, 1949), 15.

[17] David Michael Levin, *The Opening of Vision: Nihilism and Postmodernism* (London: Routledge, 1988); cited in Berry and Wernick (eds.), *Shadow of Spirit*, 2. Similarly, Heidegger cites Fragment 123 of Heraclitus, 'phūsis krūptesthai philei', and (in Reginald Lilly's translation) renders the saying thus: 'being loves (a) self-concealing' or 'to being there belongs a self-concealing' (Heidegger, *Principle of Reason*, 64–6).

the dependence of truth upon the seeker after it, and the power of unsatisfied desire. Few of WBY's famous rhetorical questions, one of his favourite poetic techniques, admit of either–or answers, and to translate this issue into black-and-white terms is to reduce a contrary to a negation, to use Blakean terms, or to strip it of its antitheticality, to use a Yeatsian one.[18] GY wrote in the course of an automatic session, then copied into a notebook, a definition that she considered crucial for the dynamism of the system she was shaping: 'A *philosophy* created from experience, burns & destroys; one which is created from search, leads.'[19]

It is no more possible to frame a non-temporal, non-discursive issue in linear terms than it is possible to bring concealment to light: when the hidden is brought into the open, the quality of hiddenness disappears. The supersensual in the Yeatses' system serves an integral function as a repeated pointer to an absence at the heart of things. This absence, to speak paradoxically, is everywhere in the automatic script and other experiments, as well as in the texts that WBY published out of those researches, and its depth will surface throughout this study in various ways. So although it would be a wrong turn to ask about belief in terms that require a yes or no answer, it is important to ask what I or anyone else believes, and what belief is, as we read *A Vision,* the *Vision* papers, or any of the many related poems and other works. Such unanswerable questions are structural principles, themes, and effects in the Yeatses' *magna opera* as well as influences upon it.

Given that a number of good reasons exist to consider faith as a component of WBY's work, why is it awkward to do so? Spirituality, in the sense of an interior state instead of or in addition to sets of propositions, is difficult to accommodate in the kinds of discourse that usually feature a canonical literary figure. The kinds of religious

---

[18] On the antithetical, see Adams, *Blake and Yeats,* and *Yeats's Poems, passim.* With reference to *A Vision,* see Adams, *Yeats's Vision,* 13.

[19] *YVP*i. 252; iii. 174; see also *YVP*iii. 298–9.

thought and practice with which WBY was involved, which Auden famously categorized as 'Southern Californian', are an even less congenial discursive fit.[20] It can be downright embarrassing to talk about whether disembodied voices actually spoke to WBY and GY, and this phenomenon is a sure sign that a comfort zone of intellectual life has been disturbed. The discomfort interests me, for it raises the issue of what is being added or removed in the process of making a discussion 'academic'. Do the Yeatses' beliefs or mine (or those of other individuals or groups) make a difference to the texts, the reading of them, or the other systems of exchange in which they play a role? Do we privilege the secular? And if we do, what agendas are served by such privileging? To approach this question, I will shift focus briefly to a context in which it occurs dramatically: in the practical business of encountering WBY as many readers do, as students or teachers in a classroom. How to incorporate WBY's spiritual, parapsychological, and magical interests gracefully into a literature course is a challenge, and the reasons for this translate readily into more general concerns.[21]

When the time comes to introduce the question of WBY's religious practices and convictions, the atmosphere in my classrooms shifts noticeably, into discomfort or even low-level anxiety. Students watch me closely and look at each other to see how to behave, as if their sense of the appropriate attitude for the occasion has betrayed them. It is as if some unspoken law of secular universities has been broken, or a play has suddenly departed from its script. In that I represent the authority of the system, a social dissonance has sounded, interrupting the smooth operation of power. It is allowable under the ideologies within which a college classroom operates for students to be passionate about WBY's poetry, in other words—in fact, few poets I teach elicit more emotional participation. If the

---

[20] Auden, 'Yeats as an Example', 345.

[21] For discussions designed to be useful in teaching WBY's occultism, see Margaret Mills Harper, 'Yeats's Religion', in *YAACTS* xiii. 48–71, and the forthcoming 'Yeats and the Occult', in John S. Kelly and Marjorie Howes (eds.), *The Cambridge Companion to W. B. Yeats* (Cambridge: Cambridge University Press), 144–66.

prescribed academic distance from issues of spirituality is breached, however, the class is likely to be punctuated by titters or protests, either jokes or earnest arguments about WBY's silliness. Laughter is the easiest response, and to some extent the most appropriate, first, in that WBY himself is more humorous than he is often allowed to be, often in the magical texts.[22] As GY told Richard Ellmann, 'People don't understand that one can joke about mysticism and still believe in it, as WBY did.'[23] Second, the release of laughter may be compared to the leap at the heart of logic that Heidegger and Derrida theorize (a fact known well to Joyce, in *Finnegans Wake* especially, among others). If the joke is a shared one between readers and material, and the laughter is thus demotic or absurdist rather than patronizing or distancing, it can be downright useful as a teaching aid. The practical issue is a question of tone. With what degree of engagedness or detachment ought a class to discuss truth claims that include doctrines of the afterlife, the geometric and astrological nature of history and psychology, and direct communication between the living and the dead?

It is of course possible to put off anxiety by examining WBY's passion for hermetic truth through 'objective' points of view derived from various academic disciplines: to trace historical influences upon WBY's mysticism such as Irish folklore or the writings of Emanuel Swedenborg; to place the Yeatses' automatic writing and other occult experiments culturally amidst the widespread interest in spiritualism in middle-class Victorian and Edwardian society or the proliferation of new technologies that altered ideas about perception, communication, and memory; to examine the political relationships between WBY's Rosicrucianism and Irish nationalism, say, or between the system and the Great War or fascism; to analyse the occult experiments psychologically; or to examine them in terms of gender as a sexual dialectic or marital politics. These discussions

[22] On the topic of WBY's humour, see Adams, *Yeats's Vision*, and Helmling, *Esoteric Comedies*.

[23] Ellmann, interview with GY, 27 Aug. 1946, Richard Ellmann Papers, Special Collections Department, McFarlin Library, University of Tulsa.

are, of course, valuable and interesting (indeed, they fill a large number of the pages that follow), and they raise issues that were avoided altogether in Yeats studies for too long. Nevertheless, they also keep the distance that the academic environment enforces in discussions of religion. It is easy to fall into condescension when discussing some of WBY's passions that can seem wild or naïve: séances, Tarot readings, Golden Dawn rituals, automatic writing, and so forth.

Attitudes that instructors and students bring to class and to their reading are the first sources of awkwardness. Schools, colleges, and universities reflect positivist ways of looking at reality, and thus make assumptions about the material nature of things that WBY was passionately committed to disavowing. Academic settings, despite ideologically conservative reactions no less than postmodernist and liberationist innovations, are grounded upon a more or less empirical model: a starting position of scepticism is gradually replaced by certainty based on the accumulation of data and logical proofs. In the contemporary academy, poetry and religion are often defined in terms of science, which is then pitted against both, taking on some of their traditional qualities in so far as it is invested with the ability to answer fundamental questions, fulfil human needs and desires, and give order and beauty.[24] The recent history of the academic study of literature reflects a popular need to make reading and interpreting scientific endeavours, from emphasis on collecting historical or biographical facts, stress on poems as 'well-wrought' objects, phenomenological interest in what a text-object does, various pseudo-Darwinian determinisms based on the effects of cultural or psychological adaptations, or structuralist (or poststructuralist) hypotheses of systems of codes or laws that govern language and literary works.[25] Not that post-industrial science is really to blame:

---

[24] I am suggesting that this popular misconception exists, not that science either has little to do with the discourses of art and religion or that scientific methods are essentially religious.

[25] Some of the historical reasons for scholarly distaste of WBY's occultiana are discussed in two essays by James Lovic Allen: 'Belief versus Faith in the Credo of Yeats', *Journal*

it is only the most recent idol in a temple at least as old as logic. None the less, it remains true that, as St Paul claimed, reason cannot arrive at God.[26] Trained observers have a hard time seeing ghosts; the cognates *spectator* and *spectre* have long been uncomfortable in each other's presence. Derrida makes this point in *Specters of Marx,* for example, in glossing the scene in *Hamlet* where Horatio addresses the ghost:

There has never been a scholar who really, and as scholar, deals with ghosts. A traditional scholar does not believe in ghosts—nor in all that could be called the virtual space of spectrality. There has never been a scholar who, as such, does not believe in the sharp distinction between the real and the unreal, the actual and the inactual, the living and the non-living, being and non-being ('to be or not to be,' in the conventional reading), in the opposition between what is present and what is not, for example in the form of objectivity. Beyond this opposition, there is, for the scholar, only the hypothesis of a school of thought, theatrical fiction, literature, and speculation.[27]

The model of teaching literature in many if not most institutions resembles this putative scholar more than any 'school of thought, theatrical fiction, literature, and speculation' like occult philosophy, Yeatsian drama or poetry, or wonderment at another point of view besides oppositional logic. Teaching all too often presupposes a final point of dominance over the texts studied: by the time we finish with WBY, we will have 'gotten' him.

Such readerly superiority is difficult to sustain in a course that reads WBY seriously. His religious doctrines in particular are not supported by attitudes that are easy to pin down. Although the reasons for this situation are varied (and include his own differing views and

of *Modern Literature,* 4 (1975): 692–716, and 'Yeats, Belief, and ESP: New Critical Attitudes', *Éire-Ireland,* 24 (1989): 109–19.

[26] See 1 Cor. 1: 19–24, where Paul denounces both a Hellenistic emphasis on rationality and a Judaic demand for physical demonstration in favour of the 'folly of the gospel'.

[27] Jacques Derrida, *Specters of Marx: The State of the Debt, The Work of Mourning, and the New International,* trans. Peggy Kamuf (London: Routledge, 1994), 11.

varying levels of certainty at different moments), one significant factor points to a logical inconsistency at the heart of the academic project. A materialist universe is seemingly presupposed, but in fact the teachers and students who act as subjects to approach literature or other objects with their analytical tools assume a position of transcendence that I would characterize as fundamentally religious with regard to the material they study. When they study, they, or 'we', are not, in the perspective generated by the academic institution, specifically located in time or place, limited by our circumstances, or available for dismantling by the tools we use, to paraphrase Audre Lorde. We are immortal, lordly, unmoved. But WBY refuses to allow us our transcendence. The passage cited at the beginning of this chapter is typical of the most common strategy used in WBY's publicly religious language: the prose even at its most dogmatic backs away from its own declarations. Seekers from the Western tradition may find, he writes, not truth, but 'something attractive'. A faith that is 'a legitimate deduction . . . as I think' is at the same time not 'understandable'. Its attractiveness, the unity that is like 'a perfectly proportioned human body', is paradoxically ugly and painful, taking on the 'eye of newt, and toe of frog' of a witches' brew. The creed is undercut even in its most open expression, in a declaration written from the totalizing position of an old man remembering and making sense of his life. I will return to this passage, but I want to note here that this sly quality to WBY's prose often puts students on the defensive. His conception of faith fits into neither side of the computer logic that students have often brought to class: is he a zero or a one? does he believe in something or doesn't he? There is a radical disjunction between the questions we insist on asking and the answers that the poet is willing to give.

One means whereby to explain the resistance of WBY's occult texts to explication is to stress their relationship to mainstream philosophic idealism, as WBY himself realized before he rewrote *A Vision* for its second edition, undergoing a course of reading at the communicators' insistence. Like his predecessors Kant, Blake, and Fichte, WBY will not admit that the differences in belief between a reader and writer are a mere conflict of values—he will not allow me to say of him, as I can of Dante, that he believed in one kind of universe and I believe in another. Rather, WBY's writing suggests a different way of regarding what truth is, shifting the terms of the discussion to insist that the reliability of the system depends upon the creative imagination, not on any intrinsic difference between what is thought or believed by one person or another, or what is absolutely true. Like Kant, WBY to a large extent replaces the object of belief or inquiry with its function, since the object is inaccessible. Further, as Kant implied and Blake proclaimed, the consequence of such a universe is that all discourse becomes discourse about myself. All I know about God becomes subordinated to the human concept of freedom; in Blake's words, 'The Last Judgment is an Overwhelming of Bad Art & Science. Mental Things are alone Real.'[28]

In this sense, Kathleen Raine is correct in asserting that the guiding principle unifying WBY's spirituality is 'the *philosophia perennis*' which 'in all its branches holds that not matter but mind—consciousness—is the ground of reality as we experience it. . . . Theosophy and magic, psychical research and the popular beliefs of the Celtic race, Blake and Swedenborg, Neoplatonism, Indian philosophy and the supernatural drama of the Japanese Noh plays—all these concern the exploration of a mental universe.'[29] The material world of external circumstances, including history, destiny, and time, become one element in an equation, dependent upon other elements and not givens or absolutes. Alternatively, to use terms from *A Vision,* the Body of Fate is one of the four Faculties of each human being, the part of the human condition that is 'forced upon us from without' (*AV A* 15) and thus out of our control, but that also belongs to us only as one part of our personhood considered in entirety. Thus, although we may be unaware of the source of our circumstances in ourselves and do not choose those circumstances, they are still ruled by our imagination. To return to the topic of WBY's rhetoric, it makes sense that a world like this would express itself

---

[28] Blake, *Complete Writings*, 617.   [29] Raine, *Yeats the Initiate*, 106–7.

in language that is creative and paradoxical, that describes a reality that is apparently external, and even predetermined, in wayward, ambiguous, or poetic terms.

So far, so good. But WBY's occult beliefs are not finally reducible to a parallel with mental processes, as Raine is also aware. Function may replace object in WBY for the purposes of comparison or explanation, but a wild card of supersensual otherness remains. The shivering traces of another, unrepresentable world in poems like 'The Cold Heaven', 'The Second Coming', and 'Byzantium' are examples of a less readily assimilable universe. WBY's universes are neither solipsistic nor closed: they end in a face, of ghost, rough beast, or image-begetting images, but it is not our face. As he wrote through the voice of his seance-suggested Other Leo Africanus in a manuscript not intended for publication:

Yet, the formulas of science, though necessary as a mechanism of much reasoning, precisely because the known is much less than the unknown, ensure that a scientific exposition can but have temporary value. In your heart you know that all philosophy, that has lasting expression is founded on the intuition of god, & that he being all good & all power it follows [as] Henry More the Cambridge Platon so wisely explains that all our deep desires are images of the truth. We are immortal & shall as it were be dipped in beauty & good because he cannot being good but fulfill our desires. Yet desire is not reason & that intuition, though it can arouse the intellect to its last subtlety, is but the deep where reason floats, or perhaps the light wherein the separate objects of our thought find colour & definition.[30]

The 'intuition of god' is the step we find most difficult to take. The difficulty is the cause of some of the rather curious prevailing ideas about the *Vision* experiences, such as the notion that when WBY tells readers in the introduction to the revised edition that the instructors who spoke through his wife came 'to give you metaphors for poetry' (*AV B* 8), they, and he, mean by that phrase that they

---

[30] 'Leo', 28. A cancelled passage following the word *know* in the second sentence replaces 'god' with the occult tradition: 'that tradition enforced by the experience of the soul is the nearest you can come to truth & that lasting philosophy is expression' (45 n. 70).

were not to be believed (an interpretation that confuses messengers with message first of all, and then assumes, amazingly, that material that provides metaphors for poetry is by definition unreal).[31] What WBY was about will become relevant later. Meanwhile, I would like to continue examining the difficulties of navigating Leo's 'deep where reason floats' with the charts available in academic life.

In political terms, questions of belief, or at least its sister field, ethics, have historically cut to the heart of the institutionalized study of English literature, derived as the discipline is from nineteenth-century aesthetics and coloured as it is by twentieth-century economic realities. Lecturers participate in a system of pedagogy and scholarship that has a long history of presuming, with the faith of Kant, Schiller, and Coleridge, that art improves people's lives. In the United States, for example, the Modern Language Association may not officially share in a public apprehension of the arts and the humanities as socially endorsed replacements for institutional religion in social life, but it uses such conceptions in outreach programmes in defence against an attitude that finds literary study meaningless. The same argument has been used to try to save the National Endowments for the Arts and the Humanities from legislators who profess to be offended by esoteric or daring subjects for study. Perhaps especially in educational settings in the United States, where 'church' is firmly separated from state-funded public schooling, high art (defined as the sort assigned in college classrooms, and poetry perhaps more readily than prose) is still marketed, as it has been for several generations, as one of the prime places to go in the academy for answers about the human condition.

---

[31] On this famous quotation, Alan S. Marzilli notes, correctly, that 'This single remark may have led many critics away from studying a work that occupied a significant part of WBY's time and energy for many years' ('Masking of Truth in W. B. Yeats's *A Vision*: A Comparison of the Two Editions in Relation to the Original Automatic Experience' (M.A. thesis, Emory University, 1993), 66). Balachandra Rajan also makes the point that 'to Yeats himself, who had cast his life into his rhymes, the strange designs which the communicators dictated and the frustrators confused were the climax of a thirty-year search for synthesis' (*W. B. Yeats: A Critical Introduction* (London: Hutchinson, 1965), 80).

Matthew Arnold articulated eloquently and influentially the late nineteenth-century hope that 'the spirit of our race will find, . . . as time goes on and as other helps fail, its consolation and stay' in poetry, given that 'there is not a creed which is not shaken, not an accredited dogma which is not shown to be questionable, not a received tradition which does not threaten to dissolve'. Looking back at Arnold is one way to make plain an important distinction between a Romantic 'religion' of art, which forms the genetic material of the academic way of thinking about poetry, and WBY's seemingly similar but ultimately contradictory views. Arnold believed that he witnessed a kind of second coming at the end of a materialistic era, and that the new faith would be poetic, so that 'more and more mankind will discover that we have to turn to poetry to interpret life for us, to console us, to sustain us'.[32] Whether or not we agree with Arnold, share his fears at the dissolution of Christianity or the desolation of a scientific world, we should remember that we are his heirs. We may react against our history and protest that we are no longer regarding reading as a moral or spiritual exercise, but we cannot be unaffected by such views. As Terry Eagleton has remarked, students of English literature remain 'irremediably altered by that historic intervention. There is no more need to be a card-carrying Leavisite today than there is to be a card-carrying Copernican: that current has entered the bloodstream of English studies in England as Copernicus reshaped our astronomical beliefs, has become a form of spontaneous critical wisdom as deep-seated as our conviction that the earth moves round the sun.'[33] And this unexamined conviction should give us pause. Eavan Boland has described Arnold's vision of the new moment when 'most of what now passes with us for religion and philosophy will be replaced by poetry' in terms that resemble 'The Second Coming' more than the benign new world foreseen by her Victorian predecessor. Boland prophesies danger: 'The line

---

[32] Matthew Arnold, 'The Study of Poetry', in *idem*, *Essays in Criticism, Second Series*, ed. Noel Annan (London: Oxford University Press, 1964), 47.
[33] Terry Eagleton, *Literary Theory: An Introduction* (Minneapolis: University of Minnesota Press, 1983), 31.

between religion and poetry has given way. And what comes forth, monstrous to my eyes anyway, is neither religion nor poetry, but the religion of poetry.'[34] The gods are not easily banished: they may merely have taken up residence in a different temple.

Eagleton's metaphor implies that contemporary assumptions resemble faith in science more than science as the absence of faith; extending it, we might say that the difficulty with WBY is that he never accepted the new heliocentrism. To cite again the passage from 'A General Introduction for My Work' cited at the head of this chapter, it is not accidental that WBY equates 'a new science' with 'faith'. At any rate, literature is not substituted for religion in WBY, for the simple reason that a live belief in extra-material reality remains. However, a crucial ontological detail disallows any simple binary between materialism and non-materialism. In one formulation or another, WBY's beliefs in supersensual reality always include a proviso for the human mind, individually or in concert with others in a Great Mind, in the system. In the 1920s his poem 'The Tower' claims, in words that resemble the beginning of the 1901 essay 'Magic' and 'A General Introduction for My Work':

> ... I declare my faith:
> I mock Plotinus' thought
> And cry in Plato's teeth,
> Death and life were not
> Till man made up the whole,
> Made lock, stock and barrel
> Out of his bitter soul,
> Aye, sun and moon and star, all,
> And further add to that
> That, being dead, we rise,
> Dream and so create
> Translunar Paradise.
>
> (*VP* 415)

---

[34] Eavan Boland, 'When the Spirit Moves'. *The New York Review of Books*, 12 Jan. 1995.

In this regard WBY's faith in art resembles Blake's claims of divine status for the human imagination more closely than it does other versions of the Romantic commonplace. As WBY put it in an essay from the heady decade of the 1890s, when his hopes for occult renewal were at their height, Blake

had learned from Jacob Boehme and from old alchemist writers that imagination was the first emanation of divinity, 'the body of God,' 'the Divine members,' and he drew the deduction, which they did not draw, that the imaginative arts were therefore the greatest of Divine revelations, and that the sympathy with all living things, sinful and righteous alike, which the imaginative arts awaken, is that forgiveness of sins commanded by Christ. (*E&I* 112)

WBY here transforms a rhetorical device into a spiritual truth, regarding Blake's system genealogically in order to stress its connection with occult tradition and deducing the sacredness of art from an a priori assumption of active, commanding divinity. He arrives at a widely used metaphor, with his own versions of sacramental symbols and artist-priests, from the opposite direction from Arnold, Coleridge, and others, by transferring literal faith into the realm of the aesthetic rather than raising the aesthetic to the language of faith. Although WBY had no great love for the Catholic Church in Ireland, his symbols are animated by a rather more Catholic than Protestant variant of the artistic faith, in that they function more as Real Presence than convenient shorthand for spiritual abstractions. To be more precise, and to use language that the later WBY would have preferred, his aesthetic spirituality has a pre-Schismatic or Orthodox colouring, Byzantine rather than Roman.[35]

---

[35] WBY connected Irish Christianity with pre-Roman orthodoxy on several occasions: e.g., in the 'Commentary on Supernatural Songs', in *The King of the Great Clock Tower* (Dublin: Cuala Press, 1934). Discussing Irish Christianity 'before the Great Schism that separated Western from Eastern Christianity in the ninth century', WBY comments that 'In course of time the Church of Ireland would feel itself more in sympathy with early Christian Ireland than could a Church that admitted later developments of doctrine' (*VP* 837). Romanticizing and orientalizing, of course, characterize his need to find Catholic and Orthodox qualities in the religion of art, a need that also identifies his Anglo-Irish

In WBY's scheme, the parishioner at the temple of art does not dominate the interaction between worshipper and god: the poet is modernist to this extent, prizing difficulty, as well as anti-low church, rejecting the altar call. The purpose of the experience is not for the attender or reader to attain the right emotion or thought, to adopt the proper attitude towards and understanding of the rituals and symbols. Rather, sacramental objects and acts are iconic (the word *icon*, of course, derives from *eikōn*, 'image', in Greek): they have power in themselves, in excess of the ability (or lack of ability) of the believer to appropriate them.[36] But at the same time, crucially, they are creations, of an individual artist and of a tradition, the concept through which a reader is brought into the system. A mosaic or painted Christ is more than an aid to personal meditation. It is Christ acting, albeit through the gaze and prayer of the beholder: the eyes of an icon look back at the viewer from traditional poses that are designed to bring her or him to a transformed state. The

Protestantism. Similarly, the exoticism with which English Pre-Raphaelites represented medieval Catholicism displays their own background in a Church of England–dominated nineteenth century. See R. F. Foster, 'Protestant Magic: W. B. Yeats and the Spell of Irish History', in *Paddy and Mr Punch: Connections in Irish and English History* (London: Allen Lane–Penguin Press, 1993), 212–32, for the Anglo-Irishness of WBY's occultism and the related tradition of Protestant gothic with its 'mingled repulsion and envy' of Catholic magic.

[36] WBY had long held theories of the symbol that emphasized its magical qualities: see 'Magic', sects. VI and VII (*E&I* 44–50). See also Allen R. Grossman, *Poetic Knowledge in the Early Yeats: A Study of* The Wind Among the Reeds (Charlottesville, Va.: University of Virginia Press, 1969), for an examination of this concept in an important volume. Elizabeth Bergmann Loizeaux, *Yeats and the Visual Arts* (New Brunswick, NJ: Rutgers University Press, 1986), is the most important treatment of the interconnectedness between the visual and the written in WBY. Describing the techniques used in painting (or 'writing', the term used by iconographers) icons, John Baggley uses a magical metaphor relevant to the parallel with Yeatsian practices:

the suspension of . . . colours in the egg medium and laid over a gesso or gilt-gesso ground, allowed the light to pass through the materials and be reflected into the eye in a series of events that are almost alchemical in that they demonstrate a transformation of matter, or rather, of vibrations of light. The transformation of matter by the finer vibrations of light can be regarded as more than the ultimate spiritual symbol: it is a demonstration of the actions of divine energy manifested on the physical plane. (John Baggley, *Doors of Perception—Icons and their Spiritual Significance* (London and Oxford: Mowbray, 1987), 104–5)

paradox of action and detachment is revealed, in that meditation is simultaneously necessary and unnecessary, since the object of thought is that which cannot be conceived, and the goal of the practice is already perfected. God became human precisely in order that humans might become God; the human soul is an essential, if not the pre-eminent, component of a relationship with that which (or who) requires nothing.[37] This knowledge is similar to that which Derrida isolates as an 'unthought' quality of Western religion; that since the dominance of Christianity, the moral imagination represses both the demonic or orgiastic sacred and Greek abstraction, and incorporates them into the idea of 'a person as transcendent other, as an other who looks at me, but who looks without the subject-who-says-I being able to reach that other, see her, hold her within the reach of my gaze.' Quoting and commenting on Jan Patočka, Derrida adds:

In the final analysis the soul [in the Christian mystery] is not a relation to an object, however elevated (such as the Platonic good) [which implies, therefore, 'such as in Platonism where the soul is the relation to a transcendent Good that also governs the ideal order of the Greek *polis* or the Roman *civitas*'], but to a person who fixes it in his gaze while at the same time remaining beyond the reach of the gaze of that soul.[38]

It is difficult to generalize about WBY's use of symbols, given the number of changes that his usage underwent over the course of his long career. In his mature periods, however, symbols most often function within this kind of system, in which the object as such disappears, taking the subject, that I-saying being defined in terms of the object, with it, only to return freighted with the alterity that we might think of as that which Sartre believed he had located in the

[37] I have been influenced in my understanding of the use of icons by Gregory Collins, OSB, *The Glenstal Book of Icons* (Blackrock, Co. Dublin: Columba Press, 2002); Henri J. M. Nouwen, *Behold the Beauty of the Lord: Praying with Icons* (Notre Dame, Ind.: Ave Maria Press, 1987); and Leonid Ouspensky, *Theology of the Icon*, trans. Anthony Gythiel, 2 vols. (Crestwood, NY: St Vladimir's Seminary Press, 1992). See also Baggley, *Doors of Perception*, and Leonid Ouspensky and Vladimir Lossky, *The Meaning of Icons*, trans. G. E. H. Palmer and E. Kadloubovsky (Crestwood, NY: St Vladimir's Seminary Press, 1983).
[38] Derrida, *Gift of Death*, 25.

gaze of the Other and which has arguably been a part of the subject all along. Symbols function as gateways, or jumping-off points, through which the human imagination can approach a transmaterial world. But they also operate in reverse, as if they were conduits through which that world can come to this. This back-and-forth quality not only delineates a system based on correspondences, the principle 'as above, so below' of Hermetic tradition, but suggests a destabilizing uncertainty about which of those two elements is in power at any moment. The incantatory images of the poem 'Parnell's Funeral'—for example, 'A beautiful seated boy; a sacred bow; / A woman, and an arrow on a string; / A pierced boy, image of a star laid low' (*VP* 541)—illustrate a Parnell whose symbolic reality as sacrifice is at least as real as his historical existence, but they do not allow a determination of which one is primary. The Irish hero as symbol is neither strictly representational, a sign that may distil but ultimately serves a material reality, nor allegory, an image of a transmaterial truth that ultimately disdains materiality.

Symbolism in this poem and others resembles sacred drama, as the poem itself recognizes, the speaker comparing political murders and chaos to 'a painted stage', but then exchanging theatre for ritual action, the devouring of a heart. The poet gives actors masks and directs their actions into stylized, unnatural patterns that claim to be real, in a complex relation to daily life. Such use of symbol is also reminiscent of astrology as it has been practised since the advent of the scientific study of astronomy; the practitioner assumes a system of calculations that are traditional rather than personal or realistic to be genuinely indicative of human character or universal destiny.[39] To return to a religious metaphor, this language is not

---

[39] Paul de Man's distinction between image and emblem, outlined in 'Image and Emblem in Yeats', in *idem*, *The Rhetoric of Romanticism* (New York: Columbia University Press, 1984), 145–238, is relevant here. De Man defines two kinds of symbolism in WBY: a 'symbol' is a natural image, and an 'emblem', in the poet's words, may be described as 'having its meaning by a traditional and not by a natural right'. Further, de Man notes, 'in this context, "traditional" is synonymous with "divine"' (p. 165). Elizabeth Heine notes that even within his use of astrology, WBY was partial to symbolic rather than real progressions of planets as he charted predictions for his own life, a practice that

art conceived as helpful to human beings, the church of art as an essentially service-oriented institution; WBY's art serves mysterious powers that people do well to regard with awe, even though those powers are ultimately human.

My emphasis on transcendent humanity is not to claim that WBY was a Christian; his thought ran in directions considerably more outside orthodox religious traditions than within them.[40] But it is to propose that WBY's lines of thinking do not so much operate outside the main channels of Western thought as highlight qualities within it that tend, for a number of reasons, to remain untheorized or recognized, whether in the experiences of students or the ruminations of their teachers. Students in high school or university classrooms, no less than other mortals, do not actually define themselves or their world as neatly as they may think they do. Delineations between subject and object, individual will and group behaviour, material and non-material, active and passive, and even positive and negative, are not the stable footholds on what we regard as real that it is easy to imagine that they are. The issue finally is not so much that WBY should not provoke laughter as to recognize that laughter is both the response of discomfort with an irritant to the system and potentially a release of the tensions that have held that system locked in place. The poem with which WBY chose to end *The Tower* recognizes that strange truths may provoke their hearers to derision, but suggests that an appropriate response might be a sort of laughter that indicates a more complicated emotional state:

borders on magic (Elizabeth Heine, 'W. B. Yeats' Map in his Own Hand', *Biography: An Interdisciplinary Quarterly*, 1 (1978): 37–50).

[40] WBY was Christian if by that term is meant that he was a man of his milieu, which was saturated with Christianity. He had religious inclinations, if no regular profession, and his family history was steeped in Anglo-Irish Anglicanism. His explorations to a large degree take their tone from the church that his father rejected and that he tried to replace. Mysticism, which my analogy of meditation on icons suggests, is another issue. WBY certainly had mystical experiences, and he never renounced his claim to John O'Leary in 1893 that 'The mystical life is the centre of all that I do and all that I think and all that I write' (*L* 211). However, WBY equates mysticism here with magic, the topic that is the context for this often-quoted remark (the paragraph begins, 'Now as to Magic', and asserts that magical study is, 'next to my poetry, the most important pursuit of my life').

I have mummy truths to tell
Whereat the living mock,
Though not for sober ear,
For maybe all that hear
Should laugh and weep an hour upon the clock.

('All Souls' Night', *VP* 474)

Power

The central principle of all the Magic of power is that everything
we formulate in the imagination, if we formulate it strongly
enough, realises itself in the circumstances of life, acting either
through our own souls, or through the spirits of nature.

WBY, 'Is the Order of R.R. & A.C. to remain a Magical
Order?'[41]

WBY's published works about his occult practices function themselves
like words of power, speech acts designed to change the universe in
which they are spoken, and the ambitions and ambiguities of such a
project saturate his *œuvre*.[42] One way to approach this phenomenon
is as knowing subject to inert object: we can analyse WBY. My use of
the traditional plural pronoun is deliberate, to make obvious that a
standard method assumes a common, unbiased, learned community
of peers, and the shared values that are a constitutive quality of this
kind of writing. As I have been arguing, though, it is also possible
to read from a position that takes into account the possibility of its
own instability. Such an analysis includes in its logic the affectedness

---

Among WBY's critics, Virginia Moore is one of only a few who ascribe Christian belief to
him. In a late chapter that argues overtly with general opinion on this subject, Moore
also names GY in making her animated counter-argument: 'After Mrs. Yeats had read this
chapter so far, I asked her if she thought I had overstressed her husband's Christianity.
Her answer was "Certainly not"' (Moore, *The Unicorn*, 431).

  [41] G. M. Harper, *Yeats's Golden Dawn*, 265.

  [42] For a study of the rhetoric of WBY's prose, see Susan Martha Dobra, 'Collaboration
and Consensus: Constructing a Rhetoric of Abnormal Discourse for Composition from
the Esoteric Prose of William Butler Yeats and Annie Wood Besant' (Ph.D. diss.,
University of California, 1993).

of readers, who function in the system as objects for the subject WBY, who shapes us, no less than as subjects who consume him. As he wrote in another late introduction, 'A poet is justified not by the expression of himself, but by the public he finds or creates; a public made by others ready to his hand if he is a mere popular poet, but a new public, a new form of life, if he is a man of genius' (*E&I* x). The design of the writing, particularly of the late works, when WBY was speaking to a posterity he felt sure would listen, is to create us as WBY's public, no less than those who bought his books when they first arrived on booksellers' shelves. This conception of writing as power over strangers is another aspect of the discomfort that the works produce. It's not pleasant to be worked on, and in various ways, all of WBY's occult prose puts its readers in the position of the base metal in an alchemical experiment. Our transformation is the goal, whether we like it or not; even the attractive qualities that lure us into paying attention in the first place serve a function well beyond the author's desire to please. We are in something of the position of the narrator of the early story 'Rosa Alchemica', a reflexive strategy that is part of the story's considerable interest. We must choose to accept or refuse the empowerment offered, and we gain power by first relinquishing control.

This kind of power seldom moves in a straightforward trajectory. WBY's occult non-fiction, by which I mean essays like 'Magic' or 'Swedenborg, Mediums, and the Desolate Places', the short monograph *Per Amica Silentia Lunae*, and *A Vision*, in this regard bears a noticeable resemblance to books from Western magical or mystical traditions which WBY read and studied, sometimes in the contexts of organizations to which he belonged.[43] From the cabbalah to the

---

[43] Among critics of WBY, Harold Bloom discusses *A Vision* as 'a Gnostic scripture' most expansively (*Yeats*, 240). But see also A. Norman Jeffares, who claims that *A Vision* is most important for 'the role it plays as Bible to Yeats's religion of poetry' (*W. B. Yeats: Man and Poet*, 204). Terry Eagleton hints at 'a remote connection' between WBY and a mystical strain of Irish orthodoxy, specifically a line of theological and epistemological thought as old as Eriugena that stresses the paradox of humanity's knowledge of the unknowability of God (*Heathcliff and the Great Hunger: Studies in Irish Culture* (London and New York: Verso, 1995), 50–1).

works of Madame Blavatsky, this diverse assemblage has in common qualities that WBY's prose often shares. Exposition is densely
allusive, dotted with obtrusive scholarly references. The operating
principles of the style are expansiveness and inclusivity, mirroring
the usually sloppily defined and syncretistic theologies presented, yet
the very encyclopaedism of the surface is part of its resistance and
unknowability. For example, doctrines of any number of religious
systems appear—Gnosticism, Hermeticism, cabbalism, Neoplatonism, Manichaeanism, Zoroastrianism, and Rosicrucianism, among
others—but they are systems about most of which little evidence
remains, if much publicly disseminated knowledge was ever available.
Syntax is frequently complex, featuring thoughts that are connected
through correspondence and association rather than sequential logic.
The more ancient occult texts are frequently incomplete, a fact that
adds little to their readability but much to their tantalizing quality.
Perfect doctrine is now, with the partial loss of the text, forever
lost to mortal seekers. As above, so below: as a text is difficult,
multi-voiced, or damaged, so a reader is puzzled, disunified, and
defiled. As the reader is initiated, so the text reveals its fullness in
order for the act of reading to correspond to the sacred and conjugate
act of communicating truth. (The relation of truth to humanity,
as Paracelsus wrote, is conjugal indeed: 'the things beneath are so
related to the things above as Man and wife'.[44])

Like any marriage, this *logos* means desire as well as satisfaction.
Occult rhetoric must entice, since being generous in sharing the light
with a benighted world is a sign of its godliness, but not reveal, since
enlightenment is an interior phenomenon that cannot be gained
through reading *about* it. This gesture of simultaneous offering
and withholding is common to most Gnostic-influenced texts and
at least as old as the *Corpus Hermeticum*, which presents Hermes
Trismegistus explaining that God did not distribute mind (*nous*) to

---

[44] Paracelsus, *His Archidoxes: Comprised in Ten Books, Disclosing the Genuine Way of
Making Quintessences, Arcanums, Magisteries, Elixers, & c.*, trans. J. H. [?James Howell],
2 vols. (London: printed for W. S., 1661), book x, ch. viii; i. 154; cited in Kathleen
Raine, *Blake and Tradition* (London: Routledge & Kegan Paul, 1969), i. 361.

all men, 'not from begrudgery, for grudging does not begin in heaven but is composed below, in the souls of men who do not have mind'. God is at once the cause of the absence of true understanding but not to blame for it, since blame is part of the mindlessness that is God's absence. Similarly, God is both plain throughout the universe but not seen there (*Corpus Hermeticum*, IV. 3, V).[45] Lack functions unsteadily in two logical positions: that of the opposite of presence, and therefore the state that disciples are to be lifted from, and that of a dynamic accompaniment to the acts of attainment and bestowal of blessedness. Like ancient literature or modern poetry, these books demand the labour of scholarly research or translation as well as the creative activities of synthesis and interpretation to be intelligible. The reward of all that discipline, like that of Torah in the midrashic tradition, is collected in the heart of the reader who accomplishes the difficult and creative work of reading. Equally, although occult texts are often authored, which is to say that they identify themselves as having been generated by a figure of writerly authority, who is presumably an adept, they often present themselves as impersonal compendia. Authors are not named or given pseudonyms; material is ordered and labelled or numbered like a manual or the Bible, and thus figured as traditional or universal.[46] To read is to be schooled, to compound one's knowledge arithmetically, but also to school oneself, to create a new whole from the fragments. The wisdom of the author is proved by the withdrawal into anonymity, about which I will have more to say later, as God's is by invisibility.

Bibliographic codes also assert the push-and-pull of occult power.[47] Arcane knowledge is often housed in books that either are or look

[45] Walter Scott (ed. with trans. and notes), *Hermetica: The Ancient Greek and Latin Writings which Contain Religious or Philosophic Teachings Ascribed to Hermes Trismegistus*, 2 vols. (Oxford: Clarendon Press, 1925), i. 150, 156–65; trans. mine. The explanation in the *Timaeus* of imperfection in human souls as the result of *anankē*, necessity, intruding into the creativity of the gods (69a) may also share in this rhetoric.

[46] See Leon Surette, *The Birth of Modernism: Ezra Pound, T. S. Eliot, W. B. Yeats, and the Occult* (Montreal: McGill–Queen's University Press, 1993), esp. 3–36, for a useful introduction to the topic of occultism and literature, esp. of the modern period.

[47] The term *bibliographic code*, coined by Jerome McGann, refers to the physical qualities rather than the ideational content of a book. See McGann, *Critique*; Jerome

like hand-copied codices or incunabula, rare because old as well as marginal, perhaps even banned, dotted with words or passages in Greek, Latin, Arabic, or Sanskrit, difficult of access in look as well as in language. They assert power by their physical as well as ideational inaccessibility.[48] Yet, in that the appeal of such books also partakes of the romanticization of the antique that swept Europe in the wake of industrialization, exploration, and empire building, their rarity is a sign of the power of the consumer at least as significantly as it is the sign of the power of the artefact. Like ownership of ancient keeps or archaeological treasures, the possession of old knowledge, in old books, bestows value on the owner. So does the possession of newly written knowledge in limited editions, of course, like the tiny press run for the first edition of *A Vision* or the volumes printed by the Cuala Press (as WBY knew well). We should also note that such value is essentially religious or, more particularly, magical. In one generalized sense owning anything is a religious experience, in that commerciality since the rise of advertising is closely akin to spirituality through a similarity of function in offering fulfilment. But more particularly, the owner of books participates in the same bi-directional flow of power noted above with reference to the *Corpus Hermeticum*. The book functions as an agent of gnosis by turning the owner into a magus, one who controls history by possessing its

J. McGann, *The Textual Condition* (Princeton: Princeton University Press, 1991), and, for an overview and analysis of recent textual theory, Peter Shillingsburg, *Resisting Texts: Authority and Submission in Constructions of Meaning* (Ann Arbor: University of Michigan Press, 1997).

[48] The bibliographic codes of the 1st edition of *A Vision* especially engage in this rhetoric. Published by a small idiosyncratic press, in a small edition of 600 copies, with margins and type that suggest medieval books and antique-looking woodcuts, it clearly announces itself as occult. Incidentally, these codes had been well read when the Library of Congress and other libraries catalogued the critical edition of the book. According to Abby Yochelson, a reference specialist in English Literature at the Library of Congress, 'While we have chosen to assign a PR literature classification to Yeats's *Vision*, we have given it a subject heading of 'occultism.' Other libraries may choose to classify the work within a religion context. ... [A] number of libraries ... classified this work under BF1411.Y4 1978, assigning it a designation beginning BF, with works on religion, instead of PR, literature, with the rest of Yeats's works' (personal communication, 13 Jan. 2003).

meaning. The more idiosyncratic and wide-ranging the gathering, of books or allusions or quotations within them, the greater this power. It is worthwhile remembering that power over the course of events, over history itself, is a moving force of WBY's occult writings.[49] The writer as mage asserts this power, and it is accessible ongoingly to the reader as disciple as well. The authority of the past, the absent, and the intangible resides in contemporary possessors of occult truths that act as mediatorial spirits from ages past. Walter Benjamin also uses this metaphor which, in that it delineates a mysterious phenomenon, is something more than metaphor, when he proposes that such a possessor is indeed possessed: 'inside him there are spirits, or at least little genii, which have seen to it that for a collector—and I mean a real collector, a collector as he ought to be—ownership is the most intimate relationship that one can have to objects. Not that they come alive in him; it is he who lives in them.'[50]

The uncanny ways in which people dominate the history in which they live by means of texts and the ways in which, paradoxically, the same people are given the life they naïvely call their own by those same texts, to use Benjamin's language, may be teased out using the passage from 'A General Introduction for My Work' quoted above. WBY is not only recalling his own spiritual journeys but actively rewriting them and expecting that his readers, whom he presumes to own the never published edition that the introduction was written to open, will be changed through that act of proprietorship. He uses a ringing period to hammer home a message that has the sound of evangelical witness ('I was born into this faith, have lived in it, and shall die in it'). He may be playing upon contemporary anxieties, activated by social disruptions from mustard gas to motor cars, women's suffrage to Stalin's regime, when he chooses vague words like 'dangerous fanaticism' to describe what needs to be escaped. He

[49] Helmling argues for the relation between WBY's sense of powerlessness in the face of Irish history, which he saw as being written without him in the years from the Rising through the Treaty, and his renewed interest in spiritualism during these decades.

[50] Walter Benjamin, *Illuminations*, trans. Harry Zohn (New York: Schocken, 1969), 69.

marshalls for support an impressive list of fellow believers starting in Ireland, perhaps with a nod to his large Irish-American readership, and broadening to the arcane East. Common Yeatsian motifs like 'Unity of Being' and reference to Blakean imagination further underline the argument for a lasting commitment to readers familiar with his works already, as many purchasers of the collected works for which the essay was written would certainly be. Presumably the works introduced by the essay would comprise a kind of initiation into power over the tension-ridden times. But another mood also haunts the declaration. Talk of 'a new science' sits uneasily with the sense that WBY's faith has differed from the person he was at one moment to that of another ('from man to man and age to age'), never resting in a doctrine that is 'intellectually understandable'. The final citation, 'eye of newt, and toe of frog' (*Macbeth*, IV. i. 14) draws upon the authority of characters in an imaginative work, not 'real' people, whose sanity is dubious and whose power may be devilish, whose apparitions, summoned by the spell whose words WBY quotes, speak words that mislead and destroy through their hearer's own temptation to believe them.

The whole passage is prefaced by a reconstruction of WBY's experiences with spiritualism that is carefully tailored for a sceptical audience. This description reduces WBY's many years as a theosophist, a Hermetic adept, a student of spiritualism, and an analyst of psychic phenomena to an editorial research project, 'an investigation of contemporary spiritualism' undertaken after 'Lady Gregory asked me to annotate her *Visions and Beliefs*, . . . that I might understand what she had taken down in Galway'. The seriousness of the time he claims to have spent, 'several years', is undercut by the description of 'those mediums who in various poor parts of London instruct artisans or their wives for a few pence upon their relations to their dead, to their employers, and to their children' (*E&I* 517). Class, always a sensitive issue with WBY, receives the major emphasis here, and it is interesting to recall that WBY usually took care to traffic with the more 'respectable' spiritualists, women like Elizabeth Radcliffe, who were not in the business for money, and men like F. W. H. Myers and Andrew

Lang, who pursued psychic phenomena within the academy-like atmosphere of the Society for Psychical Research.[51] In this late retrospective essay, even upper middle-class mediumship and scientific clubbiness seem not to serve to establish the position that WBY intends to occupy with regard to his material and his public. In the 1930s, when the sacred Pound and Eliot were yielding their place in the public imagination to the materialists Auden and MacNeice, WBY chooses neither the gentility of country drawing-rooms nor London libraries to persuade. Lest any reader mistake the poet's own status, he changes the scene immediately from working-class London to a remembered conversation held while walking though the stately Coole woods with Gregory, himself and his aristocratic Irish friend safely in a subject position *vis-à-vis* an 'old man' whom they passed and commented upon, a 'gamekeeper' and his visitation by ghostly deer, and a 'certain cracked old priest' who talked of the dead haunting the neighbourhood. Spiritualism may be *déclassé*, these people not my or our kind, WBY seems to be saying, but we in Ireland can bypass social considerations to recognize that it bears the wisdom of the ages nevertheless.

The words that follow the *credo* are as interesting as the ones that precede it. Just after the Weird Sisters' incantation, WBY brings up

---

[51] Spiritualism was slightly risky for adherents with a middle- or higher-class status to maintain, a fact which explains the deep interest that its gentrified wing had in establishing its own respectability. For example, *Light*, the publication of the London Spiritualists' Alliance, included in every issue a list of eminent people who could vouch for the movement, a roster that included churchmen, politicians, heads of state, titled gentry, and men of the professions. The editors of the journal also felt the need to remind advertisers that its readers had purchasing power, telling prospective buyers of space that *Light* 'has a very large and world-wide circulation among the most cultured, thoughtful, and intelligent people of all classes' (37 (1917): 209). 'All classes' here, of course, means all above a certain level. Implicit class prejudice probably played a role in the disapproval of mediumship, states of trance, and hypnotism by theosophists as well as Rosicrucians. WBY may be subtly defending his descent into spiritualism to magically inclined readers as well as a sceptical general public. On class distinctions within the spiritualist movement in England, see Logie Barrow, *Independent Spirits: Spiritualism and English Plebeians 1850–1910* (London: Routledge & Kegan Paul, 1986). On Elizabeth Radcliffe, see George Mills Harper and John S. Kelly, 'Preliminary Examination of the Script of E[lizabeth] R[adcliffe]', in *Yeats and the Occult*; *YVP*i. 2–5; Foster, *Apprentice Mage*, 487–90; and Saddlemyer, *Becoming George*, 48–50. On the culture of the Society for Psychical Research, of which WBY was a member from 1913 to 1928, see Alan Gauld, *The Founders of Psychical Research* (London: Routledge & Kegan Paul, 1968).

A Vision, his own contribution to the literature, for the first time. 'Subconscious preoccupation with this theme brought me *A Vision*, its harsh geometry an incomplete interpretation,' he notes, in a paragraph that immediately moves to consider the warring emotions that accompany Irishness (p. 518). *A Vision* surfaces again only in one phrase at the end of the essay as essentially a distancing device, allowing WBY to hate the modern age without being damaged by his own attitudes. Despite poets who are 'determined to express the factory, the metropolis, that they may be modern', and WBY's repugnance, 'When I stand upon O'Connell Bridge in the half-light and notice that discordant architecture, all those electric signs, where modern heterogeneity has taken physical form', the contrary of any movement is always implied for someone 'accustomed' as he is 'to the geometrical arrangement of history in *A Vision*' (pp. 525–6), he asserts. In these final words WBY appropriates the occult philosophy of his book for purposes of keeping emotional equilibrium, making peace with the political and artistic scene of Europe in the 1930s. The earlier remark is similarly distancing, using the sensitive word 'subconscious' to describe a book that WBY described in the introduction to its second edition as brought by spirits and 'the creation of my wife's Daimon and of mine' (*AV B* 22), not the result of his own 'preoccupation'. He also relegates the book to the secondary position of 'interpretation' of one of his major themes—as opposed, perhaps, to creative expression—and then drops the subject altogether, despite its position in the lead sentence of the paragraph.

The topic of faith in this essay, then, acts as WBY's other occult prose does, as an enchantment, beat to a rhythm of sound and rhetoric reminiscent of spoken ritual or oral rhetoric, syncopated by a tone that vacillates between assertion and imaginative contrariety, and bracketed by social and political contexts that do not define the subject, as culture might be expected to do, but rather are used by that subject. Irishness, Anglo-Irishness, opposition to modernity, occult collaboration with his wife, and the many versions of self present in the autobiographical account, not to mention the collected works that were intended to follow the introductory essay, are all appropriated for WBY's purposes. So are we, who in our ownership of the essay and the collection that was to follow it will determine its fate, and our own, through its agency. To ask what such a man believed, and to try to answer that question from reading an essay such as 'A General Introduction for My Work' without reflecting on our own beliefs, is to be deceived. Such a path would be *Hodos Chameliontos,* in a phrase WBY liked, a path of the chameleon, which changes its colours depending upon the tricks of the light that readers shine on it and eludes the grasp even after it is caught.[52] The way out of the shifting smoke and mirrors is to find that one's answers reflect one's own issues or convictions, and to learn to adopt the position of the magus who asserts personal will, preposterously, on even the most recalcitrant of material.

The rhetorical shifts in the late essay actually have a long history in WBY's prose about the supernatural. The scenes in his unfinished novel *The Speckled Bird* that depict the various London occultists with whom the autobiographical protagonist works to create a new religion are full of sly digs at alchemists, Swedenborgians, Rosicrucians,

---

[52] *Hodos Chamelionis* is the title by which the Introducing Adept in the Adeptus Minor (5 = 6) Ritual of the Golden Dawn is known, and also the name given to the newly installed Aspirant to the rank: at the climax of the ceremony, the Chief greets the new Adeptus Minor with the words, 'And therefore do I greet thee with the Mystic Title of "Hodos Chamelionis", the Path of the Chameleon, the Path of Mixed Colours. . .'. (Israel Regardie, *The Golden Dawn: A Complete Course in Practical Ceremonial Magic. Four Volumes in One. The Original Account of the Teachings, Rites and Ceremonies of the Hermetic Order of the Golden Dawn* (*Stella Matutina*), 6th edn. (St Paul, Minn.: Llewellyn Publications, 1989), 225, 242). The phrase has a negative tint in the title of a section of *The Trembling of the Veil,* written as WBY worked on the system: he describes being 'lost' in 'that region a cabbalistic manuscript, shown to me by MacGregor Mathers, had warned me of' (*Au* 215). In the Dedication to *A Vision* (1925) the term has the positive resonance appropriate to its source, as WBY recalls studying 'how so to suspend the will that the mind became automatic, a possible vehicle for spiritual beings', a state 'we had learned to call *Hodos Chameliontos*' (p. xi). See G. M. Harper, *Yeats's Golden Dawn,* 177 n. 30. Note the similarity to a description of automatic writing given by GY to Harbans Rai Bachchan: 'It meant writing after suspending the will.' However, she did not mention her husband's 'spiritual beings' when she told Bachchan the purpose: 'it aimed at evoking the "subconscious", through which, it was believed, revelation was possible' (*W. B. Yeats and Occultism: A Study of his Works in Relation to Indian Lore, the Cabbala, Swedenborg, Boehme and Theosophy* (Delhi, Varanasi, Patna: Motilal Banarsidass, 1965), 239).

spiritualists, Martinists, cabbalists, utopianists, astrologers, and chiromancers; believers in haunted houses, odic light, or magic elixirs; as well as liberal Catholics and mystically minded Anglicans. Yet the early work also contains passages of deep seriousness about folk beliefs, visionary experiences, and mystery religions. Foster notes the similarity between the satirical tone in *The Speckled Bird* and the voice that WBY had recently been developing in his correspondence with Augusta Gregory,[53] but early letters to other friends like Katharine Tynan or even the intensely spiritual George Russell (AE) also tend toward dry wit about serious spiritual matters. The stories 'Rosa Alchemica', 'The Tables of the Law', and 'The Adoration of the Magi', that trilogy of WBY's best-known occult fiction, derive a fair part of their power from the uncertainty of the reality of the action, the unanswerable question of whether the narrator's witness is reliable, and the nagging sense that he is a fool, and perhaps we are, too, for either believing or not believing in the miraculous events.

The essay 'Swedenborg, Mediums, and the Desolate Places' (finished in 1914) argues a theory of the soul's survival of death that WBY had spent the years he mentions in the 'General Introduction' developing, linking learned occult sources with the folk beliefs collected by Lady Gregory. Here, too, though, self-consciousness to the point of humour and acute consciousness of audience act as antithetical counters to the serious proposals being advanced. WBY comments on Swedenborg's pedestrian style, 'his abstraction, his dryness, his habit of seeing but one element in everything, his lack of moral speculation' (*Ex* 42), and his 'gift for evidence' (*Ex* 49), and by implication presents his own contributions in language and imagery that are presumably closer to Blake's 'impulse towards what is definite and sensuous' (*Ex* 50):

In describing and explaining . . . I shall say very seldom, 'it is said', or 'Mr. So-and-So reports', or 'it is claimed by the best authors'. I shall write as if what I describe were everywhere established, everywhere accepted, and I had

---

53 Foster, *Apprentice Mage*, 175.

only to remind my reader of what he already knows. Even if incredulous he will give me his fancy for certain minutes, for at the worst I can show him a gorgon or chimera that has never lacked gazers, alleging nothing (and I do not write out of a little knowledge) that is not among the sober beliefs of many men, or obvious inference from those beliefs, and if he wants more—well, he will find it in the best authors. (*Ex* 50–1)

At which point a footnote refers us to just those authors, and informs us that WBY '[has] myself been a somewhat active investigator' in the sort of research carried out by the Society for Psychical Research. We are to approve a discourse that offers stories instead of empirical evidence as being superior to the merely logical, knowing that WBY could stoop to proof if he so desired. Similarly, we will give him our 'fancy for certain minutes', if not belief, although we are marginally (via the note) informed that fancy could be supported by demonstration if we were energetic enough to do the research that WBY has done. The demarcation between poetic essayist and psychical researcher, art and science, is blurred, in precisely the same way that the boundary between stage magician and fearsome mage, between, say, Harry Houdini and Aleister Crowley, is erased a few pages later:

We speak, it may be, of the Proteus of antiquity which has to be held or it will refuse its prophecy, and there are many warnings in our ears. 'Stoop not down', says the Chaldean Oracle, 'to the darkly splendid world wherein continually lieth a faithless depth and Hades wrapped in cloud, delighting in unintelligible images', and amid that caprice, among those clouds, there is always legerdemain; we juggle, or lose our money, with the same pack of cards that may reveal the future. The magicians who astonished the Middle Ages with power as incalculable as the fall of a meteor were not so numerous as the more amusing jugglers who could do their marvels at will; and in our day the juggler Houdini, sent to Morocco by the French Government, was able to break the prestige of the dervishes whose fragile wonders were but worked by fasting and prayer. (*Ex* 57)

'Sometimes, indeed', WBY concludes, 'a man would be magician, jester, and juggler', and demonstrates his point with a story of a strange Irishman who does word tricks, fooling and pleasing his audience by describing acts that can be done with absurd simplicity as if they require magic, before offering 'the moment of miracle' (*Ex* 57). Are we witnessing WBY promising to wag one ear and not the other and then wiggling one with his hand, or is this the moment when he produces real animals and people out of his silk bag?

Even the essay 'Magic', written in the immediate aftermath of WBY's most agonizing period of involvement with the Order of the Golden Dawn, and when he was 'throwing myself into' work on his never completed Order of Celtic Mysteries,[54] is as notable for its hesitancies as its boldness in the matter of belief. It could hardly begin with more gauntlet-throwing certainty: 'I believe in the practice and philosophy of what we have agreed to call magic' (*E&I* 28). Yet the essay allows for naturalistic explanations for most of the phenomena described, principally in suggesting that magical symbols are at root the same as poetic ones, that strong minds are capable of impressing their thoughts upon weaker ones by an act more of will than theurgy, and that a great memory, common to all, is the explanation for effects that seem telepathy or transformation. This supposition adds power to poetry, but it simultaneously dilutes some of the power of esoterica, making it possible for the readers of the *Monthly Review*, where the essay was first published, to read the words of the young claimant as those of a poet in an English Romantic tradition, not a wild Irish occultist whom the editors made the error of allowing into their relatively new and eminently respectable magazine.[55] WBY informs his readers, with little humility, that 'all men, certainly

---

[54] During this period, WBY spoke of 'throwing myself into' his project to create a 'native' mystery cult to his friend Fiona Macleod (William Sharp), quoted in Foster, *Apprentice Mage*, 245.

[55] The magazine, founded in 1900, was aimed at men of the liberally educated British upper middle class. It featured mostly economic, political, and military essays, on such topics as imperialism and defence (in 1900–1 a number of essays concerned the Boer War), as well as artistic contributions from poems and serialized fiction to criticism of painting and drama, with the occasional piece on popular scientific topics such as archaeology and astronomy (or racial theory, like an essay by Havelock Ellis on 'The Fair and the Dark'). Despite a few contributors like Arthur Symons, WBY is definitely in unusual company. WBY was very good at placing his work, though; as Yug Mohit Chaudhry reminds us, 'As a young man with neither an income nor a professional training, and a family living in impoverished conditions, [WBY's] overriding concern during the 1880s and '90s was publishing his work in periodicals and thereby securing

all imaginative men, must be for ever casting forth enchantments, glamours, illusions; and all men, especially tranquil men who have no powerful egotistic life, must be continually passing under their power' (*E&I* 40), and the essay as a whole works to further literary, not magical, aspirations. One of its most notable stylistic characteristics is a tendency to undercut assertions by parenthetical comments, subjunctive verbs, and immediate retractions. A paragraph near the end of the essay, which is the central assertion of the poetic/magical correspondence, is typical.

Men who are imaginative writers to-day *may well have preferred* to influence the imagination of others more directly in past times. Instead of learning their craft with paper and a pen they *may* have sat for hours imagining themselves to be stocks and stones and beasts of the wood, till the images were so vivid that the passers-by became but a part of the imagination of the dreamer, and wept or laughed or ran away as he would have them. Have not poetry and music arisen, *as it seems,* out of the sounds the enchanters made to help their imagination to enchant, to charm, to bind with a spell themselves and the passers-by? These very words, a chief part of all praises of music or poetry, still cry to us their origin. And just as the musician or the poet enchants and charms and binds with a spell his own mind when he would enchant the mind of others, so did the enchanter create or reveal for himself as well as for others the supernatural artist or genius, the *seeming transitory* mind made out of many minds, whose work I saw, *or thought I saw,* in that suburban house. He kept the doors, too, *as it seems,* of those less transitory minds, the genius of the family, the genius of the tribe, *or it may be,* when he was mighty-souled enough, the genius of the world. (*E&I* 43–4; italics mine)

While asserting a 'mind made out of many minds', WBY also admits that the enchantment of which he speaks affects not only the 'passers-by' but also the dreamer of 'past times' and the poet now. If the readers of his essay as well as the poet are influenced by the illusion of power in the text, then no amount of careful reading will unbind the spell. The repeated phrase 'as it seems', thanks to the ambiguity of the

---

a regular income' (*Yeats, the Irish Literary Revival and the Politics of Print* (Cork: Cork University Press, 2001), 42).

adverb, indicates the rhetorical complexity. It is both a throw-away concessive tag, allowing WBY to plant suggestions without requiring agreement (he does not have to supply demonstrative evidence; he is merely talking about how something 'seems'), yet it also begs the question of agreement, allowing him to assert without asserting that things 'seem' the same way to his readers as they do to him. They are put in the position of needing both to believe and not to believe in order to follow the logic of the thought. Part of the intent of such language is to require that its hearers confront their own predispositions and, importantly, that they not resolve tensions within those predispositions. Part of the power—and power is the central issue here—accrues from readers not being sure whether the impact of WBY's writing results from his mind, his and his readers' minds mutually, or a greater whole: the mind of the culture or Anima Mundi, 'the genius of the world'.

The phrase 'supernatural artist' comes from an earlier passage in the essay that also makes this point: an experience with an 'evoker of spirits' gave WBY visions and leaves him inclined to believe that 'One mind was doubtless the master, I thought, but all the minds gave a little, creating or revealing for a moment what I must call a supernatural artist' (*E&I* 36). Sources of thought are impossible to articulate adequately, as are distinctions between minds and the difference between 'creating and revealing'. These issues inform the automatic script and the universe of multiple forces projected in *A Vision*, but they also suggest that readers should be aware that we are contained in this 'supernatural artist', in the moments when we read and the ones in which our reading affects us, in ways that we may or may not consciously recognize. Thus WBY passes the contents of the vision on to his audience, not merely to retell his story but to intimate that it is theirs as well. Pierre Bourdieu links the authority that accompanies all effective discourse with just such a joining of minds and the seeming diminution of power (the word *ministry*, after all, derives from the Latin *minor*) through which one speaks for many. What occurs is a complex sending out of magical power through symbol or symbolic action:

The mystery of performative magic is thus resolved in the mystery of ministry (to use a pun close to the heart of medieval canonists), i.e. in the alchemy of *representation* (in the different senses of the term) through which the representative creates the group which creates him: the spokesperson endowed with the full power to speak and act on behalf of the group, and first of all to act on the group through the magic of the slogan, is the substitute for the group, which exists solely through this *procuration*. Group made man, he personifies a fictitious person, which he lifts out of the state of a simple aggregate of separate individuals, enabling them to act and speak, through him, 'like a single person'. Conversely, he receives the right to speak and act in the name of the group, to 'take himself for' the group he incarnates, to identify with the function to which 'he gives his body and soul', thus giving a biological body to a constituted body. *Status est magistratus*; 'l'État, c'est moi'. Or, what amounts to the same thing, the world is my representation.[56]

The pregnant word *representation* should remind us that these stylistic effects are of course a performance, a show dependent upon the audience's will to believe no less than a display of the appropriative magic of word power. In this respect, wby's occult essays resemble the work of any professional trader in spiritual mysteries, all of which fall into Derrida's category of 'theatrical fictions' unavailable to the scholar. Not every sermon, every piece of sacred music, every chiromantic prediction is equally inspired. Analysis cannot help us determine the level of genuineness in any given performance; if we go down that road, we find ourselves on the *Hodos Chameliontos* again. Frank Hardy, the faith healer in Brian Friel's play with that title, very nearly loses his way among these questions:

Was it all chance?—or skill?—or illusion?—or delusion? Precisely what power did I possess? Could I summon it? When and how? Was I its servant? Did it reside in my ability to invest someone with faith in me or did I evoke from him a healing faith in himself? Could my healing be effected without faith? But faith in what?—in me?—in the possibility?—faith in faith?[57]

---

[56] Pierre Bourdieu, *Language and Symbolic Power* (Cambridge, Mass.: Harvard University Press, 1991), 106.

[57] Brian Friel, *Faith Healer*, in *Selected Plays* (Washington: Catholic University of America Press, 1984), 333–4.

Frank, another Irish wonder-worker, is also a figure of the artist and of the dramatic form, simultaneously a liar and a vessel of power. His questions are unanswerable in terms of his gift, but they are the same questions that performative artistry raises in secular terms, and the power of the play derives in good part from the audience's sense that they/we are an essential part of the system that sustains Frank's/Friel's morally dubious force. Likewise, WBY's stylistic manipulations in various rhetorical settings provide a key to his uses of occult, as well as aesthetic and dramatic, power. This principle should be kept in mind in reading the texts that are the focus of the next section.

It should be noted that WBY is at his best with a public that, while it might be doubtful about occult truths, presumably does not resent the imperialism inherent in assertions of magical power. Such resentment is precisely the issue in the privately printed essay 'Is the Order of R.R. & A.C. to Remain a Magical Order?', written for fellow adepts in the Golden Dawn and published in the critical year for the order of 1901 (interestingly, the same year as 'Magic').[58] This futile attempt to convince his sorores and fratres of the evil of forming separate secret 'groups' within the society is noteworthy for the discomfort of the mage-author, who feels the need to assert not power over but sacrifice on behalf of others, and to do so in clear terms in order to counter the secrecy and vague doctrine of the 'groups'. Conscious of the likelihood of failure, WBY nevertheless pleads,

If we preserve the unity of the Order, if we make that unity efficient among us, the Order will become a single very powerful talisman, creating in us, and in the world about us, such moods and circumstances as may best serve the magical life, and best awaken the magical wisdom. Its personality will be powerful, active, visible afar, in that all powerful world that casts downward for its shadows, dreams, and visions. (p. 267)

---

[58] The essay is printed as Appendix K in G. M. Harper, *Yeats's Golden Dawn*, 259–68. For accounts of the crisis of 1901, see ibid.; Ellic Howe, *The Magicians of the Golden Dawn: A Documentary History of a Magical Order 1887–1923* (London: Routledge & Kegan Paul, 1972); and Israel Regardie, *What You Should Know About the Golden Dawn* (Phoenix, Ariz.: Falcon Press, 1985), ch. 1.

But of course there was little unity within the Order. The 'talisman' that the institution was to be, its corporate 'personality', did not exist in the wreckage of the 1901 débâcle. Unlike such flourishes as 'Magic' or the 'General Introduction', which work the crowd like a travelling preacher because of a confidence and skill in the power of the master to charm the uninitiated, this essay addresses a closer relation between author and audience but does not succeed stylistically. Each point raised also raises the spectre of a counter-argument, and WBY cannot move beyond the oppositions into the unity within diversity that would be his only route to agreement. Yet this is an important essay, not least because it represents an early attempt to meld matter with presentation, to speak not as a solitary genius but as a personality joined to the minds of others and linked by correspondence to higher authors on the chain (which 'casts downward for its shadows, dreams, and visions'), both groups of which would be both co-authors and audience. The resulting tonal, ideational, and spiritual complexities and delights were beyond the distressed writer of the pamphlet, but the multifoliate possibilities of such a project re-emerged with the correspondence with Leo Africanus and blossomed fully in GY's automatic writing. WBY's occult truths, dependent upon such concepts as links between minds and a common store of memories, are expressed with an added layer of interest when to the relationship between author and audience is compounded a relationship at the heart of authorship itself. His most fruitful forays into the opportunities suggested by these arrangements of power and desire, besides the poetry that gained in strength as he made his experiments, occurred on the two occasions on which he not only asserted a supersensual reality but looked hard into the face of the Other who regarded him from that inexplicable place.

First Interlude

Double Visions: Two Manuscripts and Two Books

We know what to call people who hear voices. A number of pathologies feature such behaviour as a likely symptom. Some groups of people allow for an occasional mystic. What is an appropriate response to someone like WBY, who wants to hear voices but is not sure, or not for long, that he does? who searches out situations in which contact with a spiritual Other might occur, listens, and believes, and at the same time doubts, tests, and examines the various possibilities of deception and self-deception? More relevant to the purposes of this study, when he writes energetically of the process, and if writing is indeed inextricably a part of that process of contact, how should the writing thus produced be regarded?

An analysis of the Yeatses' automatic writing or the compositions derived from it needs to take account of some of the presuppositions that the texts imply before going very far. No less significant than questions of beliefs brought by readers or author to Yeats's magical works are questions begged by genre. Different kinds of texts deliver different sorts of messages. That is to say, considerable networks of predetermined information exist in the categories themselves, for example, of religious or literary, philosophical or personal, poetic or technical discourses. Of course, categorization raises other familiar questions, and the boundaries between kinds are not always distinct. It is often less simple than it appears to determine what markers make a sacred text recognizably different from a secular one, or the extent to which philosophy or history is poetic or fictional. Moreover, a single text can happily blend more than one kind of discourse, drawing attention, for example, to the personal quality of its matter as well as its general claims.

For *A Vision*, genre has been problematic from first to last. Indeed, the history of the book's reception might reasonably be written as a history of argument over what kind of thing it might be.[1] Nor did its author tend to diminish the confusion. Writing to the prospective publisher Werner Laurie in 1923, WBY suggested that Macmillan would probably release it from his contract with that company 'as the book is entirely unlike any other work of mine and will not appeal to the same public. When you see the specimen pages you may reject it on the same grounds.' His next letter voices his concern more openly, as well as the generic difficulty:

I send you the first big bundle of my new book. I sense it will alarm & shall not be surprised if you will have nothing to do with it. Here & there—in certain passages of the analysis of the 28 phases into which I divide human life there is perhaps good writing but good writing is not my object & Part I (?The Curtain?) can only be dry and technical. My object is the exposition

---

[1] Graham Hough would disagree: he begins his analysis of the book with its genre, since it is 'the end we understand most easily'. According to Hough, *A Vision* is an apocalypse (Hough, *Mystery Religion*, 89–90). Harold Bloom agrees, calling it an apocalypse or a 'Gnostic scripture' (Bloom, *Yeats*, 270). Northrop Frye retained a serious interest in the book in terms of the genre he called an anatomy (Northrop Frye, 'Yeats and the Language of Symbolism', in *Fables of Identity: Studies in Poetic Mythology* (New York: Harcourt Brace and World, 1963), 218–37; *idem*, 'The Rising of the Moon', in *Spiritus Mundi: Essays on Literature, Myth and Society* (Bloomington, Ind.: Indiana University Press, 1976), 245–74). Frye's approach has been elaborated upon by Adams, 'Symbolism', 431; *idem*, *Yeats's Vision*, 3; and Helmling, *Esoteric Comedies*. Other critics of his generation tend to treat *A Vision* as a sort of strange reader's guide, useful for explaining otherwise opaque references in the poems, a 'system of references' (Brooks, *Modern Poetry and the Tradition*, 176) or a 'symbology' (Richard Ellmann, *The Identity of Yeats* (New York: Macmillan, 1954), 163). Other studies stress its use as a guide to WBY's aesthetics more generally, a 'visual pattern . . . transformed into a philosophical or metaphysical system' (Georgio Melchiori, *The Whole Mystery of Art* (London: Routledge & Kegan Paul, 1960), 3), a myth or an allegory about poetics. See e.g. M. I. Seiden, *William Butler Yeats: The Poet as a Mythmaker* (East Lansing, Mich.: Michigan State University Press, 1962), 13, and Helen Vendler, *Yeats's Vision and the Later Plays* (Cambridge, Mass.: Harvard University Press, 1963), 29. Michael J. Sidnell stresses the phantasmagoric, calling the book a 'vast imaginative construction' unifying WBY's poetry, fiction, and philosophy (*Yeats's Poetry and Poetics* (London: Macmillan, 1996), 108).

of certain symbols. There is a public, for a book of this kind but you may not think it is your public.[2]

The problem of an audience is a recurring concern in this correspondence, with good reason.[3] Generic expectations are of prime importance in the business of selling books: people buy new works based on the kind of writing they know that they like or want. WBY was keenly aware of such practicalities, and he knew that this book would probably confound the literary, aesthetic, and political expectations of his carefully nurtured public. He also knew that he had on his hands a hybrid, different in kind from one section to another. At one point, he even toyed with the idea of printing some parts in a smaller typeface, in italics, or perhaps in red ink, to help 'the reader's mood', since then 'he would know when to expect beauty of form, or my attempt at it, and when to expect mere explanation'.[4]

The difficulty continued through the preparation of the second edition as well. WBY wrote to Harold Macmillan in March 1934 that he would send the copy of the revised *A Vision* 'in a week or two'. Trying to pave its way, the author explained, 'It is a book which will be very much wanted by a few people—I get letters already asking for it—but will puzzle the bulk of my readers.' None the less (asking for the impossible), WBY told Macmillan, 'I want it to be taken as a part of my work as a whole, not an eccentricity. I have put many years of work into it.'[5] Macmillan replied favourably to WBY (although offering a royalty rate that was lower than usual until the book had sold 2,000 copies), but nine months later, after a visit

---

[2] W. B. Yeats Collection, Special Collections and Archives, Robert W. Woodruff Library, Emory University.

[3] Laurie was not sure that the intended print run of 500 would sell, although he wrote to WBY on 18 Aug. that he did not mind that some orders were being cancelled. WBY wrote back to assure him that 'Your letter was not unexpected. I think however that you will sell the 500.' As it happened, Laurie did increase the run to 600, and the copies sold out, but the response to the book was (predictably) minimal. W. B. Yeats Collection, Special Collections and Archives, Robert W. Woodruff Library, Emory University.

[4] Letter to Werner Laurie, 11 Sept. 1924; W. B. Yeats Collection, Special Collections and Archives, Robert W. Woodruff Library, Emory University.

[5] Unpublished letter to Harold Macmillan, 9 March 1934. BL Add. MS 55003.

from WBY, wrote a worried letter to WBY's agent A. H. Watt. Surely, Macmillan complained, 'you will realize that the subject matter of the book is one that makes a very limited appeal. To most ordinary minds it appears to be quite mad, and I cannot believe that the sale will be anything but a very small one. I rather gathered from Mr Yeats that he shared this view.'⁶ So he did. In May 1937, while correcting proofs for the second version, WBY wrote to Edith Shackleton Heald about *A Vision* (which is 'not to be confused with its first edition published years ago'): 'This book is the skeleton in my cupboard. I do not know whether I want my friends to see it or not to see it. I think "Will so-and-so think me a crazed fanatic?" but one goes on in blind faith. The public does not matter—only one's friends matter'. (*L* 888–9).

Whether the book is 'mad' and its author 'a crazed fanatic' is a question of whether the book makes claims that it can demonstrate to the satisfaction of its readers—and one complexity of *A Vision* is that it makes competing claims. A significant part of the book's strangeness results from a number of mixed signals about what sort of messages it contains. This phenomenon was, of course, immediately obvious. One of the first reviewers of the revised edition, Mary Colum, wrote in the pages of *The Forum and Century* in April 1938 that WBY 'flings in the face of the public one of the most fantastic constructions of the intellect that has ever been produced, a remarkable medley of astrology, spiritualism, philosophy, Hermetic wisdom, poetry, credulity, and necromancy'—yet 'he is willing to admit, too, that the mysterious instructors in *A Vision* may also be "created beings", an invention of his dream life'.⁷ Luckily, though, some of the generic confusion can be lessened for contemporary readers by making a few critical distinctions between the two versions of the book, while remembering that although the second edition is to some extent a new book, it also to some degree contains the older book within it.

---

⁶ Unpublished letter to H. Watt of A. P. Watt & Son, 31 Dec. 1934. BL Add. MS 55003. Quoted in Finneran, 'On Editing Yeats', 120–1.

⁷ Mary M. Colum, 'Life and Literature: The Individual vs. Society. Rev. of *A Vision*', *Forum and Century*, 99 (1938): 214–15.

In other words, the skeleton in WBY's cupboard should be regarded as not one but at least two related skeletons, a piece of information that should make it a little easier to sort through the jumble of bones.

In purpose and form the second *A Vision* is very different from the first. The revision was not merely a clarification or elaboration; the book changed in kind between 1925 and 1937. In order to appreciate the shift from one *Vision* to the next, it may be instructive to recall that *A Vision* is not the only occult text that underwent such reworking. The pages that follow compare the revision of *A Vision* with two other texts begun in similarly ambiguous and engaging experiences: the unpublished manuscript titled 'Leo Africanus' and the monograph *Per Amica Silentia Lunae*, which grew from the experience with a mysterious entity whom WBY came to identify as an anti-self. Both pairs of texts, 'Leo' and *Per Amica* and the two versions of *A Vision*, represent movement in time from an encounter (to whatever extent imaginary) with a non-corporeal world in the form of voices or written communication toward retrospective synthesis in a published product. Both also travel a distance away from discursive immediacy and toward the kind of transcendental appropriation with which WBY was more comfortable, the tonal mastery that he had for years practised in his other occult essays. For both pairs, the former text, the least finished, can be greatly intriguing, and I find it unfortunate that most readers of WBY encounter *Per Amica* and the second edition of *A Vision* and not their quirky predecessors. The later works, and not their odder cousins, are easily available. This fact has limited not only appreciation of the unusual events out of which the books arose but perhaps even interest in the books themselves, at least for those readers who might prefer the rawly emotional and concrete earlier texts to the smoothly allusive *Per Amica* and the philosophical 1937 *A Vision*, with their confident and sly narration and their impersonal tone.

Per Amica is often regarded as a kind of preface to *A Vision,* a simpler (and, many claim, superior) version of the ideas fleshed out more elaborately in the later book. The opening paragraphs of WBY's introduction to the 1937 *A Vision* endorse such an attitude, and *Per Amica* is indeed the jumping-off point for the first two numbered questions in the automatic script, one by WBY and one by GY, as if the newlyweds had discussed before the session began the idea of organizing the rather formless script to carry further the ideas sketched out in that book (*AV B* 8; *YVP*i. 65). Broadly considered, the system explodes into multiplicities the dualities of the 1917 monograph. For example, four Faculties, then four Principles beyond them, replace the self and anti-self of the earlier book; and the 'two realities, the terrestrial and the condition of fire', in *Per Amica* shift to relative states in *A Vision*, dependent upon opposition and expressed in expanding and contracting gyres, renamed Destiny and Fate (*Myth* 356; *AV A* 129).

Indeed, *Per Amica* is not only a predecessor but in some ways a prophecy. A Prologue addressed pseudonymously to a woman whom WBY would have married ('Maurice' or Iseult Gonne) represents the book as arising from conversations between them, foreshadowing the birth of *A Vision* in the automatic script. The famous opening poem of *Per Amica*, 'Ego Dominus Tuus', is set at the foot of Ballylee, the Norman tower in Galway whose purchase as WBY's and GY's symbolic home would not be finalized until a year and a half after the final draft of the poem was complete. The professed themes of the monograph, the existence of daimons ('Anima Hominis', the title of the first of two linked essays) and a supernatural source of common images ('Anima Mundi', the parallel title for the second essay), are an elaborate set of possible explanations for the messy mechanics of direct encounters with a spiritual world; *A Vision*, similarly, draws the lines and curves of its system over an obsessively researched and questioned direct encounter. The final sections of *Per Amica* mention the return to self from the daimonic realm as occurring in the winding motion of gyres that do not appear until *A Vision*, even using the distinctively Yeatsian word *pern* to describe it (*Myth* 364). As a whole, *Per Amica* shares in the emotional stock-taking that is a prominent theme of the winters that WBY spent with Pound at Stone Cottage, feeling his age and the age of the world as it moved into war. During this period WBY wrote the first instalment of his memoirs, the ghost play *The Dreaming of the Bones*, the play *The Hawk's Well* with its prominent conflict between youth and age, and the poems of *Responsibilities*.[8] *Per Amica* reads as 'half a prayer or desperate plea for some outward sign of regeneration', as Lawrence Lipking has described it.[9] It features a poet at midlife hoping for continued inspiration, a man used to his life and habits of thought longing for connection with history through a Great Memory and with what is alien to his finite self through a daimon, who 'comes not as like to like but seeking its own opposite, for man and Daimon feed the hunger in one another's hearts' (*Myth* 335). Read in the context of the automatic script, which began a few months after publication, it is hard not to feel that WBY's prayer was answered.

However, if *Per Amica* is a prayer, it is more a public than a private one, the measured convictions of a well-known poet in mid-career, not for many moments or very intensely revelatory of personal loneliness or grief. The book is filled with a generalized subjectivity even when the first person singular pronoun is used. The daimon, the mysterious Other, is evoked by conscious fabrication of a mask, but it is the mask, that famous Yeatsian aesthetic concept, and not the supersensual Other, which receives the emphasis. At times the daimon is sensed involuntarily in fleeting moments that are immediately appropriated by the man into his own desires: 'I am in the place where the Daimon is, but I do not think he is with me until I begin to make a new personality, selecting among those images, seeking always to satisfy a hunger grown out of conceit with daily diet' (*Myth* 365–6). WBY allows his readers few glimpses of another relation although he evokes it at key moments, such as the present-tense admission near the end of the book that 'yet as I write the words "I select", I am full of uncertainty, not knowing when I am the finger, when the clay' (*Myth* 366). Another such resonant

---

[8] See the accounts of 1913 and 1914 in Foster, *Apprentice Mage*, 502–31. For the best account of the creative outcome of the time spent with Pound, see James Longenbach, *Stone Cottage: Pound, Yeats, and Modernism* (Oxford: Oxford University Press, 1988).

[9] Lawrence Lipking, *The Life of the Poet: Beginning and Ending Poetic Careers* (Chicago and London: University of Chicago Press, 1981), 49.

moment occurs in a section when hero and mask, two concepts that are Yeatsian trademarks, converge, and the hero, having donned the mask, 'knew another's breath came and went within his breath upon the carven lips and that his eyes were upon the instant fixed upon a visionary world: how else could the god have come to us in the forest?' (*Myth* 335).

Even so, the rhetorical question gives away the public nature of this discourse. Richard Ellmann is correct in characterizing *Per Amica* as an evasive manœuvre, a way of presenting a supernatural theory as 'an extended and elaborate metaphor' to forestall objections to its metaphysical qualities. According to Ellmann, WBY in *Per Amica* 'seems not so much to convince the reader as to take him in'.[10] The monograph does work to incline that reader to agreement through lush, imagistic prose, using anecdotes and quotations from poets or Henry More in lieu of declarative linearity. In an early unpublished draft of *Per Amica* WBY complained of his early style 'where there is little actual circumstance, nothing natural, but always an artificial splendour', but it is hard to see that this prose has travelled far from the elaboration of a work like 'Rosa Alchemica' or, for that matter, 'Magic'.[11] WBY, the old conjuror, is up to his old tricks. Probably the most famous statement in *Per Amica* is the assertion that 'We make out of the quarrel with others, rhetoric, but of the quarrel with ourselves, poetry' (*Myth* 331). WBY did make poetry out of quarrels with himself, but his prose was not generally so lucky. Certainly *Per Amica* is not, for all its sensuous beauty. Even when WBY endorses doubt and the sacrifice of pleasant self-deception in the paragraph that follows the quotable sentence above, the argument is couched in impersonal terms: 'We must not make a false faith by hiding from our thoughts the causes of doubt, for faith is the highest achievement of the human intellect, the only gift man can make to God, and therefore it must be offered in sincerity' (*Myth* 332).

Compare to this sentence the passage from the 'Leo Africanus' manuscript from which it was derived:

[10] Ellmann, *Man and Masks*, 199. [11] Quoted in Ellmann, *Identity*, 305.

Even the wisdom that we send you, but deepens your bewilderment, for when the wisest of your troop of shades wrote you through the ignorant hand of a friend 'Why do you think that faith excludes intellect. It is the highest achievement of the human intellect, & it is the only gift that man can offer to god. That is why we must leave all the winds of time to beat upon it'[,] you but sought the more keenly to meet not your own difficulties but the difficulties of others. Entangled in error, you are but a public man, yet once you would put vague intuition into verse, & that insufficient though it was might have led you to the path the eye of the eagle has not seen. ('Leo', 28)

Not only is the passage vivid with imagery, figuring 'the winds of time' beating upon human faith, WBY as 'entangled in error', and the road he has not taken being 'the path the eye of the eagle has not seen'; it is also self-revealing in ways that WBY would use to great effect later. The phrase 'public man', of course, reappears in 'Among School Children' to complicate the speaking subject of that poem as a ridiculous figure, a scarecrow of a 'sixty-year-old smiling public man' (*VP* 443). Familiar Yeatsian language—'public man', 'eagle', and even the word 'bewilderment' (put to good use in 'Easter, 1916', composed less than a year later)—occur here, but in a discourse distinct from any of his published work. The authorial voice is direct, castigating (as neither 'Easter, 1916' nor 'Among School Children' is, despite their poses of self-conscious deflation) and demanding to be heard.

Yet the authority upon which the voice draws seems at first glance to rest upon the slimmest of suppositions. The author is identified with the source of disembodied vocal messages given during a series of seances, which may or may not be from a spirit, who may or may not be who he claims to be, written through the conscious intention of WBY, who may or may not believe that he is ventriloquizing. Even further, this personage is not alone, but one of a 'troop of shades', who do not speak directly but avail themselves of automatic writing 'through the ignorant hand of a friend' of WBY's to make their messages known. The spirit is ostensibly that of Leo Africanus, the sixteenth-century travel writer and adventurer Al Hassan Ibn-Mohammed al-Wezar Al-Fasi, who was summoned mediumistically in seances beginning in 1912 (after a false start in 1909) and who developed into a figure that WBY conceived as a kind of *alter ego*, a symbolic opposite.[12] By late 1916, when the private essay was written, WBY was sufficiently convinced of the value of Leo as guide to engage in an experiment with highly significant ramifications for his later work: to suspend authorial control and write as if through the personality and agency of another.[13]

The essay is in the form of two letters, one from WBY to Leo and the other from Leo to WBY, written at Leo's suggestion 'as from him to me', as WBY remembered the request. 'He would control me ~~if he could~~ in that reply so that it would be really from him' ('Leo', 13). The cancelled words are significant, as is a cancelled passage from the opening section of the essay: 'If I would write out my difficulties in a letter addressed to you as though you were still living in the east & then wrote another letter in your hand you would see to it that the second letter was but in seeming mine. I should be overshadowed in my turn' ('Leo', 21). The process of writing the letters would put WBY in the borderland between traditional Western authorship, presided over by the strong myth of the stable self, and the uncharted territory of writerly mediumship, with its resonances of femininity, darkness, the irrational, and the non-Western. It is furthermore no accident that Leo is identified with the Orient as an enslaved Arab only partially converted to Christian ways, and that he travelled in and wrote about Africa. His 'overshadow[ing]' of WBY from the East, as well as the importance of his book *Descrizione dell' Affrica* or *Africae descriptio* (originally written in Arabic) to the orientalist studies of WBY's day, suggest links with the powerful ambivalences of the exotic Other and the so-called Dark Continent and their tantalizing and threatening promise of release from the control of the ego.[14] WBY

---

[12] See Foster, *Apprentice Mage*, 464–7, and the introduction and notes in 'Leo' for accounts of the relationship between WBY and Leo.

[13] The composition is dated by Foster (*W. B. Yeats: A Life, ii: The Arch-Poet 1915–1939* (Oxford: Oxford University Press, 2003), 72).

[14] Leo's book, translated into English by John Pory in 1600, was edited in 1896 by Robert Brown and Sir E. Denison Ross. Ross, a friend of WBY, was director of the School of Oriental Languages at London University. A few years later he would provide WBY with a transliterated (and slightly inaccurate) title for the fabricated book that was

would emulate the female mediums of his experience and relinquish ownership of his own pen (with all of its sexual associations) so that his words would be 'but in seeming mine'.

The words are still WBY's, of course, for all of his attempt to free them from his own governance. The dream of freedom from self occurs only within the framework and volition of that self; the Other exists as such only because of the subject that places it in an imagined location outside that identified with the subject. WBY remained sceptical of his own efforts to replace conscious with anti-self as he wrote. The essay is full of his doubts: 'I~~ think probable~~ I am not convinced that in this letter there is one sentence that has come from beyond my own imagination but I will not use a stronger phrase ... there is no thought that has not occurred to me in some form or other for many years' ('Leo', 38–9). Leo has his doubts too, explaining that he had better stick to general topics because when he focuses on specific events 'I am full of doubt. I am not even certain, that I am not certain that I did not mistake the images I discover there [in WBY's mind] for my own memories' ('Leo', 33). None the less, the essay is distinctly bold and direct in comparison with Yeatsian public prose, a tonal quality which (paradoxically, given that two personages speak) derives from a less multiple authorial self than a work like *Per Amica*. In splitting himself for the two parts of

supposedly the source for *A Vision:* TARĪQUAT UN-NUFŪS BAYN AL-QUMŪR WA'L SHUMUS or 'The Way of Souls between the Moon & Sun'. See *YVP*iv. 49 n. 24. Connections between Yeatsian self- or group identities and orientalism have been examined most often in contexts of WBY's nationalist politics. See e.g. Seamus Deane, 'Heroic Styles: The Tradition of an Idea', in *Ireland's Field Day* (London: Hutchinson, 1985), 45–58; *idem*, 'Yeats and the Idea of Revolution', in *Celtic Revivals: Essays in Modern Irish Literature 1880–1980* (London: Faber, 1985), 38–50; Richard Kearney, 'Myth and Motherland', in *Ireland's Field Day*, 61–80; *idem*, *Transitions: Narratives in Modern Irish Culture* (Manchester: Manchester University Press, 1988); David Lloyd, 'The Poetics of Politics: Yeats and the Founding of the State', in *Anomalous States: Irish Writing and the Post-Colonial Moment* (Dublin: Lilliput, 1993), 59–87; Marjorie Howes, *Yeats's Nations: Gender, Class, and Irishness* (Cambridge: Cambridge University Press, 1996); and Edward Said, 'Yeats and Decolonization', in Seamus Deane (ed.), *Nationalism, Colonialism and Literature* (Minneapolis: University of Minnesota Press, 1990), 69–95. On the connection between Western mediumship and orientalism, see London, *Writing Double*, ch. 4. It should be noted that overshadowing is an interesting concept in the script and in poems in *Michael Robartes and the Dancer*. See Ch. 3 below.

the essay, the persona who writes each part is less multiple than the chameleon WBY of the later work, who drifts into danger when he focuses on sincerity, from which he has escaped hitherto only by the 'theatrical, consciously dramatic' donning of a mask.

Leo represents a leap forward for WBY, even though that leap was anticipated by many years of artistic growth. The interplay among masks in *The Wind Among the Reeds*, with its cast of named speakers in the first edition representing 'principles of the mind' (*VP* 803) is relevant, for example. So is the move toward ritual in drama, replacing fiction with myth and substituting traditional-seeming words and gestures for the autonomy of playwright or actor; and so also is the practical knowledge gained from collaborative ventures like the co-writing of *Cathleen Ni Houlihan* with Lady Gregory. The increased separation of WBY from Leo ironically accompanies more rhetorical engagement than these other experiments. In dialogue with a (perhaps) independently existing anti-self rather than declaration through an invented mask, WBY speaks from a more engaged, less distanced location; his overt splitting of psychic and spiritual self results in less fragmentation of authorial self. Leo's title for himself is revealing of this new relation:

I know all & all but all you know, we have turned over the same books—I have shared in your joys & sorrows & yet it is only because I am your opposite, your antithesis because I am in all things furthest from your intellect & your will, that I alone am your Interlocutor. ('Leo', 38)

The interlocutor, whose speech (*locutio*) is defined by its 'between' quality (*inter*), whose statements exist only as part of a dialogue, and whose position is defined by its relation to another who stands opposite, is a fitting descriptor for Leo. Further, one interlocutor implies another, which is to say that in the seances and written experiments with Leo, WBY also summoned a self that may be defined by the fact of its dialogue with a spiritual counter-self: an *Ille* and not a *Hic*, to use terms from 'Ego Dominus Tuus'. The knowledge of Anima Mundi and the influence of spirit 'secondary personalities', the major themes of the 'Leo Africanus' essay, are written into the authorial subject.[15] As Leo puts it, for the spirits as well as for WBY (whose mind seems 'broken, & your will doubled' when he writes a play, or whose images are more than merely 'jetsam from your more hidden thoughts' ('Leo', 29–30)), 'our message [is], as it were built in the whole structure of our body & our mind' ('Leo', 29). In this regard, 'Leo', and not *Per Amica*, is the most significant predecessor of *A Vision* as well as WBY's later work in its shadow, because the unpublished letters and not the more commonly known text lay the groundwork for the great experiment, to use the phrase from the monograph, in 'quarrelling', in which it is a question not so much of whether one holds a position against others or argues internally but of whether a position that is not one's own is entertained. Leo's ambiguous status as neither demonstrably self nor Other adds to his value, for he, like GY's communicators and perhaps GY herself, cannot be pigeon-holed as friend or frustrator, bringer of agreement and ease or the shock of the new and unassimilable.[16]

Almost all criticism of *A Vision* refers to the second edition, a state of affairs that is probably appropriate given WBY's patent endorsement of that text rather than the earlier version. His 1937 introduction confesses as much:

The first version of this book, *A Vision*, except the section on the twenty-eight phases, and that called 'Dove or Swan' which I repeat without change, fills me with shame. I had misinterpreted the geometry, and in my ignorance of philosophy failed to understand distinctions upon which the coherence of the whole depended, and as my wife was unwilling that her share should be known and I to seem sole author, I had invented an unnatural story of

---

[15] On the concept of Anima Mundi in WBY, see Christopher Blake, 'The Supreme Enchanter: W. B. Yeats and the Soul of the World' (Ph.D. diss., Georgia State University, 1997). The term, deeply associated with *Per Amica* and WBY's life before his marriage, seldom appears in the script. In Dec. 1917, WBY approached the topic, asking if his ideas about life after death were correct, but he was told that 'Anima mundi is too vague' (*YVP*i. 153). On another occasion Thomas objected after WBY used the phrase in a question, replying 'I hate that term' (*YVP*i. 234).

[16] On Leo as frustrator in the automatic script, see Ch. 5.

an Arabian traveller which I must amend and find a place for some day because I was fool enough to write half a dozen poems that are unintelligible without it. (p. 19)

It is quite appropriate to be wary of WBY's confessions in this essay—I would not want to accept without hesitation, for example, the assertion that his only reason for continuing and in fact adding to the outlandishness of the fantastic story of Michael Robartes, the mysterious Arab tribe, and all its other trappings was so that readers could understand a few poems more easily. Nevertheless, years of revision and plans to include the second edition in the collected works projects of his late years, as well as numerous letters suggesting that the first edition was unfinished, all encourage readers to focus on that book rather than the much rougher earlier work.[17] So does the 1925 *A Vision*: in the dedication WBY admits, 'I could daresay make the book richer, perhaps immeasurably so, if I were to keep it by me for another year, and I have not even dealt with the whole of my subject, perhaps not even with what is most important' (p. xii) and hints that more is to come: 'Doubtless I must someday complete what I have begun' (p. xiii). Moreover, the first version was 'horribly expensive', suitable for a piece of drawing-room–tabletop art but hardly for a widely read book.[18]

Furthermore, in some respects the 1937 *A Vision* seems to reveal more of the spiritualistic collaboration that lies behind the book than the 1925 edition, which hides the fact of GY's automatic writing behind an elaborate and transparently false story of old books, chance discoveries, and a strange nomadic sect from the Arabian

---

[17] For textual histories of the revision, including its intended place in the two abortive editions of WBY's complete works, Macmillan's Edition De Luxe and the edition proposed by Charles Scribner's Sons of New York, see Finneran, 'On Editing Yeats', and esp. Hood, 'Search for Authority'. See also letters to Olivia Shakespear, Edmund Dulac, and Frank Pearce Sturm: *L* 695 and 699–700; and Richard Taylor (ed.), *Frank Pearce Sturm: His Life, Letters, and Collected Work* (Urbana, Ill., and London: University of Illinois Press, 1969), 93.

[18] Foster cites a letter to 'an importunate correspondent' from WBY lamenting the 'horribly expensive' price (£ 3.3.0) and also its unfinished status: 'It is only a first draft of a book & intended for students of Plotinus, the Hermetic fragments & unpopular literature of that kind' (Foster, *Arch-Poet*, 313).

desert. By 1937, WBY had added new prefatory material including an introduction telling the story of the automatism as well as a long tale, 'Stories of Michael Robartes and his Friends: An Extract from a Record Made by his Pupils', which subsumes the hoax material of 1925 into a seemingly allegorical if highly unusual fictional experiment.[19] The 'Stories', about 'a group of strange disorderly people on whom Michael Robartes confers the wisdom of the east', as WBY described it to Dorothy Wellesley (*L* 859), have baffled critics both of *A Vision* and of WBY's fiction ever since. The introduction is not without its ambiguities, either. The story of the automatic script and other experiments is told years after the fact, with the luxury of recollection and the concomitant blurring of fact into the fabrications of memory. WBY has had time to make sense of his 'incredible experience', to put it in a larger context than he could have done in 1925. To some extent, distance may provide clarity, but the essay also tells more about WBY in the 1930s than necessarily re-creates the events of 1917 and beyond with a high degree of accuracy. The 1937 introduction, like the book in general, is a public repackaging of material that was much closer to the private experiences of the Yeatses in the first edition.

The journey from 'Leo Africanus' to *Per Amica* includes a movement away from emotional engagement with an Other and toward the appropriation of that otherness into an authorial self whose multifaceted nature contributes to its assertions of power. The distance from the 1925 to the 1937 version of *A Vision* covers similar ground. In 1925 the discourse contains within it traces of someone else, mediated though that presence is by a number of factors. In other words, GY's active participation is still traceable there, and so are the voices of the various controls and guides of the automatic script. By 1937 the text has been reworked into a book whose author contains

---

[19] In reality, the way for the 1937 edition had been paved in the public mind (or at least that portion of it purchasing art press books) by the publication of the new framing material separately. The *Packet for Ezra Pound* was published by the Cuala Press in 1929, the 'Stories of Michael Robartes and his Friends' in 1931. However, 1937 marked the widely distributed Macmillan edition of the book as a whole.

vacillations and variations within himself, whose analysis of history uses its own historical moment as part of its authority, and the very form of whose book also illustrates the ideas of interlacing cones and alternating movements.[20]

The change results in a more masterful presentation: in 1925 the authority for the system is hidden, and wby presents himself as responding to initiatives that he does not explain except through obvious fictions. The book is riddled with omissions, statements without contexts (including unattributed quotations, usually from the script), and abrupt shifts of subject. Generally speaking, the focus in 1925 is more personal, sexual, and psychological than philosophical, social, or historical.[21] The book is also more lyrical, by which I mean that it is more dependent upon image than explanation and more likely to follow associative than logical progression, although the 1937 book is more literary, in that it is aimed at wby's literary public and not a small coterie of fellow occultists. Significantly, the 1925 book is dedicated to 'Vestigia', the Golden Dawn motto of Moina (Mrs MacGregor) Mathers, the widow of the founding Chief of the Order; in 1937 the book is prefaced by an emotive essay about and a public letter to Ezra Pound.[22] In 1937 the authority for the system is not the now freely mentioned communicators but the motions of the gyres, a more impersonal source. The system is situated smoothly in a long history of ideas, buttressed by statements from the numerous philosophers wby read in the years between the two editions, and organized more clearly thanks to the years of refinement since the first edition. In 1937 the spirits no longer play the role of the hidden teachers; they too take their place in the wheels upon wheels, which become not only subject-matter but processes that affect all things: ideas, author, the times in which the book was composed, and the times to come.

[20] On the fictional author 'Yeats' and the form of his book, see Adams, *Yeats's Vision.*
[21] On the differences between the two versions, see esp. Barbara L. Croft, *Stylistic Arrangements: A Study of William Butler Yeats's* A Vision (Lewisburg, Pa.: Bucknell University Press, 1987), and Seiden, *William Butler Yeats.*
[22] For this and other points of comparison between the two versions, see Marzilli, 'Masking of Truth'.

Moreover, and crucially, wby accrues power to himself by setting the wheels in motion formally and intellectually. He is again the mage, the knower, and even the mover of those gyres, in the important sense that it is he through whom their creative representations have come. The gyres not only foreordain but also depend upon wby's knowledge, creative expression, and interpretative exposition. The 1937 *A Vision* knows that it will be read as part of the *œuvre* of a major literary figure. It anticipates being read and analysed; it expects to be influential; it expects to contribute to the posthumous assessment of wby as the book of his life and work becomes a historical document.

Appropriately, its final words are magisterial.[23] The three parts of the conclusion contain a summing up of wby's age and the turbulence of the times, a transcendence into knowledge by means of a mysterious Thirteenth Cone beyond the unceasing cones of the intelligible system, and a final, very Yeatsian rhetorical question: 'Shall we follow the image of Heracles that walks through the darkness bow in hand, or mount to that other Heracles, man, not image, he that has for his bride Hebe, "The daughter of Zeus the mighty and Hera shod with gold"?' (*AV B* 302). 'Then I understand', wby comments; 'I have already said all that can be said', and now what 'shall we' choose, man or image? The only authority above this wise man, who knows what questions to ask to send readers on their way, is that Thirteenth Cone. It 'can do all things and knows all things', but 'has kept the secret' of the consequences of its freedom (p. 302). None the less, it is wby who knows of it and who informs us of its secrecy. The secret is less powerful for being available as a subject of his discourse, just as the communicators and gy are also diminished by their change in status from 1925 to 1937, from concealed sources of truth to characters in a story by wby about the beginnings of his book.

---

[23] This magisterial quality is paralleled by the archly conservative political stance that wby often took in his last years. The 1937 *Vision* recalls the fascism of the 1930s, as Stephen Spender was the first to notice. The 1925 book is as different in this regard as 1920s fascism was from later embodiments (Spender, review of *A Vision*, *The Criterion*, 17 (1938): 536–7).

Two of the most commonly quoted phrases from the 1937 edition both contribute to the hegemony of the impersonal gyres as a vehicle for their poet-expositor in this version of *A Vision*: the statement that WBY makes at the beginning of the tell-all introduction that the communicators came to give him 'metaphors for poetry' and a passage from the end purporting to answer the question of 'whether I believe in the actual existence of my circuits of sun and moon':

To such a question I can but answer that if sometimes, overwhelmed by miracle as all men must be when in the midst of it, I have taken such periods literally, my reason has soon recovered; and now that the system stands out clearly in my imagination I regard them as stylistic arrangements of experience comparable to the cubes in the drawing of Wyndham Lewis and to the ovoids in the sculpture of Brancusi. They have helped me to hold in a single thought reality and justice. (*AV B* 25)

Both 'metaphors for poetry' and 'stylistic arrangements of experience' are rhetorical pauses for effect and also convenient ways to deflect a question about occult truth into the safer territory of art.[24] Interestingly, the automatic script from which the phrase derives was not located among the rest of the manuscripts, and it has long been assumed that WBY invented the words, putting them in quotation marks as if quoting the instructors but instead reporting from faulty memory, wishful thinking, or imperious afterthought. Such an action is compatible with the 1937 *A Vision*, but the truth is slightly more complex. In the original context, WBY appears not as powerful bard but as humbled student. The script from which the phrase was taken was filed, or misplaced, among the manuscript pages of the *Packet for Ezra Pound*, for which it has been used. In this record of an early session, the unnamed instructor(s?) tells WBY that the 'mystical work' is filled with images and their meanings, but the spirits 'will not do

---

[24] GY told Donald Pearce that WBY's posturing was meant to be read ironically: that the reference to Brancusi, whose work did not impress WBY ('all those ovoids . . . seemed to put him off'), 'is made with a certain amount of humor, you see—which you earnest Americans never seem to catch!' (Donald Pearce, 'Hours with the Domestic Sibyl: Remembering George Yeats', *Southern Review*, 28 (1992): 494).

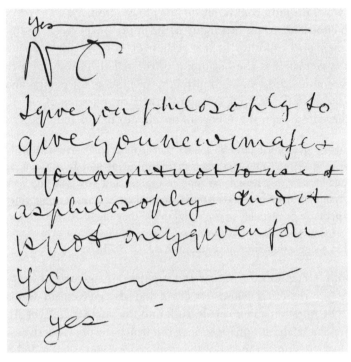

1. George Yeats, automatic script, undated [1917](NLI MS 36,260/4)

your work for you you must think things out for yourself'. Although 'they are all anxious to get through', the messages would come, 'but never clearly always in images not understood till later'. WBY was clearly told it would be 'good' 'if you don't set up as a philosopher', that it would 'be the end of it & her' if he did not use the script 'for art only'. To an unrecorded question, GY wrote 'NO' in large letters, followed by the genesis of WBY's famous remark in his introduction, written a decade later: 'I give you philosophy to give you new images you ought not to use it as philosophy.' The next words complete the thought: 'and it is not only given for you yes'.[25]

[25] See Introduction, n. 10.

Virginia Moore records a conversation with GY that corroborates the distancing from the original context of the 'images' or 'metaphors' remark, although neither Moore nor her informant take the further step, implied in much Yeats criticism, of appropriating both images and forms for the poet alone:

> Though shying a little from the subject—understandably, for she has been hounded—she told me in 1952 that, whereas, in the beginning, Yeats (and presumably herself) did think the messages spirit-sent, and therefore proof of communion between the living and the dead, he saw them later as a dramatized 'apprehension of the truth.' If not from the dead, from whom, from what, this 'truth'? From their own higher selves.[26]

Such claims that the system is useful for metaphor or image and stylization or dramatization are to some degree counterbalanced, for example, by strange stories in other sections of the 1937 introduction (which are not cited nearly as often) of sounds, smells, and such materializations, and by the presence in both editions of *A Vision* of direct quotations from the script, which imply volitional speech by the presence of the punctuation itself. Nevertheless, just as the difference between 'Leo' and *Per Amica* is the contrast between direct encounter and suggestive essay, the two versions of *A Vision* are also distinct in kind as well as in level of polish. The one is closer to reportage, an account by an author who later remembered being 'overwhelmed by miracle'; the other presents much of the same material but at a distance from its feathered glory, as the measured thoughts of an old man turning the symbols over in his mind while readying himself for posterity.

The 1925 *A Vision* is not written for a crowd. In comparison with the ending of the 1937 book, the last two numbered sections of the first edition, a short paragraph called 'The Herring Fishers' and a final statement entitled 'Mythology', are as modest a conclusion as WBY ever wrote. 'The Herring Fishers' contains almost an apology and a hesitant question:

---

[26] Moore, *The Unicorn*, 277–8. Ch. 6 of Anne Saddlemyer's biography (*Becoming George*, 105–33) is the most informed and well-reasoned account of the experience and what each of the recipients believed to be happening.

Much of this book is abstract, because it has not yet been lived, for no man can dip into life more than a moiety of any system. When a child, I went out with herring fishers one dark night, and the dropping of their nets into the luminous sea and the drawing of them up has remained with me as a dominant image. Have I found a good net for a herring fisher? (*AV A* 251)

The final paragraph is a statement of purpose that ends with a sentence in which WBY's will is literally buried in the modal verb, in a play on the older, strong meaning of *willan* and the blurring of a distinction between subjunctive and optative moods in English: 'That we may believe that all men possess the supernatural faculties I would restore to the philosopher his mythology' (p. 252). Does this *would* indicate tentative hope, slight inclination, urgent wish, or active intention? The amount of choice that WBY has in the matter is left obscure.

Perhaps the submerging of the authorial will in language that casts not so much a spell as a net, with the intent less to control than to discover, is appropriate for the quirky 1925 *A Vision*, imperfect and disjunctive, presented as if it claims to be a revelation of preternatural truth but also countering that claim in a number of ways, such as citing as authority for its information an obviously fictional and oddly humorous story or suggesting that its author is inadequate to his task ('Having the concrete mind of the poet, I am unhappy when I find myself among abstract things' (p. 129)). WBY ends this book which he knew was unfinished by depicting himself hoping to catch something in a luminous sea and relying not on his own well-defined mask but on herring fishers who are as indefinable as the skilled adults he went out with as a child. The fishers have some of the defamiliarized, and therefore the more desired, 'cold and passionate' quality of the central figure in the poem 'The Fisherman'. The fish may partake of the magic of longing that characterizes the fish-become-glimmering-girl in 'The Song of Wandering Ængus'. As it often does in WBY's work, the sea, along with pools, wells, and watery depths, symbolizes the unfathomable as well as the Anima Mundi, that store of collective memory and knowledge that is often described as a reservoir. WBY plays the child in the automatic script more than once, and both husband and wife are like children at different moments in the thinly disguised autobiographical poem 'Desert Geometry or the Gift of Harun Al-Raschid' that opens Book II of the 1925 book. In rhetoric and in images, the first *A Vision* registers the uncertainty of a book without the kind of authorship to which its famous author was accustomed. It may even be a book that argues against the authorship of its writer. At the very least, it complicates the idea of individual, willed creativity as well as suggests that the magisterial WBY, for all his decades of spiritual and aesthetic explorations and all his experience in writing out of that experience, could not control his material.

This lack of control is far from merely a weakness in the book. Indeed, the earlier *A Vision*, like the 'Leo Africanus' letters, has as both a defining quality and an abiding theme the unsettled relationship between authority and authorship, and the equally dynamic relationship between creativity and externally originating truths. The book is shot through with structural and topical issues that might be described, using its terms, as the relative positions of Will and Mask (that is, authority and the fictive construct 'author'), Creative Genius and Body of Fate (that is, invention and discovery), on the Great Wheel. These conjunctions and oppositions are best understood by directing attention to the complex genesis of the text, since the reception/creation of the automatic script and other documents was an embodiment or dramatization of them. Coming to terms with the automatic script by such a route is the next task.

2

Nemo the Interpreter

Surely the automatic script and the other texts associated with it are the product of GY. They began with her, on that autumn day in 1917, and they arguably ended with her efforts to correct *A Vision* years after her husband's death. This chapter focuses on her authorship, but it does not follow a straight route, since the automatic script is no straightforward text. This text creates its own author and authors; it problematizes responsibility and authority; it reduces distinctions between the personal and the abstract as well as between the mundane and the supernatural. It resists direct discussion, as do many other occult texts and, for that matter, as do many manuscript drafts that represent pre-composition for later published works. They problematize linearity. Thus, after an initial discussion of the collaboration, the chapter will be organized by role, or rather by possible meanings for the roles suggested by GY's motto in the Order of the Golden Dawn. However, to begin, the assertion of authorship made in the first sentence above needs to be adjusted. Arguing with it is the first order of business.

It is a postmodern truism that the primary referent of any text is itself, but the *Vision* materials are about themselves in striking ways and to an unusual extent (even among occult writings or other automatically produced texts, which often incorporate claims for validity into their messages). The documents are as concerned with their own status as they are bearers of messages that make up their ostensible matter—the gyres, phases, historical material, descriptions of post-mortem states, and so forth—of the system. Moreover, these two components are strikingly enmeshed. The system emanates from practices that have the same deep structure as intellectual content, so that, for example, opposites at play formulate how dynamic opposition defines all forms. Phases are comprehensible when the right phasal energy explains them. Destiny can be rendered intelligible only when it is destined that comprehension occur. As any reader of the script can see, a significant proportion of the energy of the automatic experiments, from the first sessions to the last sleeps, was spent exploring the nature of what was happening, an exploration often couched in personal terms. Page after page, session after session, the script concerns itself with what desires prompt or obstruct the messages, who or what is sending them, how and how well they are received or translated, and how the abstractions being explained are at work in the Yeatses' lives (and the lives of others who are close to them). Readers will also recognize the difficulty, if not the impossibility, of culling the impersonal from the personal, or the intellectual from the emotional. The necessity of the intimate and relational quality of the truths received saturates the whole project. I suspect that when WBY announces in the dedication of the 1925 book, 'I have not even dealt with the whole of my subject, perhaps not even with what is most important, writing nothing about the Beatific Vision, little of sexual love' (*AV A* p. xii), the 'BV', as it is abbreviated in the script, has to do with the unity of action and thought, life and work, medium and message, that is an ever-present aspect or aspiration of the experiments, as it was the goal for WBY in his poetry, but which he found impossible to translate adequately into his published text.

Looking at the Yeatses' occult project in its personal and intimately collaborative aspect is a convenient way to approach some of the issues of creativity and power that are critically important for the automatic script. I will suggest later that much is to be gained by approaching in collaborative terms other work by WBY written after the *Vision* experiments had become part of his experience. For now, it is useful that the procedural issue is not only a salient characteristic of the script, but an explicit topic in it. Abstractions having to do with the nature of the experiment, like many others, present themselves in the documents in precise terms, sometimes even in personalized form. The project itself is given phasal characteristics, including relative positions of the four Faculties in a phase; its astrological placement is discovered; its development is divided into stages; it requires specific kinds of feeding and care; it has its own sexual characteristics and erotic needs; and it has its own daimons or personal genii.[1] This is not to suggest that the Yeatses' collaboration was personified or even envisioned as a single entity. It was not, although collaborative energy as a topic in the script attracts issues of identity appearing in various guises, beginning with that of the hand that wrote the script.

In general terms, collaboratively written ventures often raise questions about identity, beginning with the naming of their authors. A text with more than one producer, whether co-written by known writers, someone with no literary pretensions but with a story to tell and a ghost writer, one known figure and one or more silent partners, unnamed writers with a *nom de plume*, or even one person with two personae (such as William Sharp and Fiona Macleod), takes liberties with conventions of authorship in the modern West. As Holly A. Laird puts it in her study of female co-authors, 'today's social systems of authorship are not designed to cope with variability in the number of authors involved'.[2] Collaborations can bring to the surface various literary assumptions clustering around the idea of the named author as well as posing practical difficulties in economic and

---

[1] See, for a few examples of such characteristics, *YVP* i. 197; ii. 183, 243, and 249. For a discussion of daimons, see Ch. 5 below.

[2] Holly A. Laird, *Women Coauthors* (Urbana, Ill., and Chicago: University of Illinois Press, 2000), 2. For other studies of writerly collaboration, see Lisa Ede and Andrea Lunsford, *Singular Texts/Plural Authors: Perspectives on Collaborative Writing* (Carbondale, Ill.: Southern Illinois University Press, 1990); Wayne Koestenbaum, *Double Talk: The Erotics of Male Literary Collaboration* (New York: Routledge, 1989); Holly A. Laird, 'Forum: On Collaborations I', *Tulsa Studies in Women's Literature* 13, (1994): 285–91; *idem*, 'Forum: On Collaborations II', *Tulsa Studies in Women's Literature*, 14 (1995): 11–75; London, *Writing Double*; Jack Stillinger, *Multiple Authorship and the Myth of Solitary Genius* (New York: Oxford University Press, 1991); Helen Sword, *Ghostwriting Modernism* (Ithaca, NY: Cornell University Press, 2002); and Lorraine Mary York, *Rethinking Women's Collaborative Writing: Power, Difference, Property* (Toronto: University of Toronto Press, 2002).

legal terms. Both sorts of issues, aesthetic and material, have the same family tree, which can be traced back through the rise of copyright, the notion of legal ownership of written texts, and, further still, to presumptions about individuals and writing or speech in Western societies.[3] Authorship suggests control over the messages of a text as well as any financial or political gain it might generate, although it also carries with it the risk of a message beyond the range of influence of its sender. Thus, collaborations also point to issues of power, over written material as well as of one participant over others. In practical terms, one writer may (or perhaps must) have less authority than another, as is the case with a number of slave or colonial narratives. Collaboratively written texts sometimes find their place at the margins of literary practice, in that they do not participate in the validated form of single, named authorship. Such texts may be more likely to be derived from one set of social margins or another to begin with; they may indeed be signs of writing that occurs outside institutional power, as are native narratives, pseudonymous collaborations by women, or books in popular as opposed to élite genres. Further, and also relevant to the Yeatses, joint exercises of imaginative power suggest a rich field for explorations of the erotic. A sexual economy is often, if not always, at play in collaborative ventures.[4]

---

[3] See Roger Chartier, *The Order of Books: Readers, Authors, and Libraries between the Fourteenth and Eighteenth Centuries*, trans. Lydia G. Cochrane (Stanford, Calif.: Stanford University Press, 1994); David Saunders, *Authorship and Copyright* (London: Routledge, 1992); Martha Woodmansee, 'The Genius and the Copyright: Economic and Legal Conditions of the Emergence of the "Author" ', *Eighteenth-Century Studies*, 17 (1984): 425–48; and *idem* and Peter Jaszi (eds.), *The Construction of Authorship: Textual Appropriation in Law and Literature* (Durham, NC: Duke University Press, 1994). The genealogy of theoretical explorations of authorship includes Roland Barthes, 'The Death of the Author', in *Image, Music, Text: Essays Selected and Translated* (Glasgow: Fontana, 1977), 142–8; Jacques Derrida, *Of Grammatology*, trans. Gayatri Chakravorty Spivak (Baltimore: Johns Hopkins University Press, 1976); Michel Foucault, 'What Is an Author?', trans. Josué V. Harari, in Harari (ed.), *Textual Strategies: Perspectives in Post-Structuralist Criticism* (Ithaca, NY: Cornell University Press, 1979), 141–60; and Raymond Williams, *Marxism and Literature* (Oxford: Oxford University Press, 1977).

[4] See the range of examples explored in Whitney Chadwick and Isabelle de Courtivron (eds.), *Significant Others: Creativity and Intimate Partnership* (London: Thames & Hudson, 1993); see also Koestenbaum, *Double Talk*.

The automatic script is not like other collaborative texts in a number of ways, of course. It is neither intended nor suitable for publication (no less true for the papers' having actually appeared in print, as readers can probably attest). It may be an error even to regard as a single entity documents that are more like field notes, a diary, a series of letters, or a laboratory report of an ongoing experiment. Doing so may lead to artificial assumptions of unity as well as completion, with any number of conceptual mistakes following in their wake. Yet the script does represent a definable project, begun under remarkable circumstances and carried out for distinct purposes. That project was spiritual, although for both GY and WBY the spiritual, the personal, the social, and the literary were never easily separable. The sessions were driven by the possibility of joint and individual enlightenment and transformation. Literary benefits were inextricably linked to spiritual growth, and literary power was joined to occult expansion for WBY, among whose most committed purposes was to join word and work in a project he approached magically as often as not. According to Michael J. Sidnell, part of WBY's greatness resides in just this conjunction, so that, 'Far from being an essentially lyric poet who happened to be interested in holistic philosophies, WBY strove constantly to overcome the limitations of the lyric in the creation of more expansive and inclusive structures.'[5] The gradually widening gap between the provinces of the cognates *grammar* and *grimoire* over the centuries was, in other words, a historical and spiritual condition that WBY was determined to change. GY had similar interests: a student of Pico della Mirandola, with his insistence on the endless possibilities of the free human will and the efficacy of all religious studies, she created a series of experiments that suggest a belief that 'the unity of the intellect may be reconciled with the immortality of the soul',

[5] Sidnell, *Yeats's Poetry and Poetics*, 108. Sidnell has taken this general point further than many in suggesting that 'In Yeats, vision and belief, more than informing the "content" of the poetry, determine its structural conventions', including predominantly the use of personae in numerous works. Sidnell's analysis of dramatized personages in the published work is relevant to the discussion that follows of personae in the automatic script.

as Paul Oskar Kristeller writes of Pico.[6] Pico, like his friend Ficino, connected rhetoric and magic and thereby provided the automatic script with a pedigree and imprimatur.[7]

Transformative identities are at work in the automatic script, assumed names and roles to fit the purposes of the matter of their communication. The most important of these belong to GY, and are particularly appropriate emblems for the couple's experiment in multiple or anti-authorship.

Nemo Sciat

When she was initiated into the Hermetic Order of the Golden Dawn in 1914, sponsored by the adept Demon Est Deus Inversus—a.k.a. WBY—GHL took as her motto and magic name the Latin phrase *nemo sciat*: let no one know. It was inevitably shortened to Nemo ('no one' or, suggestively, 'no man') in the shorthand used by Order members who called each other only by mottoes. It survives as such in one list.[8] Several years later, GHL married her former sponsor, and

---

6 Paul Oskar Kristeller, 'Giovanni Pico della Mirandola and his Sources', in *L'Opera e il pensiero di Giovanni Pico della Mirandola nella storia dell'umanesimo: Convegno internazionale, Mirandola: 15–18 settembre 1963*, i (Florence: Istituto Nazionale di Studi sul Rinascimento, 1965), 63, and *idem, Renaissance Concepts of Man and Other Essays* (New York: Harper & Row, 1972), 57–8. GY's serious interest in Pico had much to do with his importance to the Western magical tradition as the first scholar in Western Europe to become acquainted with the cabbalah and try to reconcile it with Christianity and Platonism. On her translation, see *MYV* i. 41–2 and 273 n. 5. See also Saddlemyer, *Becoming George*, 60, 121.

7 The relationship between rhetoric and magic, which has often been remarked on by Kenneth Burke (e.g., *A Rhetoric of Motives* (Berkeley: University of California Press, 1969), 82), is explored by William A. Covino, *Magic, Rhetoric, and Literacy: An Eccentric History of the Composing Imagination* (Albany, NY: State University of New York Press, 1994). Covino mentions Ficino's definitions of the orator and the magus 'as similar figures' (p. 42).

8 The motto 'Nemo' is added in pen to one of several keys to members of the various temples kept by Gerald Yorke and provided to my father, George Mills Harper. Until recently Nemo was thought to be Hyde Lees's motto. I am grateful to Ann Saddlemyer and Warwick Gould for pointing me to the complete name, which R. A. Gilbert has discovered in a card file of Order members. According to Gilbert, 'For George Yeats there are two cards: one records her as Mrs W. B. Yeats, adding only her address at 16

Nemo became the author of GY's *magnum opus*. Nemo is still at work in the matter, if only in the sense that no one may know still the extent of that work, despite all the discussions that include the tale of the automatic script and even the publication of an edited form of the script itself. GY's daughter was fond of recalling that her mother used to say that she was constitutionally unable to answer a direct question. According to Anne Yeats, her mother would always take a question and 'send it back to you', one manifestation of the high value she put on privacy, her own and also that of others.[9]

As most readers of WBY quickly discover, most of the scholarly attention paid to GY occurs in the course of retelling the story of the first days of the marriage and the start of the 'incredible experience' of automatic writing.[10] GY plays a number of different roles in these stories, from bit part to supporting actress: a self-effacing young bride and mediumistic helpmeet; an unconscious Sybil, ignorant of the wisdom that comes unbidden from her lips or hands; the smart perpetrator of the perfect hoax for a depressed bridegroom with magical inclinations; or yet another silenced woman behind a literary genius. Past the honeymoon, though, the critical notice has tended to wane. After some mention that the experiment of the automatic script continued for several years, the attention generally shifts to the texts that WBY authored and back to WBY the author of them.

This state of affairs is understandable, of course. After all is said and done, literary interest is regularly related to interest in authors.[11]

Montpelier Square, Knightsbridge, S.W., and her motto, Nemo Sciat. The other card is more full. On this she appears as George Hyde Lees, with the same address and motto, but with these additional details: "No. 471 on roll. 24.7.1914 5–6. 1916. Pledge dated 21 June 1914." ' See R. A. Gilbert, 'Seeking that which was Lost: New Light on the Origins and Development of the Golden Dawn', in *YA* xiv. 46. For a more specific focus on GY's motto and issues of naming and anonymity, see my 'Nemo: George Yeats and Her Automatic Script', *New Literary History*, 33 (2002): 291–314.

    [9] Personal communication, 30 June 1996.
    [10] The quotation is from *AV B* 8. For several widely influential versions of the story see Ellmann, *Identity*, 149; *idem, Man and Masks*, 219; Jeffares, *Man and Poet*, 191; and Moore, *The Unicorn*, 253–78.
    [11] Jack Stillinger's explanation of this phenomenon remains one of the most articulate; see Stillinger, *Multiple Authorship*, 3–24.

Yeats studies are likely to be pulled toward WBY—the poet, that is, not the wife who took on his surname with their marriage. The difficulty of moving in a direction other than towards WBY in an examination of the *Vision* papers or any of the many texts associated with them has much to do with intellectual reliance on the notion of authorship, as we know.[12] But it is more than merely interesting to notice that unwary readers are led away from the ambiguities of multiple and nameless authorship back to the relative security of 'Yeats' in trying to make sense of texts that have their source in communications the writers believed were held with beings from beyond this world and/or their higher selves, in a setting that is utterly, if confusingly, collaborative. Nor do the multiplicities and confusions stop with the script as such. The system itself is wrapped in the clouds of such ambiguities, from the innocuous abstractions of the four Faculties and Principles in *A Vision* to more disturbing threats to self-possession in settings such as WBY's poems 'Leda and the Swan' or 'The Second Coming'.

Multiple lines of creative force move beneath imperfect authorial or subjective control in WBY's late work generally. This phenomenon prevents 'Yeats' from becoming a stable textual element in the works derived from the automatic script, contributing both to a number of the mixed signals in *A Vision* and also to the dynamic subjectivity of the later poetry. The effects that the automatic experiments had on WBY's poetry will get more of my attention in later chapters, but it is worth noting the common phenomenon of a shifting subject in the late verse: think of 'Among School Children' with its bemused and bewildered old man sliding into youthful image-worshipping mother and beyond, the restless motion enabling the triumphal last apostrophe that blends subject and object in the images of chestnut tree and dancer. Unpredictable personae and flexible subjects abound, from the experimental voice of the Crazy Jane series to the *tour de force* of 'Byzantium' with its final apocalyptic send-off of subject and

---

[12] In *Writing Double*, London considers the automatic script as collaborative authorship and situates it in the context of other nineteenth-century mediumistic writing.

world alike, or the multiple gendering and transpersonal ecstasy of 'Supernatural Songs'. And so forth: examples multiply. WBY knew what he was talking about when he opened the introduction to the 1937 version of *A Vision* claiming that his poetry 'has gained in self-possession and power' (*AV B* 8). It is tempting to read this 'self-possession' as a *double entendre*, for the experience to which WBY attributes his change involves possession in a magical, daimonic sense as well as a psychological one. Indeed, the power accrues from this dual sense—self-possession as something like Stephen Dedalus's 'subjective and objective genitive', flowing to the self partly through the self being possessed by an unnamed other.[13]

Such power cannot be traced back to any of the commonly told stories about the momentous autumn and winter of 1917–18. WBY did not invent this phenomenon alone, and it is far too great to have come from a GY who provided for her husband nothing but feminine self-effacement, unconsciously prophetic wisdom, clever fakery, or patriarchally coerced subordinacy. The usual narratives have become fixed with retelling (even the variations fall into a well-defined and narrow range).[14] Their rigidity is an obstacle to understanding. It may even be that narrative is not the best mode through which to explore

[13] James Joyce, *Ulysses*, ed. Hans Walter Gabler (New York: Vintage, 1986), 170.

[14] The stories of the Yeatses' experiences, it should be noted, also participate in a fairly narrow and well-defined discursive range of recitals of automatic experiences. Most emphasize the imposition of an alien power, as does Edward T. Bennett in describing the onset of automatic writing: 'The most frequent experience is that illegible scribblings, or endless convolutions, are made, often with considerable energy. It is as if a new force was trying to control the hand. After a few trials, definite letters, words and sentences are frequently evolved out of the chaos' (*Automatic Speaking and Writing: A Study*, iii: *The Shilling Library of Psychical Literature and Enquiry* (London and Edinburgh: Brimley Johnson and Ince, 1905), 5).

The narrations often stress surprise and speed: e.g., 'the chosen agent suddenly finds herself (or himself) writing rapidly and continuously without conscious volition' ([Mrs Desmond Humphreys] Rita, *The Truth of Spiritualism* (London: T. Werner Laurie, 1919), 59), or 'the pencil would then write easily and rapidly, expressing opinions, conveying information, and answering questions' ([John G. F. Raupert] A member of the Society for Psychical Research, *The Dangers of Spiritualism: Being Records of Personal Experiences, with Notes and Comments and Five Illustrations* (London: Sands, 1901), 82). Sir Oliver Lodge's widely read book *Raymond* also participates in the number of accounts of automatic writing that are echoed in descriptions of the Yeatses', including WBY's own in the introduction to the 1937 *A Vision*:

GY's work. The familiar stories are more than usually infected with their subject's intentions for them, after all. Since she took charge of her husband's effects at his death, she to a large degree orchestrated which stories were told, and by whom, for thirty years thereafter, as indeed she had done to a significant extent long before. When one deeply involved informant is the source of information about events for which little independently verifiable data exist, what is ostensibly history or literary biography leans toward autobiography, or an intentional avoidance of it. Of course, autobiography, like historical narrative in general, tends toward fiction, since stories require not only a reigning self-consciousness to tell them but also individualized heroes and heroines within them. Moreover, if these narratives are self-referential, they are so at an extraordinary slant: they feature an author who arranges not to be identified as such, a main character interested in making sure that she is not the focus of the tale.

Inquiry into the automatic script and the Yeatses' occult system is going to wreak havoc with story-telling in a number of ways: since it blurs the boundaries between individuals as well as their integrity as singular (the Yeatses would say 'daily') selves, it makes difficult the easy assumption of a cast of characters. In that it reconceptualizes the linearity of time and questions the finality of birth and death, those quintessential beginnings and endings of narratives, and in that it does not begin with its own beginning (as any reader of *Per Amica* knows) or end with its ending (extending well past WBY's death, among other things), it spells trouble for the imposition of a regular plot. Moreover, the messy business of the occult experiment did not move in a single trajectory, although it was envisioned as a process with goals and stages. For all of these reasons, I will not approach

In most cases of fully-developed automatism known to me the automatist reads what comes, and makes suitable oral replies or comments to the sentences as they appear: so that the whole has then the effect of a straightforward conversation of which one side is spoken and the other written—the speaking side being usually rather silent and reserved, the writing side free and expansive. (Sir Oliver J. Lodge, *Raymond, or Life and Death* (London: Methuen, 1916), 355)

it narratively. Instead, if you will, I will look into the Yeatses' collaboration as if meditating on symbols. To put this less mystically, I will follow some etymological peregrinations of GY's magical name and the title given to her role in the script (extending the method in a later chapter to consider the names of some of the other personalities involved in the creation of the system), since examining these descriptors suits the matter of her creativity and the intricacies of the experiments that underlie the sea change in her husband's work.

No Man

Upon entering the Order of the Golden Dawn, GY would have chosen her motto to symbolize the essence of her personal myth, to 'define her personal search for meaning and her link to the Divine', as Mary Greer describes the act of self-naming. 'The motto became her magical name, because in naming herself after the image of a central principle, each [member of the Order] strove to make herself over in that image.'[15] It is helpful in understanding her work to recognize that GY was also Nemo Sciat, or Nemo, and to tease out the implications of that mythic identity.

The rare Latin phrase *nemo sciat* occurs twice in the Vulgate. In one of the stories about David's early career (1 Sam. 21: 2), the canny young man is on the run from King Saul, misleading a priest about his reasons for being at a holy place. The outlaw David thus keeps the priest Ahimelech from realizing that the king's former favourite is now a fugitive, and he also manages to procure not only sacred

---

[15] Mary Greer, *Women of the Golden Dawn: Rebels and Priestesses* (Rochester, Vt.: Park Street Press, 1995), 4–5. One of the first tasks that candidates for admission to the Order were asked to undertake was to suggest secret mottoes for themselves, by which they would be known by their fellow members. In addition to representing aspects of the higher self, of course, the mottoes had practical value in maintaining secrecy within the Order and between the Order and world outside it. See R. A. Gilbert, *Golden Dawn: Twilight of the Magicians* (Wellingborough, Northamptonshire: Aquarian Press, 1983), 33; and Howe, *Magicians*, 56. It should also be noted that some Order mottoes may have originated in the Esoteric Section of the Theosophical Society, which WBY joined in 1888.

bread for his men to eat but also the sword of Goliath for himself to wield. David replies to Ahimelech's inquiries about why he is alone thus: 'Rex præcepit mihi sermonem, et dixit: Nemo sciat rem, propter quam missus es a me, et cuiusmodi præcepta tibi dederim' (in the King James translation, 'The king hath commanded me a business, and hath said unto me, Let no man know any thing of the business whereabout I send thee, and what I have commanded thee'). The chosen one, the anointed king, lives paradoxically outside the bounds of both secular and sacred law and speaks to a representative of power in vague terms or *double entendre* (what king, it might be asked, in a culture deeply ambivalent about human royalty, has sent him, and on what errand?) in order to achieve a higher good. This scenario presents suggestive parallels to a 'business' about which Nemo Sciat—that is, GY—allowed few to know, which was both an exercise of power and a foray outside the boundaries of regularized and publicly endorsed authority.

The second biblical occurrence of the phrase is equally suggestive. Jeremiah 36: 19 occurs in the middle of a story featuring a dictated book of great power. The prophet and his scribe must hide in order to escape the king's wrath when he reads the unpleasant truth, his officials warn: 'et dixerunt principes ad Baruch vade et abscondere tu et Hieremias et nemo sciat ubi sitis' ('then said the princes unto Baruch, Go, hide thee, thou and Jeremiah; and let no man know where ye be'). The book receives the punishment intended also for the men: it is slashed with a knife and then burned. The passage is a fine example of slippage between book and writers that goes beyond metaphor to physical substitution, body of book for human bodies, in addition to the more common elision of writing and authority, in which the king's anger is directed at God, Jeremiah, and Baruch, all of whom share responsibility for the book, indiscriminately. Like the biblical book, GY's project would have bodily consequences for her, as well as outcomes in the areas of power and mind.[16]

---

[16] I am grateful to Ann Saddlemyer for the reference in Jeremiah (Saddlemyer, *Becoming George*, 66–7 and 682–3 n. 21) and to Herbert F. Tucker for the one in 1 Samuel.

Although rare in Latin, the phrase *nemo sciat* occurs fairly often in one highly suggestive neo-Latin author: Emanuel Swedenborg. He even seems fond of the expression. It occurs some 252 times in the *Arcana Coelestia*, for example, an unwieldy exegesis of the books of Genesis and Exodus, a familiar source to any occultist. This twelve-volume work represents, as well as promotes, a bold elision between text and writer. An essential part of Swedenborgian doctrine holds that Jehovah is present in this world in scripture, so that text assumes almost an equivalence to divine author. As the eleventh edition of the *Encyclopædia Britannica* puts it, the New Church believes that God has appointed 'a visible representative of Himself in the word of Scripture. This word is an eternal incarnation.'[17] Among the many passages in which the phrase appears in the *Arcana Coelestia*, several might have caught the eye of the future 'interpreter' of the *Vision* experiments. For example, the story of Joseph, in Genesis 37–50, includes a prominent account of dream interpretation. Swedenborg explicates Gen. 40: 8, in which Pharoah's baker and butler, imprisoned with Joseph, complain that they have had dreams but there is no one to interpret them. Swedenborg explains that the message is applicable for everyone: ' "Et interpretator nullus illi": quod significet quod nemo sciat quid in illis, constat ex significatione "interpretationis" quod sit explicatio quid in se habeat' (' "And there is no interpreter for it": that this means that no one knows what is in them, is certain from the signification of an "interpretation" as an explanation of something held within itself').[18]

People need to have something explained that they already have within them. 'Let no one know', in other words, yields 'let the interpreter know', as she serves as translator for her own difficult text. For GY, a similar blending of two roles occurs. The motto plays with its own language to suggest a similar game. Nemo Sciat in its shortened form, Nemo, as name, blends back into the

---

[17] *Encyclopædia Britannica*, 11th edn., s.v. 'Swedenborg', 223.
[18] Stairs Project, *The Heavenly Doctrines* (Academy of the New Church, 2004); <http://www.theheavenlydoctrines.org>. The passage above is n. 5105; trans. mine.

Latin suggestively, swerving from the implication that no one may understand something to the sense that she is the (no) one who may: let Nemo know.

The motto certainly suggests anonymity, but it is important to notice that to be Nemo is not to be nameless. It is to be *named* nameless, a difference that has been part of Western culture at least since Homer made the word *Outis* a central feature of the story of Odysseus and Polyphemus. Assumed namelessness is in fact a sign of Odysseus's cunning, which is his source of power, the quality that attracts gods to him. He is *polytropos*, a man of many turns and devices, but he is certainly no less Odysseus for his multiplicity. In fact, his hidden name, like his hidden identity, is a sign of his personal strength and a test of character for those around him. To assume anonymity is the opposite of having anonymity thrust upon one.

Indeed, Nemo insisted on it. WBY was always careful to give his wife credit, as he did most notably in the introduction to the 1937 edition of *A Vision*, ambivalent though that account is about her agency.[19] From the beginning, however, he was instructed to keep quiet about the mediumistic sessions and her participation. As early as 25 November 1917, Thomas of Dorlowicz told WBY that 'the information is not to be betrayed as to *source*—all else may be done ... you can say it is a sequence[20] & your original thought—that is to

---

[19] In this context, G. M. Harper cites an unpublished letter of 31 Dec. 1919 to John Quinn in which WBY mentions that his wife has been 'every evening in my study helping me at my work', but is silent about the occult nature of her help (*MYV*ii. 386). Having promised not to talk about the script, WBY was willing to imply that her collaborations were merely literary. Later, of course, he revealed her role in the experiments, over her objections. She felt strongly about the issue, and it precipitated 'their first and only serious quarrel' (Richard Ellmann, interview with GY, 17 Jan. 1947, Richard Ellmann Papers, Special Collections Department, McFarlin Library, University of Tulsa; Saddlemyer, *Becoming George*, 405–6; and Foster, *Arch-Poet*, 384).

[20] In the script, 'sequence' and 'allusion' are loaded terms. The definitions given by the controls do not make these ideas very clear: 'Sequence is an intensity produced by association of words ideas & images' (31 Aug. 1918); 'Allusion is the impact of the objective image idea or thought upon the subjective' (2 Sept. 1918) (*YVP*ii. 36–7). Sequence, associated with phase 15, desire, and symbolic art, is a positive term. Allusion, its opposite, is associated with phase 1, 'cessation of desire', and allegorical or abstract art (*MYV*i. 200).

a degree true' (*YVP*i. 123). Thomas referred to a 'pledge of secrecy' and 'private script always' soon after, on 23 December 1917 (*YVP*i. 175). In an important session on 4 March 1918, just before the couple left England for their first trip to Ireland together, all of the guides and controls who had taught them previously gathered for a spiritual send-off.[21] Their first item of business was a strong warning for wby (whom gy would dub 'William Tell' for his tendency to be indiscreet[22]):

we are not pleased because you talk too freely of spirits & of initiation—you may *yes* not speak of any personal thing we give—you may speak of the actual system but ye may not tell of any personal thought image or information we give nor of the forms & processes we give for your own contemplation nor of such demand & restrictions as we make nor of the life we demand that you should live—only speak of those actual machineries of the philosophy that may be in the book

Yes [responding to an unrecorded question] but do not imply that it is through your own initiation or psychic power

imply *intervention* if need be

Yes dream—*yes* but not *guidance of spirits in your own life*

That is always wrong—because you speak to unbelievers you destroy our help. (*YVP*i. 369)

gy may have felt as strongly as they did, if it was she, or something close to her, who broke into their plural voice to state in first-person singular 'I do not *wish* the spirit source revealed'. It is revealing that this statement is followed immediately by insistence that the intimate parts of the script be kept private: wby must 'Never mention any personal message' although 'these (*no*) are the most important of all our communications' (*YVP*i. 369). On numerous occasions the poet was instructed not to allow visitors to the sessions. Even though it gradually became obvious that the system would have to be put into some written form, in order to make its bewildering complexities

---

[21] No fewer than six communicators, some of both varieties, were present on this occasion, which was also the day on which the issue of having a child was raised intently; see also Ch. 5 below.

[22] Ellmann, *Man and Masks*, 168.

clear to WBY, if for no other reason, his collaborator was not nearly as keen as he to expose it to the general public. As late as 1922, he wrote in the notebook in which he was keeping a record of their 'conversations' (the method of the moment) that they were to engage in the system in their lives: 'We perhaps prepare' for a supernatural manifestation of the Four Masters, WBY noted, an event that would be 'more than teaching as in Nietsche'. However, 'She does not want me to write system for publication—not as exposition—but only to record & to show to a few people' (*YVP*iii. 110).

In keeping with her interest in secrecy, it is telling that GY's hand penned the first mention of the fabricated author of the 'Speculum Angelorum et Hominorum',[23] the book outlining the system which Michael Robartes found in Krakow in the story that WBY invented for the introduction to the first version of *A Vision*. Although WBY wrote out the over-elaborate hoax, Fish clarified that tinctures lay behind the tale-within-a-tale of Giraldus and the Judwali tribe, and Thomas gave the other reason for the whole business: 'Supernormal origin received through a person we will call Gyraldus' (*YVP*i. 250; ii. 183).[24] Like Thomas himself, Giraldus has more than a passing relationship to the actual hand that penned much of the system. His portrait presides over the first book, and his turbaned and sharp-eyed pose, holding out a scroll which remains closed, may be the most visible of the many guises behind which not only WBY, to whom he bears a striking resemblance, but also GY, his sharp-eyed

[23] The Latin title was problematic for WBY. The final word is spelled *Homenorum* (possibly a typographical error) under the portrait of Giraldus which WBY commissioned his friend Edmund Dulac to create for the 1st edition of *A Vision*, but *Hominorum* in that book's introduction (p. xvii). Neither spelling is correct. WBY uses the proper spelling, *Hominum*, in a letter dated to Lady Gregory dated 4 Jan. 1918 (*L* 644), but left blank spaces for the fictional title in two unfinished MS versions, and filled in one of the spaces with 'Speculum Angelorum et Hominis', a spelling he retained for a third MS and the Robartes–Aherne typescript (*AVA*, Editorial Introduction, pp. xxxi, xlix n. 21). By 1937, he had settled on the best choice of the four spellings: *Hominum* is the only variant there (pp. 38, 39). See Foster, *Arch-Poet*, 312.

[24] Who the historical Gyraldus (or Giraldus: the Yeatses spelled it both ways) was has been a matter of critical debate. For an account of the possibilities see Raine, *Yeats the Initiate*, ch. 13. See also the note to the Frontispiece in *CVA*.

collaborator (who was fond of clothes), is hidden. Giraldus was created as a masquerade, to usher in a book that comprises a series of masks and poses as importantly as it contains straightforward exposition.

With biographical considerations in mind, the assumption of anonymity looks like a show of independence or idiosyncrasy, somewhat like the childhood nickname 'Dobbs' (which became a favourite with her husband), or the figure of a square with which GY

2. Portrait of Giraldus, frontispiece to *A Vision* (1925), woodcut by Edmund Dulac. Reproduced by permission of Hodder & Stoughton Limited.

identified herself in letters to Dorothy Shakespear and Ezra Pound.[25] In that names carry with them complex codes of conduct and group identity, as well as self-imposed definitions and restrictions, to assume a new name is always to lay aside a familiar self—personal, familial, and social—for a new freedom or a new allegiance. Such an act might well have appealed to a young woman from a social environment like that in which GY was reared. R. F. Foster suggests that she chafed against being a member of one of England's 'upper-middle-class county families, well-off and independent, with an inclination to the bohemian and slightly rackety'.[26] Like other members of the Order of the Golden Dawn, most of whom were from middle or upper middle classes, she assumed a secret name from an old and alien language and culture, in part as a sign of escape from the petty provincialism and frivolity of Edwardian and Georgian England into a more cosmopolitan and cultivated culture. Nemo is GY's sign, then, and it is also a sign of its times. Nemo, with her sly pun on identity as well as gender and perhaps aural hints at 'no more' or even 'name-o', chose a name that resonates slightly with a sense of the worldly and (ironically) the new, more like the planned dissonances in the use of ancient myths by her relative contemporaries Pound or Joyce than her husband's nostalgic summonses.

The word's antiquity brings to mind not only Latin and Homeric Greek but also Judaic tradition, including a strong sacral tone. In any Western religious tradition, but perhaps especially in a group as cabbalistic as the latter-day Rosicrucianism with which the Golden Dawn identified itself, to be named as nameless is to assume a kinship, of whatever kind, with the most ineffable of names, the Tetragrammaton. The possessor of the name YHWH claims power by the way in which the word rejects the ordinary business of proper nouns in favour of philosophical or theological statements. The four

---

[25] Pound and Litz (eds.), *Pound and Shakespear*, 59; Saddlemyer, 'George, Ezra', 8, 9 n. 6, and *passim*.
[26] Foster, *Apprentice Mage*, 437.

letters do not give information, since telling occurs at a distance from, and interferes with, the pure existence that is the deity; instead, they gesture toward the impossible act of speaking about being. Similarly, Nemo also enacts a linguistically playful swerve away from identifying marker to emphasize instead the insufficiency of language to identify. The god says 'I am' to Moses' query about his name (Exod. 3: 13); Nemo responds 'I am not' to a question to which a name is the answer.

This response is itself a spiritual exercise. Any Golden Dawn motto is not merely an identifier but a requirement for membership in a secret society whose goals centred on self-improvement through personal transformation. The magic practised by initiates reconstructed a spiritual path upward from one 'I' to another, from ego to Ego, as it were. The particulars of the rituals derive from sources as far-flung as ancient Hebrew and Christian Gnosticism, strands of Indian philosophy (filtered for the most part through theosophy), Hellenistic and pseudo-Egyptian Hermeticism, and Western Christian cabbalism and alchemy. More immediately, the project of self-transformation also occurs in the context of nineteenth-century social discourse shaped by the positivist paradigm of natural science. The debate over the place of humanity in a materialist universe forms a prominent part of the backdrop for the Order of the Golden Dawn in both reactionary and collusive senses. The rituals and the rhetoric surrounding the Order are clothed in ancient dress, appropriately enough for a spiritual system aiming to re-create a supernatural world adequate to the needs of its latter-day practitioners, in a period when religion was widely felt to have lost its power. Equally, though, members of the Order assumed possibilities of endless expansion and progress in their private spiritual lives, though these notions are deeply imbued with the materialist values and the industrial age that the practice of magic decried. As Israel Regardie, one of the most articulate public expositors of the Order, describes it in an introduction to its teachings, Golden Dawn magic not only refers historically to 'the Divine Theurgy praised and reverenced by antiquity' but is also a 'quest spiritual and divine, . . . a task of self-creation and reintegration, the bringing into human life of something eternal and enduring'.[27] The pre-eminent goal of any magician was the cultivation of a kind of second self, a next evolutionary stage of humanity. In Regardie's words, 'At the commencement of his career, the Magician is obliged to comprehend that his one aspiration is to his Higher Self, to his Holy Guardian Angel, and that any faculties which are obtained must be harnessed to that aspiration.'[28]

Order mottoes symbolize a route whereby an initiate may purify and expand consciousness to become finally a divine version of her- or himself. Such identifiers are not merely replacements or alternatives for other names, but special titles that are sanctified—set apart—from old identity. Nemo, then, points toward a future reality that would be thought to transcend this physical plane. The term emphasizes its status as both a paradox and an agent of change: a description of an existence that does not exist in this time or world as well as a tool for furthering the purpose of leaving an old life behind. In generic terms, this is what any Order motto does. Still, this particular example is a rather curious choice. It is unlike many of the others from the Golden Dawn, most of which proclaim their meanings with much less subtlety, such as Maud Gonne's appropriately flamboyant Per Ignem Ad Lucem (Through Fire to Light), or, for that matter, WBY's own assertive identification with Demon and Deus.

GY's magical name comments on identity and identity change, suggesting both the 'one aspiration' to the 'higher self' that Regardie mentions and that such loyalty is to an empty signifier. Progress to the next stage may not be an exercise in control; the self and its knowledge may not be in charge of its transformation, even a transformation it has set in motion. GY's automatic writing, which poses various potential disturbances to stable selfhood, seems also to have been designed for her benefit in just this area, or so it is suggested

---

[27] Israel Regardie, *The Tree of Life: A Study in Magic* (York Beach, Me.: Samuel Weiser, 1972), 31.

[28] Ibid. 37–8. The identification of 'higher self' with 'guardian angel' has obvious affinities with the Yeatsian daimon. See Ch. 5 below for a discussion of daimons.

by a question and answer in a session a few weeks after the beginning of the script. WBY asks, 'Why were we two chosen for each other?' and is told that the 'emotional protection' his bride is destined to receive from their union is 'from her own distrust of self' (*YVP*i. 110).[29]

In an essay about the colourful magician Aleister Crowley, Alex Owen has argued that the magical intention to develop a magical self reflected contemporary cultural trends at the turn of the twentieth century, a pivotal point in the history of the Western self, at which the boundaries that had been thought to define that culturally central entity, including gender identity, were being problematized in a number of ways.[30] Magical inner exploration is expressed in terms that sound like physical journeys from one realm to another. Owen notes that adepts 'sought to develop a powerful and effective second self which would explore the spheres beyond conscious awareness. This second self, however, was not the dissociated personality of spiritualist mediumship or psychological disorder.'[31] Rather, it was a demonstration of will: the magician overcomes the habitual instability and dissociation that lie between the ordinary and the magical selves. Part of the self is split from another part, and power flows through the lines of communication between them.

GY, a dedicated magician practising a form of spiritualism, was experimenting with practices that highlight complexities in both magical and spiritualist notions of the self. Magical celebrities like Crowley, stressing active control rather than receptive illumination, do not represent the only, or even the most common, attitude. Many initiates of the Golden Dawn had a strong sense of fragments of self that the Order existed to help integrate rather than overcome. Magic, according to Regardie (in a book that devotes a good deal of space

---

[29] They will also be helped by two images: eagle or hawk and butterfly.

[30] Alex Owen, 'The Sorcerer and his Apprentice: Aleister Crowley and the Magical Exploration of Edwardian Subjectivity', *Journal of British Studies*, 36 (1997): 99–133. See also Joy Dixon, 'Gender, Politics, and Culture in the New Age: Theosophy in England, 1880–1935' (Ph.D. diss., Rutgers, 1993), and Alex Owen, *British Occultism and the Culture of the Modern* (Chicago: University of Chicago Press, 2004).

[31] Owen, 'Sorcerer and Apprentice', 121.

to criticizing Crowley, among others), is a much more humble and aesthetic experience: its variety of rituals and symbols exist precisely because it 'recognizes the many-faceted nature of Man. . . . Each part of the soul, each elemental aspect of the entire man must be strengthened and transmuted, and brought into equilibrium and harmony with the others.'[32] Nor was spiritualism concerned simply with getting a simple self out of the way to make way for separate entities to take over. Organizations like the Society for Psychical Research and writers like Theodore Flournoy had replaced passive mediumship with speculations about the nature of the plastic mind. Flournoy, a Swiss professor of psychology, collected data from dozens of mediums in the course of his investigations, which WBY read with interest when the translation *Spiritism and Psychology* appeared in 1911.[33] Flournoy suggests that although 'nothing is more rare than to find a true medium', the real thing is no less real for originating not only in the Beyond but in the mysterious realms of the psyche in the here and now: 'the ordinary self is only a fragment—a portion, more or less mobile and unstable, of a larger individuality from which it is differentiated'.[34] GY's motto comments on these sorts of problematizations as well as reflecting them. In her ambivalence, Nemo may be more modern than her husband. Furthermore, in that the interrogation of self as the formation of a higher self flowered into fullest expression in the experiment in transcendental auto-creation that is the automatic script, the script may be the most modern of his works as well.

GY was a full generation younger than her husband (her father was born in 1865, the same year as WBY). Indeed, James Joyce, author of the famous and fabulous remark that WBY was too old, was ten years older than the ancient one's wife.[35] Saddlemyer reports that WBY characteristically 'relied upon her as the sounding board for

[32] Regardie, *What You Should Know*, 93.
[33] Foster, *Apprentice Mage*, 463.
[34] Theodore Flournoy, *Spiritism and Psychology*, trans. Hereward Carrington (New York and London: Harper & Brothers, 1911), 59.
[35] WBY recorded the much-debated conversation that took place the first time he and Joyce met; see Richard Ellmann, *James Joyce*, rev. edn. (Oxford: Oxford University Press, 1982), 101–3.

the younger generation'.[36] Through her aunt by marriage, Olivia Shakespear, her close friend Dorothy Shakespear, and Dorothy's beau and future husband Pound, GY was in first-hand contact with the intellectual and aesthetic ferment of the pre-war years in London. In a penetrating analysis of the Shakespear circle, John Harwood lists visitors to Olivia Shakespear's salon in Brunswick Gardens, including 'Wyndham Lewis, the sculptor Henri Gaudier-Brzeska, the pianist Walter Morse Rummel, Richard Aldington, Hilda Doolittle ('HD'), William Carlos Williams, T. E. Hulme, John Cournos and others'.[37] Of course, younger modernists than WBY, like his wife's near contemporaries Joyce, Picasso, Pound, and Woolf, were also experimenting with the implications for art of the constructedness and multiplicities of human identity, the secular breaking of subjects into constituent parts that do not necessarily cohere, and representing in various ways a consequent fracturing of meaning. GY, like her husband, blended the progressive inclinations of international modernism with more conservative-tending interests, as well as holding firmly to various forms of occult thought. (These seemingly contrary tendencies are not as unusual as they might appear, of course: the occult was one of many dimensions seemingly antithetical to the new era, like primitivism or madness, whose expulsion or repression from discourses of modernity are in fact essential components of it.[38]) In a letter of 24 April 1913, Dorothy Shakespear tells Ezra Pound that her cousin GHL's copy of *Poetry* has arrived, doubtless the famous March 1913 issue in which Pound and F. S. Flint published the first Imagist manifesto.[39] Imagism's emphasis on the image itself, hard-edged and seemingly objective, rather than on symbolic or rhythmic resonance, is compatible with

[36] Ann Saddlemyer, 'Looking for Georgie: Research Still in Progress' (Paper presented at the Annual Meeting of the Modern Language Association, Chicago, 28 Dec. 1990).

[37] John Harwood, *Olivia Shakespeare and W. B. Yeats: After Long Silence* (London: Macmillan, 1989), 130.

[38] On this phenomenon, see, e.g., John Jervis, *Transgressing the Modern* (Oxford: Blackwell, 1999), and Marianna Torgovnick, *Gone Primitive: Savage Intellects, Modern Lives* (Chicago and London: University of Chicago Press, 1990).

[39] Pound and Litz (eds.), *Pound and Shakespear*, 210.

the mood of many sessions of automatic script: WBY asking about emotional, experiential, or symbolic truth and receiving diagrams, numbers, or abstractions that occur in pairs or sequences with neat categorical precision. On a trip to Rome in 1914 with Dorothy, GHL attended an exhibit of Futurist paintings. Another letter from Dorothy to Ezra records laughingly that GHL felt 'her ferment inside, being calmed by the ring of blue & green' in works by Balla and Severini.[40] These artists' emphasis on destruction of static materiality, dynamic malleability, and multiple, simultaneous consciousness must have resonated with her sense of herself and the world.

Spiritualism was changing as well, as the Victorian period faded into the Edwardian, and as Europe slouched toward the huge transformations of the Great War, waning and then reasserting itself in the 1890s and through wartime, when bereaved women and men on the home front flocked to mediums for hope of life beyond the grave for slaughtered sons, lovers, husbands, brothers, and friends. The renewal featured a greater emphasis on voices, either spoken or written, and correspondingly somewhat less on physical phenomena, so that Arthur Conan Doyle could suggest in 1926 that 'materialisation may have been more common in the past than in the present', and that 'in these days complete materialisation is very rare'.[41] The gradual shift away from dramatic physical embodiments

---

[40] Letter of 16 March 1914, ibid. 328.

[41] Arthur Conan Doyle, *The History of Spiritualism*, 2 vols. (New York: George H. Doran, 1926), ii. 209–10. Doyle's wife Jean had conducted automatic writing a few years earlier. See *idem*, *Pheneas Speaks: Direct Spirit Communications in the Family Circle, Reported by Arthur Conan Doyle* ([London]: Psychic Press and Bookshop, [1927]). See also Ruth Brandon, *The Spiritualists: The Passion for the Occult in the Nineteenth and Twentieth Centuries* (New York: Knopf, 1983), 226. In 'Swedenborg, Mediums, and the Desolate Places', WBY laments the passing of materialization in latter-day mediumship: 'Most commonly, however, especially of recent years, no form will show itself, or but vaguely and faintly and in no way ponderable, and instead there will be voices flitting here and there in darkness, or in the half-light, or it will be the medium himself fallen into trance who will speak, or without a trance write from a knowledge and intelligence not his own' (*Ex* 54).

in favour of spoken or written communication reflects the subtle tastes of middle-class practitioners. There are significant exceptions to this general trend, though. It should be remembered that William Stainton Moses' widely influential *Spirit Teachings* (1883) was the result of automatic writing, which he had developed in the 1870s.[42] Similarly, the physical medium Elizabeth Guppy-Volckman, who was active in WBY's time, was a well-known levitator (see *CL*ii. 292). For decades since its beginnings with table-rappings in upstate New York, spiritualism had worked for social respectability, attempting to found itself as a mainline variant of Christianity, a safe and wholesome activity, and a repository for genuine intellectual investigation for the educated professional classes. Such periodicals as the newspaper *Light, Two Worlds, The Occult Review, The Medium and Daybreak* (volumes 2–4 of which are in the Yeatses' library), *Borderland* (edited by William T. Stead), and even the *Proceedings of the Society for Psychical Research* reflect the upward mobility of the movement, as did hundreds of books and the successful marketing of various products of potential interest to spiritualists, from planchettes and crystal-gazing globes to cures for rheumatism and special hymnals for use at seances.[43] One important area of change is linked to the heavy impress of 'science', including developments in the sciences of the mind. Spiritualist phenomena were analysed in scholarly detail by the likes of Frederic W. H. Myers, Frank Podmore, Sir Oliver Lodge, Sir William Barrett, and other members of the Society for Psychical

---

[42] [William Stainton Moses], *Spirit Teachings* (London: Psychological Press Association, 1883). See also Arnold Goldman, 'Yeats, Spiritualism, and Psychical Research', in *Yeats and the Occult*, 109, and Oppenheim, *Other World*, 77.

[43] See Harry Price, *Short-Title Catalogue of Works on Psychical Research, Spiritualism, Magic, Psychology, Legerdemain and Other Methods of Deception, Charlatanism, Witchcraft, and Technical Works for the Scientific Investigation of Alleged Abnormal Phenomena from circa 1450 A.D. to 1929 A.D.* (London: The National Laboratory of Psychical Research, 1929). Among the books published in the decade before the Yeatses began their experiments, the more interesting and possibly influential include Bennett, *Automatic Speaking and Writing*. Hanson E. Hey, *The Seven Principles of Spiritualism; with a Brief History of the Spiritualists' National Union* (Halifax, The Spiritualists' National Union, 1910), uses the significant Yeatsian term Anima Mundi in connection with the movement (p. 37).

Research, who were critical of the more dramatic manifestations and favoured subtler forms.[44] C. G. Jung, interestingly, analysed mediumship and occult phenomena in his inaugural dissertation for the medical degree; the case involved, *inter alia*, automatic writing that resulted in a circular diagram of the forces and laws of the universe.[45]

GY, who, according to Iseult Gonne Stuart, 'had a certain wildness about her', developed a process and a self that both used her magical training and participated in mediumship, particularly of the more intellectualized, higher-brow variety preferred by the Society for Psychical Research.[46] She thus joined older and newer conceptions of the self, womanhood, and authorship in a blend that bears her personal stamp no less than does the Yeatses' system, although her automatism also of course bears the mark of her time and station. The blend was inherently fluctuating and unstable in terms of subjectivity, gender, and the role of the writer.

One way to understand the power politics of her automatic script is to notice the paradox mentioned above, of someone practising both mediumship and magic. Although the Yeatses certainly did not share simple interpretations of these vocations, the two were commonly

---

[44] For connections between spiritualism and the new sciences see Oppenheim, *Other World*, 199–390; on the epistemological suitability of the Society for Psychical Research for its founding members, see John Peregrine Williams, 'The Making of Victorian Psychical Research: An Intellectual Élite's Approach to the Spiritual World' (Ph.D. diss., University of Cambridge, 1984). Further discussion of the interconnections between new technologies and spiritualism may be found in the interlude on automatic performance below.

[45] C. G. Jung, *Psychiatric Studies*, trans. R. F. C. Hull, ed. Sir Herbert Read, Michael Fordham, and Gerhard Adler, in *The Collected Works of C. G. Jung* (London: Routledge and Kegan Paul, 1957), i. 40.

[46] Richard Ellmann, interview with Iseult Gonne Stuart, 21 Sept. 1946, Richard Ellmann Papers, Special Collections Department, McFarlin Library, University of Tulsa. Ellmann, writing up the notes afterward, was not sure of the adjective 'wildness': 'I don't think Iseult used quite that word—strangeness perhaps.' It should be noted that GHL had been to many sittings with mediums such as the famous American Mrs Etta Wriedt (in the Wednesday sessions of 'Julia's Circle', organized by W. T. Stead) and the equally well-known Mrs Gladys Osborne Leonard (who is best known as the medium for the sittings recounted in Lodge's *Raymond*), beginning probably in 1912. See Saddlemyer, *Becoming George*, 55–7.

understood in magical and spiritualist circles to be incompatible. After all, mediums yield the conscious will to outside forces in order to admit influences from beyond, while magicians harness the will in order to travel beyond their rational selves. Mediums, as it were, stay at home and open windows to allow breezes from the Beyond to blow upon them; magicians open doors and venture into larger worlds. That of magician was generally considered the superior vocation, both functionally and socially: mediums, who were as often from working classes as not, were lower in social status than, for example, the more genteel and professional members of the magical Order. Both magic and theosophy were the sorts of occupations for which one might, for example, need the reading-room of the British Museum, to brush up on one's Egyptian history. Indeed, the Golden Dawn actively excluded mediums. The pledge that all candidates requesting admission to the Outer Order signed contains a specific cautionary note:

The Chiefs of the Order do not care to accept as Candidates any persons accustomed to submit themselves as Mediums to the Experiments of Hypnotism, Mesmerism, or Spiritualism; or who habitually allow themselves to fall into a completely Passive condition of Will; also they disapprove of the methods made use of as a rule in such Experiments.[47]

The automatic script echoes this warning when in January 1918 the Yeatses were told by the control that communication '*through a medium in trance . . . is wrong*' (*YVP*i. 227).[48] The injunction in the

---

[47] See R. A. Gilbert, *The Golden Dawn Companion: A Guide to the History, Structure, and Workings of the Hermetic Order of the Golden Dawn* (Wellingborough, Northamptonshire: Aquarian Press, 1986), 45. It should be noted that GY was not the only member of the Golden Dawn to engage in automatic writing, which was often regarded as less potentially dangerous than trance mediumship: e.g., Elsa Barker, who wrote the popular 3-vol. series *Letters of a Living Dead Man* (London: William Rider and Son, 1914–19) from automatic scripts received from a soldier killed in the Great War, was an active member of the Order in England and the USA. See Gilbert, 'Seeking', 42 and 49 n. 24.

[48] Interestingly, the reasons for the communicators' injunction against trance mediumship have to do with the free participation of the spirits in a true collaboration, not any danger to the human participants in the exercise. The spirits must come of their own volition to people they know, the Yeatses learned: 'All mediumship which aims at

Golden Dawn was no light matter: the tone with which Regardie describes the 'spiritualistic trance' as 'nothing more or less than an unnatural descent into inertia and the animal consciousness', in which 'all humanity and divinity is abdicated', is clear enough. 'Magic therefore', he reaffirms, 'has no association from any possible point of view with passive mediumship.' He explains:

the medium cultivates a passive and negative trance which hurls her centre of consciousness below into what we may call the *Nephesch*. The Magician on the other hand is intensely active from both a mental and spiritual point of view, and though he too strives in noetic trance to hold the ratiocinative processes in abeyance, his method is to rise above them, to open himself to the telesic rays of the Higher Self rather than to descend haphazard into the relative slime of the *Nephesch*.[49]

As these descriptions make more than clear (even in their pronouns), the gendered implications of GY's exercise in self-conquest as well as self-cancellation are deeply significant.[50] As both magician and medium, Nemo aligned herself with both the conqueror and the vanquished, the dominant masculinized position and the subordinate feminized one. The key issue is submission: magicians in the Golden Dawn, for example, frequently 'travelled' to other planes through what was known as skrying or travelling in the spirit vision, using Tattwa cards or other techniques. However, they were trained to remain in control of their projections and active in defence against the dangers of attack from 'any hostile force' that could arise during

obtaining contact with newly dead is wrong because it disturbs & obsesses the spirit This is very important But if the spirit wishes to contact with some special individual *he can always do it in some* way or another without going to a medium—they hate mediums they *dont know*' (*YVP*i. 252; see also Card S74, *YVP*iii. 409). Saddlemyer points out that this exchange very probably concerns the issue of trying to contact the spirit of Hugh Lane, the nephew of Lady Gregory, whose will and unsigned codicil caused considerable controversy. WBY and others had made unsuccessful attempts to locate the will through contacting Lane (Saddlemyer, *Becoming George*, 146).

[49] Regardie, *Tree of Life*, 38.

[50] In psychoanalytic as well as feminist terms, parallels exist between late nineteenth- and early twentieth-century mediumship and a revived interest in female mysticism. See Amy Hollywood, *Mysticism, Sexual Difference, and the Demands of History* (Chicago: University of Chicago Press, 2001).

the potentially vulnerable crossing. Mediumship required the skills neither of sending out a 'Thought-Ray ... sent like an arrow from the bow' nor of protection of the potentially vulnerable body; on the other hand, it was conceived as opening oneself to the realm of the other, as feminized an idea as the militarized terminology of the magical way of astral travel was masculinized.[51]

Further, GY's chosen form of mediumship, automatic writing, was by all accounts the one requiring the least effort and skill of any. Magicians must be learned and practised, but not automatic writers. Stead described the practice as 'a familiar and simple form of mediumship'; Lodge called it 'the commonest and easiest method of communication'; 'among the great variety of phenomena broadly classed as psychical, there is no other that appears to be so easily elicited as that of automatic writing', according to Edward Bennett. Automatic writing requires no special training or equipment. However, even though 'it can be practiced by a large proportion of intelligent persons' and thus has 'some advantages superior to those of any other class of psychical phenomena' (making it appealing to a person of good breeding), it nevertheless has a pleasing hint of feminized obedience to it. 'One thing is clear. The automatic writer frequently finds himself in the presence of an intelligence which he feels compelled to recognize as superior to his own normal intelligence.'[52] Despite the attribution of male gender to the automatic writer in this description, the alliance with feminity is clear.[53]

---

[51] See Regardie, *Golden Dawn*, 108–9, for these instructions.

[52] Bennett, *Automatic Speaking and Writing*, 5; Lodge, *Raymond*, 365; William T. Stead, *Letters from Julia, or Light from the Borderland: A Series of Messages as to the Life beyond the Grave received by Automatic Writing from One who has Gone Before* (London: Grant Richards, 1898), p. xiii.

[53] Analogies common in discussions of the feminine, such as physical weakness or illness or weak-mindedness, appear commonly in discussions of automatic writing. One striking example may be found in the writing of one Dr C. Williams, a physician whose book *Spiritualism and Insanity* was published in 1910. Dr Williams places automatic writing within a deeply gendered discourse of mental illness. He warns that the passivity required for automatic writing is dangerous: in one case, he reports, an automatic writer 'became so weakened in will-power that a most insane act, attended by the most lamentable consequences, was the result' (C. Williams, *Spiritualism and Insanity: An*

GY's magical name corroborates such spiritual hermaphroditism. It shares its masculine form with the name George, which GY apparently liked, happily trading in 'Georgie' for the name WBY preferred when she married. Incidentally, the most famous popular uses of the name are also decidedly masculine: Jules Verne's Captain Nemo, that famous explorer of the depths whose books had been a well-established part of a child's repertoire of reading material by the last decades of the nineteenth century, or the comic-strip character 'Little Nemo'.[54] Dickens's *Bleak House* (1853) also features a mysterious and tragic character known by the name, a figure with additional potential resonance for a young reader like GY. He is the lost father of Esther Summerson, who dies alone and in disgrace, of opium addiction; GY lost her own adored father, who died estranged from her mother and among strangers, to alcoholism when she was 17.[55] The ironies are parallel and multiple of a masculine gender for a young woman calling herself 'no man', a mysterious fictional superman named 'no one', and a name to call a father-figure as well as a bereft daughter. The 'not one' that suggests a domain outside the Western male self slips easily from none to more than one, from lack to excess, and this movement is also significant to an informed view of the automatic script. To be No Man may be to be variously No One, super-man, and more than one man: perhaps, as writer, not a single author but the two collaborators, who multiply into four as their daimonic selves are considered, then into more selves and others until a single person begins to look like a bewildering multiplicity of beings.

Essay Describing the Disastrous Consequences to the Mental Health which are Apt to Result from a Pursuit of the Study of Spiritualism (London: Ambrose, [1910]), 19). The Yeatses were not immune to such analogies: the record of a sleep from 29 Nov. 1920 speaks of the 'sentimental other-world Kindergartenism of spiritualism' and illustrates it with a dramatic sign: 'While communicater was speaking of this spiritualistic folly, interpreter began blowing & saying her mouth was full of fluff' (*YVP*iii. 58).

[54] The death of Jules Verne, prompting a flurry of renewed attention to his works, occurred in 1905, the same year that Winsor McCay's strip *Little Nemo in Slumberland* began. The name is far from uncommon. See Saddlemyer, *Becoming George*, 67.

[55] Ibid. 24–5.

Various accounts suggest that in GY's non-magical life as well, she presented herself in ways that highlighted some play with received gender roles and social categories. Although she seems to have enjoyed the 'woman's work' of poet's wife—for example, creating pleasant domestic spaces and running her house 'like clockwork', as Frank O'Connor told Richard Ellmann in 1946—she was also a somewhat unusual angel there.[56] She created effect by painting astrological night skies on the ceiling, as well as keeping flowers on the table.[57] Guests and family members were treated to a 'mocking and iconoclastic sense of humour', according to Foster, as well as a marked disinclination for dullness or small talk.[58] By all accounts GY was slightly androgynous-looking in presentation, tall and tanned—with colouring 'almost as dark as a gypsy's', according to one biography of her husband—with a square jaw and an unsettlingly direct gaze.[59] It is no accident that the communicator Ameritus described her phase, 18, as having 'too much self control & too much emotion for beauty' (*YVP*ii. 409). Contemporary portraits often feature her looking directly at the viewer, not dramatically, dreamily, or modestly to the side, as was popular for women's portraits.

The vivid difference between her preferred pose and those of some of the other women in WBY's life may be illustrated by comparing a studio portrait of GY taken in 1920 with photographs of Maud Gonne, Florence Farr, Constance and Eva Gore-Booth, and Olivia Shakespear, or even the much younger Dorothy Wellesley.[60] Hatted, as GY often was, with one arm akimbo, in a loose-fitting

[56] Richard Ellmann, interview with Frank O'Connor, 13 Oct. 1946, Richard Ellmann Papers, Special Collections Department, McFarlin Library, University of Tulsa.

[57] The number of times she painted the various houses in which the Yeatses lived during the decades of their marriage is one of many striking details in Saddlemyer's biography.

[58] Foster, *Apprentice Mage*, 438. Jaffe also mentions 'a tremendous sense of humour' (Grace M. Jaffe, *Years of Grace* (Sunspot, N. Mex.: Iroquois House, 1979), 164), a quality that is also prominent in Saddlemyer's biography.

[59] Keith Alldritt, *W. B. Yeats: The Man and the Milieu* (New York: Clarkson Potter, 1997), 255. The gaze is often commented upon; see Saddlemyer, *Becoming George*, 34.

[60] The portrait of GY appears in Pierce, *Yeats's Worlds*, 200. The other photographs mentioned appear in Foster, *Apprentice Mage*, plates 10, 13, 14, and 16, between pp. 160 and 161, and in Pierce, *Yeats's Worlds*, 247.

and slightly bohemian-looking satin overblouse or jacket, scarf, and fur wrap, she has turned her head so that the effect is of an intended silhouette momentarily interrupted by the sitter glancing back at the camera. The focus of the photograph is on piercing dark eyes emerging from the shadow of the hat brim; a soft cloudy backdrop is countered by the structural emphasis on the large left hand against her hip. The overall impression is one in which the subject of the photograph is an assimilable object only ambiguously and partially: the voyeuristic pleasure that is a structural feature of female portraiture is complicated by that reciprocal gaze, the partially hidden features, the slightly dramatic or exotic clothing, and the pose that suggests impatience with being captured on film. Of course, photographic poses are to some degree directed by photographers, as well as studio styles or other forces. Agency is difficult to ascribe; like the automatic script, a photograph is the product of a range of dynamics and intentions. Nevertheless, the direct look at the camera gives the viewer less of GY than if she had turned away. Sartre's description of this paradox puts it neatly: 'to perceive is to *look at*', he remarks, 'and to apprehend a look is not to apprehend a look-as-object in the world (unless the look is not directed upon us); it is to be conscious of *being looked at*. The look which the eyes manifest, no matter what kind of eyes they are is a pure reference to myself.'[61] GY typically gives her viewers themselves as referents, adding to the magic effect of her appearance. We are under her power.[62] This witch-like effect is heightened in counterpoise with the complementary portrait of WBY taken at the same time, which is arranged so as to enable the viewer a less compromised freedom to look at the displayed object. Bare-headed, with greying hair swept

---

[61] Jean-Paul Sartre, *Being and Nothingness: An Essay on Phenomenological Ontology*, trans. Hazel Barnes (New York: Philosophical Library, 1956), 258–9.

[62] With regard to the notion of her tendency to withhold part of herself while engaging directly, compare an early impression by Iseult Gonne: 'There is much in her of the quality of the sphinx, and she has awoken greatly not only my admiration but my curiosity. . . . She is (it seems to me) one of those minds who can give generously and, which is even a finer quality, hold back more than they give' (Jeffares *et al.* (eds.), *Letters from Iseult Gonne*, 89).

3. George Yeats, 1920 (reproduced with permission of Rex Roberts)

4. W. B. Yeats, 1920 (reproduced with permission of Rex Roberts)

gracefully away from his face, WBY looks modestly, even demurely, through a pince-nez away from the camera in a proper silhouette, a sober black suit softened by the characteristic (and often caricatured) poet's flowing tie, with his hands closed gently upon a pair of gloves in his lap.

GY's chosen work displays similarly disruptive poses. First, in producing her major creative accomplishment through automatism, she chose an occupation that had from its beginnings in the mid-nineteenth century simultaneously emphasized and subverted dominant ideologies of femininity. In general, the spiritualist movement in England and North America, as a number of studies have emphasized, was a bellwether for unstable conceptions of gender, which were highly class-specific, unworkably prescriptive for a fairly wide percentage of the populace, and internally inconsistent.[63] Many mediums were female, and the seance rooms of these sensitives from a generation before GY were located on a number of social fault lines. Women who contacted spirits were quintessential examples of a supposedly natural superiority of women to men in spiritual matters. Since women were believed to be more naturally passive, empathetic, and imbued with Christian morality than men, it would follow that they were more likely to be receptive vessels for spirit communication. The power that some mediums wielded over their sitters or in wider social spheres could be considerable (as were some of their incomes). At the same time, mediumship also usually depended upon attitudes of submission and physical containment within a domestic and familial sphere, or at least required that mediums advertise themselves as so restrained. In fact, a number of spiritualists in the nineteenth century were also public figures, advocates of such issues as women's rights, vegetarianism, and pacifism.

---

[63] See Diana Bashan, *The Trial of Woman: Feminism and the Occult Sciences in Victorian Literature and Society* (New York: New York University Press, 1992); Ann Braude, *Radical Spirits: Spiritualism and Women's Rights in Nineteenth-Century America* (Boston: Beacon Press, 1989); Alex Owen, *The Darkened Room: Women, Power and Spiritualism in Late Victorian England* (Philadelphia: University of Pennsylvania Press, 1990); and esp. for its sensitivity to issues of class Oppenheim, *Other World*.

Some mediums were famous for producing dramatic physical effects or possessing inexplicable knowledge.

None the less, despite the personal attention given to the stars of the profession, mediumship at its core advertised and required an act of self-renunciation or even eradication. This quality remained as the practice developed in the decades before GY tried automatic writing, 'advancing' (with all that this descriptor implies) from working-class neighbourhoods to the drawing-rooms of the well situated, and from sensationalism to subtlety. Thus Bette London, arguing that mediumship was a form of marginalized authorship, can assert that when GY began her automatic writing in 1917, mediums 'were increasingly of the same sort (in class, education, and professional aspirations) as those who became conventional authors'.[64] This situation does not necessarily indicate 'progress' of the sort that respectable spiritualists might have desired, but rather that the number of well-situated mediums remained relatively steady, depositing the kinds of records that people of some means leave behind them, while the numbers of spiritualists in the self-educated upper working classes waned with the gradual decline of that group as a whole.[65]

A suggestion of class consciousness remains, however, in GY's refusal to broaden her mediumistic practice from the reception of the script with her husband to other projects. On several occasions, the spirits stressed that this experience would happen only once, that they were sent for a specific purpose. On 10 November 1917, less than a month into the experiments, the Yeatses were informed that 'The automatic script will only continue for a time because it will be too bad for her—that side of the anti should not be developed too greatly'. On the next day, Thomas reiterated: 'I was sent to

[64] London, *Writing Double*, 8.
[65] As Janet Oppenheim notes, accurate numbers of spiritualists are difficult to come by, for a number of reasons. Members of working classes often could not afford subscription fees. Equally, not all middle-class spiritualists wanted to be publicly recognized as such (Oppenheim, *Other World*, 49). None the less, Barrow is persuasive in arguing for the decline of spiritualism within working-class culture by the early decades of the twentieth century (Barrow, *Independent Spirits*).

the medium for various reasons of which I have fulfilled one—My coming is not for the reason you ask I was sent as part of my duties' (*YVP*i. 78). A year later, he was still insistent: 'no no no', he answered an unrecorded question from WBY; 'nothing will be accurate with this medium but the philosophy' (*YVP*ii. 42). In fact, the spirits, and the medium, were curiously ambivalent about their activities on more than one occasion. One strong message, again from November 1917, is a strong humanistic urging, with a further injunction to WBY to be sure to take it in:

the reliance absolute reliance on the supernatural and the consequent abandonment of personal judgment is as great a temptation as any other—Artistic Genius & moral Genius are the two works of man and in these he has to develop his own powers—I will go on when you have read this. (*YVP*i. 99)

No One

In keeping with the simultaneous evasion and assertion of her motto, the automatism that GY practised did not include eradication of personality, even though she wrote directly as 'GY' (carefully noting the change from automatic to direct writing) relatively seldom in the automatic script. Quite the opposite. W. T. Stead's opinion about automatic writing, his own form of mediumship, is suggestive for GY's script:

Automatic writing, I may explain for those unfamiliar with the term, is writing that is written by the hand of a person which is not under control of his conscious mind. The hand apparently writes of itself, the person to whom the hand belongs having no knowledge of what it is about to write. It is a familiar and simple form of mediumship, which in no way impairs the writer's faculties or places his personality under the control of any other intelligence.[66]

---

[66] Stead, *Letters from Julia*, p. xiii.

Rather than self-renunciation, then, it may be more accurate to think of the script as, first, a multiplication of personalities that widens into a complication, not a diminution, of self. Authorship in the script is like a network of channels through which agency flows in many directions more than like a single, originary creative act or a passive reception of external information. One channel consists of the two human partners, who were required to interact with each other as WBY described years later: 'Except at the start of a new topic, when they [the communicators] would speak or write a dozen sentences unquestioned, I had always to question, and every question to rise out of a previous answer and to deal with their chosen topic' (*AV B* 10–11). The disembodied participants also acted in congress, with each other as well as with the Yeatses. On the third day of recorded automatic writing, 7 November 1917, before developing the question-and-answer format, the control groped for a way to describe the process in which the Yeatses and he were engaged. Assuring them that the communicators are by no means the only sources of knowledge—'most of us are only forms under the reflection of real spirits'[67]—the control used vocabulary that suggests collaboration on a level that approaches amalgamation. Spirits and people were 'intermingling so *incroached* on each other', and the topics covered were 'interpretations'; information came from 'two spirit thoughts' in an 'imperfect telepathy' or 'intercommunication', between 'intermediaries'. The script entailed 'radiation of thought'; the knowledge presented by the ghostly partners was 'prompted . . . in your own thought' or 'taken from the inner wisdom of your own consciousness by selection' (*YVP*i. 62–3).

In the momentous early spring of 1919, after the birth of Anne Yeats, Thomas described the role of controls in the proceedings with a metaphor that one might have expected him to use about GY's role

---

[67] A notebook entry corroborates the idea that the instructors' communication was always mediated: 'Thomas thinks that all communications come through spirits at 1 or 15', it reads. Nor do the voices of the dead escape except by going through this gate: the 'newly dead seem to communicate but think through spirit at one or through trance medium' (*YVP*iii. 148).

in the project, not his own or that of his fellows. To a question about what the controls' 'relation to the teaching' was, he replied, 'Mouthpieces & trumpets' (*YVP*ii. 250).[68] In other words, the spirits were 'mediums' for the system no less than GY, bearing the same relationship to the teaching itself as the vibrating mouthpieces of trumpets do to the music produced by the instrument as a whole. More specifically, and typical of the complicated relations between the parties involved in the effort, Thomas explained that the guides attached to the Yeatses 'collect' the controls—'me or others', who then transmit the information to the waiting hands or voices of the human participants. The only other function of the guides is to '[look] after you', he averred; thus a circular relationship is posited in which guides, controls, and human beings all perform tasks for each other.

The script features frequent shifts into meta-discourse, on intentional and also unintentional levels. Details about the system are interwoven with commentary on and questioning of the method: there are instructions about where messages come from, who sends them, and through what channels, as well as occasions of self-talk such as a moment when, in the same early session mentioned above, the control wavered: 'no—yes—no—I cannot tell you here—yes' (*YVP*i. 62). This remark looks like a response to an unrecorded question, but whether it is a response to a query by one of the Yeatses or to voices beyond the control is impossible to know. At any rate, the slippage between levels of discourse rapidly develops into a defining characteristic. Considered genetically, the system itself changes from its expression in the script to its shape in the published book. The philosophical material is a different entity in its first, raw form from the potentially intelligible and thus objectifiable body of thought that it reaches for in *A Vision*, despite a counter-rhetoric (especially in the 1925 version of the book) which suggests that sort of expository clarity to be impossible. In the originating documents,

---

[68] Mrs Etta Wriedt was widely known for her use of a tin trumpet in seances; see Saddlemyer, *Becoming George*, 55–6.

the system is a network of interpretation, a consortium of opinions, a number of voices arguing and building on each other's arguments.

The system of the automatic script is also striking for the way in which it continually implicates its writers in its concepts. Their changing levels of awareness, abilities to comprehend, and relationships with each other are an intrinsic part of the truth it tells. Its abstractions have human faces in a more or less Blakean sense. The patterns it suggests in gyres and cones, Moments of Crisis and Lightning Flashes, Faculties and Principles, afterlife stages and daimonic influences, are designed to instruct through knowledge of the intimate nature of truth. WBY was told relatively early in the process of receiving it that this philosophy would be unlike other philosophical speculation because it would not be 'bred in stagnation' but instead be 'a light which you follow', because 'all that matters is to lead or be led, to renew or be renewed' (*YVP*i. 252). In developing the system, the Yeatses develop themselves; in forming their own lives, they embody it and can only thus possess and transmit it. In writing it out in a book, WBY reduced and simplified this aspect of the script more than any other. The intensely personal quality of its truths, one of the most remarkable qualities of the script, is almost completely absent from the public presentation.[69]

In fact, given all of the personal material in the script, it remains curious that its primary writer has not become more available to critics trying to make sense of her than has occurred in the near decade since the materials' publication, despite the healthy state of the Yeats industry on both sides of the Atlantic. I have often wondered why I have never felt particularly voyeuristic when reading the script, either in manuscript or now in its edited form. One explanation (which happily does not depend upon my personal morality for its force) is reminiscent of the photograph described earlier (and shown in Plate 3) and the complication that occurs in viewing it. I cannot invade a privacy that is actually the landscape of what occult vocabulary might name a higher self, a willed and nameless or renamed source

---

[69] See Ch. 4 for more on this topic.

of authority over the material I scan. This subject, unavailable for my consumption and in fact a source of power over me, might be described as Sartre does the Other, who 'is in no way given to us as an object. The objectivation of the Other would be the collapse of his being-as-a-look.'[70] The Latin *sciat* blurs into the sense of the Greek *skia*, a shade or shadow: in searching the script, even searching for its authors, I see what I do not know much more vividly than I discover palpable identities for its writers. Still, this sense of peering into darkness does not imply lack of authorial personality: far from it. My sense of command over the fixed idea of an author may suffer, but not my sense of the text being driven.

The success of the script, then, did not depend upon GY's mediumistic absence; on the contrary, it required her presence, although a particular kind of presence. She did need the abilities to clear her mind and consciously enter an altered state (using skills she would have gained in her years of magical training) to allow her 'antithetical self' to dominate her 'daily self' and the force to flow through her.[71] She was not to relinquish control by, for example, allowing herself to be hypnotized, a state expressly forbidden in a late script (*YVP*iii. 510). Indeed, in so far as the outcome relied on her abilities to control her mind, the script is as much a demonstration of her personal expertise as it is an act of the sort of mediumistic selflessness popularized in nineteenth-century spiritualism. As Thomas informed the Yeatses in the first week of script (in a message that WBY copied out carefully on an index card later), 'we take from the medium that quality which is lacking to our dream state . . . we can think & elaborate our thoughts in as far as it is possible for us to find that necessary help from the medium' (*YVP*i. 75; iii. 235). A stream of script from the couple's first trip to Ireland together, in which questions were not recorded, explores the paradox of the medium's willing a relaxation of will, including the difficulty of maintaining this necessary 'voluntary

---

[70] Sartre, *Being and Nothingness*, 268.
[71] The degree to which GY entered a 'trance' is not clear. See the interlude on performance for further discussion.

passivity' in the midst of the dialogic method: 'The questioning makes the voluntary difficult because it cannot easily be assumed by will in the questions & talk & so on going on.' None the less, the communicator was insistent that the dialogue be maintained. In answer to an unrecorded question, presumably about whether GY should be kept in the dark, so to speak, to cut down on the difficulties of attaining the proper state, Rose was unequivocal: 'No,' the guide insisted, 'the medium must know question' (*YVP*i. 415–16).

As GY had more agency than they might have expected, WBY had rather less. On 20 November 1917, a few weeks after the sessions began, WBY asked and was told that he was correct in assuming that his questions were guided from the other side (*YVP*i. 92). The model was one of collaboration rather than possession, however. During the first week of recorded script, WBY suspected a deeper level of influence; he asked about the extent to which his mind was occupied by these new presences in his life: 'Do you only come when you are questioned,' he asked, 'or do you live for a time within our life or our thought. For instance do you enter into my dream when I am writing or thinking of writing?' Thomas replied that the spirits did not arrive unless bidden, leaving WBY presumably free to write out of his own dream, but the control did add in answer to an unrecorded question, 'I get them from your subconscious' (*YVP*i. 77). Whether by 'them' was meant the spirits' answers to the questions, or perhaps WBY's questions themselves, is not clear. It is certain, however, that the human participants were joint creators with the spirits in the system. At another session rather early in the proceedings (3 December 1917), a control known as Marcus excused his inability to answer a question by explaining, 'I told you I cannot ask those questions'. Ask of whom? WBY wanted to know. 'Those about you?' 'No', Marcus replied; 'I ask from your minds.' Receiving a positive answer to his next question, 'Do [you] obtain all your knowledge through us?', WBY wondered again whether he and GY were used without their knowledge: 'Do you obtain through us more than we know of' Marcus's answer was, 'No' (*YVP*i. 136). However, the questioner was directed both by spirits and his human partner, as the Yeatses learned in exchanges such as this one, from 1 February 1918. WBY asked if the control was 'satisfied with our method of questioning'. 'Yes quite' came the answer; 'there may be some points you do not think of—if so I will put them in mind of medium' (*YVP*i. 324).[72]

The medium's active participation was overt from the outset. In early January 1918, as she was working on lists of phasal characteristics, the guide could not help WBY place his old friend Florence Farr in a phase because, he or she explained, 'Medium never saw her but twice & I can't place her from that' (*YVP*i. 204). A few weeks later, on 31 January, a comment by WBY records GY objecting to a formulation by the control: 'medium finds it incredible that 2 persons who shared in same passion do not meet in P[assionate] B[ody]' (*YVP*i. 319). As time passed, the medium and the questioner obviously discussed the communications outside the sessions themselves, and their analyses sometimes enter the script, for example when Thomas notes that on a particular point 'medium wrong' (*YVP*i. 464). As time passed, the script, 'more & more influenced by her will', would 'therefore become less automatic', Thomas informed them on 11 November 1918, although he wrote this critical message in mirror writing, undercutting his own announcement with letters designed to demonstrate automatism and keep the contents of their message from the hand writing them (*YVP*ii. 120).[73] Near the end of GY's first pregnancy, in a session on Christmas evening 1918, upon hearing

---

[72] Not only did GY provide some of the questions, but WBY provided some of the answers. He often, with the spirits' approval, asked questions which implied their own answers, so that the communicators needed only to confirm or deny what he had already formulated. His active role in answering his own questions has on occasion been overemphasized, sometimes by readers wanting not to find a gullible poet taken in by sideshow spooks: e.g., Denis Donoghue mentions 'Yeats, not George, who asked the questions and took charge of the themes', as part of a counter-argument to Brenda Maddox's theory that GY was in effect hoodwinking her husband throughout; Denis Donoghue, 'The Fabulous Yeats Boys', *The New York Review of Books*, 11 May 2000, 32–6, review of Maddox, *George's Ghosts*.

[73] Mirror writing, in which the letters and words are written in reverse so that they can be read normally if viewed in a mirror, is scattered throughout the script. It occurs most often after particularly personal questions or at other points that might be likely to distract the writer from the open state of mind she needed in order to register the

that they were making little headway 'because mediums vitality low & sensitive', her husband seems to have suggested that he take over some of her tasks. Despite her fatigue and perhaps boredom, he was not allowed to continue alone. Thomas answered an unrecorded question mentioning 'writers *nerves*' (referring to GY as 'writer', an interesting term) and declined WBY's offer: 'No no because we cant use you alone—must have you & medium *equally*' (*YVP*ii. 152).

At the start of the first session after Anne Yeats's birth on 26 February 1919, her mother's title was changed. 'No longer the medium', Thomas announced, 'different name/Interpreter' (*YVP*ii. 200). By June, GY dropped the convention of running the letters and words together when her pen was moved.[74] This unremarked change in her handwriting merely reflected what none of the participants had denied from the outset: she was a full-fledged member of the company of co-creators, though her role was different in kind from the rest. The distance that automatism implies between the message written and the writing hand gave her role a structural objectivity: while questions were asked and answered, she was in a position to look on and evaluate as well as take down the dictated messages. 'Interpreter', of course, implies a more active level of participation than 'medium', the common spiritualist term for entranced and unconscious transmitters of spirit messages.[75] The new term refers

communications accurately. In a working typescript of Book IV of what would become *AV A*, WBY describes the purpose of mirror writing along with another technique:

An automatist . . . will sometimes answer questions . . . with quotations in some classical language, correct even to the accents, and will fall into confusion when a quotation is impossible. . . . Such quotations are used often to convey precise information requiring present thought as clairvoyance, and desires to keep the subconscious from interference from the conscious mind as 'mirror writing' does. (NLI MS 36,270)

[74] She also began recording the questions as well as the answers at this point, on 16 June 1919 (*YVP*ii. 299), a significant moment in the script.

[75] Geraldine Cummins suggests that 'a medium is, in most cases, *an interpreter*' (*Unseen Adventures*, 133). London claims that Cummins preferred the term and that it was common among mediums and psychic researchers (*Writing Double*, 163, 193), but I have seldom seen it used in spiritualist literature, including Cummins's books. The Society for Psychical Research tended not to refer to automatic writers as mediums (perhaps, as Saddlemyer suggests, to distinguish itself from the less prestigious spiritualists

to a human agent only, as opposed to the depersonalizing of the human subject in 'medium', implying as it does the first meaning of the word, which refers to a substance or mode through which an event occurs. Although mediumship was recognized to require a certain degree of knowledge, 'interpreter' probably suggests a higher level of skill. However, the new designation also carries with it some ambivalence in the degree of personal intervention it connotes. One common meaning of the term, the one likely to have been meant by Thomas, suggests familiarity with two usually separated regions: since the Middle Ages, an interpreter has been a translator, making ideas from one language intelligible to speakers or readers of another. This sort of interpreting, like good civil engineering, is best when least visible, when the ideas of the sender reach the recipient of the message without addition by the middle party. Like the poet in WBY's 'Adam's Curse', this sort of interpreter must hide the difficulty of her work: she must be learned but must not display her erudition. Any translator knows that simple transference of meaning from one language to another is impossible, a state of affairs included in the other common sense of the term. An interpreter is a producer of evaluations and analyses, a task that may require some deference to the subject-matter but which also presumes a rather high degree of subjective intrusion. In the early twentieth century in England and Ireland, interpretation certainly had both critical and creative

---

(*Becoming George*, 108)), preferring *automatist*. Regarding the term *medium*, there was considerable debate. In 1919, Percy Dearmer wrote to the editor of the *Journal of the Society for Psychical Research* lamenting the term. However, *Interpreter* was not one of the proposed replacements. Dearmer asks:

Ought we not . . . to discard the term 'Medium'? It will never get rid of the associations of Mr. Sludge [the satiric figure of Robert Browning, based on the American medium D. D. Home], and does great injustice both to the subject with which we are concerned and to a respectable class of people. 'Sensitive' is better; but I think we could improve upon it, before it has come into general use. This is not a small matter. We hardly realize how necessary good terms are, and how much harm is done by bad ones. (Percy Dearmer, ' "Nomenclature": Letters to the Editor', *Journal of the Society for Psychical Research* 19, (1919): 105).

More correspondence on 'nomenclature' followed, including the suggestion 'transmittor', a 'perfectly clear, good, and intelligible word' (p. 180).

connotations, referring to the making of meaningful distinctions and judgements as well as constructing versions of truth from raw materials provided by others. Interpreters cannot operate alone, but must stay between or among other expressive agents, as the *inter-* of the word indicates. Yet they also display personal style as well as produce meaning as their influence spreads (*pret–*) abroad.

Despite WBY's decades of participation in the Order of the Golden Dawn and his long experience in collaborative enterprises with strong women such as Lady Gregory and Maud Gonne, this distribution of power seems to have been somewhat problematic for him. His depictions of the experience, for instance in the seemingly straightforward introduction to the 1937 *A Vision* and in the fictionalized narrative poem 'The Gift of Harun Al-Rashid', published in the earlier edition, both feature a medium overcome by spirits who 'entranced' her (*AV B* 10), who keeps 'childish ignorance of all that passed' (*AV A* 125). Perhaps the expectations of marriage, for husband and possibly wife as well, jarred with the masculinity or multiple gendering of the role GY played in the couple's nightly experiments. Nevertheless, WBY, who had for many years been as fascinated by adventures in losing spiritual, political, or sexual power as in attaining it, was enthusiastically drawn to his and his wife's variants of automatism. At any rate, both he and she promulgated various dissonances between his public versions and the experience itself. The documents suggest a very different dynamic from the ones familiar to readers of WBY's published material.

Like the part played by Nemo, the operations of power in the script may be suggested more readily through the exploration of identity and authority than in narrative or dramatic accounts, which must rely on singular, separable actors. In Chapter 5, I will return from etymology to fabula to tell the stories of the controls, who were most often masculine and who were to some degree related to GY or, less frequently, to WBY. Here, it is enough to note that the large number of communicators of male gender may imply the importance of GY's position as subject as well as the necessary deflection from her daily self. The relations among participants (human and non-human)

and between their personalities and the matter being communicated underscore the need for intimate partnership. And the changes
in communicators (different instructors and changing kinds and
numbers of spirits for different material and changing conditions)
demonstrate a constant awareness that all names and personalities
are provisional, and that an effort dependent upon partnership and
subjectivity is necessarily fluid. Behind the names in the script is
always the sense that revelation is beyond the fixed knowledge of
the most adept of spirits or human beings. That revelation is linked
to mutual exploration of a multilayered reality, and that reality is
simultaneously highly sacred and grounded in joint daily life.[76]

To Allot

The Yeatses certainly carved out their automatic practice to suit their
own creative means. This is not to say, however, that in taking up
automatic writing to begin with, GY chose a form of discourse with
a standard pattern. In fact, although there are standard descriptions
of the start of the process, the writing itself varies widely. Automatic
texts produced in England and the United States from the spiritualist
revivals of the mid-nineteenth century to the present are of many
kinds. Differences abound in the speed of the writing, the sizes and
kinds of letters (such as 'mirror writing', words spelled backwards,
run together, or written in tiny or oversized script), different styles

[76] A considerable amount of discussion of the nature of controls exists in spiritualist
literature, which is relevant here only to suggest that the Yeatses had many examples
and analyses of multiple controls available to them: e.g., Lodge notes in *Raymond* that
controls are usually a function of trance mediumship, not ordinarily untranced automatic
writing. They may be 'the subliminal self of the entranced person', but whatever their
source, 'the dramatic character of most of the controls is so vivid and self-consistent, that
whatever any given sitter or experimenter may feel is the probable truth concerning their
real nature, the simplest way is to humour them by taking them at their face value and
treating them as separate and responsible and real individuals.' Sometimes, as when a
medium is tired, they are absurd, 'but undoubtedly the serious controls show a character
and personality and memory of their own, and they appear to carry on as continuous an
existence as anyone else whom one only meets occasionally for conversation' (p. 357).

of handwriting, the employment of foreign languages (which may or may not be known by the medium), the presence of vocal messages, the use of single or multiple controls, the attribution of messages to telepathy with living people or communication with the dead, and so forth. These variables are signs of deeper structural variances such as the degree of conscious awareness or will (sometimes rendered as interference, sometimes as helpfulness) or the suggestion of telepathy or other effects of other minds. In addition, the degree of private or public drama or spectacle associated with the written texts, the assumed relationship between the body and the mind, and analogies with dreaming and the imagination or, alternatively, with such relatively recent innovations as typewriting or telegraphy, are all relevant. The differences among all of these variables, in turn, suggest determinants such as class, religious affiliation, degree of professionalism, gender, and individual personality. Automatic writing was also a form of mediumship given to change over time: as 'Melchior' communicated to his chosen medium in 1931, the method employed by any automatic writer is not 'a fixed thing. It is continually being changed by improvement, and increased ability on both sides [that is, the human and the spirit] resulting from practice.'[77]

Of particular relevance to Nemo is a basic distinction based on the level of willed authority: although any automatic writing involves the presumed surrender of control over the writing hand, some mediums are entranced, and some are fully awake, indicating not only how far the session is to be regarded as performance but also how present and controlled the medium and sitters believe her waking mind to be. As E. W. and M. H. Wallis assert in their 1903 *Guide to Mediumship, and Psychical Unfoldment*, some writing is 'automatic', in which 'the hand does the work [while] the mind may be separately engaged', while some is 'impressional', meaning that 'the sensitive knows beforehand what will be written, or is conscious of what is

---

[77] Melchior, *The Teaching of Melchior* (London: Herbert Joseph, 1933), 122.

being given as the hand writes'.[78] In fact, as Nandor Fodor points out, 'there are many degrees of the two states, blending is frequent, the important point apparently being to bar the interference of the conscious mind'.[79]

For GY, the malleability of the method was part of its appeal. As 'Demon' found that frustration and opposition fulfilled his needs, Nemo was, I believe, attracted to the elasticity and variety not only of content but of self implicit in automatic writing. 'Melchior', again, notes that 'advanced Occultists, however, do not use this method of obtaining information', but goes on to describe automatic writing in these terms:

It consists of a human mind attuned, by desire and psychic development, to perceive the thoughts which are given to it from the individual world. Selection, conscious or unconscious, is made by the individual at work as to the particular type of teaching he will receive. He becomes attuned to that alone.

Not only are automatic writers inclined to be psychically gifted people who want to make their own 'selections' from among various truths, 'Melchior' claims; they are also predisposed to blur subject and object:

you find difficulty in separating that which is given to you from that which you yourself create. The reason for this is that there is no exact line of demarcation between the two, owing to the creative power of thought. The creations of your thought become objective realities around you, with *life in themselves*. Are their activities yours, or theirs? Do you see?[80]

This is not to say, of course, that all automatic writers 'fragment' or split into primary and secondary personalities, or, pathologic-ally, into genuinely split personalities (some famous mediums like

---

[78] Wallis and Wallis, *Guide to Mediumship*, 64. These are both types of automatic writing, not to be confused with 'spirit writing', which occurs at a seance, in which the whole personality as well as the writing hand is possessed by an intelligence not the medium's own.

[79] Fodor, *Encyclopædia*, s.v. 'automatic writing'.

[80] Melchior, *Teaching of Melchior*, 122.

Hester Dowden did not apparently do so). The practice does, however, suggest doubling or multiplying of personality, as do secular performances featuring more than one voice.

Appropriately, perhaps, GY did not use one consistent method or level of trance. Mediumship in the script was itself a creative act, participating in the creativity stressed by some writers on the subject. A book written in the mid-1920s, for example, stresses that 'the right kind of passivity [for mediumship] is emphatically *not* a state of mere vacancy', and that clear distinctions are to be drawn between 'higher' and 'lower' types of mediumship. 'On the higher levels of mediumship', the writer, L. Margery Bazett, continues, 'it is at least worth consideration whether a strong affinity exists between the mystic, the artist, and the medium, as to certain basic qualities, quite apart from their development and manifestation. All three endeavour to transcend the limitations of objective life; all are in the highest degree sensitive.'[81] GY was one of the 'higher' sort. At times she may have been in an altered state, similar to hypnosis; as time went on, the couple experimented with different methods, including writing down complementary dreams or somnambulistic activity. In the summer of 1922, WBY noted that they shifted from one type of 'sleep' to another: ' "Philosophic sleaps" have ceased to avoid consequent frustration, but two nights ago George began talking in her sleap. She seemed a different self with more knowledge & confidence' (*YVP*iii. 108). At other times, as when she interrupted a script to insert a comment or attend to the correct labelling or numbering of a session, question, or response, she was clearly aware of what was or had been going on. It is impossible to know what roles the Yeatses presumed her conscious mind to play in the proceedings, although it is clear that her state changed as the script advanced. For example, we might note that a fair number of the terms and metaphors used to describe the method of the script constantly redistribute power: daimons

---

[81] L. Margery Bazett, *Some Thoughts on Mediumship* (London: Rider, [1926]), 5–6. This book was endorsed (and introduced) by Sir Oliver Lodge, whose name presumably added respectability and sales.

'collect' images as guides 'collect' controls, who are mouthpieces and flesh to cover bones already in the world of the living. The living are 'guided', 'controlled', or 'looked after', but the others are 'dependent' on them. Authority over the system and the other participants in receiving it emanates from any of several directions. It would be incorrect to argue that GY unabashedly asserted power, however: even when she was most active, the terms of the relationship between the partners in their automatic script remained characterized by the partial effacement of one of them. Until the final day of recorded script, any personality that could be identified as GY is a presence beneath or behind the surface of the vast majority of words written by her hand.

Such an act, and such an issue or distinction, may be classified under more than one heading in Western intellectual and popular history. One is religious, or rather in the no one's land between religion and psychology, that intellectual terrain whose shifting ground in recent centuries Foucault has famously travelled. Literature and popular narratives teem with stories of holy men and women without control over their words, from the Hebrew prophets or the Gerasene demoniac of the New Testament gospels to the Delphic Pythia, Platonic descriptions of possession, Teutonic ecstatic utterances, and various examples from Indian spiritual literature. The Yeatses would have been familiar with compendia of such phenomena, from the budding fields of comparative mythology and cultural anthropology as well as the more esoteric libraries of theosophical and Rosicrucian material.[82] Such accounts range along several continua. Some cultures and subcultures have stressed the 'out of self'-ness of ecstasy,

---

[82] Two such works were Sir Walter Scott's *Demonology and Witchcraft*, which GHL had owned since 1914, and Ennemoser's *History of Magic*, a catalogue of various forms of magic and a historical account organized by culture, which Pound read aloud to WBY during the winter of 1913. See Walter Scott, *Letters on Demonology and Witchcraft, Addressed to J. G. Lockhart, Esq* (London: John Murray, 1830). GY's copy is in the Yeatses' library (O'Shea, *Descriptive Catalog*, 1860). WBY's library also contains a copy of Joseph Ennemoser, *The History of Magic: To which is added an Appendix of the Most Remarkable and Best Authenticated Stories of Apparitions, Dreams, Second Sight, Somnambulism, Predictions, Divination, Witchcraft, Vampires, Fairies, Table-turning, and Spirit-rapping*, trans. William Howitt, ed. Mary Howitt, 2 vols. (London: Henry G.

while in others it is relatively commonplace for a shaman or saint to move beyond one state into another without considering it a sacrifice of the essential being. Different individuals and groups also make different distinctions between the sacred and the demon-possessed or the insane. No clear cross-cultural or atemporal line is easy to draw between losing oneself and finding a more enlightened self, or between inspiration and illness.

GY's automatic writing occurred in a popular and intellectual climate that had long been heated by questions that join the general area of ecstatic states with the act of writing. A number of issues that preoccupied nineteenth-century hermeneutics and popular debate derived largely from biblical interpretation, and the volatile intermingling of textuality and belief that fired Romantic art and criticism also informs the production of a system like the Yeatses', sitting uncertainly as it does on the fence between secular art or philosophy and religion or magic.[83] In arguments over inspiration and textual integrity, different positions claimed varying degrees of direct involvement by God in the act of writing. Some claims for scriptural writers and other visionaries used as instruments of God's will envisioned ancient authors almost as automatic writers themselves, serving as mediums for a ghostly author whose true name never appears. A few persuasions, like a number of contemporary spiritualists, the Theosophical Society, and the Society for Psychical Research, attempted to find a middle ground between science and

Bohn, 1854) (O'Shea, *Descriptive Catalog*, 636). For WBY's introduction to this book see Longenbach, *Stone Cottage*, 56.

[83] One line of thought in spiritualist circles connected the rise of mediumship directly with the ravages to religion brought about by the new biblical criticism. Hanson G. Hey, writing in 1910, waxes eloquent on this point, pointing a rhetorical finger at this sign of general decay:

Modern Spiritualism came before the public about the middle of the nineteenth century, when men were being borne fast away from their old moorings of faith, out towards a blank, drear materialism, by destructive, so-called higher criticism, which made no attempt to build again upon the ground it had laid waste; and it was to save humanity from the morass of doubt that this grand revelation from God came, as in the days of yore, to lift us up to higher things. (*Seven Principles*, 3)

religion, using concepts like the subconscious, evolution, and the nature of matter, among others. Throughout the nineteenth century, historical or scientific 'fact' had butted against spiritual or theological 'fact' in various ways, and interpreters and believers frequently resorted to a variety of contortions to prove one position or another. Literary forms as well frequently express fear as well as excitement, looking back as well as forward and registering uneasy blends of emotion and intellectualism, the realm of the uncanny erupting into the discourses of science and realism in modes ranging from gothic tales to detective fiction. The authors of the Yeatses' automatic script wear both modern and conventional masks, existing in a frame that proposes itself as a repository for bold new thought as well as the wisdom of the ages, acting as experimenters of a new science as well as participants in ancient communion. It is keenly appropriate that the symbol for phase 18, GY's phase in the system, is a two-faced figure (*YVP*iii. 401), and that the True Creative Mind of the phase—the way of thinking in which it most fruitfully expresses itself—is 'Emotional Philosophy' (*AV A* 79), two seemingly uncongenial states joined to create something entirely new.

   The purpose of the names of the Yeatses' instructors begins with Nemo, the un- or multi-named motto of their primary 'interpreter'. On the one hand, the more clearly the ghostly communicators are identified, the more real they seem, with presumed personalities from which their voices emanate and specific, if indefinable, locations in the reservoir of images of Anima Mundi. The more real they are, of course, the more GY is effaced or, rather, undefined as one capturable source. The livelier the characters of the voices answering WBY, arguing with him, refusing him information, steering him away from undesirable topics or toward more fruitful ones, the less focus there is upon the medium, and therefore the more objective or transparent she may seem. In other words, her disappearance or fragmentation as a subject is, in the script, a sign of her validity: the less she is there, or the less singly she appears, the more 'real' she is as credible automatist. She gains authority as author to the very extent to which she loses it as named solo writer. (And this is another secret of the misinformative frustrators of the script: the more the process is replete with mistakes, or the more the voices disagree with one another, the more authentic it becomes.) On the other hand, however, as a collaborator who acted more as stage manager than star actor, GY is emphatically not a Florence Farr, Maud Gonne, or even Lady Gregory, those charismatic presences on the stage and scene. She is self and Other, both medium and magician, agency without visibility or traceable location, blurring gender and generational boundaries to receive and create a system that is itself dynamic and multiplex, which will provide for her human collaborator images and voices to explore in his own work.

The Latin meaning of *Nemo* may not, in fact, be the only or the most apt referent for issues of agency in the automatic script. In Greek it is a complex verb meaning to distribute, apportion, or allot.[84] In the middle voice it has the sense of dwelling in or occupying, later accruing a sense of possession or habitation. Nemesis, distributive or retributive justice, is derived from it.[85] Perhaps it is more accurate to think of the script not as anonymous but as many-named, the distribution site of many voices and the seat of judgement about which of them is speaking at any one moment. At issue is not absence or hidden agency but choice and the ability to distinguish among many speakers and personalities, a phenomenon whose importance to WBY's late work is instantly recognizable. The automatic script is redolent with intricacies of authority that only begin with the active un-naming of 'GHL' or 'GY'. The spirit controls especially have distinct personalities to accompany the presumption of individuality that their various names bestow. The names of the instructor(s) for each day appear at the heading of every day's script, carefully noted along with the date, time, and place. Such a practice was common to seances, and the location in time and space would of course be important for later astrological interpretations of a day's script.

---

[84] I am grateful to Marie Markoe for pointing me in the direction of the Greek *nemo*, with its rich associations.

[85] A Yeatsian connection I will not trace here concerns Leda, who in some sources was the daughter of Nemesis. See 'Leda', *AVA* 179.

The importance of documenting the name of the instructor is a bit harder to fathom. As I will suggest later, however, the truth of a communication would presumably be altered if Leaf were to give it or accompany a control at a session, rather than Fish or Apple. WBY might ask different questions, leading to different answers, if Thomas instead of Ameritus were presiding over a session, although it is difficult to say precisely just what such differences would be.[86] Further, indications throughout the script suggest that the named communicators are themselves 'mouthpieces' (*YVP*ii. 250), and not the final sources for the messages they convey. Other personages stand behind them, who themselves are sometimes named. The messages are variably anonymous, but whether or not they are named, who or what the communicators are remains a mystery, in the process of revelation no less than in WBY's carefully worded retrospective descriptions. It is never clear whether or to what extent the names are invented, for the nonce or permanently, or by whom.

Such complexities are far from unknown in spiritist literature. In the course of his investigations, Flournoy reports two examples (one of supposed posthumous contact with F. W. H. Myers), repeating from his sources two striking analogies to make the point that even firm believers often admit to inherent difficulties:

Hodgson compared the communication which he held with the deceased through the channel of the medium (Mrs. Piper) to the conversations which might take place in this world between two persons widely separated from each other who are compelled to exchange their messages by means of two messengers, both of them drunk.[87] And Mr. Graham, convinced that it is indeed Myers who is revealed in these message of which I have just spoken, declares, nevertheless, that to attempt to obtain a reply is equivalent almost to 'writing a letter in the darkness and giving it to a messenger who is half asleep to carry across an unknown country bristling with obstacles . . . to an

---

[86] On personalities of communicators, and the reasons for them, see Ch. 5 below.

[87] At this point in the text, the translator has inserted the following comment: '[The drunken persons on this analogy would be the medium on this side and the intermediary on the other, both presumably in a trance-like condition]' (Flournoy, *Spiritism and Psychology*, 184).

address which is temporary and changing, and carry back replies dictated to an illiterate secretary who does not always understand what he writes'.[88]

It may perhaps seem surprising, given such difficulties of clear communication, that the names of controls in spiritualist literature are so often known. It is far more common for hearers to know the names than to have clear information about the nature of the disembodied speakers. Of course, there might be commercial value, or at least value in public relations, for a medium to speak with someone famous. It tended to increase the recognition, say, of Mlle Helene Smith, a Swiss medium about whom Flournoy wrote his most widely read book, when she spoke with a reincarnated spirit who claimed to have been Marie Antoinette. Presumably, a spirit with name recognition would also be taken more seriously than one from the masses of anonymous figures in the other world. Even if the spirits were not of famous people, names that indicated sources in foreign places had appeal in a culture deeply impressed with the Orient and exoticism. For GY, fame was not an issue: indeed, she was firmly committed to keeping the script, as well as other parts of her life and contributions to her husband's work, as private as possible. WBY was often told not to talk about the script, and with the notable exception of Anne Hyde, none of the named personalities who spoke during the hundreds of sessions of script was—waiving all question of their celebrity—even locatable in the Bodleian Library or *Chambers' Biographical Dictionary*.[89]

Yet the naming of the instructors is both consistent and insistent, no less than if each control were a queen or maharajah. This state of affairs suggests that it is centrally important to the script both that it be filled with authors and, equally, that they signify something other than authorship in the usual sense. Like other authorial presences in the script and *Vision* documents, as well as in *A Vision* itself,

---

[88] Flournoy, *Spiritism and Psychology*, 184–5.

[89] On WBY's efforts to locate the historical Anne Hyde, see Ch. 5. For the location of Leo Africanus, see David Patrick and Francis Hindes Groome, *Chambers's Biographical Dictionary* (London: W. & R. Chambers, 1911), s.v. 'Africanus, Leo'. See also Foster, *Apprentice Mage*, 465.

including daimons, frustrators, Giraldus, Robartes, and 'Yeats', they suggest both their own ephemeral state and that such named agents betray little of the hidden authority behind them; it is impossible to gain sure access to that authority. The communicators bespeak a text that seems to resist control and practically to author itself, by which odd phrase I mean hold discourse with and against the Yeatses as well as its other producers. In the documents that comprise the automatic script, meaning is finally generated not through a tight fit between hand and pen, or even a loose impression of an authorial presence guiding the whole, but by an unworkable *mélange* of symbolic excess and omission in which the valid is indistinguishable from the unreliable and both are in active engagement with writers or readers, automatic or otherwise. The automatic script relocates agency as it overdramatizes and under-realizes it, disjoining both authority and identification in the process. In this regard, the manuscripts and notebooks throw responsibility for their sense and status as meaningful discourse on to those of us who have contact with them, slyly offering the recommendation that interpretation is action and suggesting that this was always so. These scripts, unlike their theatrical namesakes, play scripts, do not direct their actors to perform for us: instead, they meet our gaze, and thus vanish from our subjective space.

Second Interlude

Automatic Performance: Technology and Occultism

> Was he [the communicator] constrained by a drama which was part of conditions that made communication possible, was that drama itself part of the communication?
>
> (*AVB* 13)
>
> I suspect that there may be an element of drama essential to communication & that this may not be more than dramatic machinery.
>
> WBY, sleep notebook, 18 February 1921 (*YVP*iii. 85)

Early evening. A sparely furnished sitting-room, rather dimly lit. Fresh flowers on a table scent the air faintly, adding their fragrance to a lingering heavier smell: incense is regularly burned here. A woman enters from the dining-room, from which clinks from cutlery and crockery announce that dinner is being cleared away. She retrieves a small notebook from a stack in a cabinet, retrieves a pen and ink from a box in the same cabinet, and sits down at a table in the centre of the room. Her husband, a middle-aged man with flowing grey hair, follows her. He sits in a chair opposite hers. They pass a few last remarks as she fills the pen and positions the paper in front of her. At her signal, they fall silent and sit quietly, as if waiting for something. Then, slowly, as if taking part in a ritual, she lifts the pen, puts it to the paper, and begins to write.

Fade-out and flash forward: a figure sits in a cluttered room at a nondescript desk, fingers over a computer keyboard. She stares out of the window and wonders what she might learn about the Yeatses' automatic script and related materials if she thought of them not necessarily as texts, but as performance. The papers do record any number of stage-setting-like instructions, indicating precise ways in which the couple had to arrive, invoke, communicate, and conduct themselves during the sessions themselves. More broadly, directions are given for sleeping, eating, love-making, burning incense, taking walks, topics for conversation or research. The Yeatses and their communicators constructed a discipline that reached even to issues like whether WBY should, for example, accept invitations to lecture or work on the writing of plays or poetry. Conceptually, the Yeatses' automatic adventures point to various theoretical slippages between performance and performativity—that is, between theatricality and a quality of language in which, as Judith Butler puts it, 'a word . . . might be said to "do" a thing, [so that] the word not only signifies a thing, but that this signification will also be an enactment of the thing'.[1] The automatic script certainly fleshes out notions about identity being constructed by means of iteration, and about how language is altered in ritualized behaviour, whether it be religious chant, words spoken in a play, or poetic recitation.

In the introduction to the collection of essays *Performativity and Performance*, Andrew Parker and Eve Kosofsky Sedgwick outline a consequence of performative language that begins with J. L. Austin's distinction between constatives and performatives and stretches past Derrida's consequent critique. In *How to Do Things with Words* (1st edn. 1962), Austin famously distinguishes between constatives, which describe an existing state, and performatives, which call something into being. He stresses a surprising relationship between words and references in the latter. If the action of a performative statement fails to accomplish what it intends, the result is not untruth, as it would be in a constative statement, but failure, something like sadness or illness. If, for example, a priest says, 'I now pronounce you

---

[1] Judith Butler, 'Burning Acts: Injurious Speech', in Andrew Parker and Eve Kosofsky Sedgwick (eds.), *Performativity and Performance*, (New York: Routledge, 1995), 198. See also *idem*, *Bodies that Matter: On the Discursive Limits of 'Sex'* (New York: Routledge, 1993), 121–3 and *passim*. Speech and event are at issue also in the statement that I have used as the second epigraph to this section, an aside in a sleep notebook responding to a troubling message from frustrators who 'would like to kill "the fourth daimon" ', i.e., the Yeatses' unborn child, Michael.

husband and wife', and a marriage does not take place, something unusual has happened, but the priest has not lied. Austin explains this phenomenon by suggesting that 'Language in such circumstances is in special ways—intelligibly—used not seriously, but in ways *parasitic* upon its normal use—ways which fall under the doctrine of the *etiolations* of language.'[2]

The word *parasitic* in this statement struck a chord. Derrida expanded the diagnosis of this performative malady in an early essay ('Signature Event Context' of 1972): 'Therefore, I ask the following question: is this general possibility necessarily that of a failure or a trap into which language might *fall* . . . or indeed is this risk, on the contrary, its internal and positive condition of possibility?'[3] Parker and Sedgwick emphasize the perverse quality of Austin's and Derrida's famous parasite, a concept to which I must return when I consider the bodily qualities of the script in Chapter 4. In other words, the performative illuminates a quality present in all linguistic situations. These concepts are useful for understanding the Yeatses' script, because they point to interconnections between three phenomena there: first, performance (the dramatizations of the script, or the script as drama), performativity (the language therein, which creates the system, and indeed the occult marriage, by *fiat*), and a third concept that grounds the first two historically. Derrida refers to this third term when he comments, a few pages before his remarks on Austin, on the iterability, or repeatability, of language and the way that language looked at in this way reduces the old emphasis on individual people from whom or to whom an utterance is sent.

All writing, therefore, in order to be what it is, must be able to function in the radical absence of every empirically determined addressee in general. And this absence is not a continuous modification of presence; it is a break in presence, 'death,' or the possibility of the 'death' of the addressee, inscribed

---

[2] J. L. Austin, *How to Do Things with Words*, 2nd edn. (Oxford: Clarendon Press, 1975), 22, cited by Parker and Sedgwick (eds.), *Performativity and Performance*, 3.

[3] Jacques Derrida, 'Signature Event Context', in *Margins of Philosophy* (Chicago: University of Chicago Press, 1982), 325.

in the structure of the mark. . . . What holds for the addressee holds also, for the same reasons, for the sender or producer. To write is to produce a mark that will constitute a kind of machine that is in turn productive, that my future disappearance in principle will not prevent from functioning and from yielding, and yielding itself to, reading and rewriting. When I say 'my future disappearance,' I do so to make this proposition more immediately acceptable. I must be able simply to say my disappearance, my nonpresence in general.[4]

This postmodern turn sees language functioning through non-presence figured as 'death' and described with a significant metaphor, 'a kind of machine'. A conjunction between death and technology is brought to the surface by paying attention to performativity. Just so, although with a stress on this conjunction as historically mediated—in other words, more modernist than universal—we can trace a link between beyond-life experience and technology in order to make intelligible the Yeatses' nightly performances and the performativity of the language and form of the script. Mediumistic automatism is an activity that is figured as expression divorced from its usual human cause, 'a kind of machine'. To study automatism is to see something of what the language of the script accomplishes beyond any of its matter. In an entry in a sleep notebook from 18 February 1921, WBY wrote about his and GY's revelatory experiments, 'I suspect that there may be an element of drama essential to communication & that this may not be more than dramatic machinery' (*YVP*iii. 85). The 'dramatic machinery' of GY's automatic performance had much to teach.

As a performance, the automatic experiments were amply prepared for in the lives of the human co-producers. The Yeatses were both deeply involved with theatre, she with contemporary Italian drama and playwriting as well as new drama in English. She would serve for many years as honorary secretary and, with Lennox Robinson, effective head of the Dublin Drama League. Her husband was of course an experimental playwright and co-founder of a national

---

[4] Derrida, 'Signature', 315–16.

theatre. Furthermore, they were adepts in a highly theatrical occult order, skilled at staging spiritual development with aids such as costume, set, props, and ritual speech and action.[5] Unlike more established religious organizations, whose rituals and texts are likely to be set by tradition or institutional prescription, the Order of the Golden Dawn and other occult societies retain some sense of formation; groups within the Order might (and did) believe that they could revise documents or rites. Indeed, WBY's rituals for the Celtic Mysteries project are examples of this sort of compositional freedom.[6] More generally, the poet had been well schooled in the aestheticism in the last decades of the nineteenth century, with its celebrated emphasis on drama and display, and had for many years been practising the publicly staged arts of political life, confessional poetry, and the career of a man of letters. For her part, GHL left a set of highly self-conscious English drawing-rooms to embrace a career as the wife of a famous man, and for the first few years of her married life at least, she also added private mediumship to her role, a combination that required considerable management of appearances. Although the Yeatses tended not to use many of the appurtenances common to many seance rooms, the script does mention on occasion such props as a 'small crystal' or other talismans, and the burning of preparatory incense or lighting of candles.[7] Both embodied the truth, to use WBY's phrasing, that 'one must be both dramatist and actor & yet be in great earnest', a proposition that Foster rightly claims is an important concept in making sense of WBY's life.[8] It is important to make sense of GY's life as well: in her phase 18, as she and WBY understood it, 'The Head uses the

---

[5] In his retrospective analysis of the Order of the Golden Dawn, even as sympathetic a writer as Israel Regardie has criticized it as a true product of the *fin de siècle* in its self-dramatizing: 'The fact that it admitted numerous theatrical people to the ranks of its membership indicates the presence of superficiality and self-satisfaction' (*What You Should Know*, 39).

[6] For the text of these unfinished rituals see Lucy Shepard Kalogera, 'Yeats's Celtic Mysteries' (Ph.D. diss., Florida State University, 1977).

[7] See, e.g., *YVP*ii. 452 and 298, among other references.

[8] 'Maud Gonne' notebook (1912), quoted in Foster, *Apprentice Mage*, 477.

Heart with perfect mastery & begins to be aware of an audience' (*YVP*iv. 199). It was news to neither when, in one of her sleeps, the 'Sleeper insisted that in the very nature of passion there is a spectator' (*YVP*iii. 10).

The couple committed themselves to theatrical performance and performative occultism as well as symbol and written language at a time when Western imaginations were undergoing the shock of new technologies that recorded and transmitted symbolic and linguistic information, such as photography, film, and recorded sound. WBY wrote plays that consciously emulated older or non-Western forms of theatrical spectacle, avoiding modern technical effects in favour of ritualized movement and symbolic language. The Golden Dawn required members to make instruments, paint symbolic images, and copy texts by hand, and both WBY and GY engaged in the slow labour and stylized antiquity of these tasks.[9] At the same time, however, they were far from immune to newer kinds of 'twice behaved behavior', to use Richard Schechner's working definition of performance, in their occult research.[10] WBY sat for spirit photographs, in which spirits invisible to the naked eye seem to appear on the photographic plate. He first encountered Leo Africanus in a session with a medium who famously used a phonographic 'trumpet'. He was also part of a team of psychic investigators examining a machine that claimed to receive and emit the voices of the dead.[11]

He also bought his wife a typewriter, with which machine she became the medium, interpreter, and co-producer of his texts in

[9] Reproductions from GY's Golden Dawn papers appear in G. M. Harper (ed.), *Yeats and the Occult*, plates 6–11, between pp. 122 and 123.

[10] Richard Schechner, *Between Theater and Anthropology* (Philadelphia: University of Pennsylvania Press, 1985).

[11] On an experience with spirit photography, see Foster, *Apprentice Mage*, 519. For a reproduction of a spirit photograph of WBY, see G. M. Harper (ed.), *Yeats and the Occult*, plate 1, facing p. 122. On WBY's seances with Wriedt, whose trumpet was part of her fame, see Goldman, 'Yeats, Spiritualism', 114–16. See Christopher Blake, 'Ghosts in the Machine: Yeats and the Metallic Homunculus, with Transcripts of Reports by W. B. Yeats and Edmund Dulac', in *YA* xv. 69–101. For another example of the blurring of representation and the real in WBY's occult experience (and an episode in his life that is deeply sexualized and gendered), see Harper, '"A Subject of Investigation": Miracle at Mirebeau', in G. M. Harper (ed.), *Yeats and the Occult*, 172–89.

mundane as well as occult ways.[12] The thousands of pages of manuscript and typescript representing draft after draft of versions of the system as it was shaped into *A Vision* show GY's typing as a critical aspect of the book's composition.[13] She used the typewriter to put her husband's practically illegible handwriting into clean copy, to make notes for them to use in clarifying various details of the system, to organize sequences, and to make obvious various weaknesses or gaps in the exposition. At some of these gaps in the typescripts are parenthetical notes by the Yeatses to remind themselves to go back to the communicators for help in sorting out the elaborate concepts ('certain . . . help can only be obtained from embodied 1 and embodied 15', notes one page, typed by GY. 'If so, what is that help? I can make shots. But I prefer not to do so, I want the help of a different mind from my own.' Another page mentions in passing that a communicator seems to have made a mistake: 'the Dionertian account . . . is not quite accurate'). A few stray manuscripts and typescripts of late sleeps answer various questions. Given that the typist was also the co-receiver of the ideas, the creator of many of the entries in the notebooks they used as aids in organization, and the member of the couple most adept at detail (added to the difficulty that her husband sometimes had in reading his own drafts), it is inconceivable to suppose that her typewriting was simple reproduction, any more than her spiritual automatism. The Yeatses worked together to turn script or sleeps into notes, notes into drafts, drafts into further drafts, and further drafts into 'final' copy—which then, as often as not, would be changed in proof. Some typescripts are

---

[12] London discusses mediumship and stenography (*Writing Double*, 165–72). See Friedrich A. Kittler, *Discourse Networks 1800/1900*, trans. Michael Metteer with Chris Cullens (Stanford, Calif.: Stanford University Press, 1990), for an extensive consideration of new media and the production of discourse, including considerable attention to the irrational and the uncanny. For an analysis of gender and the changes the typewriter in particular made to referentiality and textual production, see Friedrich A. Kittler, *Gramophone, Film, Typewriter*, trans. Geoffrey Winthrop-Young and Michael Wutz (Stanford, Calif.: Stanford University Press, 1999).

[13] The Yeatses employed other typists as well, and many of the hundreds of pages of typewritten drafts of *A Vision* that remain (some were destroyed; see Saddlemyer, *Becoming George*, 535) were typed by others.

marked with his corrections, some with hers, and some with both. As a writer, WBY was engaged in a brand new kind of compositional process for him, in which creative and reproductive elements in textual production wove themselves together in a highly complicated dance.

Accurate notation of dance, though, like completely faithful reproduction of live performances of drama or music, is of course impossible. So too it is with the script. As the Yeatses worked together at their many-times-repeated automatic sessions, they enacted a long and varied series of events whose husk (to use a term from the system) is the automatic script, just as a dramatic script, Labanotation, or a musical score may be thought of as an incomplete record of live performance. Readers of the script cannot know the extent to which the couple discussed beforehand topics to be raised in the automatic sessions, or indeed talked things over afterwards. A few scattered comments exist, like the typed 'RECORD' from one of the sleep note-books, which explains, 'Since we gave up the sleeps we have worked at the system by discussion, each bringing to these their discoveries' (*YVP*iii. 120). In general, we cannot tell how often a question posed by WBY might have been suggested by GY, or, alternatively, how often messages received in the session proper were conditioned by conversations outside it.

One way to come to terms with factors that leave no written record is to bear in mind at least that the relationship between action and script is never one merely of inadequate recording. As Friedrich Kittler, following Marshall McLuhan and others, reminds us, 'A medium is a medium is a medium', and therefore 'cannot be translated'.[14] The automatic script points to the richness of the interplay between performance and preservation. These documents exist between the immediacy of receiving mysterious messages and the commemorative and creative acts of writing those messages down and shaping them into a single philosophical system. The script gestures toward the live moment in the unconscious look of handwriting, with dashes to indicate pauses or truncated thoughts

---

[14] Kittler, *Discourse Networks*, 265.

and interruptions of the words by diagrams or pictures, and in spaces left in typed pages to be filled in later, but it also prepares for being kept, reread, and used later in the lengthy process of shaped composition. Questions and answers are numbered, and dates, times, places, and names of communicators are scrupulously noted. Concepts are carefully worded: precise phrasing no less than supernormal truth is a dimension of the meanings asserted by the system.

Part of the value of the documents (to later readers as to the Yeatses themselves) lies in the way that they point to this dialectic, if you will, between movement and form. Both WBY and GY regarded human life as a series of staged actions shaped by a self large or dynamic enough to throw itself into multiple roles—to be playwright, stage manager, actor, and scenario, to use the metaphor of the *Commedia dell'arte* used to good effect in both versions of *A Vision* (*AV A* 17–19; *AV B* 83–4), and whose structure was first given through GY's hand (*YVP*i. 270). Both knew well also that written words raise the dead, and not only for adepts in magical orders, and that this miracle changes the dead as well as the living into some third state. Writing operates like memory to bring to an altered life in symbol or vision that which is absent from physical apprehension. This act is not always pleasant, of course. Like Frankenstein's monster, Count Dracula, and other gothic dramatizations whose horrifying similarity to the humans around them is manifest in their use of language, texts change human utterance as well as humanity itself as they perform their acts of reanimation.[15] Dramatic texts, which evoke theatrical events, have even more obvious affinities with the world of the occult. These texts are designed to be brought to life

---

15 John Paul Riquelme, 'The Female Collaborator: Issues of Property and Authorship in Bram Stoker's *Dracula* and the Yeatses' *A Vision*' (Paper presented at the Modern Language Association, Chicago, 2000), is an interesting meditation on *A Vision* and the Irish gothic via the issue of collaboration. *Dracula* is a gold-mine of connections waiting to be made among Anglo-Irishness, the gothic, gender, and communications technology, including the typewriter. See the essays in Bram Stoker, *Dracula*, ed. John Paul Riquelme, Case Studies in Contemporary Criticism (New York: Palgrave, 2002), esp. Jennifer Wicke, 'Vampiric Typewriting: Dracula and its Media'.

immediately and directly, evoking an apparitional world in which voices seem to speak from the page and visions appear out of the dark of an imagined theatre. Plays themselves are ghostly, in that they bring forms from beyond the world of the living to a shadowy mimicry of life.[16] Indeed, Joseph Roach suggests adopting 'a way of thinking about performance that discloses an urgent but often disguised passion: the desire to communicate physically with the past, a desire that roots itself in the ambivalent love of the dead'.[17] Plays also feature doubles, human beings standing in for imaginary beings, actors who are, we might say, possessed by the characters they play. To the degree that performances are designed to suggest actualities from a realm beyond the theatre, actors standing in for truths they do not in themselves embody, they might more precisely be described as mediumistic. Roach also uses this terminology, speaking of 'the performer as an eccentric but meticulous curator of cultural memory, a medium for speaking with the dead'.[18] Of course, the reverse is also true: mediumship is theatrical.

It might be more accurate to say that both mediumship and theatre participate in a cultural dynamic of representation, that features a changing, alienating sense of what it is to be human. The Yeatses' experiment fits itself into two large streams of discourse in the last few hundred years of European history. First, the machine, a powerful cause, effect, and symbol of the displacement of older ways of life by rationalism, urbanism, industrialism, and technological change in general, owed some of its attraction and terror to the ways in which it doubled for, as well as distanced people from, a sense of their humanity. The idea of the machine performed a kind of collective

[16] David Savran, noting that theatre 'has long been linked to the occult and populated by ghosts', analyses this similarity as trope: 'The Haunted Houses of Modernity', *Modern Drama*, 43 (2000): 585.

[17] Joseph Roach, 'History, Memory, Necrophilia', in Peggy Phelan and Jill Lane (eds.), *The Ends of Performance*, (New York and London: New York University Press, 1998), 23.

[18] Joseph Roach, *Cities of the Dead: Circum-Atlantic Performance* (New York: Columbia University Press, 1996), 78.

mental function as *doppelgänger* for the manual energy it replaced. In the generations preceding the moment when GY began to write automatically, this discursive engine gained steam, so to speak, until it became one of the ruling metaphors of the time, for the human body, including the brain and the senses, as well as entities from the body politic to divisions of thought. Various new forms of technology were uncanny in a Freudian sense, having replaced only incompletely what Freud called, in his famous essay on the uncanny, 'primitive beliefs', so that old and familiar fears recur, disguised as the new.[19] Old demons appear in new forms; demonic machines, similar to, but disturbingly different from, their human counterparts, move faster, work harder, see better, and produce more efficiently and consistently than mere mortals.

As the nineteenth century gave way to the twentieth, advances in technology related to communication and reproduction of images and sound, in particular, tumbled over each other making their way into public awareness. By mid-century, reproducible photography was possible, and within a few decades there were photographic portraits in most middle-class homes in Western Europe and the United States. Bell's first telephone took place in 1876, and Edison's phonograph was invented in 1877. The 1870s also witnessed photographic studies of movement by the physiologist Étienne-Jules Marey in France and Eadweard Muybridge (who created the famous sequence of a trotting horse) in the United States. Muybridge's zoöpraxiscope, which projected photographic sequences on to a screen, was first used in 1879. In 1888 (the year of the founding of the Hermetic Order of the Golden Dawn), Hertz discovered radio waves, the first kinetoscope was produced, Berliner introduced the gramophone, and Eastman introduced roll film and the box camera, making it possible for people to take their own photographs. The Lumière brothers

---

[19] Sigmund Freud, 'The "Uncanny" ', in *The Standard Edition of the Complete Works*, ed. James Strachey (London: Hogarth Press, 1959), xvii. 245. Freud's essay, written in 1919, was exactly contemporaneous with the Yeatses' experiments. No less than their explorations, it is the product of a world that highlighted performative qualities in the wake of technological change.

developed the film projector in 1895, the year that Marconi broadcast a first message by radio and Röntgen discovered X-rays. Speech was transmitted by radio in 1904. Profound shifts in perception, including perceptions of time and space, memory and motion, of the human body as well as human abilities, co-occurred with these developments.[20] Images that dissembled reality seemed to create doubles, with disquieting relationships to the original subjects of photographs; people who were absent, changed by time, or even dead, could look at the living. In the case of an X-ray, people could look at their own skeletons.[21] In the world of sound, language was amputated from human bodies (and its meanings, bereft of integrity by analogy with human

---

[20] For studies of such developments that are especially relevant to an occult context, see Eduardo Cadava, *Words of Light: Theses on the Photography of History* (Princeton: Princeton University Press, 1997), on 'the conjunction of death and the photographed' (p. 10), including the haunting of the present moment through the photographic image. Jonathan Sterne, *The Audible Past: Cultural Origins of Sound Reproduction* (Durham, NC, and London: Duke University Press, 2003), esp. ch. 6, considers the relationship of reproduced sound, memorializing, and preservation of culture. Stephen Kern, *The Culture of Time and Space, 1880–1918* (Cambridge, Mass.: Harvard University Press, 1983), examines the links between technological changes and conceptual shifts relating to time and space across Europe and the United States in four critical decades. Sara Danius, *The Senses of Modernism: Technology, Perception, and Aesthetics* (Ithaca, NY, and London: Cornell University Press, 2002) analyses three modernist novels and their constitutive nexus of perceptual shifts and technological change. For a model that describes assumptions I make here with regard to the relationship between social forces and changes in technology and science, see Bruno Latour, *Science in Action: How to Follow Scientists and Engineers through Society* (Cambridge, Mass.: Harvard University Press, 1987). For a description and application of a similar analytical mode to post-Saussurean linguistics and the institutional study of the humanities, see Ronald Schleifer, *Analogical Thinking: Post-Enlightenment Understanding in Language, Collaboration, and Interpretation* (Ann Arbor: University of Michigan Press, 2000), as well as *idem*, *Modernism and Time: The Logic of Abundance in Literature, Science, and Culture, 1880–1930* (Cambridge: Cambridge University Press, 2000). Briefly, by bypassing the chicken-or-egg question of whether machines cause or are determined by social forces (whether, to use the terms of Deleuze and Guattari (*Anti-Oedipus*), machines are social before they are material, or, in a more common formulation, that autonomous changes in technology cause changes in society in their wake), Latour prefers a model based on allegory, translation, and a network of forces, and Schleifer uses notions of analogy and collaboration. For other reformulations of the relationship between humanity and the technological, see Donna Haraway, *Simians, Cyborgs, and Women: The Reinvention of Nature* (New York: Routledge, 1991).

[21] Danius notes that radiographs were often called 'ghost pictures' or 'shadowgraphs' (*Senses of Modernism*, 78). They are still referred to as *skiagraphs* or *skiagrams*.

form, correspondingly dis-organ-ized).[22] Disembodied voices could be heard over untold distances; voices of the dead could speak again.

Along with the rhetoric of machines, a second discursive field enfolds the Yeatses' experiments: a century or more before GY took up her pen, the replacement of orality or written knowledge through the hands of public scribes by silent literacy had created ghostly voices in human heads just when the rise of rationalism relegated spirituality increasingly to the margins of people's lives in the West.[23] As Terry Castle has suggested, by the eighteenth century Western Europe was well on the way to re-creating the supernatural world in the new imagined world of the unconscious, so that 'one cannot speak in the end . . . of a "decline of magic" in post-Enlightenment Western culture, only perhaps of its relocation within the new empire of subjectivity itself'.[24] In other words, as the medium Elsa Barker puts it in the introduction to the last book in her popular series *Letters from a Living Dead Man*, 'In childhood our parents guided us—or tried to. Then science guided us—a little too far. And in the reaction we turned inward, to find (sometimes) the unconscious more troubled than the conscious.'[25] By the time mainstream science

[22] This point is made by Juan A. Suárez, 'T. S. Eliot's *The Waste Land*, the Gramophone, and the Modernist Discourse Network', *New Literary History*, 32 (2000): 751.

[23] WBY is by no means alone in stressing the differences from other Western national cultures caused by the relatively late arrival of modernity in Ireland, of course; see Angela Bourke, *The Burning of Bridget Cleary* (London: Pimlico, 1999), for a case study of a woman's murder influenced by a violent clash between two worlds in late nineteenth-century Ireland. WBY's distance from old ways is, however, as noticeable as his advocacy of them in passages such as the following, published in *Samhain* of 1906:

Irish poetry and Irish stories were made to be spoken or sung, while English literature, alone of great literatures, because the newest of them all, has all but completely shaped itself in the printing-press. In Ireland to-day the old world that sang and listened is, it may be for the last time in Europe, face to face with the world that reads and writes, and their antagonism is always present under some name or other in Irish imagination and intellect. (*Ex* 206)

[24] Castle, *Female Thermometer*, 189.

[25] Barker, *Last Letters from the Living Dead Man*, 25. Barker's books register not only the connection between, in Castle's terms, the old and new empires of external and internal states, but also the discourses of empire and war that are ubiquitous in late nineteenth- and early twentieth-century spiritualism. They are exceedingly partisan and patriotic.

had severed relations with its occult cousins, divine heat and light having been displaced into physics, with magnetism and liquids differentiated from auras and mesmeric fluids, the human brain had itself become haunted, if you will, peopled by mental phantoms displaced from their archaic place in exterior reality. For writers, this possession of the imagination has everything to do with Romantic explorations of its power and the figure of the alienated artist, cursed by the demon of a fertile brain and cast out of the *polis* because of the danger that those uncontrollable forces unleash. It is as if an artist were by nature double, not only because the artist is possessed by imagination but also because the artist must be projected into the imaginations of readers, doubled or multiplied in their minds, in order to exist at all.

This doubling registers itself in WBY's work most notably in the use of masks, which are at once theatrical images, suggestions of the uncanny, and intimations of ancient mysteries that link self and non-self in a pre-Cartesian, perhaps even pre-Platonic whole. Like the mask, the act of writing is always a gesture in the direction of possession: as 'Anima Hominis' asks rhetorically about the mask put on by the hero, 'how else could the god have come to us in the forest?' (*Myth* 335). Writing as Leo, on the topic of the identity of the Other in dreams, WBY's hand wrote to himself about his experiences as a dramatist: 'So too when you write a play, the characters seem to move & live of themselves. Is your own mind broken, & your will doubled. Is this too a beginning that might grow with a little stress upon the nerves into one of those secondary personalities which it may be, you believe perhaps, animates us till it be [indecipherable word] & yet be but a moiety of our mind' ('Leo', 29). Secondary personalities animating spirit controls, of course, were exactly what the script developed, and it is also plausible to suggest that the theory of secondary personalities moved the Yeatses toward their ideas of their own doubling of mind and will. It is important to remember, however, that such doubling does not necessarily undo an assumption of conscious volition. Unlike popular nineteenth-century hermeneutics, trapped in notions of authenticity and origin, occultism often entertained the idea of doubled will as well as assumed personalities without opprobrium: it was not necessarily true that mixed sources indicated fakery. No less reputable a practitioner of automatic writing than Stead, whose letters from Julia were some of the most famous productions of the spiritualist community, admitted readily that, 'as was remarked by a friend, my spook writes Steadese'.[26]

Likewise, late personae like Crazy Jane or the hermit Ribh speak Yeatsese, just as the communicators of the Yeatses' automatic script spoke George-Yeatsese. Of course, the Yeatses would have allowed this. How could words not borrow voice from the channel through which they come? GY's script develops this phenomenon into a finely honed skill. The voices of various communicators, sometimes simultaneously more than one, are each kept carefully separate from her own personality. The documents address repeatedly the ever-present issues of how strongly her own will, or her husband's, or that of the mysterious others, were acting upon each other. She wrote fluently even though the confident truths of one session might well be as confidently claimed to be false in another, a sure sign of multiple personalities at work. The whole exercise was for her at once aesthetic and religious, with some suggestion of a yearning for ecstasy. She copied into the back cover of one of her books a message to herself: 'In my solitary and retired imagination remember I am not alone. . . .'[27]

GY was happy to allow the active participation of her own mind, but she was never comfortable positing that the communicators were only secondary personalities or the products of her own memories. As late as 1931, she wrote to her husband criticizing the second part of his introduction to *The Words upon the Window-Pane*, about

---

[26] William T. Stead, 'My Experience in Automatic Writing. The Story of "Julia", and Others', *Borderland*, 1 (1893): 40.

[27] The quotation finishes, 'and therefore forget not to contemplate Him and his attributes who is ever with me'. It is written on the back flyleaf of Miguel de Molinos, *Guida Spirituale*, trans. Kathleen Lyttleton ([London]: Methuen, [1911?]), signed 'Georgie Hyde Lees. August. 1913'. This item appears in O'Shea, *Descriptive Catalog*, but this quotation is missing from the entry there (1332a).

mediumship. Three critical points were at issue. To begin with, WBY claims in the essay that 'every voice that speaks, every form that appears . . . is first of all a secondary personality or dramatisation created by, in, or through the medium'. Next, using the hurtful word *cheat*, he asserts that 'Because mediumship is dramatisation, even honest mediums cheat at times either deliberately or because some part of the body has freed itself from the control of the waking will, and almost always truth and lies are mixed together'. He also supposes that the personalities that appear in a seance are products not of their own memoried selves but of the 'sub-conscious or unspoken thought' of the medium (*Ex* 364, 365). To all three suppositions, she is opposed:

I think that the reason I did not very much like Part II Windowpane is that your argument—the dramatisation the secondary and tertiary personalities of the medium, seem so close to the old psichical [*sic*] research theory of the subconsious [*sic*] or at least that I cannot personally understand what you mean except in those terms. If I had to interpret that "commentary" I could not say that any "spirit" were present at any seance, that spirits were present at a seance only as impersonations created by a medium out of material in a world record just as wireless photography or television are created; that all communicating spirits are mere dramatisations of that record; that all spirits in fact are not, as far as psychic communications are concerned, spirits at all, are only memory. I say "memory" deliberately, because "memory" is so large a part of all psychic phenomena. I dont remember any case in which a spirit (communicating through a medium) had during the latter part of his life or during any part of his life been cut off from that every day faculty of memory. those people who were wounded in the head during war—they dont come—the insane dont come???—the spirits who tells [*sic*] us about their houses, their horse racing, their whiskeys and sodas, their children, their aunts and God knows whatnots, their suicides, were all mainly preoccupied during their lives with those things. Have we any record of a spirit communicating who had been at any period of his life . . . so physically or mentally incapacitated that memory, even "subconscious" memory, had been obliterated?[28]

[28] Unpublished letter dated 24 Nov. 1931.

Note, incidentally, the comparison of the 'world record' tapped by mediums with 'wireless photography or television'. GY's acts of mediumistic interpretation are not, in her opinion, as simple as tuning in to some pre-set station. (Thomas informed the Yeatses as much on 18 September 1918, explaining that 'The automatic faculty does not so much make pictures as present a surface on which pictures can be reflected & only those pictures which have a correspondence to some portion of the egos experience can be seen by the ego' (*YVP*ii. 59).) WBY, interestingly, responded to his wife's letter by correcting himself: he did not intend, he says, to suggest utter lack of volition by the use of the terms 'secondary personality' and 'dramatisation'. He makes a distinction based on the analogy with theatre:

I am more moved by the correspondents statement that I have turned a seance into a kind of wireless apparatus & denied that the spirits are there at all. If I drop that word 'unconscious' adopted out of mere politeness I may be better understood: the Daimon of a living man is a dramatist—what am I but my daimons most persistent drama—it dramatizes its fancies, characters out of fiction have written through the planchette—it dramatizes its knowledge, & when that is knowledge of other daimons it is as though it has lent them its dramatic power. The Spirit is thus present in a representation which is the child of the living & the dead.[29]

As much as WBY may have wanted to reanimate the process, using live drama as metaphor and claiming a kind of parental office for spirits (so that a 'representation' at a seance is 'the child' of both living and dead participants), automatism, GY's method, evokes machinery, even in its name. However, it also carries the suggestion of the uncanny by virtue not only of its claim to be in contact with the worlds beyond but also in its methods. When writing automatically, or engaging in vocal or enacted mediumship, a person becomes an automaton, acting like a mechanized figure or doll, the figure that Freud had singled out for examination only a few years before

---

[29] This comment and another, along with a long passage from GY's letter, are reproduced in Saddlemyer, *Becoming George*, 432–3.

the Yeatses' experiments for its uncanny qualities.[30] Mediumship was disturbing to many because of its supernaturalism, with the suggestion of demonic possession or madness, and also because a medium was a human machine, lacking in freedom and will. The automatic script makes this connection explicit in a discussion of the terms 'sequence' and 'the automatic', the difference between the two being that one 'implies individual choice' but the other 'is a mechanism' (*YVP*ii. 36). Incidentally, I suspect that unease with automatism applies more to mediumship in the 'respectable' classes than other groups: the fear of losing freedom was less a threat to people whose choices had long been circumscribed than it was to upper classes whose ways of life reaped the benefits of industrialization without suffering as many of its ill effects, who could take personal autonomy for granted, and who had the leisure to indulge in meditating on preserving the integrity of their interior lives. A threat of stolen humanity did not provoke the same fears in those who did not view themselves through such genteel-liberal lenses; plebeian spiritualists were generally more invested in the possibilities of the movement for millenarianist or other forms of socially progressive politics. As Barrow notes, spiritualism was 'strategically attractive to people of any reforming cast of mind'.[31] Be that as it may, the performance of mediumship generally elicited responses from the public that were like reactions to the popular spectacles of mechanized toys or magic-lantern shows, modern miracles that were fascinating both for their mysterious and paranormal aspects and also because of the possibility that they could be explained as exciting new technologies.

Indeed, mediumship was often described in language borrowed from the sciences—often enough to be a source of comment at the time no less than in later accounts.[32] The famous naturalist Alfred Russel

---

[30] Freud, 'The "Uncanny"', 233. See also Castle, *Female Thermometer*, 10–11.

[31] Barrow, *Independent Spirits*, 110.

[32] See Oppenheim, Other World, Part 3, 'A Pseudoscience', for a detailed overview of the relationship between the sciences and psychic research. Daniel Cottom, *Abyss of*

Wallace was consistent and confident in his claims that 'Spiritualism is an experimental science', and that ridiculing spiritualist inquiry was thoroughly irrational: 'whenever the scientific men of any age have denied the facts of investigators on *a priori* grounds, *they have always been wrong*'.[33] Non-believers used scientific language no less than believers. Millais Culpin, for example, a sceptic who ascribed all spiritualistic phenomena ultimately to 'a neurotic "Will to Power"', echoed a common observation when he noted in 1920 that 'The phenomena of wireless telegraphy and of radioactive elements have led people to think that some direct means of communication of energy from one brain to another may be possible, that is without intervention of the special senses'.[34] Culpin's diagnosis of the trouble with telepathy as, first, faulty analogy, and second, desire for power, parallels the dual aspects of GY's automatic writing as mechanized performance that I am suggesting. First, the script operates like an allegory, doubling the lives and the work of the Yeatses by putting these things into quasi-performative space, dramatizing big issues like writing, creativity, marriage, and the self, not to mention a myriad of smaller ones, from characters in WBY's plays to individual symbols like sun, moon, tower, or gyre. Items are enacted as well as discussed. Second, the issue of power or authority is of course at the core of GY's automatism, as it is for automatism in general. The phenomenon sits uncertainly in a blurred zone among the possibilities that it is a mechanization of human activity or fakery, in which cases it would diminish or debase human potential, or (like the enlarged

Reason: Cultural Movements, Revelations, and Betrayals (New York and Oxford: Oxford University Press, 1991), examines spiritualism and surrealism as movements that both explored the cultural meanings of scientific discourse.

[33] Alfred Russel Wallace, *On Miracles and Modern Spiritualism: Three Essays* (London: James Burns, 1875), 221, 17; emphasis original. Wallace is fond of analogies with advancing technology, citing, e.g., the new communicative worlds of telegram and photograph, and the new perceptive ones of telescope and microscope (pp. 37–8). See Oppenheim, *Other World*, 296–325, for a useful overview of his blend of evolutionary theory and spiritualism.

[34] Millais Culpin, *Spiritualism and the New Psychology: An Explanation of Spiritualist Phenomena and Beliefs in Terms of Modern Knowledge* (London: Edward Arnold, 1920), pp. 154, xii.

will sought by magicians) a transfiguration of humankind into a heightened, supernormal state, rising above the mechanical world even as it emulates it in its method.

Technological metaphors had been common within the spiritualist movement since its beginning. The first article of the first number of *Light*, subtitled 'A Journal of Psychical, Occult, and Mystical Research', gives a new spin even to its reigning symbol, suggesting that in cool appraisal of its subject-matter the periodical would be like electricity: 'seeking thus to emulate, if we may so say, the qualities of that newest form of illumination which has been found capable of affording—Light *without Heat*'.[35] Moreover, the essay argues, occult research represents a logical extension of scientific inquiry:

By telescope and microscope, by scalpel and chemical analysis, the Physicist has successfully invaded from all sides the kingdom of Nature, and widened the domain of human knowledge; but with all his weapons and all his resources, including those which nature herself has of late yielded up to him, the realm of Spirit has so far successfully withstood him. . . . The idea of it is to him as something hopeless—it may almost be said abhorrent—for in relation to that of which no rational conception can be formed there can be to the rationalist no hope; and where Hope is not, Mistrust and Fear are not far off.

However, 'The Spiritualist, while rendering willingly all honour and homage to the great works accomplished by his brother, the

[35] [William Stainton Moses], 'Our Principles and Purposes', *Light*, 1 (1881): 1. Although Edison's carbon-thread incandescent lamp, patented in 1879, did not, strictly speaking, produce light without heat, it did away with a flame, which may have been enough for Moses' rhetorical purposes here. Such illumination was not unidirectional: not only did spiritualists employ scientific ideas, but scientists also made use of esoteric thought. In 1874, Edison explained a phenomenon he could not otherwise explain by suggesting that it was '*a true unknown force*', possibly the 'odic' force proposed as the scientific basis for spiritualism in the 1860s by the German chemist Karl Reichenbach. By 1878, Edison was looking to theosophy for explanation and exploring practical telegraphic applications for his 'etheric' force (Paul Israel, Edison: *A Life of Invention* (New York: Wiley & Sons, 1998), 111–12; Peter Washington, *Madame Blavatsky's Baboon: Theosophy and the Emergence of the Western Guru* (London: Secker & Warburg, 1993). Phosphorescence had been explained some decades before, and phosphorus lamps were in use at the time (indeed, the first investigation of a mediumistic materialization by members of the Society for Psychical Research was undertaken with the aid of such a lamp); Gauld, *Founders*, 81.

Physicist, declines to accept them as final.'[36] Science, defined as the study of the physical world, and spiritualism, which expands that study into the non-physical realms, are akin, siblings even, and both alike will pursue the progressive dream of domination of both nature and Spirit. It should be noted that the rhetoric used here by William Stainton Moses, the editor of *Light*, certainly suggests not only that there are connections between mediumship and Victorian notions of progress and empire, but also that spiritualism, unlike its reputation, is, like physics, essentially masculine. Its gender is most evident in the military metaphors: spiritualism uses 'weapons' and 'resources' to 'invade' a terrain that has 'yielded up to him [the scientist]'. This new journal had no intention of allowing readers to think that its topics were of interest only to women, a rhetorical act that demonstrates that such a danger was thought to exist, and also that scientific language was thought to be an effective tool in preventing such potential feminization. To be scientific, of course, was to be manly as well as reputable.

Some spiritualist discourse leans toward biology, suggesting that contact between the world of the living and that of the dead results organically, from natural growth or evolution. A few noted opinion leaders like Wallace were men of the natural sciences, and they were inspirational for a variety of opinions on the matter. The spiritualist George P. Young asserted in 1909 that the movement was at a 'chrysalis stage of existence', that humankind indeed had 'larval characters'.[37] In *The Drama of Love and Death: A Study of Human Evolution and Transfiguration* (1907), the mystic reformer and poet Edward Carpenter begins with single cells and ends with the after-death state.[38] Any number of writers suggested that it might be possible to isolate the physiological processes at work in extrasensory perception, most of them tending with Lodge to locate these processes

---

[36] [Moses], 'Our Principles and Purposes', 1.
[37] George P. Young, *The Soul's Deepest Questions: An Introduction to Spiritual Philosophy* (Halifax: The Spiritualists' National Union, 1909), 61.
[38] Edward Carpenter, *The Drama of Love and Death: A Study of Human Evolution and Transfiguration* (London: George Allen, 1907).

where he supposed automatism to originate, in 'nerve centres not in the most conscious and ordinarily employed region of the brain', that organ whose mysteries continued to elude both anatomists and psychologists.[39] Such biological and anatomical talk tends to slide into the language of religion, evolution equalling teleology, the brain sounding suspiciously like the soul, and it should be noted that positive descriptions of science occur simultaneously with profound distrust of advances in technology in particular. Proponents of the new 'science' often commented on its appearance in the rapidly industrializing nineteenth century, and interpreted this conjunction not as a sign of progress but as a salve to the ills that progress had caused.

Other spiritualist language borrows from physics and mechanics. Physicists seemed more likely than other men of science to be attracted to paranormal exploration, as a number of writers noted, citing names like Sir Oliver Lodge either admiringly or disparagingly.[40] The analogies are multifold: communication with spirits is like radium rays or radio waves, invisible channels through which unknown forces or messages might travel.[41] Spiritual essences might someday be measured when science catches up to mediumship, as the existence of other new measuring tools gives reason to suppose:

The invention of scientific instruments of precision—the bolometer (which measures the heat of the distant stars), the spectroscope (which tells us what

---

[39] Lodge, *Raymond*, 356.

[40] See Edward Clodd, *The Question: "If a man die, shall he live again?" Job xiv.14: A Brief History and Examination of Modern Spiritualism* (London: Grant Richards, 1917), for an example of the latter. In this book, published in the year the script began (and reviewed, as Saddlemyer notes, in an issue of the *Irish Times* that the Yeatses probably read (*Becoming George*, 156)), Clodd writes with reference to Lodge, 'An expert in physics may be ignorant of biology and psychology; he may never have read a book on anthropology and hence remained ignorant of the invaluable material bearing on the history of Spiritualism in such classics as *Primitive Culture* or *The Golden Bough*, wherein are supplied antiseptics to Spiritualism' (p. 270). Physicists, according to Clodd, are likely to believe in spiritualism because they are used to dealing with unvarying universals, not variations or exceptions that are inevitable in the experimental material of other scientists. In terms the Yeatses might have used (and signalling one reason for their approval of such approaches), physicists are the Platonists of the scientific community.

[41] See Hey, *Seven Principles*, 17, and Viola Gertrude Rich, *Thought Radio and Thought Transference* (repr. New York: Elizabeth Towne, 1927), *passim*.

other worlds are composed of), and the microphone (which makes the tread of the house-fly to resemble the march of a cavalry regiment)—have enlarged the boundaries of human imagination, and revealed the narrowness of our sense-world.[42]

Automatic writing from the hand of Mrs Cora L. V. Richmond, by a spirit called 'Zollner', sounds a bit like WBY in its bold rhetoric: 'I announce the existence in the world of a new thought that shall take the place of all other scientific thought; a new formula that shall take the place of all other formulae: That matter possesses a power, or rather capacity and capability, of being acted upon unknown to material science.'[43] Terminology derived from theosophy or Indian spirituality, such as expansion into astral planes or perception of 'etheric vibrations', echoes the language of physics in describing explorations into different states of matter, measurement of waves, and so on.[44]

[42] George P. Young, 'The Attitude of Science Toward Psychic Phenomena', in *Essays on Spiritualism* (Halifax: The Spiritualists' National Union, 1910), 23.

[43] '"Zollner" on Spirit, Matter, Time, Space, The Fourth Dimension', collection of clippings donated to the BL by Peter Anderson, 4 Jan. 1928, entitled 'Spiritual Science Vol. I, by James MacDowall' (London, 1881–92).

[44] For automatic writing as tapping into the astral plane and 'waiting for the spirit entity to take control of the etheric vibrations', see Swami S. D. Ramayandas, *Mediumship: Its Laws and Phenomena* (London: L. N. Fowler, [?1927]), 56. Electricity was another popular topic for 'scientific' explanations of occult phenomena. A report in *Light* from 26 Oct. 1895 offers evidence to demonstrate that astrology is verifiably true from an experiment that measured the electric influence of planets—their 'electromotive force' (Arthur Butcher, 'Welcome News for Astrologers', *Light*, 15 (1895): 517). Similarly, an essay from the start of the year of the Yeatses' marriage, on 13 Jan. 1917, suggests that they might have had more dramatic results if they had pursued their studies regularly in a drier climate than England or Ireland:

It is a well-known fact that the physical phenomena of spirit manifestation are much more powerful and much more easily produced in countries where a dry electrical condition of the atmosphere prevails. This is almost certainly the cause of the superiority of American voice and materialisation phenomena compared with those obtained in this country. . . . Travellers inform us that the electrical conditions in many parts of the United States are of such a nature that an electric spark can be drawn from the face or finger after sliding over the carpet of an ordinary room, and sparks are often drawn from metal articles in the room which happen to be insulated, these conditions prevailing during a good part of the year. (Revd Charles L. Tweedale, 'Electrical Conditions and Psychic Phenomena: A Suggestion', *Light*, 37 (1917): 10)

With great frequency, mediumship was described as a new mode of communication, like those that were proliferating in the last decades of the nineteenth century. Stead described his automatic writing using one of the many metaphors of new technologies that are rampant in the literature. When waiting for a letter from Julia, he explains, he must 'make my mind passive, and wait for the message; I do not receive any communication any more than I should receive a telephonic message if I never went to the telephone. The analogy between the method of communication and the telephone is very close, but with this difference—in this system it is always the recipient who rings up, so to speak, the transmitter at the other end of the line. . . . I am never rung up by the Invisibles.'[45] In her exposition of mediumship, Margery Bazett makes the point that mediumship is common in ordinary communication by equating two meanings of the word: 'A medium is necessary even if you want to send or receive a telegram. You require either an instrument or an operator or both.'[46] In the Yeatses' script, Dionertes used the same metaphor to explain why he remained odourless while the house was filled with various spirit-associated fragrances: 'He himself has no special fragrance associated with him as he is in the shiftings[47] & therefore is a kind of telephone between us & a central group of spirits' (*YVP*iii. 96). Viola Gertrude Rich's book *Thought Radio and Thought Transference* explains the related phenomenon of mental telepathy using another commonly applied analogy: like radio waves, invisible and inaudible thoughts can be received with the proper 'aerial' or 'antenna' of psychic training. 'Man's mind is a broadcasting-station of thought,' she writes, 'also a receiving-station of thought; therefore, we have mental telepathy, or thought-transference.'[48]

The typewriter, a machine and metaphor for various crises in popular understandings of gender, technology, written communication (including authorship), and human identity, is especially interesting.

[45] Stead, 'My Experience', 39.
[46] Bazett, *Some Thoughts on Mediumship*, p. xv.
[47] On the shiftings, one of the afterlife states, see *AVA* 229–34.
[48] Rich, *Thought Radio*, 12–13.

Indeed, as a sign it works as beautifully as clerical work itself as a way to understand some of the contradictory social requirements of gendered work during this period: as Zimmeck has claimed, 'had it not existed, it would have been necessary to invent it'.[49] By the time that Hanson G. Hey's account *The Seven Principles of Spiritualism* (1910) had been in print for one year, there were more than 166,000 clerical workers in offices in England, and more than 300,000 in the United States. These workers, a great many of whom were women, represented huge changes to the workforce generally: in Britain, as Simonton reports, the number of men in white-collar professions rose sevenfold between the 1870s and 1920s, but the number of women by a factor of eighty-three, when some 80 per cent of typists were women.[50] They were also overwhelmingly from groups with a claim to some privilege. In the United States, for example, in 1890, 90.8 per cent of clerical workers were native-born, and only a shadowy 0.4 per cent were non-white.[51] Thus, when Hey explains that 'Trance speaking can be the more readily understood if you imagine the brain of the speaker, a typewriter, and the control a typist rapping out the message by means of the different keys', his use of the writing machine as passive medium fits with common images that almost completely feminized and eroticized the new apparatus in the world of bourgeois imagination, although Hey's account also gives those images a twist in having the control, the agent in charge of the message, in the position of the female typist.[52] There is a voyeuristic quality to descriptions of the typewriting woman, well dressed and attractive, on display for the pleasures of curious men. For women, the reality of typewriting as a profession included very

[49] Meta Zimmeck, 'Jobs for the Girls: The Expansion of Clerical Work for Women, 1850–1914', in Angela V. John (ed.), *Unequal Opportunities: Women's Employment in England 1800–1918* (Oxford: Basil Blackwell, 1986), 158.

[50] Margery W. Davies, *Woman's Place is at the Typewriter: Office Work and Office Workers, 1870–1930* (Philadelphia: Temple University Press, 1982), appendix, table 1, 178–9; Deborah Simonton, *A History of European Women's Work, 1700 to the Present* (London and New York: Routledge, 1998), 236; Zimmeck, 'Jobs for the Girls', 154.

[51] Davies, *Woman's Place*, 74.

[52] Ibid. 10; Hey, *Seven Principles*. The huge percentage of women relative to men occurred in Europe as well as the USA.

real private benefits from the portability of the machine. A woman who could purchase her own typewriter could work at home, like many a medium, thus preserving the ideology of separate spheres (which was rigidly observed as well in segregated working environments), and also bypassing ordinary routes (and barriers) to getting a job. (If she were married, for example, in an era when marriage bars were the norm, she could still work.)

References to typewriters in occult discourse often display uncertainty as to how much agency might be ascribed to mediums. On the one hand, both female clerical workers and mediums presumably reproduce words or ideas not their own. On the other, it is not always easy to differentiate dictation from authorship (not nearly as easy, in the immediate moment of production that typewriters make possible, as it had been since Gutenberg to make distinctions between written texts and later reproduction in typeset form). Female workers, visible in the public spaces of offices or session-rooms, 'rapped' out messages, coming dangerously close to the line between the dainty, mechanical tasks which their male employers thought were proper to them and intellectual work, for which they were meant to be unsuited (and for which they might have to be paid appropriately).[53] When Geraldine Cummins explains that when she engages in automatic writing, 'I feel like a secretary automatically recording words from dictation', but also that 'I am suspicious of the inventive powers of my subconscious mind', she registers this dubiety.[54] Typewriting women came dangerously close to replacing the (male) authorial hand with

---

[53] Female workers did provoke anxieties in the previously male clerical workforce. In the USA, before the Civil War, secretaries were male. After the war, with the introduction of typewriters as well as changing business practices that required much more paperwork, women were allowed into offices for the first time. By 1900, nearly a third of clerical workers in the USA and almost 20 per cent in Britain were female. In Germany, female white-collar workers comprised 30.5 per cent of the labour force by 1911; in 1906, 39.8 per cent of commercial workers in France were women (these last statistics, it should be noted, include other professions, such as retail assistants) (Zimmeck, 'Jobs for the Girls', 236). The huge demographic shift throughout Europe and the USA to women making money and, in the male popular imagination at least, being able to live independently from men, were perceived as potential dangers to the family as well as to male jobs.

[54] Cummins, *Unseen Adventures*, 54, 133–4.

mechanical (and diffusely zoned) replacements for phallic pens and unsettling the process of creation by acting as automatic speakers or writers.[55] Women touched erotically charged keys to produce the children of men's creative brains, but the question of textual paternity was more open than was often comfortable for the men involved.

As has been commented upon any number of times, the feminization of the machine itself is handily seen in the word *typewriter*, which referred in the early decades of its use to both the physical apparatus and the (female) operator. Part of the trouble with typewriters (the machines or the women) derives from the uncertain connection they represent between two already unstable categories: gender and new technologies. These mysterious women and their mysterious machines enact a sort of cultural neurosis: 'typewriter girls' symbolize considerable social dis-ease in the ways they complicate to whom words belong (men or women, capitalists or workers, and so on) and how connected words and ideas may be with human brains and bodies. In occult literature, which posits as perceivable realities currents that remain in the unconscious of the culture at large, these connections reveal themselves dramatically. In the automatically composed *Letters from Julia*, for example, Julia describes to Stead how she uses him for her messages in language that points exactly to automatism as frustration of a desire to control a text, a desire that in Western tradition has been gendered as male. Julia writes through Stead's hand, 'All your stored-up ideas, memories, associations, are like the letters inside a typewriter. I strike whatever I need. The alphabet was yours, but the touch was mine,' hinting of intimacy as well as impersonality in the typing process.[56] The alphabet, with its abstract symbolism, may be his, as writing has been the province of the literate and powerful, those who direct themselves

---

[55] The figure of the woman at a typewriter was highly sexualized, spawning any number of erotic items, from postcards for tasteful viewers or romantic novels to jokes in music-halls and on the vaudeville stage, to a thriving trade in pornographic photos and novelettes. See Christopher Keep, 'The Cultural Work of the Type-Writer Girl', *Victorian Studies*, 40 (1997): 401–26.

[56] Stead, *Letters from Julia*, 81.

toward the blank female page. What matters now, though, is not one symbol or another, but this experience: the conjunction of symbol with physical touch, of automatism with gendered sensuality, makes possible the release of the 'stored-up ideas, memories, associations' that are otherwise inaccessible.

Much more obviously than Stead's experience, the Yeatses' automatic writing depended upon touch and intimacy, the enactment of trust and flow of language that could be shaped into linear form only later, in the notebooks and card file, and later the drafts of *A Vision*. In an important session on 12 February 1918, Rose elaborated on the specific way in which action made meaning in the script. WBY asks and Rose responds:

16. What special quality is given to communicati[on] by my touching medium.
16. It is necessary to establish an interchange of a psychical nature for one thing to enable certain future work to be done
17 Do I then recieve [*sic*] as well as give?
17. Yes more than you give & also it enables me to write more quickly because I then have a double force
18. Do[es] it make a difference what part of body I touch Is body a kee-board?
18. Any sensitive point will do equally. (*YVP*i. 349)

In an apparent paradox, the daily performance of automatism, with its pseudo-scientific experimentation and its analogical relationship to a machine-like undoing of human will, actually relaxed the rigid controls of the idea of authorship enough to make immediacy and openness possible for the new occult couple. The script makes meaning not only by words, but by an extra-literary phenomenon like typing. GY's body acts as a keyboard, which her husband touches, and which then generates the written script without his hand holding the pen. As we might expect, the script registers an unusually high level of frustration and uncertainty when the question arises as to just what the relation is between the medium's conscious mind within her automatism. On 10 January 1918, the guides Leaf and

Fish, trying to explain the distinctions between 'subliminal' and 'conscious', made several attempts to make the methodological issue clear. At one point they affirm that 'memory' creates 'a grammar', a structure outside meaning, like Julia's alphabet. Then they suggest that 'often we leave medium to write answers quite independently of us from conscious mind or subliminal—no medium can tell difference—we only do it when message can be correctly [received] without us but there are hundreds of cases'. To WBY's anger at a phenomenon that seemed neither clearly willed nor not willed ('You understand process no better than we do!'), the guides try again to answer—'You wont admit subliminal but you will have to before the philosophy is through'—and then seem to give up. Seeming to forget for the moment that they were two rather than one writerly voice, or perhaps silent while GY speaks in her own willed voice, they—or she—announces, 'I am upset by this stupid subject—wait a few minutes' (*YVP*i. 238).

It took WBY some time to work out the extent to which just this interaction is the point. The generation of truth occurs when experience, the grammar or automatism of pre-existent pattern, is awakened by creativity. '*All spirit communication all illumination ecstasy vision etc*' results from an intrasubjective split, when, in one way of describing the process, 'the excarnate part of the soul is conscious of the automatism of the incarnate portion'. The dialogic form of the script, the drama of questions provoking answers provoking further questions, symbolizes this generated truth. In a series of sessions in early September 1918, Thomas explains the equation another way: the 'momentum that drives the automatic faculty'—that is, the apparatus through which human beings can discover pre-existent reality—comes from 'the action of the pf [Persona of Fate] on the creative genius'—in other words, the pressure of the inexorable world on the human will. Thomas continues, 'The greater the strength of the pf the more does the automatic faculty take possession of the cg [Creative Genius].' However, genius is by no means to be overtaken by fate: 'The cg should use the auto[matic] faculty and not be used by it.' If creativity is brought to bear, and 'another faculty' called 'unity of being' is present, then what results, GY wrote, is 'Blake'. 'We get the conscious visionary?' WBY asked. Apparently so. Things arrive that both pre-exist (in the world and in the psyches of those who write and read, who ask and answer) and are at the same time being created by the couple saying, in their 'unity of being', what they mean.

The result is described in language that sounds like a happy marriage between a man with a complex sense of destiny and a woman who did not look initially like his fated lover: 'the freeing from fate which is destiny is the controlling of the automatic faculty which is done by will of heart', i.e., 'freeing from passion by the choice of emotion' (*YVP*ii. 40–7; see also *YVP*iii. 242). This result also sounds like the poetry of the late WBY, in which the pressures of reality, including the pressures of consciously limited language, exert considerable force against the poet's creative and emotive counter-pressure. The poet exerts himself, the maker of meaning and chooser of emotion, in the face of the resistant chaos which is also represented in the poetry. The resultant performativity is typical: as David Lloyd notes about the poem 'Byzantium', 'it is scarcely accidental if what are from every perspective the obscurest lines of the poem seem to evoke, as if in response to their very obscurity, a set of performative speech acts which are exceptionally common in the later Yeats'.[57]

To engage deeply in mediumship, then, is to perform various uncertainties about the willed self, the male and female dynamics of co-authorship, the creations (conscious or not) of the human brain, and a reality external of them. No wonder, then, that spiritualism and new media technologies seemed drawn to each other like magnets to iron: they enact various ontological as well as epistemological difficulties of their time with great precision. Recorded voices change perception of the real, whether or not they store sounds from people who are actually dead; spirit photographs are only slightly more troubling than any other photographs to belief in a material world

---

[57] Lloyd, *Anomalous States*, 64.

with an unmediated relationship to the human eye.[58] Likewise, automatic writing complicates notions of how connected writers are to the words they produce, just as typewriters do. As the Yeatses discovered, the apparatuses of automatic writing do not so much separate the human agent from the written product as they work at cross-purposes to another system, uncovering its fictions. Human beings may always be separate from the words they speak, generated by 'automatic faculty' out of pre-existing social and psychic splits. A paradigm of unalienated writing and thought, authoritative rhetoric, and the production of meaning that uses technologies of communication without being changed by them, is one way of imagining language. Another way leads to what William Covino has called 'dialogic magic' in his study of the relationship between rhetoric and magic. 'Dialogic magic' is an engagement with forces beyond human control that puts events into motion without regulating the outcome. This sort of magic is dangerous (and is one reason for ritual magicians' disapproval of spiritualism), since it operates 'outside any regulative text that would arrest the principles of proliferation that language enacts'.[59] It is language not so much in its role as a fixed entity, on a page but not displaying the page. Rather, it is language

---

[58] In an unusual passage, WBY engages with a conception of the visual that parallels advances in photographic technologies as well as theories of the subconscious in its meditation on the reach of the human eye. The typescript of 'The Discoveries of Michael Robartes', an early draft of what would become *A Vision*, contains a 'note' ostensibly composed by 'J. Ahearne' to explain a passage in the manuscript he is editing:

It is one of the doctrines of Kusta ben Luka that the retina of the eye has an incalculable range and that it is limited by our expectations alone. He explained many miraculous phenomena in this way and ROBARTES when he quoted his opinions accustomed to deduce a like range for hearing and for touch. The body is sensitive to all things that exist but can only report to the consciousness what the mind will accept or so at least I understand him. (*YVP*iv. 38)

This topic was apparently discussed in the script and may derive from GY; it is summarized by her in a notebook entry that makes clear the psychological dimension in supernormal exploration: 'Physical retina far more sensitive than we know, using actual light can see through a stone wall but is not recorded by *conscious* memory. Spirits see what is recorded in unconscious memory' (*YVP*iii. 155).

[59] Covino, *Magic, Rhetoric, and Literacy*, 46. In ch. 4, Covino categorizes WBY as a magician of the authoritative variety, a point of view that is valid only to the degree that the *Vision* experiments are not taken into account.

as an event, expressing interaction with other voices and exceeding its frame. It makes mouthpieces or keyboards of the living, and it speaks the words of the dead.

At one point in her 1919 book *The Truth of Spiritualism*, the spiritualist author 'Rita' [Mrs Desmond Humphreys] complains about sceptics who want to get rid of the technical apparatuses used by mediums in their work, 'darkness, a circle, a table, a cabinet', and so forth, and then see whether the spirits still come. These are 'the sort of people', she protests, 'who would demand a photograph's development without chemicals or a darkened room! Who had declared that to run a tramway by electricity or harness the waves of the air to a machine that should deliver and accept messages were schemes fit for madmen.'[60] The problem to which Mrs Humphreys points is more intellectually defensible than might appear: the performance of mediumship is essential to mediumship, just as chemistry or physics are necessary to the new technologies she mentions. The performative quality of the script is not only how it goes about its business: it creates the effects it describes. Polymorphous sexual desire and discourse beyond death, as well as a human self that operates automatically, beyond reach of the conscious will, not only find expression in, but also, crucially, are after-effects of the nightly ritualized, automatic writing. The 'dramatic machinery' of the performance, the woman at the table writing automatically, the man asking her questions, and the personal and intellectual events that they orchestrate in order to allow the words to come, also make something, which does not exist until the experimenters are again and again shown the way toward it. They do not arrive: there is no closure in these textual traces or the events that produced them. Rather, this is ritual, that old way which human beings have of approaching that which is inevitable though not conceptualizable, a way of effecting change without ordinary self-determining action. The Yeatses summoned powerful ghosts and allowed them to speak, hearing their voices mingle with their own.

[60] [Humphreys], *Truth of Spiritualism*, 29.

3

'To give you new images': Published Results

All last night the darkness was full of writing, now on stone, now on paper, now on parchment, but I could not read it. Were spirits trying to communicate? I prayed a great deal and believe I am doing right.

WBY to Lady Gregory, announcing his intention to propose to GHL, 19 September 1917 (*L* 633)

GY affected the texts that bear her husband's name profoundly and variously. The pages that follow examine some of the professional literary results of the collaboration—that is to say, effects of the script and other documents that appear in WBY's published works. Even so, the emphasis will not fall exclusively on specific words or ideas in poems, plays, and prose that belong to GY and can be separated distinctly from the parts written by her husband. Such an approach tends to separate the two co-writers into neater subjective categories than I am inclined to believe represents them accurately.[1] GY's authorship is not neatly divisible into singly composed texts

---

[1] Interestingly, WBY was initially eager to undertake more conventional co-authorship with GY, of the sort, for example, that he had done successfully with Lady Gregory (see Pethica, 'Our Kathleen'). After the first few months of script, he turned on 4 Jan. 1918 to the question of literary collaboration. It would be possible with several phasal combinations, he was told (notably 17, his own, and 12 or 24, those of Ezra Pound or Lady Gregory), but he could not work with GY: 'you and medium could not do practical work together'. 'How would shoe pinch if we tried practical work?' he asked. 'Different natures' was the reply; 'neither would adapt to the other'. He pressed: 'Could we not

or fragments of texts: the communicators get in the way, as do daimons (however these entities are construed), as does the dialogic method, as does the fact that the written documents do not represent the whole praxis, and so on. Not only did she influence WBY, of course, but her husband's work also had great impact on hers. *A Vision* itself relies on *Per Amica*, to take the most obvious example of the general observation that the matter of the script shows great familiarity with and use of WBY's pre-system texts; but it also echoes preoccupations like the masks and erotic ghosts of *The Player Queen* and *The Dreaming of the Bones*, both of which were finished in 1917 before the automatic script began.[2]

To call GY an author is to stretch the term, and to make this stretch requires that a critical approach also be extended into new territory. Not only adding words or images to her husband's *œuvre*, her work also, we might say, subtracts: it subjects WBY to undoing and rethinking. For example, *Per Amica* is exploded, its dualities multiplied as quaternities, its achievement rewritten as a promise. In biographical terms, Terence Brown suggests that for WBY 'the issue was whether or not in the therapeutic exchanges on which he had embarked with a loving, sexually vital, self-dramatizing young woman, he could release a new wave of creativity which would carry him as an artist over the shoals of middle life and the sterile rocks of encroaching old age'.[3] Such a release was possible only by means of a

---

colaborate when ever the creative power came in?' But the answer was insistent: 'Yes but *not* over practical' (*YVP* i. 197–9).

    Two weeks later, they learned that GY should not lend a hand with business at the Abbey Theatre either. WBY apparently hesitated to ask for her help and requested guidance: 'I think of asking medium to help with plays etc. If so should I postpone it?' The response was decidedly negative: 'Not good—not enough constructive ability.' Unclear about the meaning of *constructive*, he asked for clarification: 'Do you mean she cannot design costumes Etc.?' The answer was either vague or part oral: 'Not well done', it came; 'yes—yes'. The work on the system was all she should undertake: 'She cant do anything till this is done—no good trying/plenty of activity but we use it all' (*YVP*i. 273).

   [2] With reference to these influences, I am indebted to R. F. Foster for drawing my attention to the fact that proofs of *The Player Queen* would have been in the study, on the desk, or nearby, when the script began.

   [3] Brown, *Life*, 258.

reworking not only of themes and styles but of his very writerly self and what it could produce. For her part, GY made her own writerly self, as the previous chapters have suggested. She also reworked WBY the poet, that multiplex aesthetic and spiritual construct, into a different entity than had existed before, by creating and expressing it in mutual terms. This change was the task, and so it is constantly at play in the texts, from the earliest fragments of script to the most polished belletristic work generated from it.

The texts authored through and concerned with 'this form of revelation through 2 people' are different in kind, as the Yeatses were informed the revelations themselves were, from texts written by two individuals contributing distinct parts to a joint project. (GY copied this fact into a late notebook: WBY 'asked if this form of revelation through 2 people had taken place in the past & said there appeared to be no well-known instance. He [the control] said that in the past solitary revelation was still possible. . . . Solitary revelation was now almost impossible & so this method was adopted' (*YVP*iii. 40).) Thematic, verbal, and structural shifts abound, all of which also comment in some way on the new 'method'. The chapter that follows examines WBY's published texts in two categories: it begins on the level of words, themes, and images in individual works, then moves to consider one volume of poetry as a whole (*Michael Robartes and the Dancer*).

A Vision and its Literary Cousins

A Vision is of course saturated with contributions made by and through GY, the communicators, and the joint revelation. It is difficult to find a part of the book that does not bear the imprint of her automatic writing, to such a degree that it is arguable that in writing it out WBY served as secretary or medium for her work no less than she served in that capacity for him. The book's genesis began almost simultaneously with the automatic script. In the first two days of writing that the Yeatses preserved, GY (and Thomas) initiated a discussion of sun and moon, warning her distinguished bridegroom that his nature was too lunar or subjective, and should be influenced by solar or objective forces. These cosmic polarities, elaborating as they did on WBY's ideas of antinomic impulses within human beings, came to constitute the basic psychology of the book. Less than a week later, on 10 November 1917, the discussion turned to the differences between antithetical and primary, the great opposites which inform the whole system.[4] Two weeks later, GY again steered toward an idea whose germ had apparently already entered the couple's conversations. At the end of a late afternoon session on 24 November, WBY asked, 'What are the 28 stages'. Thomas, the control for the session, was perhaps reflecting GY's readiness for dinner when he replied, 'I will give their meanings later' (*YVP*i. 115). True to his word, Thomas returned at 8.30 that evening to tackle this centrally important concept.

---

[4] This day's interchange features questions from (and initialled by) GY, as well as answers through her hand, as if it were important to her to give greater direction than would become usual as the experiments went on. The remarkable session takes up other major topics such as the memories of ideal lovers in the Anima Mundi, 'as a photograph . . . a long living series of images of their love and dreaming' (*YVP*i. 73), the fool, or the action of the daimon, as well as people who become representational figures in *A Vision*, such as Walter Savage Landor and Iseult Gonne. A sample of the script will illustrate:

1. Is not the antithetical self (when the Primary is the stronger) sometimes a temptation? Is not the converse of this true? GY

2. In the dream life after death does not the primary self produce itself in memory dreams? Are not these dreams the more lasting, the more the event was permeated by the antithetical self? Ideal lovers, Paris Helen, might dream of one another for centuries. Does not the disappearance of memory-dreams mean the absorption of the Primary in the Antithetical & final end of motion? GY

The antithetical self is necessarily always the temptation because it offers a contrast to the primary If the primary had no contrast to look upon there would be consequent absorption in a morality outside itself which would be accepted as a thing against which there could be no conflict—in the case where either the primary or *antithetic* is almost predominant it produces the idiot or the fool as distinct from lunacy

Genius is implied in the conflict for domination—where the antithetical is *much stronger* but not predominant it has the practical force of the primary self to control it—it is when the primary becomes submerged that lunacy ensues—And learn this

The fool is born so—the predominant self submerges him from birth—nothing changes that

The lunatic is gradually predominated by *one or the other* & therefore *may be cured*

The fool is predominated by the *antithetical* or dream self from birth—the lunatic may be predominated *by either* (*YVP* i. 69–70)

A circular diagram on which GY appears to have begun to draw the four cardinal directions and the diagonal lines indicating the locations Head, Heart, Loins, and Fall (Blakean terms used in *A Vision* which first entered the discussion two days earlier, the fourth term supplied by her[5]) is interrupted by the instructions 'No—draw circle for me into 28' (*YVP*i. 115). The numbers appear over the sketched lines of the circle, and the sheets that follow list the descriptions of the Ego (later called Will) for each of the phases of the moon.[6] This list appeared with few changes in the 'Table of the Four Faculties' of *A Vision* (*AVA* 30–3). In the next few months, GY's hand drew up lists of qualities for Good and Bad Mask (later called True and False Mask) of each phase, as well as descriptions of Evil and Creative Genius (changed to True and False Creative Mind) and Persona of Fate, all of which are also reproduced in the table without much alteration.[7]

---

[5] WBY brought the first three terms into the discussion on 22 Nov., asking Thomas 'Do you know Blake terms Head, Heart Loins'. GY wrote 'Yes—but thus—' and a fuller answer with explanations and two diagrams, one of which dissects a circle into quarters labelling the sectors Head, Heart, Loins, and Fall, the new fourth term. She then wrote in answer to an unrecorded question, 'No–but if I can get it from yourselves I may be able to—'. WBY's next question, predictably, was, 'What do you mean by fall', to which she wrote, 'The beginning of anger and the departure from wisdom' (*YVP*i. 103). WBY had fretted with the triad of terms earlier in his and Edwin Ellis's edition of Blake, adding to complete a tetrad first *Womb* (i. 262) and later doubling the term *Loins*. He explained there that the Loins'

region is double and implies both water and earth—both procreation and excretion, both vegetation and death. In Blake, however, the symbol of loins is divided into desire and fruition in the world of mortality. . . . The sequence Head Heart Loins deserves to be noted as every triad has appropriate relations with it and with its connection with the Zoas. Creation, Redemption, Judgement is the great triad; but even here the last member is double. (William Blake, *The Works of William Blake*, ed. William Butler Yeats and Edwin Ellis, 3 vols. (London: Bernard Quaritch, 1893), i. 347)

WBY was uncomfortable with sets not easily divisible into four here and in *A Vision*. See, e.g., his note to the table entitled 'General Character of Creative Mind affecting Certain Phases': 'This and the following Table are divided into ten divisions because they were given me in this form, and I have not sufficient confidence in my knowledge to turn them into the more convenient twelve-fold divisions' (*AVA* 34 n.).

[6] This list is reiterated in the records from 24 Oct. 1919 (*YVP*ii. 463).

[7] The lists for Mask and Evil Genius were received on 3 Jan. 1918 through Fish (*YVP*i. 192). On 26 Jan. Thomas gave a number of descriptions of 'PF' (Persona of Fate) amid numerous questions about the ideas upon which the Faculties are based (*YVP*i. 289). The complete list for Persona of Fate (as well as Creative Genius) was

Many, if not most, of the historical personalities, literary figures, or members of WBY's circle that serve as examples of each phase, which seem when they occur in *A Vision* strikingly illustrative of WBY's opinions about their personalities, style, or thought, were also placed by GY's hand. Her husband for the most part chose *who* would be included, and she put down *where* such figures as Whitman (6), Nietzsche (12), Blake (16), Shakespeare (20), Dostoyevsky (22), Synge (23), AE (25), Luther (25), and Socrates (27) should appear. Almost all of these examples were male, as might be expected of a list of famous persons in Western history and culture; other than immediate friends, there are few women. WBY was not solely responsible for this state of affairs: he was given a vague answer when he asked the phase of Florence Farr Emory, and when he asked for placement of Jane Austen, he was given in reply a straight bold line, the sign throughout the script for refusal to answer, along with the words 'do not want to' (*YVP*i. 196–7). As early as January 1918, the controls were forthcoming with the important information that there is 'no human being at either' phase 1 or phase 15, although it was WBY who suggested that 'spirits at 15 [are] very beautiful' (*YVP*i. 188). However, GY's hand placed her husband at phase 17, the most auspicious phase for artists, and also put Maud Gonne at phase 16 (with Helen of Troy, though Helen was later moved[8]), answering WBY's question about 'the phase of supreme human beauty of the Helen of Troy' by affirming that it was also 16. The instructors were more than willing to place women important in WBY's life among the examples and to give the questioner detailed information about their relationships to him as well as their symbolic resonances in his creative work, from Iseult Gonne (14) and Lady Gregory (24) to GY herself (18).

Book I of the first *A Vision*, 'What the Caliph Partly Learned', which sets forth the Great Wheel, is matched in inventiveness if

given much later, begun by Ameritus on 25[?] Oct. and Dionertes on 22 Dec. 1919 (*YVP*ii. 466, 522). By this late date GY and the controls were apparently anxious to get the table organized: they merely gave lists, refusing to allow WBY to ask any potentially distracting questions during these sessions.

[8] See *YVP*i. 524 n. 77.

not polish in the second book, 'What the Caliph Refused to Learn', a rather confused and loosely organized presentation of ideas that underpin the Wheel: gyres, the Great Year, and the Four Principles, among others. The third and fourth books, 'Dove or Swan' and 'The Gates of Pluto', elaborate the system's use of gyres and history, continuing the astrological idea of the Great Year and explaining the application of the Principles and other matters concerning life after death. Many of the ideas in these books as well arrived through GY, with textual evidence that suggests her husband supporting the formation of the ideas more out of intense eagerness to receive more regularly than by directing the terms of the discussions.

For example, Christmas Day 1917 saw the arrival of a valuable gift: the image of a 'funnell' to be used 'as a symbol'.[9] The explanation following a drawing of a spiralling cone introduced the idea of 'Stability at base only', and suggested that WBY 'apply it to your own meditations'. The communicators added, 'This method is only a machinery but you can use it.' Use it he did, of course, and the circles that define lunar phases, human life, and history appear in such poems as 'The Cat and the Moon', 'The Second Coming', 'The Hero, the Girl, and the Fool', and 'His Bargain' from *Words for Music Perhaps*, 'There' from 'Supernatural Songs', 'The Gyres', and 'Under Ben Bulben'. Elements that turn and change as they do, gyre-like, or history reckoned as cycles, are also present in such plays as *The Cat and the Moon, Calvary*, with its final image as soldiers 'Join hand to hand and wheel about the cross' in a dance (*VPl* 787), in the conjunction of time, death, sexuality, and dance in *The King of the Great Clock Tower*, and in the repetitive structure of *Purgatory*. In the workshop of the automatic sessions, the Yeatses worked at length on the meaning of the symbol they variously called *funnel, spindle, coil, watch spring, hour-glass, spiral, shuttle, cone*, or

[9] The term *funnel* was first mentioned on 25 Nov., apparently in response to WBY's request for 'symbolism in this system of diurnal motion of ⊙' (his next question mentions the funnel, asking for clarification of the previous answer), but the answers to this part of that evening's session were misfiled (*YVP*i. 119, but see NLI MS 36, 253/2). Luckily the idea was taken up again a month later.

finally *gyre*.[10] GY also supplied the image of two moving circles, one inside the other, representing the relation between individual personality and human civilization, in a diagram given at Stone Cottage in Ashdown Forest during the amazingly productive first month of script (25 Nov. 1917, *YVP*i. 116–20). This image, which WBY was told was also symbolic of the relationship between primary and antithetical (since 'all signs have 2 meanings', another principle of the script that resonates through *A Vision* and much of WBY's late work (*YVP*i. 117)), underlies the premiss basic to *A Vision* that the same principles regulate each human being and collective humankind.

Actually, it was some four months after the concept of the funnel first entered the dialogue that the couple shifted from considering the symbol in relation to the individual soul to the far more fruitful subject of the gyre and the movements of civilization. It is worth noting that the former topic, which appears relatively infrequently in *A Vision*, contributes to retrospective poems such as 'The Circus Animals' Desertion', with its image of the poet's remembered life as a climb through thesis and 'counter-truth' to find the base of the ladder it climbed at the end (*VP* 629–30) as well as meditations on remorse and destiny in settings like *The Words upon the Window-Pane* or *Purgatory*. The latter topic was broached at the beginning of one of the first sessions in the west of Ireland, to which the Yeatses travelled during the first spring of their marriage. In obedience to an instruction a few days earlier to 'do funnell' (*YVP*i. 415), WBY asked the question that opened up the first major theme to emerge at Coole: 'Can one apply funnel to human history' (8 Apr. 1918, *YVP*i. 420). The control's positive reply, which may have been anticipated by both partners, set off

---

[10] It is tempting to multiply possible sources for this symbol, from GY's knowledge of vorticism to such occult locations as Eliphas Levi, as quoted in a typescript compiled by Christina Mary Stoddart in 1922 for the use of members of the Hermetic Order of the Golden Dawn. It is Levi who mentions 'the necessity of the hour-glass symbol in the translation of Power from one plane to another as laid forth in the 'Convoluted Revolution of the Forces' (photocopy from the papers of George Mills Harper).

months of investigation which provide the theme and many of the details of 'Dove or Swan'.

GY wrote page after page with notations of tentative dates for the twenty-eight phases, diagrams of diamonds and hour-glasses, and discussions, as the complicated theory of history emerged. Incidentally, since not every detail could be given in the relatively cumbersome automatic method, spiritual collaboration at times needed to be bolstered by more common methods of joint composition. For example, the control for 18 February found it difficult to get the 'current clear' for a discussion of dates, noting that 'This is much more difficult because facts' and that 'you will have to work it out in detail by yourselves because it would be too much necessary work for script' (*YVP*i. 355–6). Gradually, the material was well enough sorted so that in late 1920 a new communicator named Carmichael could come during a sleep and give 'confirmation of classification of devisions of historical cone being devided among phases' (*YVP*iii. 60). WBY wrote in the notebook they were keeping of sleeps and meditations that Carmichael came 'last night . . . and gave following for history cone'—the 'following' being an almost complete draft of the diagram entitled 'The Historical Cones' which introduces and explains 'Dove or Swan' (*YVP*iii. 61; *AVA* 178).[11]

In the 1937 edition of *A Vision* WBY apologizes, 'I knew nothing of the *Four Principles* when I wrote the last Book: a script had been lost through frustration, or through my own carelessness' (*AV B* 187). Indeed, several pages of script having to do with Principles are missing, torn or cut out of the notebooks in which the sessions were recorded. Carelessness is thus not the most likely reason for their disappearance. I suspect frustration, very possibly not of the sort that WBY meant (attributing damage to frustrators) when he introduced the topic into his philosophical account two decades after the intense years of the script. The frustration was doubtless the 'interpreter's': the Principles originally appeared as complex analogues of her husband, Maud Gonne MacBride, Iseult Gonne, and herself, and

---

[11] See Ch. 4 for discussion of Carmichael.

much that was revealed about them was intensely personal. GY had an amazing generosity toward her husband's obsession with his complicated emotional past, recognizing well the intricacies of the connections for him between sexual desire and the artistic creativity she was committed to vivifying, but apparently some of these revelations were insupportable even though they were abstracted into cosmic proportions and furthermore recorded on pages clearly meant for no eyes but hers and his. The frustration is now ours as well, for the early documents involving the Principles contain some of the most arresting material of the automatic experiments.[12]

Three of the four Principles were first mentioned by GY on 31 January 1918, in the course of a discussion of the soul after death. In response to a question about visions of loved ones seen after death, it had been established that a spirit just separated from the body sees 'friends kindred spirits guides' immediately after the moment of death but is then left alone 'to meditate'. 'What is it set to meditate on?', asked WBY. The next several questions show him hearing for the first time of three of what would become the four Principles (and incidentally are a good example of the dialogue when it worked smoothly, question leading to answer leading to question, and so on). The soul meditates, GY wrote, 'on the dissolution of the passionate body'. 'You mean not the phisical body', he asked. No, 'The passionate body'. The next logical question was 'How many bodies are there?', and the answer propelled them into the new topic: '3—physical passionate spiritual'. Later in the evening the fourth term, Celestial Body, arose in response to a request for 'a diagram of their bodies & their degrees or planes' (*YVP*i. 312–17). With two minor alterations—the term *Husk* replacing *Physical Body* and *Spirit*

---

[12] Despite the difficulties attending the analogies between the Principles and women important in her husband's life, several of the early sleeps suggest that the Principles had a continuing poignant attraction to GY, particularly because they enable the untying of psychological 'knots' and the healing of losses in the spiritual space between lives. In the first of these sleeps, WBY recorded that she spoke while asleep of a dream in which the Principles appeared in the form of 'sleepers as if floating in air', changing into forms that distinguished them from each other, and performing their function of 'recovery' in order to 'make the next incarnation better' (*YVP* iii. 9).

replacing *Spiritual Body*— the Principles were now in place. In the next three important days many concepts that inform 'The Gates of Pluto', such as the Vision of the Blood Kindred, Dreaming Back, and the function of burial ritual to the spirit—were introduced and explored.

Notes in WBY's hand on a separate page relate the four Principles to the four elements, earth, water, air, and fire (*YVP*i. 535 n. 11), thus connecting the Principles with the tetradic relationship among WBY, Maud Gonne MacBride, Iseult Gonne, and GY which the script had elucidated in connection with *The Only Jealousy of Emer*, begun some days after the marriage and completed a scant two weeks before this session at the end of January 1918.[13] He asked that night several questions about the Passionate Body of GY and Maud Gonne, and for the next two days the Yeatses continued to explore, in addition to the universal meaning of the Principles and life after death, the symbolic identification at the heart of the play, in which GY, her husband, and two other women act out their parts as archetypes of wife/heroine, man/hero, fated love as perfected idea, and young mistress as erotic desire. In terms of Principles, GY is positioned as Celestial Body, WBY as Physical Body, Iseult Gonne as Passionate Body, and Maud Gonne MacBride as Spiritual Body. Celestial Body, the last Principle, is located on the highest plane of the four, as Emer, and not the hero Cuchulain, is the true hero of the play. The action turns on her terrible choice to save Cuchulain from death and eternal possession by the woman of the Sidhe in a shadow life beyond death, by renouncing his love

[13] WBY had apparently begun to think about the play as early as the spring of 1916 (Saddlemyer, *Becoming George*, 83). Its composition had begun by 3 Nov. 1917, or so WBY told Lady Gregory, although some time elapsed before he actually began to write (see *MYV*i. 6, 25). It was finished by 14 Jan. 1918, when he wrote to Lady Gregory that 'To-day I finished my new Cuchulain play' (*L* 645). On the autobiographical elements of the play see Herbert J. Levine, *Yeats's Daimonic Renewal* (Ann Arbor: UMI Research Press, 1983), 97–100. For two studies that emphasize the system at work in the play, see Vendler, *Yeats's Vision and the Later Plays*, and Janis Tedesco Haswell, *Pressed Against Divinity: W. B. Yeats's Feminine Masks* (DeKalb, Ill.: Northern Illinois University Press, 1997).

forever.[14] The lonely path of power wielded on another's behalf, which frees the other into a destiny beyond relationship, is the source of 'woman's beauty', according to the poem that opens the play:

> What death? what discipline?
> What bonds no man could unbind,
> Being imagined within
> The labyrinth of the mind,
> What pursuing or fleeing,
> What wounds, what bloody press,
> Dragged into being
> This loveliness?
>
> (*VPl* 531)

One of the most striking clusters of sessions among the whole body of papers is in essence a blend of genesis, critique, and personal application of *The Only Jealousy of Emer*, in which playwright, interpreter, characters, and spirits all participate in an unfolding of expression and meaning.[15] In the first weeks of automatic script, WBY had asked whether there was 'symbolism not apparent to me in my Cuchulain plays'. Yes, and it was discoverable through his new wife's help, he was told: 'There is a symbolism of the growth of the soul—If you take certain symbols & use them on the medium['s] prevision you may get information I can not give you' (*YVP*i. 91). This symbolism was developed over the course of several sittings in two very long days in January 1918, as elaborate schemes of symbolic meaning were developed for the four principal characters, who were identified by phase, element, planet, astrological sign, cardinal direction, and part of the human body,

---

[14] Not every critic has seen the emphasis on Emer that I find in the play. In her influential early study, Vendler, e.g., reads Fand as Muse: 'Fand has the poetry, and consequently the victory'. Emer, Vendler suggests, is 'touching but superfluous' (*Yeats's Vision and the Later Plays*, 236).

[15] A tantalizing reference to an invocation suggests that the Yeatses contacted the archetypal characters directly as the play developed; see *MYV*i. 27.

among other correspondences.[16] Personal struggles were clothed in conversations on such topics as the withered arm of Bricriu, the Kiss of Death, and the intense 'contact' between Fand and Cuchulain.

The emotional intensity of the play's themes of love and renunciation, in a world in which destiny and choice are embroiled in each other, is clearly derived from these dialogues, as even a short sample makes clear: 'After contact how will C be different?', WBY asked, wondering about a connection with dangerous implications for his marriage, though the risk of allowing 'contact' in order to retain a larger mystery seems to be one which the author of the script was willing to take. 'Man loses desire & seeks love', he was told, though not the love of the woman of the Sidhe, who is 'at peace so he can no longer love her'. 'Who will C love?', he posed several questions earlier. 'I cannot tell you till you know yourself,' GY wrote, 'and you do know I think but perhaps unconsciously.' His next question, 'Emer?', was not dignified with a reply, merely a straight line. 'Perhaps unconsciously' both WBY and GY did know that their relationship, with the risks of such textual and symbolic encounters as *The Only Jealousy of Emer*, was enlivening both of their imaginative lives. 'Is my play a true dream?', WBY asked, summing up. 'Perfectly true' was the reply. Could he add to it? 'Can C get contact after his renunciation of Sidhe & Emers renunciation of hope?' No, he was told: end it there: 'Your present play is complete—the new one is not yet formed' (*YVP*i. 219–20). Complete though it may have been, WBY did not understand its implications fully, I suppose, since several days later, in the mirror writing that signals intensity on a personal level, WBY's question about the meaning of the term 'contact' prompted a forceful piece of advice: 'Cuchulain refuses contact—do you not realise yourself in that refusal—Cuchulain if he had not refused would have wandered in a false world all his days' (*YVP* i. 253).

---

[16] See *MYV*i. 25–8, 42–57, 76–89, 117–19, 122–8, and 147–53, as well as scattered references throughout both volumes of *MYV* for accounts of the more important discussions of *The Only Jealousy*.

It is tempting to read this exchange as prophetic: the automatic script informs WBY that GY understands the 'true dream', which is that she will risk everything, even her expectation of domestic stability, in order to save her husband from the sterile desire for absolute beauty, a desire that is imaged in his imagination always as Maud Gonne. Like all heroes, Emer chooses fame, but the fame she chooses is not her own, and it is attained by returning her husband to the impure world of passion. *The Only Jealousy of Emer* is unusual among WBY's dramatic works in focusing on a female character without the power to allure men, and on the agonizing choice she faces because she does not have such power. When Emer makes her decision, sacrificing her dreams of a peaceful married life in order to rescue Cuchulain from the living death that would be caused by 'contact' with a woman of the Sidhe, she is as trapped as Sophocles' Oedipus, unable either to kill himself and meet his father in the underworld or remain alive and see his wife and mother here. The gods have laid a perfect trap: Cuchulain will awaken from the trance of desire for perfection into passion for his young mistress, not love for his courageous wife.

Watching the play, the audience may hope beyond the end of the play for consolation for Emer, as Sophocles provided for Oedipus. Interestingly, WBY places a poem about the wisdom found by Oedipus, in the translation 'Colonus' Praise', immediately after the final stanza of 'Among School Children' in the volume *The Tower*, so that the latter poem seems to answer the former's famous question about what lasts through time, what constitutes the 'blossoming' of labour, and whether we can separate art from artist, dancer from dance. Oedipus reappears in *The Tower* in the lyric 'From "Oedipus at Colonus"', with its final stanza counselling 'gay' bravery in the face of tragedy. This poem immediately precedes 'The Gift of Harun Al-Rashid', the transparently fictionalized story of the automatic script, transplanted from *A Vision* for reuse in the 1928 volume.

However, *Emer* ends with bitter irony as Eithne Inguba exults over her seeming power to raise Cuchulain from his death-sleep. The price of wisdom is loss. The dominant effect of the play is tragedy, but it is tragedy of a mysterious and curiously modern kind. Its shape-changing plot, its image-laden poetry, and its self-conscious artificiality as staged event all speak of its occult status. It is a play replaying an intrinsically dramatic and unstable blend of fact and fabrication, of the immediate world and something radically outside it. Thus, the play seems to foretell the Yeatses' future and to underscore GY's acute contemporary awareness of the man she married, as well as her own needs, but it also implies that both the future and the present are volitional conditions. To watch the play today is to feel its uncanny, seance-like force; we seem to witness a purgatorial repetition, reminiscent of *Purgatory* and *The Words upon the Window-Pane*, of a willed action with the deepest resonances in the life of the couple who generated the play. *Emer* thus suggests both tragedy and autobiography. We face with Emer and, behind her, GY a moment of choice that can free the creative abilities that make possible the play we are watching as well as the playwright and poet WBY's astonishingly productive body of late work. GY supports WBY in writing a play about semi-autobiographical characters, one who renounces hope in order to recover for another the ability to experience the 'Intricacies of blind remorse' (*VPL 555*) that will drive him to create as well as drive him from her bed for ever. *The Only Jealousy of Emer* is an autobiographical tragedy of art.

The Principles are in the background of another of WBY's poems in which the collaborative enterprise is most evident, 'An Image from a Past Life' (*VP* 389–90). This poem not only elaborates system-related themes, but also represents a shift in Yeatsian subjectivity, relevant in the contexts of other poems and, indeed, volumes. It will reappear as part of the latter topic later in this chapter, when it will be important to recall the intricate investigations of personal (extended into multigenerational) lives that dominated its genesis. Indeed, the subtleties, and also perhaps the high level of emotional involvement, of its themes required two distinct phases of script for full development. The first phase began on the evening of 1 February 1918. WBY reopened a discussion where it had left off the night before when he was told that he was correct in assuming that the medium

was 'controlled by an old PB' (*YVP*i. 327)—after which revelation
the control immediately shifted topic, talking around the subject for
some time with warnings about how long this subject would take to
complete, how to engage with another medium, and what to avoid
saying to her.[17] The first question the next evening, when the couple
sat down just before 6.00, suggests that the Yeatses were concerned
by the thought that an old PB controlled GY: 'What do you mean
by controlled', WBY asked, 'when PB continues into another life?'
The writing hand requested that they 'wait for ten minutes please',
then elaborated on the restriction of 'free will and choice', the PB
'forcing the ego into a repetition of its former circumstances –this
continues till death of old pb'. WBY asked 'how . . . the ego' could best
'remedy this' situation, with its fatalistic implications, and was told
that 'It can do nothing except work for the balance of the other three
[Principles]'. In the medium, he was then told, the Principles were
not balanced: 'the medium is not passionate in your sense because
the old pb forces it back.'[18] That this discussion was occurring on
several discernible planes and had deep personal implications is clear
from one of the next questions: 'Why [are] you trying to impress
upon me some contrast between Medium and M G [Maud Gonne]'
(*YVP* i. 329).[19]

The 'ego' whose actions WBY wondered about is at once the Self
of GY, which needed to balance her other three Principles to escape
domination by an old Passionate Body, and also WBY, in that ego,
another term for the Physical Body or Husk, is WBY's Principle
in the tetradic terms of *The Only Jealousy*. Similarly, the PB was
simultaneously her own from another life and also Maud Gonne.

---

[17] It is not known who this 'high medium' was; see Saddlemyer, *Becoming George*,
151 and 705 n. 95.

[18] GY obviously considered this information important: she quoted the last answer
verbatim in a notebook, substituting *G. Y.* for *medium* (*YVP*iii. 158).

[19] The answer to this question is intriguing: 'Yes', WBY was told, 'but we did not
succeed—MG is in a second journey through her phase.' His next question, 'Had that
[the 'contact' between MG and medium] to do with her second journey?', was answered,
'Yes but I wanted more than you got I think'. At this point he seems to have realized
he was in dangerous territory, suggesting 'I wont go on with that unless you wish to
comment'. Straight lines confirmed his suspicion.

It was vital that each partner separately, and both in relation to the other, avoid emotional repetition, even though, as WBY wrote in 'Under Saturn', the poem that follows 'An Image from a Past Life' in the volume *Michael Robartes and the Dancer*, comparison was inevitable: the older man's 'lost love' was 'inseparable from my thought/Because I have no other youth' (*VP* 390–1). It was not clear when or how this situation of imbalance might be remedied: 'Will old PB of medium die, & if so when or how?', WBY asked two nights later. The control's answer, 'It concerns medium in a way that makes it unfair of me to talk of the subject', suggests confusion in the issue itself, but also a sort of spiritual courtesy: one shouldn't talk about the medium in words she is writing, since she might be reading along. The life-altering issue of how to address the trouble for a couple created by passion overshadowed, the confusion of gender role, as well as jealousy when a woman feels the desire her lover felt for a past sweetheart, and the suggestion that it is she and not he who is doomed to repeat 'former circumstances', all contribute to 'An Image from a Past Life'.[20]

The next formative phase of the script for the poem occurred some eighteen months later, in a highly personal series of sessions presided over by Ameritus, the 'interpreters daimon' (*YVP*ii. 300). A tangled mesh of emotions, ideas, and connections between significant people through various incarnations explained why the poet and the interpreter were who they were, acted as they did, had their particular Moments of Crisis, and found themselves in relationship with certain key figures in their lives.[21] Chapter 5 will return to this period of script in order to discuss how the Yeatses' relationship was extended

---

[20] The poem registers palpable frustration on the part of the male character at the hint of a former life felt by his lover but unavailable to him. The mood is parallel in this session, when WBY is told that he has not been through his phase before, and so would not have old passions to untie, but that both Maud Gonne and GY have such overshadowings. On the Yeatsian tendency to form emotional triangles between himself and two women, see Harwood, *Olivia Shakespeare and W. B. Yeats*, esp. ch. 8.

[21] Moments of Crisis are discussed throughout the *Vision* materials, though they do not have much to do in the published books. They are of four types, abbreviated IM (Initiatory Moment), CM (Critical Moment), OM (never explained in the documents), and BV (Beatific Vision). See Barbara J. Frieling, 'The 'Moments of Crisis' in Yeats's

into previous and future incarnations, a context that also underlies the emotional fabric of the poem. Here, however, it is enough to note that the script of the summer of 1919 made 'An Image' possible. The Yeatses had moved to the mostly renovated Ballylee, which had been identified for them at a cluster of sessions there the previous autumn as a feminized symbol associated with GY, not the masculinized 'Ballyphallus or whatever he calls it' that Pound along with most other readers of WBY have regularly assumed.[22] On 28 October 1918 WBY was instructed in mirror writing to 'make a protective symbol round medium now—a sheltering symbol' of their square castle, and that 'the tower is for the medium alone—not for you—it is a symbol of the human arm & the human heart' (*YVP*ii. 101–2). After the Yeatses moved into the tower in June 1919, Thomas changed his 'sign' to a new one containing the astrological symbol for Venus at its base. In the same session, GY began a new practice of writing down both questions and answers, a method that put firmly to rest any notion that the interpreter was in an involuntary or semi-conscious state: she was, I reckon, thoroughly comfortable at this point in the experiments with switching into a receptive mode and back out again.

'An Image from a Past Life' is set by a 'dark stream' of a river that suits the faintly sexualized unease of the two partners in the poem. His opening remark, 'Never until this night have I been stirred', and her comment that her heart is 'smitten through' (the key word *smitten* occurring twice in the single stanza), prepares well for the suggestion of sacrifice and remorse in 'that scream' he hears. The prominent themes of the discussions of the summer of 1919, before the poem was composed in the autumn, fan out into a swirl of related ideas, all of which feed the poem.[23]

Vision Papers', in *YAACTS* x. 281–95; *MYV*ii. 228–46 and *passim*. Frieling suggests that OM, the 'moment of greatest disquiet' (*YVP*iii. 349), may stand for Objective Moment.

[22] Ezra Pound, letter to John Quinn, 1 June 1920, cited in B. L. Reid, *The Man from New York: John Quinn and his Friends* (New York: Oxford University Press, 1968), 419.

[23] See Saddlemyer, *Becoming George*, 237. Saddlemyer notes that one of GY's 'vivid and revealing nightmares' was the origin of the poem.

First, the couple discussed the purgation necessary for successful movement from one life to the next, the intertwined roles of Teacher and Victim making possible the loosening of one soul's knotted ties by another (see, e.g., *YVP*ii. 344). WBY explained what he understood of these antinomies, with slightly changed terminology, in *A Vision*: 'There are two human types found at each phase and called *Victim* and *Sage*, the first predominantly emotional, the other predominantly intellectual' (*AVA* 52). The relationship between the two is critical for the reception of truth in this life, and it also functions between lives. In the 'return', when a soul prepares for its next life by re-living its former one, 'There are therefore . . . a *Waking State* and a *Sleeping State* which alternate', WBY writes, adding in a note that 'these states seem analogous to *Sage* (or teacher) and *Victim* respectively' (*AVA* 224). The alternation of roles is crucial, part of the familiar pattern with which the *Vision* documents, *A Vision*, and late WBY is shot through of oppositions in dynamic relationship with each other. The wielding of power and knowledge trade places, tip of cone to wide end of gyre, to become forfeiture and atonement (*AVA* 93), sometimes even within one figure, such as Christ, who is sacrificial lamb in one revelation and wise teacher in the next (*AVA* 148).

Intense relationships are characterized by such positionings. If the relationship is spiritual, 'There must arise in the mind of one, where the bond is between two, a need for some form of truth so intense that the *Automatic Faculty* of the other grows as it were hollow to receive that truth' (*AVA* 248). If sexual or creative, slightly different conditions apply. As WBY explains in the technical and abstract vocabulary of *A Vision*, communion between human and spirit occurs with conflict.

When the conflict is sexual and the man and woman each *Victim* for the Dead and for the *Ghostly Self*—each miracle working idol and an object of desire, they give one another a treble love, that for the dead, that for the living, that for the never living. And if those two for whom the victimage had been undertaken be born of the man and of the woman then there is created, both before and after the birth, the position known as that of the *Four Daimons*, and each of the four has been set free from fate. (*AVA* 249)

To simplify, lovers may be victims in clashes taking place in a world of which they know nothing. If so, they are playing roles that benefit others in the shadowy realm of other lives. Most eerily, these others may be reborn as the lovers' children, a situation that leads (both in *A Vision* and in the script from summer of 1919) to daimons.

Daimons, those semi-divine ghostly selves that help to explain desire, the joining of fates, and motivations for self-expression, entered discussions in the summer of 1919 in the context of what occurs in conditions of 'very onesided love'. The energy in such a situation is explainable by way of the concept of an ideal lover, standing in for and behind the living unloved one and creating a daimonic personality: 'The one who is *not* loved *nearly always* has an *ideal* lover', the Yeatses heard on 30 July, and 'from them is born 3rd Daimon' (*YVP*ii. 346).[24] This subject was not, of course, merely academic, as the next question shows: 'Was that true of me & MG'. The answer, 'Yes of both of *you*' suggests the scenario which Solomon suggests as a sad possibility for marriage in 'Solomon and the Witch' (the poem that precedes 'An Image from a Past Life' in the volume): 'Maybe the bride-bed brings despair,/For each an imagined image brings/And finds a real image there' (*VP* 388).

The ideal lover is not the same as the overshadower, the Yeatses learned. One is an image out of personal or the great memory, the other an actual remnant of a lived life: 'Ideal lover image in memory/overshadower the CB of real person' (*YVP*ii. 418).[25] As the summer progressed, it was revealed that, unlike WBY and Maud Gonne, despite the drama of their decades (and indeed, past lives[26]) of unresolved love, GY's personal history through previous lives included passionate and tragic affairs, a revelation that both

---

[24] Daimons, among them Third Daimons, are discussed in Ch. 5 below.

[25] The term 'overshadower' is reminiscent of Leo Africanus offering to 'overshadow' WBY, and thus write by means of WBY's hand and mind.

[26] At the end of August, WBY learned that he first met Maud Gonne in 1542, in 'a high walled town' where they were lovers, and that 'the one sided devotion in this life' he felt for her was caused by the fact that 'she had to come to you—You could not go to

explained her depth of personality in this life and also suggested that she could claim intensity of experience to match the image-laden histories of her husband. In early August, thanks to the interventions of Anne Hyde (who will receive more attention in Chapter 5), the Yeatses learned that in the eighteenth century GY had been in love with someone but not married to him, and also that she had hurt someone beyond bearing. The affair required at least three incarnations to purge it of its ruinous power. It was also image-ridden, and thus caused an ideal lover as well as an overshadower in a subsequent life, during which 'The man remained so much the ideal lover *that the Image was that of the first husband*'. WBY asked, 'Was the first husband a very remarkable man' and learned that he was 'A very beautiful man— *16*', the phase of great physical beauty, to which Maud Gonne belonged in this incarnation (*YVP* ii. 361).

A welter of details suggests that the Yeatses lost momentum for learning about the more impersonal aspects of the system in favour of trying to make sense of the various ways in which their lives had connected with each other's, and with those of significant others. In the midst of this period they learned that overshadowing is behind a seemingly inexplicable loss of desire in a relationship. By September WBY could ask, 'In all loves is there overshadowing' and receive this information: 'Yes *& when that is withdrawn there is always a lack of sensual desire for a time*.' An added abstract dimension to the poem may have failed to materialize at this point when the next question, 'Do the man the woman & the overshadower correspond to genius mediumship & beauty', was answered in the negative. Overshadowing is not primarily analogy; it is painful intimacy. 'Is man always victim for the being that overshadows the

her' in that incarnation. That Gonne was of lower position than he was revealed in the following exchange:

Why did her having to come to me cause our relations in this life to have this special character

The fact that she was of a different class & status & had to come in secret to you unacknowledged with no recognized position weighed on her— She hated your wife & tried to destroy her. (*YVP* ii. 404)

woman', the poet asked, in a more profitable direction, and was told, 'Yes & vice versa'. He received further confirmation of the extended query, which would feed directly into the poem, that 'the woman who overshadows [is] always a woman who once made the lover of the overshadowed happy'. The sympathy in 'An Image', which is directed toward the female speaker as distinctly as it is to her male lover, is clearly anticipated in these sessions of script, which established by early September that GY was victimized by her husband's overshadower, although that victimage was potentially redemptive in that 'The man overshadowed causes expiatory suffering to woman' (*YVP*ii. 411–17).[27]

On Sunday, 24 August 1919, near the end of the dense period of explorations of past lives, Ameritus dismissed 'more Script' and urged that WBY '*must* write poetry'. It is frustratingly unclear what questions were being answered by the list of yes's and no's that follow this injunction, but in the midst of them, Ameritus mentioned that 'I have also given you material for a Noh play' (*YVP*ii. 387). Indeed, another play in addition to *The Only Jealousy of Emer* had been explored at some length. *Calvary* (1920) entered the discussions before *The Only Jealousy* was finished, overlapping the other drama in theme no less than chronology.[28] *Calvary* is framed and interlaced with the image of a white heron that parallels the seabird imagery of the earlier play and also echoes the private symbology of 'three birds' used to refer to Iseult Gonne, Maud Gonne, and GY in the script.[29] The stated purpose of the heron, which WBY made obvious in a

---

[27] This exchange was important enough to be summarized in the card file; see *YVP* iii. 348.

[28] *Calvary* is also connected thematically with the idea of the overshadower in its preoccupation with free choice, as opposed to God's determinations; when the Yeatses were 'codifying' the script into notebooks, WBY wrote notes on the play and the concept on the same page (*YVP*iii. 191).

[29] See *MYV*i. 91, 166–8. The session in which the characters Judas and Peter (who was omitted from the play) first appear, 23 Dec. 1917, also mentions the three birds, contains a drawing of a bird given 'in answer to your thought', and has a number of moments of emotional intensity having to do with Iseult Gonne, who visited the Yeatses for a few days that Christmas holiday (*YVP*i. 173–7 and 522 nn. 38–46; *MYV*i. 92).

note to the play, concerns the primary and antithetical tinctures that were, over the months and years of the script, one of the concepts he understood best and used most frequently. The heron, which stares at its reflection in the water in a shivering dream to set the scene before the action begins, is antithetical. WBY's lengthy note to the play explains that 'Certain birds, especially as I see things, such lonely birds as the heron, hawk, eagle, and swan, are the natural symbols of subjectivity, especially when floating upon the wind alone or alighting upon some pool or river' (*VPl* 789).

Some of the structural underpinnings of the play were touched on as early as December 1917, in a suggestive session just before Christmas, containing a stream of information from Thomas not given in response to written questions (*YVP*i. 173–7). The session is jammed with tantalizingly brief bits of important information, much of it personal. Mention is made of inner and outer circles (anticipating the discussions of history on the horizon), 'Anne' (Anne Hyde, including a reference to the 'quickening' of a pregnancy, presumably hers), the phase of Thomas of Dorlowicz (18, the same as GY's), the mechanics of the process ('we do our best', Thomas remarked, 'but all is not always too easy/if things fail do not distrust us—we are not in control—not in control but of certain psychic forces'), reincarnation, the need for secrecy, the 'three birds', including the need 'to look after Iseult' and her upcoming problematic marriage. In the midst of these light brush strokes on topics that much would be made of later, the words 'objective pity & despair at 22' are written upside down, followed by notice that 'Judas *temporal*/Peter *spiritual power*' (*YVP*i. 174), the first hint of the play, although Peter would disappear from the cast.

A month or so later, WBY opened a session asking, 'My head is full of a poem will that interfere?' George Harper believes that this poem was actually *Calvary*, based on the topics for the next two days of script (*MYV*i. 165; *YVP*i. 532 n. 239). The session transcripts, which Harper summarizes (*MYV*i. 165–9), do indeed develop key issues such as the pity of Christ, which at phase 22 is 'an objective realisation of a collective despair in the christian sense' (*YVP*i. 291). Christ, it was revealed in these sessions, is primary or objective, a soul empty of itself and doing another's will to bring all people into fated salvation. Christ pities the poor in their 'primary despair' of 'sin poverty ill health' and so on, but he does not pity 'subjective despair', which is the malady of Judas. Peter is not discussed; the energy, as so often in the script, is in the bipolar opposition. Judas is at phase 8, the phase opposite 22, Christ's phase. Thus Judas serves as Christ's Creative Genius in the 'story of 22', as WBY put it, incidentally revealing that the play in his mind would be the story of Christ, difficult though it would be to create him as a main character. The CG (as the Yeatses abbreviated it) propels the action of the crucifixion, WBY learned, since he 'synthesises this pity into a single action, a *choice*'. Judas saved WBY the early difficulty of having a helplessly victimized protagonist, since as the CG he is 'personified origin of action'—in other words, 'that which gives the impulse *never* that which enriches and thinks' (*YVP*i. 291–3).

In the play's eventual dramatis personae, Christ is in triangulated opposition to the antithetical Lazarus as well as Judas, a third character brought into focus during the second period of work on the play, in the early weeks of 1919. On 24 January, GY's hand relayed approval and a suggestion about *Calvary*: after notification that 'George feels Thomas is present', she wrote, 'I like the idea of your play—*put it much later*/Why not/Starting at the end of his life'. WBY was to write on 'the Christ', not 'the Cuchulain', because the former myth was more likely to result in 'natural heroic life' at this point in his life (*YVP*ii. 189–90). Obediently, WBY set 'the Christ' in the hours before and during the crucifixion, thereby bringing the issues into stark relief and also using the system as Thomas had suggested: WBY was not 'to write on system' *per se*. Instead, 'I would like you to write something *through which* I can give you ideas', in order to keep the poet from 'the abstract' and 'a mechanical turn'. WBY wanted to know 'What kind of thing' Thomas had in mind and learned that it should be something about triangles, like 'Christ Judas lazarus—2 maries Pilate—John Paul & Peter' (*YVP*ii. 197–8).

In the finished play, triangulation rules the day: both Lazarus and Judas desire freedom from Christ's salvific pity no less than Christ desires to save them. The antithetical Lazarus yearns for the solitude and death denied him when Christ raised him from the dead, and the antithetical Judas betrays his teacher in order to escape the domination of fate. Judas's last speech also suggests that he plays the fool in believing that he could escape his fated betrayal by the particulars of the way he accomplished it (he gloats that God could not have decreed 'that I'd go with my old coat upon me/To the High Priest, and chuckle to myself/As people chuckle when alone' (*VPl* 785)). This quality echoes discussions of the fool that had been taking place on 23 and 24 January as part of instruction about the last three phases—hunchback, saint, and fool—and, more intensely, the complexities of the relationship between Teacher and Victim, roles that Christ and Judas play for each other. In turn, this discussion developed from the desire expressed by the control and guide on 22 January: 'I am really full of 22'. GY wrote and initialled a point her husband needed to consider, that 'You do not understand the moral necessity of 8 & 22'. That necessity involved faith, found by acknowledging weakness on the part of 22 and strength on the part of 8, the renunciation of personal redemption by the saint (which may lie behind Christ's final cry in the play, with its small change from the scriptural source, 'My Father, why hast Thou forsaken Me?' (*VPl* 787)), and, finally, the double event of 'Christ betrayed as victim' and 'Christ betrayed as teacher as new avatar' (*YVP*ii. 184–9).

Despite the emphasis on patterns of three in the poem (there are also three musicians, three Roman soldiers, and 'three Marys' (*VPl* 783)), the main focus remains the opposition and linkage between Judas and Christ. The actor playing Judas turns into a virtual part of the scenery when he remains on the stage to hold up Christ's cross in the last section of the play, functioning as a visual analogue to the bond between the two characters. The last group of sessions to engage the play demonstrate not only WBY's willingness to write about subjects that engaged his occult collaborator as well as himself (I suspect that the topic of Christ was in general of more interest to

GY than to WBY), but also, in the final weeks of the first pregnancy, when the relationship between the two Yeatses was about to change in ways that they had yet to understand, and the possibility of infant or maternal mortality would have been in the air, a significant interest in coupled topics of love and betrayal, pity and despair, the roles of Victim and Teacher, and fate and destiny. Like *The Only Jealousy, Calvary* expresses as its central theme an ideologically fraught choice to suffer on behalf of another, in this play not in the realm of sexual desire and love for a husband but in the arena of sacrifice to the point of death with its related issues of fate (as embodied by the soldiers) and the possibility that the gift may not be well received.

Germs for several other poems came directly from GY's hand in the script, such as the concept of complementary dreaming and the specific images that inform 'Towards Break of Day' and 'Another Song of a Fool', which Harper and Sprayberry have analysed. A drawing and notes made by GY provided the image patterns for both poems and the basic organization of 'Towards Break of Day'.[30] The short poem 'The Four Ages of Man' restates an idea from the early months of GY's part of the script with very little change, although it was written some seventeen years after Thomas and Fish told WBY that 'in every cycle—first 1/4 circle fighting body—2nd 1/4 fighting mind—3rd 1/4 fighting heart—4th 1/4 fighting soul'.[31]

[30] George Mills Harper and Sandra L. Sprayberry, 'Complementary Creation: Notes on "Another Song of a Fool" and "Towards Break of Day"', in *YAACTS* iv. 69–85. On the same evening that these poems were generated (7 Jan. 1919), GY asked about, and then received, allusions to Cormac and Cashel, along with a strong injunction that WBY '*go to the past*—a historical & spiritual past—church the *Castle on the hill*' since he was 'drained dry—the true moment for vision'. This evening's script, marked 'Personal Only', added urgency and direction to the writing of 'The Double Vision of Michael Robartes' (*YVP*ii. 162). See also Brown, *Life*, 264–5.

[31] This idea had considerable and continuing appeal to WBY. After GY recorded it, he made notes in the card file and in a notebook, repeating the neatly symmetrical formula also in 'The Four Contests of the Antithetical within Itself' in *A Vision* (*AVA* 35). He altered the order of mind and heart (identifying the second quarter with heart and the third with mind) in galley proofs of *A Vision*, and kept the new order for the poem. For further details, see *MYV* i. 173.

In addition to these directly collaborative poems, for which GY provided an early or pre-writing stage for her husband's creative process,[32] any number of other symbols or concepts, or even turns of phrase, often thought to be specifically Yeatsian are in fact not the product of his brain alone. Among these are the idea of 'hunchback ... saint ... [and] idiot' for the last three phases of the moon, used in 'The Phases of the Moon' and 'The Saint and the Hunchback' (*YVP*i. 116).[33] Another resulted after WBY was corrected when he suggested that 'anti is sad primary gay'. He was taught a lesson recalled in 'Lapis Lazuli', which centres on the conjunction of tragic and 'gay' emotions, when he learned that the two occur together in an antithetical dispensation, the tincture most proper to imaginative art: the control asserted that 'Anti must always be sad & gay' (*YVP*i. 269). A third example of a well-known passage in WBY that he did not originate concerns Keats, a poet often mentioned in the script, who famously appears in 'Ego Dominus Tuus' as a man whose 'love of the world' and 'deliberate happiness' was caused by a displacement from 'mind' into 'art':

> His art is happy, but who knows his mind?
> I see a schoolboy when I think of him,
> With face and nose pressed to a sweet-shop window,
> For certainly he sank into his grave
> His senses and his heart unsatisfied,
> And made—being poor, ailing and ignorant,
> Shut out from all the luxury of the world,
> The coarse-bred son of a livery-stable keeper—
> Luxuriant song.

> (*VP* 370)

[32] Sandra L. Sprayberry has elucidated this aspect of the script; see Barbara J. Frieling, Margaret Mills Harper, and Sandra L. Sprayberry, 'Our Lives with Yeats's Ghosts: The Writing and the Editing of the Automatic Script', in *YAACTS* xvii. 19–34.

[33] The three terms appear together in the list of 24 Nov. 1917, although they had obviously been discussed earlier. A long session two days before demonstrates that the figures for the last three phases had been discovered (*YVP*i. 102). On 24 Nov., before the list was given, WBY asked about 'the malicious hunchback' in a context suggesting that this figure had been raised in verbal discussions that do not, of course, appear in the texts (*YVP*i. 114).

This idea was adumbrated in an early session (6 December 1917), when Keats was identified with his phase (12) because of his 'sins against anti[thetical]'. WBY asked whether Keats 'sought in life what he should have found in Anti' and was confirmed: Keats's 'sin' (a term that explains the somewhat derogatory tone in the poem) was 'that he created in anti that which he did not find in life' (YVPi. 146). On 24 January the earlier poet was moved from phase 12 to 14, and his Persona of Fate was explained in GY's hand: 'He loved or sought the material good of world' (YVP i. 287). The famous Yeatsian tower not only makes its first appearances in GY's portion of the dialogue, but was also there associated specifically with her and the work of the script. According to Frieling, the tower 'became central to the Yeatses' search for the symbolic truth of the journey of the soul in the 1918 [script]', and the images associated with a round tower narrowed into specific references to Ballylee over the course of the year.[34] That spring, during a session at Glendalough, the ancient monastic community with a striking round tower, Apple relayed the information that the symbol stood for 'life—abundant flowing life', especially the Yeatses' life together as husband and wife. It was 'incomplete', 'nothing' unless they apprehended its meaning correctly: 'it is not you alone but both—by will nothing/No you must have a full yet simple life' (YVPi. 394). Nothing could be more different from WBY's ringing tones in 'Blood and the Moon', proclaiming the 'bloody, arrogant power' of his Norman castle as phallic, patriarchal, and determinedly Anglo-Irish:

I declare this tower is my symbol; I declare
This winding, gyring, spiring treadmill of a stair is my ancestral stair;
That Goldsmith and the Dean, Berkeley and Burke have travelled there.

(VP 480–1)

However, these often-quoted verses are not his only use of the symbol, with its several and sometimes blended referents, from

---

[34] Barbara J. Frieling, 'A Critical Edition of W. B. Yeats's Automatic Script 11 March–30 December 1918', (Ph.D. diss., Florida State University, 1987).

Wicklow to Galway. Rather than male precursors travelling on a treadmill, the 'golden king and silver lady' of alchemical sun and moon go 'bellowing' and 'prancing' in the lighter-hearted 'Under the Round Tower' (*VP* 331), a poem much more in keeping with the meanings urged upon WBY in the script (this poem matching its tones to 'The Collar-Bone of a Hare', appearing before it in the volume *The Wild Swans at Coole*, as well as 'Solomon to Sheba', the next poem in the collection). The erotic imagery joining male and female in 'Under the Round Tower' is connected with the spiralling movement of history, a conjunction recalled in *A Vision*, where WBY describes the movement of the historical cones as containing 'that continual oscillation which I have symbolized elsewhere as a King and Queen, who are Sun and Moon also, and whirl round and round as they mount up through a Round Tower' (*AVA* 182).

The butterfly, symbol of wisdom in counterpose to the eagle or hawk, also flits over the script. Butterfly and eagle have been appropriated for a male voice and art in 'Tom O'Roughley', in which Tom asserts that 'wisdom is a butterfly/And not a gloomy bird of prey' (*VP* 338). Like the tower, however, the butterfly was originally associated with women; it stood for 'symbol of innocence of emotion', of 'wisdom overcoming anger', or simply of 'wisdom why not' in connection with the medium and also with Iseult Gonne in the script of 22 November 1917 (*YVP*i. 104). Indeed, 'Tom O'Roughley' is among a number of other poems in *The Wild Swans at Coole* whose fountainhead was in GY's script. The idea of Dreaming Back, that the soul after death undergoes 'as it were a smoothing out or an unwinding' (*AVA* 227) by re-living important events from its life in reverse order is of course central to *Purgatory* and *The Dreaming of the Bones*. It also plays a part in such poems as 'Shepherd and Goatherd', in which the spirit of Robert Gregory 'grows younger every second':

> Jaunting, journeying
> To his own dayspring,
> He unpacks the loaded pern

Of all 'twas pain or joy to learn,
Of all that he had made.

(*VP* 342)

'The Hero, the Girl, and the Fool' gives the last words to the Fool
by the Roadside, who knows that 'When all works that have/From
cradle run to grave/From grave to cradle run instead' (*VP* 449) once
the first movement is completed. No less explictly, 'On Woman'
praises Sheba, WBY's favourite poetic code name for GY, and makes
its wish to live 'like Solomon/That Sheba led a dance' not now 'But
when, if the tale's true, / The Pestle of the moon/ That pounds up all
anew/Brings me to birth again' (*VP* 346). It was Thomas, through
GY, who first mentioned, in a very early session, that spirits 'dream
backwards remember. . . . when they reach the prenatal they have
returned to the condition of being able to go forward' (11 November
1917, *YVP*i. 75).[35]

Finally, GY's moving hand generated the catalysing idea for what
came to be her husband's most famous poem. It was she who
first wrote that the 'soul of world [is] in centre' of the historical
gyres, and that the modern age is in chaos because 'the worlds
civilization is apart from the centres' (*YVP*i. 426, 428). In doing so,
she introduced the apocalyptic image in the opening lines of 'The
Second Coming', in which 'the centre cannot hold' in 'the widening
gyre' (*VP* 401–2).

Michael Robartes and the Dancer

According to Hugh Kenner, famously, WBY wrote books rather than
accumulating poems: that is to say, especially in the late work,
individual lyrics often interact with others in a volume, through

---

[35] WBY had touched on a similar idea in 'Swedenborg, Mediums, and the Desolate
Places', noting that 'In the west of Ireland the country people say that after death every
man grows upward or downward to the likeness of thirty years', and that 'to grow old in
heaven is to grow young' (*Ex* 39).

shared allusions and compounded images.[36] GY's collaborative work is also to be seen in these larger units, and it is especially worth examining *Michael Robartes and the Dancer*, the first volume that was shaped, start to finish, while the automatic experiments were in full flow, in order to watch for her shaping presence. In WBY's collected poems, *Michael Robartes and the Dancer* is prepared for by the last cluster of poems in *The Wild Swans at Coole*, a group that also appeared in the Macmillan incarnation of that volume (1919).[37] These seven or eight poems (depending on whether 'Ego Dominus Tuus' is included in the count) rely more directly on the system than any in WBY's corpus—are, in fact, almost inexplicable without it—and the volume that precedes them also has a sprinkle of other poems from the new revelations, but *Michael Robartes and the Dancer* (1921) is certainly the most visionary of WBY's volumes of poetry. It is visionary in the specific sense that it is steeped in the occult philosophy of *A Vision*, but it also stands out in a canon filled with poems deriving from or influenced by everything from folk beliefs, theosophy, Rosicrucianism, theurgy, spiritualism, and Vedantic doctrine, in that it does not assert so much as try on its supernatural system. It is less descriptive than dramatic, not so much using the system as theme or symbol but immersed in it, living inside its world, rather as if the system were the stage on which a drama took place.

WBY announces as much in the Preface to the Cuala edition. He writes:

After the first few poems I came into possession of Michael Robartes' exposition of the *Speculum Angelorum et Hominum* of Geraldus, and in the excitement of arranging and editing could no more keep out philosophy than could Goethe himself at certain periods of his life. . . . It is hard for a writer, who has spent much labour upon his style, to remember that

---

[36] Hugh Kenner, 'The Sacred Book of the Arts', in John Unterecker (ed.), *Yeats* (Englewood Cliffs, NJ: Prentice-Hall, 1963), 10–22.

[37] *The Wild Swans at Coole*, as it was first published by Cuala Press in 1917, contained twenty-three lyrics and the play *At the Hawk's Well*. Macmillan published a larger (and of course more widely distributed) volume in 1919, without the play but with seventeen added poems.

thought, which seems to him natural and logical like that style, may be unintelligible to others. The first excitement over, and the thought changed into settled conviction, his interest in simple, that is to say in normal emotion, is always I think increased; he is no longer looking for candlestick and matches but at the objects in the room.[38]

The woodcut of a candle on the title-page of the volume gives the same message: read the poems for themselves, but be aware of their context.[39] Watch the action, but know that it is visible because of lighting of a specific quality. Don't necessarily pay attention to the candle, but know that you can see these objects because of it.

The trick, then, is to watch the performance and pay attention to the stage business—that is, to clues in the contexts for the book that point to its being, in effect, a *mise en scène*. Being aware of the staging makes it possible to see in the poems an action that functions like an invisible subtext that the artist is proscribed from actually mentioning. That context or subtext is of course the automatic writing and other experiments, and the proscription comes from that source as well. On 26 August 1918, Thomas and Erontius reiterated the injunctions to secrecy that WBY had heard more than once, but added that he could give hints, as it were: in response to an unrecorded question, they answered 'At present no', but added, 'Yes also the work is written or must be written on another understanding than that under which you have so far spoken'. WBY asked, 'What is that understanding' and was told, 'That you must acknowledge without indicating the means the supernatural origin of the system' (*YVP*ii. 25). Although 'the work' referred to may well be *A Vision* itself, WBY sensibly took it to extend to any public document in which he used the system. Like WBY, in the pages that follow I intend to 'acknowledge' the hidden performance behind the volume and the kinds of multiple truths dramatized. Unlike him, I will 'indicat[e] the means' by way of the image of the light in the tower that appears

---

[38] *Michael Robartes and the Dancer* (Dublin: Cuala Press, 1921).
[39] The same woodcut was used for the Cuala edition of *A Packet for Ezra Pound* (1929), which introduced the mediumship of GY to the public for the first time.

in 'The Phases of the Moon', part of the coding for the *Vision* experiments in the frame poems for the visionary material. That light signals a change in the positioning of the poetic subject and a correspondingly new tonal quality in WBY's work, a change that two of the dialogue poems from the volume will begin to demonstrate.

This approach does not emphasize the volume as a thematic whole or as a carefully arranged sequence of poems, although much might be said on these topics. In *Michael Robartes and the Dancer*, system poems that are personal in scope and antinomian in tone yield to a middle section of WBY's most remarkable political poems, which he did not publish in book form for several years prior to the publication of *Michael Robartes*. These include the daring 'Easter, 1916', and although the issues surrounding the public appearance of this group or this poem are beyond the scope of this project, it is intriguing to notice that one of WBY's best-known political voices, attained through self-questioning, should find its place nestled amid poems lit by the system's radical division of self, as well as newly genuine dialogues between voices that do not fit easily into the hierarchical or imperialistic roles to which he was consistently drawn.

Following the central section are three more poems that stage a self in the context of antithetical visionary life: 'Towards Break of Day', which might be included as a fourth of the new kind of dialogue poem; 'Demon and Beast', which is a striking depiction in verse of the person of phase 17 from *A Vision*; and 'The Second Coming', which in the context of this volume announces itself as a personal and subjective vision, not (as it is often read) a universal claim. The volume is rounded off by three poems in genres that use language as a way of changing reality: a prayer, a meditation, and a dedication that curiously equates the volume of poetry with the tower in which the poet and his wife were living, in that the words on the page are written to be carved on the tower.

The drama imperfectly hidden behind the surface of *Michael Robartes and the Dancer* begins with the observation already mentioned, that this volume of poetry, like the first version of *A Vision* (published in 1925), is a censored work. Further, *Michael Robartes and the Dancer* is performative, no less than the other texts surrounding the visionary experiments. The book suggests that a non-textual event is being transferred into another medium, that the poet is in effect covering with poetry an elaborate domestic ritual, complete with masked characters and emblematic movement and, of course, its own script (making *Michael Robartes and the Dancer* doubly dramatized, like a play within a play). This is not to imply that the volume is theatrical in a narrow sense, that its speakers are simply staged characters, or, to use a more commonly misappropriated Yeatsian term, dramatic masks at a safe distance from the roles they play. For one thing, talk of masks or plays can lead to the impression that WBY was not passionate about the poetry or the events behind it, which was far from the case, especially in this part of his career. WBY's silent collaborator in the automatic script was no less skilled at such urgent double-mindedness, which can assert and deny in the same breath as a way of expressing deep convictions. Dialogical or polylogical truth was her great achievement, creating a universal system and a marriage, while coding personal anxieties in geometric symbols and hiding revelations from herself in automaticity. Like performance art, the system was both planned and improvised, both conscious and unconscious, the production of two people who knew exactly what they were doing and at the same time were engaged in radical experimentation.

Despite the surprise occasioned by the success of the automatic script, a reported emotion that is doubtless genuine, the scene had been carefully arranged so as to make the script possible.[40] Indeed, the possibility of arriving at rich occult truths by collaboration probably had something to do with the couple's reasons for choosing each other in the first place. A remarkable series of daily letters written to GHL in the weeks just before their marriage suggests that WBY had an 'imagined image' (*VP* 388) to bring to his bride-bed that

---

[40] WBY records his surprise in the introduction to *AV B* (p. 8). GY's amazement is recorded in Jeffares, *Man and Poet*, 191, and Moore, *The Unicorn*, 253.

definitely included deep joint study. On 4 October 1917, he wrote to her, 'You find me amid crowds but you will lead me to lonely places. Let us begin at once our life of study, of common interests & hopes.' The following day, he may have had William and Catherine Blake in mind: the comment 'I kiss the tops of your fingers where they are marked by the acid' shows a lover's pity but possibly also a writer's hopes that those fingers, like Catherine Blake's, would help to burn her husband's images into permanent form. On 6 October, he wrote a letter whose reception may have been mixed, mentioning that 'A letter has come from Maud Gonne praising you. She calls you "charming . . . graceful and beautiful" and adds "I think she has an intense spiritual life of her own and on this side you must be careful not to disappoint her." ' The following day, he typed, rather badly, 'I will live for my work and your happiness and when we are dead our names shall be remembered—perhaps we shall become a part of the strange legendary life of this country. My work shall become yours and yours mine and do not think that because your body and your strong bones fill me with desire that I do not seek also the secret things'—that 'magnetic ♂' will . . . not make me the less the student of your soul.'[41] The automatic script had been carefully prepared for, if not rehearsed, before it made its dramatic appearance during the Yeatses' honeymoon.

The backdrop of *Michael Robartes and the Dancer* is equally prepared for in *The Wild Swans at Coole*, a book that would have formed part of the context for the faithful reader of WBY encountering the new volume. WBY had, as it were, pre-announced his resuscitation of the character Robartes, whom he had killed off years earlier in the story 'Rosa Alchemica', by inserting Robartes into 'The Phases of the Moon', 'Ego Dominus Tuus', and 'The Double Vision of Michael Robartes', the last poem in *Wild Swans* (thus preparing as well for later collected works, in which 'Michael Robartes and the Dancer', the first poem of the new volume, would follow 'The

---

[41] Unpublished letter; quoted by Saddlemyer, *Becoming George*, 97, and Foster, *Arch-Poet*, 99.

Double Vision'). The link between volumes is not merely a named character. For example, note that 'The Phases of the Moon' raises a question about just what is happening behind a lighted window. Robartes and Aherne, whose dialogue comprises most of the poem, are travelling; they pause in a place they seem to know, and Robartes interprets the light they can see:

> We are on the bridge; that shadow is the tower,
> And the light proves that he is reading still.
> He has found, after the manner of his kind,
> Mere images; chosen this place to live in
> Because, it may be, of the candle-light
> From the far tower where Milton's Platonist
> Sat late, or Shelley's visionary prince:
> The lonely light that Samuel Palmer engraved,
> An image of mysterious wisdom won by toil;
> And now he seeks in book or manuscript
> What he shall never find.
>
> (*VP* 373)

Here WBY is alone; any knowledge he comes up with will seem his 'original thought' just as prescribed in a script that had lasting effect: 'the information is not to be betrayed as to *source*—all else may be done . . . you can say it is a sequence & your original thought—that is to a degree true' (*YVP*i. 123). 'Ego Dominus Tuus' also imagines that a lamp burns in the tower, and although neither *Hic* nor *Ille*, the speakers of that poem, is strictly speaking *alone*, since they are talking together, and *Ille* in particular also invokes a 'mysterious one who yet/Shall walk the wet sands by the edge of the stream/And look most like me, being indeed my double' (*VP* 371), still, these projections of self and anti-self are part of one poet's imagination.

However, other poems in *The Wild Swans at Coole* suggest the presence of someone else. The poem placed between 'Ego Dominus Tuus' and 'The Phases of the Moon', entitled 'A Prayer on Going into my House', mentions the tower as a place where the poet's heirs may be blessed—an anticipated life with children that might interfere with the carefully developed image of solitary study, unless their mother took care that their father not be disturbed. The love of beauty and reverence for elegance in the form of 'unspoiled' simplicity locate this poem in an intertextual nexus that reaches back to 'Rosa Alchemica', in which the protagonist, just before his 'final' meeting with Robartes, has filled his house with what must have been a visual cacophony of religious ornaments and rich colours, a pattern of peacocks in a tapestry acting as 'the doorkeepers of my world, shutting out all that was not of as affluent a beauty as their own' (*Myth* 269). This vision also stretches forward to early drafts of *The Discoveries of Michael Robartes*, an early version of *A Vision* in the form of a dialogue between Robartes and Owen Ahearne, in which Robartes apologizes to his friend for having to entertain him in mean surroundings:

But here we are at my own door and I wish I were rich enough to welcome you under a less pretentious roof. ~~I do not think this room will make upon you an impression of energy or reality as we use those words. And yet everything in it has been made amid the roar of machinery.~~ If on the second coming of Christ it were decreed that all should be as before I can imagine Him seeking among the poor and the half poor for a room simple enough ~~to share His affection.~~[42] He would be compelled to take a

before he could inhabit the room

handful of coppers from Peter's bag and change it into gold ‸~~that He might~~

to be

~~find~~‸ a fitting scenery for the Last Supper, that is one reason why the new Christ whose advent is very near will not come to the poor and the ignorant. (*YVP* iv. 18)

This Robartes, a bit more spartan than his Rosicrucian predecessor (and more right-leaning in his anti-modernism, as he prophesies a Christ for the new antithetical and autocratic age), has learned some lessons from the historical cones of the script no less than has the speaker of 'A Prayer on Going into my House', who asks for the 'blessing' of 'No table or chair or stool not simple enough/For

---

[42] WBY's revisions moved the phrase '*to be* a fitting scenery for the last supper' to follow 'simple enough'.

shepherd lads in Galilee' (*VP* 371). Incidentally, the resurrection
of Robartes was intricately connected with the script of GY, from
the early assertion that his phase was 18, the same as hers.[43] Later,
Ameritus directed WBY to write the dialogue itself: as a part of the
effort 'to get you started writing wheel', he was instructed to use
the semi-dramatic frame of having 'Robartes & Ahearne discuss
philosophy' (*YVP*ii. 485–6). As Saddlemyer has noted, Robartes,
who after 'The Phases of the Moon' becomes 'increasingly important
as the vehicle through which the statements of *A Vision* are expressed',
is 'a protective cover for GY who did not wish her part to be made
public', as well as her husband.[44] Even in 'The Phases', the figure
in the tower is not really alone: human life just outside the window
mocks that solitary toil.

Neither Michael Robartes (for all that he is double or multiple
within himself), nor the poet William Yeats, the one who invokes a
curse on any developer building near Ballylee in 'A Prayer on Going
into my House', is the only interior decorator hinted at in *The Wild
Swans*. Most notably, 'In Memory of Major Robert Gregory' requires
a bride. It begins:

> Now that we're almost settled in our house
> I'll name the friends that cannot sup with us
> Beside a fire of turf in th' ancient tower,
> And having talked to some late hour
> Climb up the narrow winding stair to bed.
>
> (*VP* 323–4)

The newer poems that filled out *The Wild Swans* between its appearances as a Cuala volume and as a Macmillan publication suggest a setting interpreted by fictional characters in two poems and depicted in
more realistic guise in other poems: an elegy for a friend's all-too-real

---

[43] See *YVP*i. 149 for the first mention of Robartes' phase, on 6 Dec. 1917. George
Mills Harper cites a second location for this information, in an unpublished notebook
(*MYV*i. 276 n. 38).
[44] Ann Saddlemyer, 'Reading Yeats's "A Prayer for My Daughter"—Yet Again'
(Paper presented at the International Association for the Study of Anglo-Irish Literature,
Otani, Japan, 1990), 7–8.

son killed in the war and a half-humorous request for rustic blessing *cum* imprecation against modern furniture and suburbanization.[45]

To return to that lighted window: if someone actually looked into it, of course, she or he would see not the poet reading but the poet and his wife sitting at a table, he devising spoken or written questions, she providing answers, or the two of them copying out revelations sent in dreams, perhaps talking over an automatic session before or afterwards. The night would be typical of hundreds of intense, lengthy sessions. As WBY mentioned to John Quinn on 31 December 1919, the intensity was great: 'My wife is very excited at the thought of America & many people', WBY wrote, 'having been practically alone with me since our marriage, every evening in my study helping me with my work.'[46] Of course, the nearly thirty months of script by no means all took place in the drafty tower: the script occurred wherever the Yeatses went, to numerous houses, hotels, and even in transit, in several countries. Nevertheless, in simplified symbolic form, the first three poems of *Michael Robartes and the Dancer* reflect this time, in that they suggest a new presence in WBY's always confessional poetic world, if only in that all three feature direct talk between a male and a female voice.

---

[45] On the critical differences between the two versions of *The Wild Swans at Coole*, see Ronald Schuchard, 'Hawk and Butterfly: The Double Vision of *The Wild Swans at Coole*', in *YA* x. 11–34. Schuchard calls the two volumes 'the sun and the moon apart—the former a solar volume, mired in the emotional realities and intellectual hatreds of the objective world, the latter a lunar volume, lifted by the recovery of a subjective reality that led the poet back to a lost visionary plane' (p. 111). Schuchard claims that in 1919, at the cost of obscuring the sequential nature of the volumes and the dramatic transformation that had taken place in the seventeen months that separate them, WBY deliberately conflated the two groups of poems and distorted their chronology, evidently to prevent people from knowing 'too much about his personal concerns', as Jeffares puts it (A. Norman Jeffares, *A New Commentary on the Poems of W. B. Yeats* (London: Macmillan, 1984), 129; Schuchard, 'Hawk and Butterfly', 111). The evidence of the script demonstrates that this impulse was not entirely WBY's own, and that the motives behind the change offer both concealment and also a hinted-at display of the Yeatses' occult life.

[46] Unpublished letter. See *MYV* ii. 386.

Alternatively, the aperture might be lighting other activities more typical of newly married folk. *Michael Robartes and the Dancer* suggests sexual wisdom, or the integration of sexuality and philosophy, much more strongly than the more expository last movement of *The Wild Swans*, initiated by 'The Phases of the Moon' with its poetic list of phases. As a volume, *Michael Robartes and the Dancer* solves the artificial dilemma proposed by the male voice of the first poem, presumably the character Robartes, to the female voice, probably the Dancer of the title, between 'thought' and the body, gendered as male and female. This book does not offer a philosophical system, but reaches toward what Solomon and Sheba almost achieve in the richly comic poem 'Solomon and the Witch'. In that poem, Solomon expounds learnedly upon the excellence of their love-making, suggesting to Sheba (who has the first and last words of the poem) what was happening when she spoke in an automatic voice 'in a strange tongue' in the midst of her pleasure the night before. The sound was not even human, he explains: it was the crow of a cock that

> Crew from a blossoming apple bough
> Three hundred years before the Fall
> And never crew again till now,
> And would not now but that he thought,
> Chance being one with Choice at last,
> All that the brigand apple brought
> And this foul world were dead at last.

> (*VP* 387–8)

A set scene featuring lit windows with sexual congress taking place behind them fired WBY's imagination later. Another such window occurs in the late play *Purgatory*, with a markedly different tone, as the old man imagines his mother begetting him behind it. Interestingly enough, an unpublished letter from WBY to GY from the weeks immediately before their marriage also suggests a lighted window. On 4 October 1917, he wrote from Coole Park: 'My beloved: I arrived an hour ago. The masons are at work at Ballylee. Lady Gregory thinks that we should get married as soon as possible

& that I should bring you here before the weather grows very cold & gloomy that we may make our Ballylee plans together while the castle looks well. She does not want us however till we are married—that one candle being I think the danger, or at least what the neighbors might say about the possible number of our candles.'[47]

The drama that takes place in this setting is one for which it serves as emblem. The lit windows of the tower burn with a flame not from an inadequate solitary lamp illuminating 'book or manuscript' (*VP* 373), but from living wisdom, of the kind available only 'when oil and wick are burned in one' (*VP* 388). The emblem on the title-page of the Cuala volume intimates as much: the single candle, blown by a heavy wind, is surrounded by an encircling swirl of wind or water. Heavily defended, unitary, male subjectivity, that imagined square tower or single candle, is enlightened not only by a feminine stream flowing by its foundations or an imagined mask or anti-self wandering in the surrounding green countryside, but by forces that redefine the fortification itself as a frame for light.[48] Later, in *The Tower*, it would become reimagined again as a home for birds or bees, ephemeral living things building in crumbling certainties and the 'loosening masonry' (*VP* 424) of an ageing body and a violent revolution. In *Michael Robartes and the Dancer* the redefinition occurs to the idea of the poet as the master of his material. The subject surrenders its authority; the poet is in a correspondingly different, antithetical relationship to his poems. This fracturing, or giving up of authority, is reminiscent of other writers, artists, and thinkers of the period, of course, but it should not be confused with the crisis in subjectivity of international modernism. In WBY, crucially, there is no accompanying fragmentation of style. This encounter with the splitting of the subject is not the result of philosophical speculation or anxiety, but the enacting in daily life of an occult truth

---

[47] Unpublished letter; quoted in Saddlemyer, *Becoming George*, 95; Foster, *Arch-Poet*, 98.

[48] The block, designed by T. Sturge Moore, appeared first in W. B. Yeats, *Reveries over Childhood and Youth* (Dundrum: Cuala Press, 1915); Allan Wade, *A Bibliography of the Writings of W. B. Yeats*, 2nd edn. (London: Rupert Hart-Davis, 1958), 111.

MICHAEL ROBARTES AND THE
DANCER, BY WILLIAM BUTLER
YEATS.

THE CUALA PRESS
CHURCHTOWN
DUNDRUM
MCMXX

5. Title-page, *Michael Robartes and the Dancer* (Cuala Press, 1920), woodcut
by T. Sturge Moore

about the multiple nature of the self, producing art characterized by dramatized possibilities of expansion in hard-edged images, relatively unstrained syntax, and conversational if resonant tone. WBY's late work implies that meaning has many faces, which may not be graspable on a rational plane, but are present none the less: *logoi* of unknown voices rather than *logos* destabilized. The combination of straightforward assertion and pregnant imagery, which extended well past the period of the script, its most important catalyst, is illustrated well by the poem 'Gratitude to the Unknown Instructors', written much later:

> What they undertook to do
> They brought to pass;
> All things hang like a drop of dew
> Upon a blade of grass.
>
> (*VP* 505)

The new subjectivity may be seen readily in *Michael Robartes and the Dancer* in 'An Image from a Past Life', especially with its automatic genesis in mind. The third poem in the volume, and incidentally also the third dialogue poem, it dramatizes the concept of the overshadower to create an effect that is new in Yeatsian dialogues. It ends with the following exchange:

> *She.* A sweetheart from another life floats there
> As though she had been forced to linger
> From vague distress
> Or arrogant loveliness,
> Merely to loosen out a tress
> Among the starry eddies of her hair
> Upon the paleness of a finger.
>
> *He.* But why should you grow suddenly afraid
> And start—I at your shoulder—
> Imagining
> That any night could bring
> An image up, or anything

Even to eyes that beauty had driven mad,
But images to make me fonder?

She. Now she has thrown her arms above her head;
Whether she threw them up to flout me,
Or but to find,
Now that no fingers bind,
That her hair streams upon the wind,
I do not know, that know I am afraid
Of the hovering thing night brought me.

(*VP* 390)

wby explains the concept in a long note to the poem in which personal reference has disappeared in a welter of over-obvious distancing devices. He begins by quoting from a letter from Robartes to Aherne about research that Robartes has done among the Judwali tribe on the Arab scholar 'Kusta-ben-Luki'. Kusta is one of the repeating figures from the swirl of framing devices for the visionary material as the thinly disguised autobiographical figure whose experiences with a mediumistic wife are the topic of the poem 'The Gift of Harun Al-Rashid', which is printed in the first edition of *A Vision*.[49] Robartes's letter reports that according to 'biographical detail, probably legendary', Kusta

saw occasionally during sleep a woman's face and later on found in a Persian painting a face resembling, though not identical with the dream-face, which was he considered that of a woman loved in another life. Presently he met & loved a beautiful woman whose face also resembled, without being identical, that of his dream. Later on he made a long journey to purchase the painting which was, he said, the better likeness, and found on his return that his mistress had left him in a fit of jealousy. (*VP* 821)

---

[49] The poem, under the title 'Desert Geometry or the Gift of Harun Al-Raschid', opens Book II of *AV A*. In 1925, indeed, the book itself is subtitled 'An Explanation of Life Founded Upon the Writings of Giraldus and Upon Certain Doctrines Attributed to Kusta ben Luka'. Like many of wby's oriental names, Kusta was given several spellings, as was Harun. wby finally settled on ben Luka for the name of the Arab scholar, b. 820 CE. See *CVA* p. xix n. 6.

WBY then mentions, as if in a pre-publicity advertisement for *The Discoveries of Michael Robartes*, 'a dialogue and . . . letters' in which Robartes sets out 'a classification and analysis of dreams which explain the survival of this story among the followers of Kusta-ben-Luki'. The poem is explicitly linked, then, to the phantasmagoria-in-process of autobiography turned outlandish mythic tale, propped on slight historical data and reaching toward heights of cosmic philosophical exposition.[50] WBY's note continues to explain that the other woman figure that Kusta saw was the overshadower of the man, a soul whose passion in a former life toward the soul of the living was not yet expiated: 'Those whose past passions are unatoned seldom love living man or woman but only those loved long ago, of whom the living man or woman is but a brief symbol forgotten when some phase of some atonement is finished.'

The poem departs from the autobiographical analogy we might expect, in which Kusta, the WBY figure, would be entranced like Cuchulain, seeing and loving the image of the woman by whom he is overshadowed. The Yeatses were both concerned that he was obsessed in the material world, after all, by what WBY asked about in more than one session: 'Why had I so wild a passion for MG?' (*YVP*i. 200; see also *YVP*ii. 390). In 'An Image from a Past Life', though, it is the woman and not the man who is haunted by the ghostly figure. WBY explains this oddity thus:

I do not think I misstated Robartes' thought in permitting the woman and not the man to see the Over Shadower or Ideal Form, whichever it was. No mind's contents are necessarily shut off from another, and in moments of excitement images pass from one mind to another with extraordinary ease, perhaps most easily from that portion of the mind which for the time being is outside consciousness. (*VP* 823)

---

[50] The term *phantasmagoria*, referring to the array of personages, images, and scenic actions assembled at the edges of the automatic experiments and the texts associated with them, was a favourite of WBY's. He first used it in the unpublished essay 'The Poet and the Actress', written in 1916. See David R. Clark, ' "The Poet and the Actress": An Unpublished Dialogue by W. B. Yeats', in *YA* viii. 135; see also Foster, *Arch-Poet*, 71.

This poem, like the first two poems in the volume, is a dialogue in which neither party has control, but in which both parties both possess and are possessed by antithetical power. They speak as if talking together, and the stanzas may be read as if they hear and respond to each other or as if they are lost in separate dreams, not answering each other's questions or even hearing them. The man believes that love brings safety: the poem opens with him wondering that 'Never until this night have I been stirred' and later asking, 'What can have suddenly alarmed you' and 'why should you grow suddenly afraid/And start—I at your shoulder', as if dumbfounded by the notion that she might be fearful while he is with her. He does not grasp the meaning of the 'poignant recollection' that strikes him in the first stanza, and the woman presumably does not understand that in describing the overshadower to the man, she is in effect bringing her rival to him in her own body. The emotional crisis is more hers than his, and the poem empathizes more with her ruined peace of mind than with his fruitless attempts to console her. None the less, the disturbing image is possible only because of the intensity of their passion for each other.

Like 'Solomon and the Witch', which precedes it, and 'Under Saturn', which succeeds it, 'An Image from a Past Life' suggests an autobiographical reading, a reading that would have been almost inevitable if an early version of the first stanza had remained intact. In its earlier incarnation, the stanza read:

> 'Neither darker night, nor the edies yonder
> Could stir a thought
> But of the kindness that you have brought
> Into my empty life—.'[51]

That kindness makes an explicit appearance in 'Under Saturn', the lines immediately following 'An Image':

---

[51] W. B. Yeats, *Michael Robartes and the Dancer: Manuscript Materials*, ed. Thomas Parkinson, The Cornell Yeats (Ithaca, NY, and London: Cornell University Press, 1994), 45.

'Do not because this day I have grown saturnine
Imagine that lost love, inseparable from my thought
Because I have no other youth, can make me pine:
For how should I forget the wisdom that you brought,
The comfort that you made?'

He and *She* may not be the Yeatses, but the poet and 'you' in 'Under Saturn' make sure that identification is made with the recent marriage of the ageing poet, he who has 'childish memories of an old cross Pollexfen,/And of a Middleton, whose name you never heard,/And of a red-haired Yeats' (*VP* 390–1). wby deleted the lines in 'An Image' that gave autobiographical weight to one character and with it the authority to define the relationship from one person's perspective. One perspective could not generate the excitement necessary for this vision. To some extent, the removal of the mention of kindness brought into an empty life is just good revision, eliminating self-pity—a kind of revision, incidentally, that wby also undertook to great effect in 'A Prayer for my Daughter', which began its life as a prayer more about himself than his daughter. That poem is still overshadowed by Maud and Iseult Gonne, for all that it rises also to be, as Saddlemyer notes, 'a hymn of thanksgiving to his wife' for the 'Plenty's horn' that is hidden in the figure of a linnet (a bird that can call in many voices), safe from hatred and therefore not to be torn from a tree whatever the 'Assault and battery of the wind' (*VP* 405).[52] Beyond removal of self-pity, the revised 'An Image from a Past Life' is striking in wby's canon in expressing fear of such overshadowing and demonstrating how that fear is experienced differently by the man overshadowed and the woman who watches his overshadowing. The poet imagines her seeing more clearly and feeling more deeply than he. The scream of terror, 'Image of poignant recollection', in the first stanza, the central symbol for the experience, is, after all, an image of her heart. Like the stages of composition of 'A Prayer for My Daughter', wby's revisions of 'An Image from a Past Life' apportion the active roles in the narrative to more than one party.

52 Saddlemyer, 'Reading Yeats's "A Prayer"', 20.

Both poems downplay the sense that one point of view only can provide the dynamism necessary for the meaning of the poem.

Another group of issues in *Michael Robartes and the Dancer* emanates from the contextual material, and occurs in the rhetoric of the volume as a whole. A curious tone begins to sound in WBY's poetry from this period. For help in listening for it in the volume of published poetry, it may be useful to swerve briefly to consider the *Speculum Angelorum et Hominum*, the non-existent book that WBY mentions in the Cuala introduction to *Michael Robartes*. He mentioned to Lady Gregory on 4 January 1918 the plan, already formulated, of 'writing it [the system] all out in a series of dialogues about a supposed medieval book, the *Speculum Angelorum et Hominum* by Giraldus, and a sect of Arabs called the Judwalis (diagrammatists)' (*L* 644), a double source that GY's hand identified as antinomies, 'Gyraldus primary/Arab Anti' (*YVP*i. 250), appropriately enough for vehicles to describe a system that proposes unending oppositions as eternal truth. The *Speculum*, then, has a symbolic role to play, as do the other parts of the hoax with which WBY tried to whet his readers' appetite for the first edition of *A Vision*. It is all, of course, an unbelievable story, and intended as such. What is most interesting about it is the way in which WBY wraps his visionary text, in both editions, in circles inside circles of introductory and explanatory material that is extremely unstable rhetorically. It is impossible to pinpoint the attitude of the authorial voice toward the material, or what the author intends a reader's reaction to be. The story of Robartes and the *Speculum*, which was discovered when the bed of 'an ignorant girl of the people' with whom he was cohabiting broke inexplicably one night, is tonally a far cry from the earlier stories of Robartes in just this aspect. Are we meant to infer anything about the love-making that took place between Robartes, 'something between a debauchee, a saint, and a peasant' (*Myth* 271) and the 'fiery handsome girl of the poorer classes' (*AV A* p. xvii) from the story of that bed? Are we meant to laugh at the portrait of Giraldus that Edmund Dulac produced for the frontispiece of the 1925 book? The woodcut is an odd combination of WBY as Italian alchemist of the Renaissance, Arab scholar, and Robartes, at the very least, and probably a hidden reference to GY as well. Giraldus, incidentally, belonged to phase 18, like Robartes, GY, and Thomas of Dorlowicz, all personalities through whom the system is brought, however slantingly, into the open.[53]

How are readers meant to react to the news that the characters Robartes and Aherne (especially the latter) are put out with WBY for killing them off in 'Rosa Alchemica'? What are they to think of Mary Bell, the character who gives herself up to the incubation of an ancient egg in the section of the introductory material that follows WBY's ostensibly confessional introduction to the 1937 edition, and then a sincere-sounding public letter to Ezra Pound? Or what about Denise de L'Isle Adam, another character in the egg story who thinks that she should have been the chosen foster swan-mother since 'I am taller, and my training as a model would have helped' (*AV B* 53)? What, finally, to make of John Aherne's letter to WBY, the last item in the introductory material to the 1937 edition, which jumbles all the stories together? Mr Aherne conveys his orthodox brother as being 'as hot as ever' with WBY for making up a ritual with 'pagan gods'. Robartes is 'bitter' too, not so much because WBY blew an incident out of all proportion and exterminated him in the process, but—or so John Aherne asserts—for WBY's stylistic sins, when in the early stories the writer 'substituted sound for sense and ornament for thought' (*AV B* 54–5). John notes some poetic licence in the dates of Kusta ben Luka, and suggests 'that your automatic script, or whatever it was, may well have been but a process of remembering'—and then evokes that window to

---

[53] In *The Discoveries of Michael Robartes*, Robartes notes that Giraldus 'considered that he was in the eighteenth incarnation of his cycle' (*YVP*iv. 24). For Robartes's placement see n. 43 above. WBY asked about the phase of 'the medium' on 30 Nov. 1917, although the separate sheet of paper with the answers to that evening's questions has been misplaced. I presume that the question was answered, since a few days later WBY asked for secondary information, 'classifications according to signs' (that is to say, the matching of twelve cycles with astrological identifiers), and received a sign for her as well as himself. Incidentally, his phase, 17, is also first mentioned in this script from the evening of 5 Dec. (*YVP*i. 141–3). Thomas of Dorlowitz was located by phase on 23 Dec. 1917 (*YVP* i. 174).

charge that WBY's light is not very illuminating. Robartes was angry,
John tells WBY, because Romanticism was dead and gone, and in
preserving it stylistically, WBY was merely playing with smoke: 'when
the candle was burnt out an honest man did not pretend that grease
was flame' (*AV B* 55).

A Vision, the partly destroyed *Speculum*, the erased dances in
the desert sand, the frustrating script, and the system itself, are
all designed to be experienced as unstable or dynamic.[54] The
rhetoric does not allow a fixed relationship between knowledge
and knower, thus making impossible the effective communication
that depends upon a clear one-way channel of information. As
Owen Aherne writes, 'the whole philosophy was so expounded
in a series of fragments ... to prevent the intellect from forming its own conclusions, and so thwarting the Djinn who could
only speak to curiosity and passivity.' However, he continues,
adding more confusion to the jumble, 'I cannot ... let this pass
without saying that I doubt the authenticity of this story' (*AV
A* 11). This material also refuses to distinguish between description and expression—that is, between objective description and
subjective intention or purpose. In grammatical terms, there is a
refusal to make clear divisions between subject and object and
between indicative and subjunctive or optative moods. To use the
terms of the system to describe Faculties of any being, the relations between Will, Mask, Creative Mind, and Body of Fate are
at constant variance with reference to each other. It only makes
sense that an immobile relationship among these linguistic and

[54] The *Speculum*, which had been used to prop up the bed of Robartes and his lover,
'was very dilapidated and all the middle pages had been torn out', according to Owen
Aherne's introduction to *AV A*. In the string of displaced authorial voices typical of the
framing material, Aherne recalls that Robartes intended to tell WBY that 'my beggar maid'
had 'torn out the middle pages to light our fire' (pp. xvii–xviii). The dances in the sand
were meant to be erased according to 'The Dance of the Four Royal Persons', by Owen
Aherne as well, in which Aherne writes out Robartes's account of the story recorded by
Giraldus about the students of Kusta ben Luka. The students ask that the marks of their
feet be smoothed over. Aherne suspects, he notes, that the story is 'a later embodiment
of a story that it was the first diagram drawn upon the sand by the wife of Kusta ben
Luka' (*AV A* 9–11).

rhetorical categories might be denied in texts that insist on multifoliate patterns within and between all people, concepts, images,
and actions.

The volume *Michael Robartes and the Dancer* both anticipates
and occurs in the context of a book of 'emotional philosophy'—to
use the term chosen to describe the true Creative Mind of GY's
phase (*AV A* 79)—that is both weighty and inconsequential,
subjective and objective, profound and ridiculous. Several of the
poems in the volume present tonal difficulties if their performative qualities are not taken into account. They in effect enact
movements and thoughts from the large, inchoate 'book' of the
system, and from the gaining of wisdom in occult partnership
that is its larger goal ('my communications are only for a purpose unknown to you & not so much for the matter contained in
them', Rose commented enigmatically, perhaps about the mysterious 'third stage' of the Yeatses' work, which required 'something
you have not yet got' having to do with 'a relation as human
beings' (*YVP*i. 354, 310)). One of the more obvious of these tonally
ambiguous poems is the title poem, which also opens the volume.
The poem is another dialogue between *He* and *She*, and *He* is the
first speaker.

> *He.* Opinion is not worth a rush;
> In this altar-piece the knight,
> Who grips his long spear so as to push
> That dragon through the fading light,
> Loved the lady; and it's plain
> The half-dead dragon was her thought,
> That every morning rose again
> And dug its claws and shrieked and fought.
> Could the impossible come to pass
> She would have time to turn her eyes,
> Her lover thought, upon the glass
> And on the instant would grow wise.
>
> *She.* You mean they argued.
>
> (*VP* 385)

The conversation continues, *He* discoursing on the need for bodies in the attainment of wisdom and *She* popping in single lines. At the end, after his thought that God gave man not his thought but his body, *She* comments, 'My wretched dragon is perplexed.' *He* responds:

> I have principles to prove me right.
> It follows from this Latin text
> That blest souls are not composite,
> And that all beautiful women may
> Live in uncomposite blessedness,
> And lead us to the like—if they
> Will banish every thought, unless
> The lineaments that please their view
> When the long looking-glass is full,
> Even from the foot-sole think it too.
>
> (*VP* 386–7)

She speaks the last line of the poem, 'They say such different things at school' (*VP* 387). The ambiguities start and end in the multiple points of view suggested by the dialogic format, and the poem is inexplicable if either party is taken to speak the truth alone, although, as in 'An Image from a Past Life', WBY makes the female voice more aware than the male of the ironies and implicit humour of the situation. WBY had written in dialogue for many years, of course, in plays, semi-dramatic poems, and poems with internal dialogue, but his use of the form at this point in his life is heavily influenced by the Socratic questions and responses that were a large part of his daily routine. It is also probably worth mentioning that 'Michael Robartes and the Dancer' is the first dialogue poem of WBY's that does not fall neatly into one of two categories. First, there are poems in which the speakers agree or form separate statements that the poem joins into a deeper idea, such as 'Adam's Curse' or 'The Saint and the Hunchback'. Others, like 'Shepherd and Goatherd' or 'Ego Dominus Tuus', feature characters who differ in opinion but one of whom has all of the poet's sympathy, creating essentially false dialogues reminiscent somehow of vaudeville, one stand-up figure feeding the other all the good lines. Incidentally, the unpublished prose piece *The Discoveries of Michael Robartes* (*YVP*iv. 13–135) falls into this category.

But in *Michael Robartes and the Dancer*, dialogues have a new twist. The characters disagree, but neither is clearly the voice of authority. 'Michael Robartes and the Dancer', for all that the character Robartes is not given to egalitarianism, is misread as covert monologue or thinly veiled misogynism, the poet speaking through a learned male character, who is wise to the old ways of Pre-Raphaelite beauty and who neatly puts a female character in her place for the modern notion that women should think.[55] On the other hand, as I suggested above, the single lines that *She* speaks can be read as undercutting his disquisitions with subtle irony. The fact that *He* ultimately argues from a 'Latin text' while *She* does not theorize but dances, an activity always valorized in WBY, also undermines the male voice's philosophy. The setting in a gallery suggests a quality of artificiality. *He* dramatizes the scene depicted in a painting of Griselda, that quintessential figure of a victimized woman, looking for hidden meaning and trying to insert the viewers into the framed scene of the painting, while *She* interrupts his theories.

His attempt to convince her—in his learned way—that she should concentrate only on her body as a vehicle for attaining and leading men to 'uncomposite blessedness' never quite seems like an attempted seduction, if only because his body is absent. He refers to an ambiguously located 'beating breast', 'vigorous thigh', and 'dreaming eye', which may be 'what your looking-glass will show' or a painted depiction, but his own body is occluded: no woman has apparently done for him what his theory proposes, in that he has to use composite and also composed wisdom, a Latin text and much talk, to prop up his arguments. *He* talks with energetic scholarly

---

[55] See Elizabeth Butler Cullingford, *Gender and History in Yeats's Love Poetry* (Cambridge: Cambridge University Press, 1993) for a nuanced reading that complicates the charge of chauvinism in the poem (pp. 86–92).

allusion about bodies, while the female voice presumably does not have to create hers from words. Her effort is rather to complement one quality with another. 'And must no beautiful woman be/Learned like a man?', she asks, placing value on a 'mere book' as well as the body, mentioning putting herself to college and the things 'they say. . . . at school' in a context that puts her into the painting by way of her body. Her problem is that body and thought are separated into two, lady and dragon.

In biographical terms, the poem participates in a complex mytho-poesis. The composite figure of Robartes is a mask for WBY no more than for a very different character like MacGregor Mathers, and the Dancer reflects Iseult Gonne, a young dancer encouraged to think, as well as Maud Gonne, an object of desire whose 'thought' WBY prob-lematically identified with shrieking, shrillness, or an 'opinionated mind' like the scream of wind in 'A Prayer for My Daughter' later in the volume. The Dancer also has affinities with GY, a young woman not content with a looking-glass and given to replying ambiguously to an older man's questions. As with the setting of the tower, which both is and is not Ballylee, the poem posits multiple correspondences that both urge identification and deflect it.

A reading of 'Michael Robartes and the Dancer' that authorizes two points of view is strengthened by noticing similarities in tone between the poem and 'Solomon and the Witch', another example of the new sort of dialogue. Solomon, the great king, a figure whose authority as a patriarch could hardly be bettered, discourses learnedly, but Sheba ultimately makes the most sense in suggesting that they stop talking and get back to their pleasure in the 'forbidden sacred grove' (*VP* 389). Sheba, known for her wisdom, is having no trouble with the 'dragon' of her thought. Neither is Solomon, although he is temporarily deflected by the many profound things he has to say. But Solomon at least knows when to quit. After his explanation of why the cock 'that crowed out eternity/Thought to have crowed it in again', she remarks, 'Yet the world stays', and he tosses off a comment about the cock—a word that crows with *double entendre*—then finishes anticlimactically with two lines that sound suspiciously like weak thinking: 'Maybe an image is too strong/Or maybe is not strong enough.' This blurring of lines between image and real begin to be comic. Incidentally, WBY added late in the composition of this poem the line that most suggests that Solomon might be babbling on a little, for all his wisdom. In the Cuala edition and *Later Poems*, Solomon is 'he that knew/All sounds by bird or angel sung'; but later editions introduce his explanation of Chance and Choice as spoken by one 'Who understood/Whatever has been said, sighed, sung,/Howled, miau-d, barked, brayed, belled, yelled, cried, crowed' (*VP* 387). A new lightening of tone, an antinomial deflation of the magisterial bardic voice existing simultaneously with the voice, is increasingly present in the poetry after this point in WBY's career. Solomon thus anticipates the scarecrow of 'Sailing to Byzantium', or the poet who had pretty plumage once in 'Among School Children', as well as the later voices in which the integration of fair and foul are intricately but not self-deprecatingly linked.

Solomon's speech, the exhilarating idea that Chance and Choice may be 'a single light', that, in other words, one's own 'sweet will' might also be 'Heaven's will' (*VP* 405), is a lesson learned in *Michael Robartes and the Dancer*. The light is too dim for clear exposition, of course, and the conjunction is impossible on a rational plane, but the poems in this volume suggest a hidden life in which great antithetical wisdom may be in the process of arriving. That life brackets even the risky political poems in the middle of the volume, beginning with the dangerous 'Easter, 1916', and suggests a context for the autobiographical material that both energizes and lightens it. Solomon is lucky to have Sheba with whom to 'try again' under the wild moon at the end of 'Solomon and the Witch', and between the lines of the volume as a whole a sense of excitement lurks, underlining fear as well as pleasure, and making possible even light-heartedness and humour, at renewed poetic possibilities that the poet owed to another.

4

Demon the Medium

I too am much better indeed better than I have been for years.
Do you know that I half think that finishing the philosophy
getting all that abstraction put in concrete form makes one
better. Perhaps I now am a medium & my force is used. I have
now quite certainly mastered every abstract element & very
surprising some of them prove to be, in their ingenuity.

WBY TO GY, [Sept. 1924][1]

Just as much may be gained from meditation on WBY's motto in
the Order of the Golden Dawn, Demon Est Deus Inversus, as
can be learned from tracing the permutations of GY's Nemo Sciat.
On a verbal level, the four-word phrase *Demon Est Deus Inversus*
overturns the expected hierarchy of the binary *Deus* and *Demon*
in two ways: first, it flattens out the distinctions between the two
terms, which after all sound all the more similar when joined by
the simple verb *Est*. Second, with the arrival of the word *Inversus*,
in its critical final position, movement is generated, as well as the
undercutting of that levelling and static form of *to be*. Something
is—overturned. The English word has the movement of turning in
it, as does its Latin counterpart: *Inversus* suggests the wheeling of
its root *verto*, from which of course English has the word *vortex*,
the system adumbrated verbally in the old magical name. The part
that WBY played in the occult collaboration that led to the system

[1] Unpublished letter from WBY to GY. Photocopy in the private collection of George
Mills and Mary Jane Harper.

parallels the structural energies of his motto. First, his role levels the expected hierarchy and muddies the distinctions between director and responder, magician and medium, author and secretary, husband and wife, male and female. Then it inverts them, suggesting different configurations of power, gender, and sexual desire. Finally, the binary itself splits or multiplies into a quaternity. Addition is replaced by multiplication; line becomes space; measurement becomes geometry. In *A Vision*, as in the documents from which it was generated, two becomes four. This chapter examines the new conceptions of power, gender, and sexual desire in turn, through brief analyses of WBY's notion of joint mediumship, changes in the gendered symbols of cosmic 'bodies' in his poetry and plays, and the sexual discourses for which the geometries of the system are an elaborate masquerade. The chapter ends with the suggestion that the move from addition to multiplication in *A Vision* is closely related to WBY's sense of history. As he abandoned line for cone or double cone, WBY tried to work out the esoteric mathematics that would let the coin toss of the times, and of his relation to them, land on both sides at once.

In 1882, a dining fraternity called The Ghost Club was founded in London 'for the confidential reporting and discussion of psychic phenomena'.[2] One of its two founders, William Stainton Moses, was one of the most distinguished men in British spiritualist circles. His automatically written books, including *Spirit Teachings* and *Spirit Identity*, were well known. He was a founding member of the Society for Psychical Research, as well as the first editor of *Light*.[3] The Revd Moses was of value to the spiritualist community at large for his sterling character. Not only that, but as Miss X reported in the periodical *Borderland*,

---

[2] After the dissolution of the Ghost Club, its records were deposited in the British Library (MS Add. 52272).

[3] Moses' automatic writing was well known to the Yeatses, who kept among their papers a typescript of his automatic notebooks (NLI MS 36, 261/2/1–3).

The fact, that . . . he was a gentleman, a scholar, and a man of recognized position and character, was, to say the least, a good letter of introduction. That many estimable Spiritualists do not share these advantages, is a fact not necessarily to their discredit, but one which must obviously subtract from the interest in their phenomena in proportion as the lack of education diminishes their capacity for exact observation, for precision of record, for profiting by the analogies and experiences of other witnesses.[4]

To Miss X and others, the reputation of spiritualism suffered from the fact that many of its adherents were working-class people. Many of the thousands of written works on the topic display their authors' lack of formal training, although a few books by the likes of Sir Oliver Lodge have a style to please Miss X.[5]

Luckily, however, the Ghost Club, which met until 1936, featured men of worth and occasionally women as well (on special evenings) as members and speakers, giving talks on such topics as the outcomes of seances or the appearances of ghosts. Among them was WBY, who spoke at meetings of the club in 1911, 1917, and 1929, and gave another address in the spring of 1932. This is a rather late date for WBY to be talking about his experiences with occult phenomena: communication with the spirit communicators of the *Vision* documents had dwindled to a mere trickle long before. In the spring of 1932 other matters besides spirits were on the agenda. His friend Lady Gregory would die before summer. He was working diligently on an 'Edition de Luxe' of all his works, as well as writing new prose, poetry, and drama, and he was reviving an intellectual engagement with Hinduism through the work of Shri Purohit

---

⁴ [Ada Goodrich Freer] Miss X, 'Note', *Borderland*, 4 (1897): 304.

⁵ Miss X was the antonym of Ada Goodrich Freer, a woman whose ethics did not match her pretentions. Although W. T. Stead praises his assistant as 'a lady of good birth and education', with 'exceptional talents and rare natural gifts', in his announcement of the publication of his occult quarterly *Borderland*, she was 'apparently self-styled "lady editor of *Borderland*"' but 'in fact was only assistant editor' (John L. Campbell and Trevor H. Hall, *Strange Things: The Story of Fr Allan McDonald, Ada Goodrich Freer, and the Society for Psychical Research's Enquiry into Highland Second Sight* (London: Routledge & Kegan Paul, 1968), 110, 21). Campbell and Hall relate the history of her falsifications of folkloric and occult research in a generally spotted career, noting that 'there is a good deal of evidence to suggest . . . that she suffered from *folie de grandeur*' (p. 97).

Swami. Or perhaps, as the list above suggests, ghosts were on his mind after all.

At any rate, WBY began his remarks retrospectively on that April evening, noting his twenty years' experience with psychic matters, but he moved quickly to the apogee of them. The secretary in charge of note-taking wrote copiously. Communicators, WBY said, 'had come to him with several communications, but always in conjunction with his wife. The best came through the medium of sleep, but were always announced by a loud objective whistle, audible to others, which told him to prepare.'[6] WBY

found that he was being instructed by a group of beings on the other side. These communicate knowledge to him in compartments. The object of this method appeared to be that his subconscious predictions should not be aroused. The subjects dealt with were as follows:

i Life of the so-called 'dead'. They would then shift to
ii History,
iii The orders of human souls,
iv Cycles of incarnation.

Until the whole process of instruction had been finished he did not understand or know their object. He was encouraged to ask questions, but these had to be exact, rapidly put, and to the point. They would say 'keep us from deceiving you. do not be vague'. By the above means a most remarkable knowledge of mysticism, and European philosophy were communicated to him.[7]

Even the abbreviated style of the secretary is more than adequate to convey several noteworthy details. First, anticipating the revision of *A Vision*, WBY's wife is unnamed and almost absent from this description: the spirits come 'in conjunction' with her, but she is

---

[6] Whistles are indeed mentioned fairly frequently in the sleeps as announcements of a spirit's arrival (see, e.g., *YVP*iii. 21, 59). The whistles were heard not only by the Yeatses: on 11 Jan. 1921 WBY records that the nurse for their daughter Anne 'has begun to hear an occasional whistle but is not afraid though she knows it is a ghost. We have of course told her nothing' (*YVP*iii. 65). WBY had long been aware of whistling as one of the signs of a ghost's presence; see, for examples, details in the stories 'Village Ghosts' and 'Kidnappers', in *The Celtic Twilight* (*Myth* 21, 70).

[7] BL MS Add. 52272, notes from 6 April 1932.

not mentioned as an active collaborator, not to mention the primary medium for the communicators.[8] It seems as if he, and not she, were playing the role of medium. The 'method' used was chosen so that 'his subconscious predictions' could remain dormant; he was kept in the dark about the 'object' of the instruction. Their roles were not switched, according to these remarks. Instead, her part is subsumed into his. He is questioner as well as the means through which the answers are received. His questions, rather than leading the discussions as they have sometimes been thought to do, look here as if they were strictly controlled by instructors subjecting him to their will: any Yeatsian vague or mystical thinking was subjected to a precise discipline ('these [questions] had to be exact, rapidly put, and to the point').

The address as a whole suggests delight at this state of affairs, and indeed gives a sense of how entertaining WBY could be on such an occasion. His remarks emphasize the supernatural nature of the communications, noting such details as smells, sounds, and apparitions. He mentions a late control, who appears relatively frequently in the sleep notebooks, as the only one of 'the group of beings who were teaching him' whom WBY could identify. The story illustrates a level of ease and intimacy with the supernatural instructors that is not often noted:

This [control] he gathered had been a clergyman, who in earth life was named Carmichael, and was the gruffest of the lot, which was saying a good deal, as they all shewed considerable irritation at times.

The identification took place under striking conditions.

He had gone to stay at Oxford in a very old house, which had been in more modern times fitted with a most antiquated form of bath-room. In fact it was all bath and no room, and he had to undress outside.

One night the aforesaid Carmichael came and chaffed him about this, saying that when he was on earth he never could endure anything but a

---

[8] She is mentioned again later in the course of her husband's remarks, although his receptivity is put on an even plane with hers. A 'note' in the midst of a description of the cone as the major symbol of the teaching mentions that 'Sometimes his wife speaks as well as writes automatically. Sometimes he gets his teaching in dreams.'

wooden tub at Oxford. W. B. Y. began to make enquiries and found out that a certain parson named Carmichael had lived there [?] years previously, and that his daughter was still alive. She was communicated with, and informed W. B. Y. that her father never would use any bath but a wooden tub.

A librarian was then discovered who has met old Carmichael and said he was of the gruffest.

Indeed, Carmichael presides over a number of sleeps beginning 8 December 1920. His arrival is accompanied by acknowledgement of his idiosyncratic personality and his interest in baths. WBY's hand recorded that the previous communicator 'said he was very "cranky"', and also that Carmichael explained that baths in his day 'were round baths some tin & some wood & added "I had a fad for wood—try it & you will find it much more satisfactory"' (*YVP*iii. 59, 61).[9]

Besides Carmichael, who was a useful control as well as demonstrable proof of spirit identity of the sort the Ghost Club would appreciate, WBY mentions earlier experiences he had had with 'a lady medium', Elizabeth Radcliffe. Radcliffe's scripts, sometimes in languages she did not know, demonstrated conclusively to WBY that mediumship was genuine.[10] At one point he remarks explicitly that 'through the combined mediumship of himself and his wife many phenomena recurred.' At the end of the presentation, comments from the other guests are recorded, about such verification of spiritualistic truth as mediumistic help in solving the case of a suicide,

---

[9] To complete the bath discussion, WBY made the following note on a blank page in this notebook: 'Carmichael was probably Dublin clergyman of that name. My sister Lilly wrote his daughter & enquired about baths. She never saw any thing but a wooden tub—supposed her father used one & knew that he hated a fixed bath. W B Yeats June 1929' (*YVP*iii. 133 n. 123). A note from 26 March 1921 proposes a connection, improbably enough, between this communicator and the unborn child whom GY was then carrying: 'The unexplained name Carmichael may be connected with "Michael"—proposed name for child if a boy. can it be *gar*—for—Michael.... This spirit was described as "cranky O very cranky" ie harsh' (*YVP*iii. 75). Carmichael is also mentioned, with his bathing interests minimized, in a letter to Olivia Shakespear from 4 March 1926 (*L* 711).

[10] See Harper and Kelly, 'Preliminary Examination'.

with WBY's additional comments about episodes that convinced him of the truth of communications from 'the other side'.

Combined Mediumship

By this point in revising *A Vision* for its 1937 republication, WBY had already written a first version of the essay that would be its introduction. In that essay, entitled *A Packet for Ezra Pound* and published by Cuala in 1929, he first reveals GY's role in the reception of the system, and then seems to reverse himself. Near the end of the *Packet*, WBY is evasive: 'Some will ask if I believe all that this book contains,' he says, 'and I will not know how to answer. Does the word belief, used as they will use it, belong to our age, can I think of the world as there and I here judging it?'[11] By the time he revised *A Packet* as the actual introduction for *A Vision* (a revision that occurred just a few months before the Ghost Club speech), WBY had back-pedalled with greater energy into this famous disclaimer: 'Some will ask whether I believe in the actual existence of my circuits of sun and moon. . . . To such a question I can but answer that if sometimes, overwhelmed by miracle as all men must be when in the midst of it, I have taken such periods literally, my reason has soon recovered.' The introduction goes on to mention modern art, dropping the names of Wyndham Lewis and Brancusi, and ends on a high note of philosophical abstraction: the gyres of the system 'have helped me to hold in a single thought reality and justice' (*AV B* 24–5). The point to notice is this: the Ghost Club speech follows these two subtle avoidances of explicitly worded faith in instruction by spirits. The

---

[11] W. B. Yeats, *A Packet for Ezra Pound* (Dublin: Cuala Press, 1929), 32. Immediately after this equivocation, WBY resoundingly endorses the importance of the communications, then ends the sentence with a return to ambivalence (and also, incidentally, claims the system as his own despite the story he has just told of its automatic arrival): 'I will never think any thoughts but these, or some modification or extension of these; when I write prose or verse they must be somewhere present though not it may be in the words; they must affect my judgement of friends and of events; but then there are many symbolisms and none exactly resembles mine' (pp. 32–3).

man whose 'reason has soon recovered' is now claiming 'combined mediumship'.[12] This is the only public occasion I know of on which WBY speaks of himself as a medium, of whatever type.[13]

As the experiments continued, the spirits were less and less insistent that WBY stick to poetry. Early injunctions such as the one he received on 12 November 1917, 'You must not allow yourself to think of development in any sense but artistic—you cannot be both a psychic & an artist' (*YVP*i. 83), become less common as the weeks lengthened into months and years. In the summer of 1919, for example, Ameritus instructed both partners on how to discipline themselves to be ready for instruction, mentioning prayer. When WBY asked, 'What do you mean by prayer', Ameritus snapped back, 'What do you', and then went on:

You must discover what *you* mean by prayer before much more script
Yes
You say exasperating—I am told you are to get script only in the degree that you become ready—turn—you have to become far more SUBJECTIVE and by the method of becoming spiritually subjective by means of objective prayer—You claim you will do as we tell you but you do nothing to make *your lives* more easy for us

---

[12] The Ghost Club speech is not the only evidence to suggest that the famous Introduction creates for rhetorical effect an older, wiser WBY, whose belief in spirits has mellowed to serve aesthetic or philosophical ends. A few typed pages transcribing a sleep dated 9 March 1928 (the *Packet* is dated a few months later, 23 Nov.), were slipped into an unpublished notebook containing descriptions of CMs, diagrams, and a few pages of automatic script. WBY added a note dated April 2, a few weeks after the sleep, to the loose sheets, recording supernatural help not only in receiving the system and even writing the first version of the book, but also in the messy process of revising it. 'Dionertes came three days ago & accepted as correct my account of "The Principles"' he notes (NLI MS 36,262/22). Incidentally, this sleep was far from the last: a fragment of automatic writing dates from as late as 1933 (NLI MS 30, 011).

[13] In *Autobiographies*, WBY relates that others claimed the distinction for him at his first seance, which frightened him badly. He began to make violent involuntary movements, and 'Everybody began to say I was a medium, and that if I would not resist some wonderful thing would happen.' The result was that 'For years afterwards I would not go to a séance or turn a table and would often ask myself what was that violent impulse that had run through my nerves. Was it a part of myself—something always to be a danger perhaps; or had it come from without, as it seemed?' (*Au* 106–7).

'I am going to leave you three problems for two days thought,' Ameritus continued. First, they were to meditate on the question, 'Why does objective prayer in *subjectives* make them spiritually subjective'. Second, they were to consider 'What is lacking in your form of prayer'. Third, and revealing the conjugal and familial issues that underlie this mutual receptivity, Ameritus wanted the couple to ponder how 'your two daimons/Third Daimon/Fourth Daimon', their whole daimonic family, was connected 'with prayer' (*YVP*ii. 353).[14] WBY was to become more subjective, more in touch with interior impressions and images, to make it possible for the communicators to use his life as their palette.

WBY was clearly convinced of the benefits of being able to relax strict divisions of labour in the sessions, and as time went on, a number of advantages were seen to accrue from the questioner playing butterfly as well as hawk. In May 1920, he interpreted a vision in terms that suggest a softening of his attempts to control meaning: Dionertes revealed, WBY writes, that 'I must not read abstract qualities into George because they would destroy her spontaneity. Because system was abstract & deliberate our lives must be happy spontaneous full of impulse. . . . I was given to expecting abstract qualities from people & when they had not them hating their abstractions instead of my own' (*YVP*iii. 17). A few months before automatic writing yielded to sleeps, WBY was moving towards normalizing a paradigm that required flexibility in daily affairs as well as in poetry. In a series of sessions on Keats that illustrated receptivity rather than control as a means to poetic power, WBY saw the principle working generally: 'You have explained to us how the transference of images is a portion of normal life—is the transference of thought equally a part of normal life', he asked. 'Of course,' Ameritus replied. 'What part does it take?', he wanted to know; 'sympathy *between individuals*' was the answer (*YVP*ii. 481). Such transference and receptivity led to unusual effects in the Yeatses' daily lives, such as the routine covering of a household ornament to signal any interference with the free

---

[14] Third and Fourth Daimons are discussed in Ch. 5 below.

flow of supernormal forces. On 29 September 1920, GY recorded, at her husband's dictation, precise instructions from Dionertes. They certainly have the sound of joint mediumship: 'When he [Dionertes] came, which he did about 11.30 pm he explained that he was always with us from about 9 o'clock, & he asked us upon any night which he was not to come to cover the little indian boat upon the mantlepiece with a black cloth. On Monday night he added to this that when he gave us meditations & we found it impossible to discuss the results about 9 o'clock we were to cover the boat for an instant with an orange cloth. If we could neither discuss meditation nor receive him we were to use both cloths' (*YVP*iii. 48). The following day, Dionertes suggested that the mediums would improve on their techniques with practice: 'the Meditation was satisfactory but that later we would get away from our own personalities more' (*YVP*iii. 49). As the days went by, various supernatural guests arrived, accompanied by smells and other strange (and sometimes disturbing) occurrences; the report comes that WBY is hearing animal calls and human voices at night, and at the same time 'George now speaks in sleap in her own character' (*YVP*iii. 52). By November, WBY is noting 'the way in which we share dreams & visions & he said this sharing came through telepathy & everything' (*YVP*iii. 57). In March 1921, at work on the writing of what would become *A Vision*, WBY refers to the 'bond' between himself and GY, and that if the bond were disturbed, 'I would write it wrong'. Writing itself had been affected by something like mediumship: he comments, 'I notice that I my self cannot bear any thing irrelevant or ornamental in my exposition of system. There is a harder & tighter influence' (*YVP*iii. 75). He was approaching the state advocated by Dionertes: 'life should be a ritual' (*YVP*ii. 535).

The importance of WBY's claim to mediumship is not primarily biographical, although the personal implications of aligning himself with the most subordinated position in occult occupations are themselves significant. In literary terms, his 'mediumship' helps to explain particular energies in the late work that derive from what might be called spiritual conviction. Unusually, WBY's late poetry that is riddled with visionary content is not only stronger than his early hermetic-laden work but also, paradoxically, quite often less 'preachy' than some of the non-religious material, less prone to defensive positions and oracular pronouncements about, for example, Anglo-Irishness. The presence of spirituality in his work tempers and complicates his tendencies to be, as Terence Brown delicately puts it, 'very vulnerable to political excitement' during his last two decades.[15] For example, hard-edged symbols from mystery religion save the poem 'Parnell's Funeral' from the difficulties that attend the Roger Casement poems. Water and swan, emblems that move into other realms beyond Lady Gregory's woods, do much for 'Coole and Ballylee, 1931'. The intoning injunction to 'Irish poets' to 'learn your trade' in 'Under Ben Bulben' is lucky to have those mysterious horsemen framing it; and so on.

   Some of the old, but still relatively common, myths about WBY are partly to blame for a lingering misrepresentation of the general observation that his faith strengthens his verse, particularly those aspects of his faith that show him consorting with the lower classes, taking wisdom from his wife, or toying with the exotic East. Luckily, the story goes, his passions for hermetic magic, spiritualism, and even the automatic experiments, not to mention his connections with Indian philosophy, including Tantrism, in the 1930s, were one by one transmuted into the more artistically promising region of 'metaphor'. In other words, he could use his religious convictions for his art. This rather neat formulation has its problems, though. The first trouble with it, as we have seen, is its own race-, class-, and gender-blind conception of art and artists. A corollary to this disciplinary liability may be equally unavoidable, but should at least be noticed. There is a tendency with a figure as complex as WBY to compartmentalize his productions and areas of activity, often with reference to pre-defined academic boundaries, so that the body of Yeats criticism contains a number of studies of the plays or the

---

[15] Brown, *Life*, 339.

poetry, WBY's work in the theatre, his nationalism, his sexuality, or his public relationships with men of letters, and so on. Relating one area to the others is a messier task, running risks of diverting clear argument into a morass of amorphous tangents.

One last problem with thinking that WBY turns belief into metaphor is that in fact he does do just this, although not in the usual sense. Denis Donoghue has noted with reference to cultural nationalism that WBY did not believe in a pre-existent Irish 'race', though he talked about one often enough. Instead, WBY conceptualizes Irish identity actively, as 'what he wants to create, by many acts of summoning and conjuring', as if he were practising ritual magic. In other words, WBY's symbols can create reality, as of course it is in the nature of symbols to do.[16] WBY's metaphors aim at a greater level of real power than most writers attempt, even at their most confident. From the time of his initiation into the Order of the Golden Dawn forward, he did not merely intend to carry meaning from one level of signification to another. He meant for his poetry to evoke presences, specifically and powerfully. He worked by analogy, magical ritual and poetic practice developing in parallel with each other throughout a long career.

Some of the strength of the late verse is doubtless due to WBY's attainment to the higher orders of this double vocation. However, some of that strength is due not to WBY the magician but to WBY the medium. WBY is famous for being élitist, as he clearly was, but he also read about, sought out, and practised with GY an esoteric practice whose presumptions locate him at a more complex paradigmatic crossroads. Magic had all the appeal of a modern world derived from Renaissance humanism, the will of centripetal Man enabling him to gain control over the universe that emanated out from him by means of specific words, objects, and actions. Mediumship, on the other hand, broke into English culture from the frontiers of North America and the British Midlands, and from the wilderness of

[16] Denis Donoghue, 'Ireland: Race, Nation, State: The Charles Stewart Parnell Lecture, 1998', in *YA* xiv. 16.

powerful table-rapping women and sensitives from labouring classes, smacking of vague immensities and threats to mainstream religious and social hierarchies, although it tried from its genesis to fit itself to a *status quo*. WBY's metaphoric mediumship changes his discursive life. As Nora Kershaw Chadwick notes in a study of poetry and prophecy, the rhetoric of magic establishes authority and arrests ambiguity.[17] The rhetoric of mediumship, as we have seen, tends to do just the opposite: it gains force from disruption and multivocality. GY took down WBY's interest in this paradox in a note appended to a report of a sleep from August 1920: 'I [WBY] forgot to say that when he [the communicator] spoke of the Daimon when famished seeing circumstance with some detail, he said "that is why you have often had very good communications when things have not been going well with you" ' (*YVP*iii. 40). In system-speak, the famished daimon feeds off emotional turbulence, not the self-satisfied clarity, the 'lack of lure', of a 'teacher Ego' (*YVP*iii. 39).

In WBY's late work, a voice intones as mage or bard, but it also impersonates marginalized characters, and characteristically renounces or doubts the power of art to the degree that such force resides in active, willed exertion. Some early poems, like 'The Ballad of Moll Magee', 'The Meditation of the Old Fisherman', or 'The Lamentation of the Old Pensioner', assume the voices of marginalized figures, and vacillation is part of the resonance of many of WBY's most moving poems (not least in the poem with that title), but in the late verse achievement through renunciation is often figured as emptiness to great effect. Hence the wisdom of the hermits in 'Meru', which grows beyond 'ravening' thought to awareness of 'the desolation of reality' (*VP* 563); hence also the gaiety of 'Lapis Lazuli' or the echo in 'The Man and the Echo'. The sequence that follows 'The Three Bushes' ends not with the triumph of spiritual love, which the lady and her lover celebrate with notions that sound like WBY's early poetry, but with the voice of the chambermaid describing

---

[17] N. Kershaw Chadwick, *Poetry and Prophecy* (Cambridge: Cambridge University Press, 1952), 22.

the departure of the lover's spirit, 'Blind as a worm' (*VP* 575). The great shapers of culture in 'Long-legged Fly' achieve their status through the non-action of the famous refrain, each mind moving upon silence 'Like a long-legged fly upon the stream' (*VP* 617). Even the commemoration of WBY's old friends in a number of the late poems rests upon such symbolic actions as Lady Gregory doing nothing but sitting at her ormolu table or Maud Gonne waiting for a train in 'Beautiful Lofty Things' (*VP* 577). Structurally and tonally, the late WBY also perfects a sense of happenstance in which a poem seems to move with its own volition, the poet's voice following rather than shaping it, a phenomenon noticeable in such works as 'The Tower' or 'Among School Children', written in the late 1920s. The automatic experiments, which began in emotional emergency and as spiritual adventures, became in that decade fully integrated into the Yeatses' daily lives, requiring flexibility, humour, and relinquishing of control on the part of both partners. The change registered in the verse parallels the couple's achievement of occult mutuality. WBY became a daily visionary at last, and the poetry finds a way to live at the intersection of natural and supernatural ('death-in-life and life-in-death' (*VP* 497)), as the system became less a matter for urgent excitement and more the stuff of ordinary experience. The miraculous arrived without fanfare only after WBY learned not to demand it.

The same *Packet for Ezra Pound* that contains WBY's softening of the bold claims of supernaturalism in *A Vision* also brings up spiritualism, of the common variety, to suggest that some readers might 'hate me for that association' (*AV B* 24). 'But', he goes on,

Muses resemble women who creep out at night and give themselves to unknown sailors and return to talk of Chinese porcelain—porcelain is best made, a Japanese critic has said, where the conditions of life are hard—or of the Ninth Symphony—virginity renews itself like the moon—except that the Muses sometimes form in those low haunts their most lasting attachments.

The gendering of spiritualism here is obvious and significant, as is the linking of spiritualism with the rich mix of gender, sexual promiscuity, class consciousness, and creativity that is familiar territory in the late WBY. In the wake of the joint mediumship of the script and other experiments, new possibilities for collaborative and polymorphous creativity were on the prowl. WBY was on the look-out for places where he and his Muses might go, well aware of the 'lasting attachments' that might be formed if one gives oneself to unknown sailors, from unknown ports of call.

Celestial Bodies

WBY's imaginative surrender to otherness in his late work, a surrender often figured in gendered terms, has an important source in the sexual politics of the script. Sexuality was, of course, indispensable to the system. When WBY asks Rose 'what special quality is given to communicating by my touching medium', the answer is plain: touching makes possible 'an interchange of a psychical nature for one thing to enable certain future work to be done' (*YVP*i. 349). The physical explorations of a newly married couple, with the added resonance of decisions about conceiving children, are intertwined with the psychic adventures of two magicians/mediums experimenting with exertion of power, submission before it, mutual efforts, and transcendental possibilities. The script varies in its attribution of authority to one party or another, its insistence upon mutuality, and its multiplicity of voices. The sexual dynamic underlying it is also marked by exchanges, between the two members of the couple, among various qualities or roles attributed to each, and between identifiable entities and a universal reservoir behind or beneath them. A notebook entry demonstrates such exploration: WBY records a curious double dream in which GY dreamed of a 'seemingly herculean christ' but 'when one came near his herculean look was all [?] appearance for he was week'. WBY dreamed of 'a hercules . . . lying naked asleep or resting. I wonder how a woman could desire such great coarse strength & then it seemed to me I became a womans mind & I felt the desire of the strength & I touched his genital organs, but this did not seem to awake. The same night George dreamed that she had had intercourse but that it was over. She was in the moment of quiet after it is over' (*YVP*iii. 87).

Sexual identity and practice, like the truths of the system themselves, are amorphous as well as embedded in rigid structures, created as well as predetermined by the geometries of destiny and choice that the Yeatses were bent on discovering. Sexual exploration (with an obvious debt to Tantrism) and the system are both obvious in an exchange from late 1919. WBY asks about orgasm, supposing that since 'instinct being stimulated to the highest point before finish, finish [is] an end not a stimulation', but he is told that the 'finish' is 'essential' because 'at End woman becomes male, man becomes female'. A shift in point of view occurs: his orgasm is for her, not him, so that her 'desire becomes positive'. Furthermore, crucially, this positive sexual desire is 'essential to script' (although '*only when between 2 who are connected*', Ameritus hastens to add). The 'transmission' of thought—or, rather, as the control corrects himself, of image—from one partner to the other is possible, and this exchange is another way of describing flexibility of gender: 'each receives masculinity or feminity from the other—that is transmission' (*YVP*ii. 484). Marital sex and the system, occurring as mirror images of each other, contribute to WBY's increasing emphasis in his work from the late 1920s and 1930s on the wisdom of the body. In the second version of *A Vision* WBY writes that the marriage is the symbol of the solved antinomy (*AV B* 52), and his work insists with growing intensity upon an undoing of the duality of body and soul, the inseparability of physicality from abstraction.

One way to see this sexual shift occurring in WBY's poetry is by following imagery of two kinds of bodies: heavenly ones that form the matter of astronomy or astrology and the corporeal forms of living human beings.[18] Connections and substitutions of these two meanings for the word, body for body, are scattered throughout WBY's poetry and drama from beginning to end. The trope is ushered

---

[18] For a more specific focus on this trope, see my 'Celestial Bodies: Sexual Cosmologies in a Collaborative Vision', in *YA* xv. 102–19.

in by the Happy Shepherd whose song, written in 1885, has opened WBY's *Collected Poems* since 1933. This poem attributes to 'cold star-bane' the dead truth of 'starry men', the bodies in the heavens both affecting and serving as metaphor for the bodies of their learned interpreters, men who peer at the stars through 'optic glass' and whose once whole, living hearts have been 'cloven and rent' by their distant attachment (*VP* 66). A final appearance of body for body substitution occurs as late as 1938 in a few pregnant comments in *The Herne's Egg* such as John's protest that his wife is 'jealous/If I but look the moon in the face' (*VPl* 1028). This remark adverts to a common use of the metaphor of heavenly bodies in literature: love poems figuring various parts of women's bodies as celestial objects, most often stars or the moon. However, in usual poetic practice the metaphor is static, referring to beauty that the lover-poet perceives as unearthly. John's worry suggests a bold change in the trope that in fact occurs in the late WBY, the vehicle encroaching upon the territory of the tenor and hierarchical distinctions between the provinces of the two fading. Woman and moon are positioned as equals, and John is helpless.

The moon starts writing back, we might say, as the late WBY expands the tradition into increasingly occult territory. The celestial bodies exert increased power over the images they suggest, and then participate with those images in a poetic system that privileges neither. The poet's stance shifts from one in which dominance over the terms of a metaphor expresses avoidance of an immediate body in favour of a vague and distant other (in this practice he is of course like the heart-damaged 'starry men' of 'The Song of the Happy Shepherd'). Direct astrological influence is evident in his middle period, as stars, among other symbols, take on increased ability to affect the scenes that they reflect. In the later verse, the speaker's overt manipulation of the scene wanes further, and the astral bodies, sometimes even dramatized into acting roles, go far enough beyond a system we might term 'metaphoric' to make the conventional poetic terms meaningless. WBY comes to incorporate semiotic excess and failure of verbal control into patterns that suggest, paradoxically, increase of power on the part of speakers who can risk travel into the unknown. Like mediums, they gain authority by being vulnerable; their seeming passivity earns them power.

In *The Herne's Egg*, as Attracta waits either to be raped by seven men or to consummate her marriage to the Great Herne—or both—she sings of her 'pale brother' coming 'Out of the moon', and asks, 'Who will turn down the sheets of the bed?' (*VPl* 1029). Her lack of hesitation in the face of an erasure of boundaries between the foully profane and the consummately sacred is her power, symbolized by the old metaphor turned inside out. No longer is a male voice envisioning a distant Love (in the service of the lover's argument) pacing overhead and hiding his face 'amid a crowd of stars' (*VP* 121). Rather, a female character chooses her fate: 'the lot of love' has become much more inexorable, as in the poem 'Chosen' from the sequence *A Woman Young and Old*, one body mingling with another in a willingly passive state, 'adrift on the miraculous stream/Where—wrote a learned astrologer—/The Zodiac is changed into a sphere' (*VP* 535). The danger of intimacy, which is palpable in early volumes like *The Wind Among the Reeds*, is still present, but there is a new willingness to engage, at the risk even of annihilation. It is significant that the later position is often expressed through the voices of women, whom WBY more than once chose as speakers in his late work for figurations beyond those manageable through his own poetic self.

WBY had an interest in female figures of astronomical and/or astro-logical import from very early in his poetic life. The skies above *The Rose*, the 1893-dated sequence in *Poems* (1895 and subsequent editions) are filled with such figures or (further highlighting their status as objects) parts of their bodies. For example, the Rose of the World in the poem with that title has a 'lonely face' that lives change-lessly 'under the passing stars', not 'amid men's souls' (*VP* 112). In 'The Rose of Peace', the archangel Michael would 'weave out of the stars/A chaplet for your head' (*VP* 113). 'The Sorrow of Love' features a 'girl' arising as a moon (*VP* 120). In subsequent volumes, 'A Woman Homer Sung' was celestial enough to have 'trod so sweetly proud/As 'twere upon a cloud' (*VP* 255), and 'Fallen Majesty' memorializes a woman by recording where 'a thing once walked that seemed a burning cloud' (*VP* 315). Of course, there is nothing new about a trope that figures an object of desire in a love poem as a heavenly body, beautiful, unattainable, timeless although potentially changeable in its course, an object on which to gaze and a part of creation whose movements have secret meaning for men's lives. In this usage, as in many others, wby is a consciously conventional poet, bending the conventions of Western lyric poetry to new uses in an age that seemed contorted with changes in the relationships between men and women. Elizabeth Cullingford has made this general point beautifully,[19] and I will not elaborate on it here except to notice that bodies of women in the air or outer space are frequent in the poetry before *Responsibilities* (1914), although wby appropriates the old trope in ways that show its uneasy application in his place and time.

The strain in the metaphor is clear in 'He Wishes his Beloved were Dead', from *The Wind Among the Reeds* (*VP* 175–6). The poem is deliberately confrontational from its title on, the speaker in his role of spurned lover easing his own pain by projecting a death wish on to the beloved, foregrounding an ever-present but seldom articulated aspect of the old dance of female objectification in love poetry. The beloved would have the perfect kind of body from which to make a heavenly object, cold and inert, if only she were not living. Only the speaker's assertion of an existence that transcends bodily life modifies the daring of his assertion. If she were dead, his beloved would come, bend her head, 'murmur tender words', and not 'rise and hasten away'. If entering into a relationship with a woman is like a hunt (and the beloved in the poem has 'the will of wild birds'), the chase presumably ends with a successful kill. Even though the speaker of this poem, named Aedh in the 1899 volume, is seemingly

---

[19] See Cullingford, *Gender and History*. On 'He Wishes his Beloved were Dead', see pp. 48–9.

passive, wishing instead of hunting, he has still done something for which he needs his lover's forgiveness, and he still plays by the rules: success in love requires the entrapment and loss of individual will of the love object. So it must be if love is devotion to perfection, worship of a statue or other lifeless object, since by definition living things cannot be perfect, completed, and timeless. The beloved in this poem would, if she would only follow the poet's wishes, 'know your hair was bound and wound/About the stars and moon and sun', a state that would presumably exalt her but also confine her, enveloping her in the images her lover has made. Further, the death wish is his own, as the lover-poet knows. His vision of the beloved has trapped him, so that he would—in the half-serious, decadent manner of the poem, or like Axel and Sara in the vault under the castle—possess her only by losing her, fulfil his biological imperative only by denying it.

In the decade and a half between Maud Gonne's marriage and WBY's own, the poet's love lyrics, like his life, underwent a series of wrenching transformations. None the less, when talk of love enters his work from this period, it continues to resonate with astronomical overtones. The poet Seanchan in *The King's Threshold* (1904) evokes celestial bodies in a half-hallucinatory moment just before his death. As he enlists his wife Fedelm's help to starve himself, he mistakes her hand for 'another hand/That is up yonder' in the heavens, where 'There is a frenzy in the light of the stars/All through the livelong night, and ... the night/Was full of marriages' (*VPl* 300, 304). After 1903, *The Shadowy Waters* features the lovers passing out of mortality, expressing their love for each other by putting the moon between them. Forgael wonders whether he should be jealous of the sky, if 'the moon/[is] my enemy', and Dectora's answer turns the trope, assuring him that her desire is to manipulate the moon on her lover's behalf. She has appropriated the heavenly body for her own purposes: 'I looked upon the moon,/Longing to knead and pull it into shape/That I might lay it on your head as a crown' (*VPl* 335). More openly powerful, the images begin to cause correspondences in the characters below. The planets reveal with prophetic force the erotic frenzy of a dying man's visions or the complex desires of a queen in love with a man who has killed her husband and taken her by force. As Elizabeth Heine has shown, WBY returned to an intensive period of astrological study during these years, working diligently at primary directions, a difficult and advanced area of study, and also invoking planets and aspects, combining astrology with the magical training he had received in the Hermetic Order of the Golden Dawn.[20] A shift in the poetry has occurred so that starry images no longer represent vagaries of emotion; now the realm of the human is a reflection of astrological forces. A woman will be drawn to a man, WBY notes in 1909 (in a passage from his journal that has Maud Gonne much in evidence), 'because she represents a group of stellar influences on the radical horoscope' (*Mem* 165). 'We are mirrors of stellar light', WBY wrote, 'and we cast this light outward as incidents, magnetic attractions, characterizations, desires' (*Mem* 167). Human beings are both mirrors and lamps, emanating as well as generating heavenly energy.

WBY's comfort with the notion of a double source for inspiration, from the self and also, simultaneously, from beyond the self, reverberates in the main principles of *A Vision*: the tinctures, waxing and waning through the cycle of phases of the moon, and the double cone, representing the idea that everything is comprised of itself and an opposing force. These principles in turn, as we have seen, mimic the process of the script: the nightly sessions were, the Yeatses believed, both a passive reception from an outside force and an active construction, resulting as a matter of course in a system of symbols that are both invented and true. Foster notes that this kind of conception was by no means new to WBY: the poet was 'from very early on . . . conscious of two kinds of truth, essential and factual', a predisposition that 'enabled him, usefully, to come down on two sides of the visionary question at once'.[21] From his early years, WBY

---

[20] Elizabeth Heine, 'Yeats and Maud Gonne: Marriage and the Astrological Record, 1908–1911', in *YA* xiii. 3–33.

[21] Foster, *Apprentice Mage*, 51.

was drawn to the idea that folk culture has it right in not being able easily to 'separate mere learning from witchcraft' (*E&I* 10), for example, or that different ages had different truths: people of ancient times 'looked as carefully and as patiently towards Sinai and its thunders as we look towards parliaments and laboratories' (*E&I* 44).

With the experience of the automatic sessions, however (and increasingly, as automatic writing yielded to the less arduous techniques for reception of speaking in sleep or writing down dreams), this handy double-mindedness appears not in the abstractions of a writer whose prose on visionary questions is filled with equivocations and rhetorical questions, or even the experiences of a magician in the planned and willed rituals of the Golden Dawn. Rather, Janus enters the everyday, becoming, as George Mills Harper has noted, 'Yeats's conviction that by recognizing, or living as though, the spirit world were everywhere at hand, it becomes so' (*YVP*iii. 1). A telling pair of entries in one of the notebooks which WBY kept after the daily automatic script ended makes this point well. On 2 May 1922, WBY noted that the control for a sleep (in which information was to be received through dreams) 'complained that the system did not sufficiently enter into all the details of my work'. The next entry revises: 'He corrected my memory of sentence in the last sleep[.] He had complained that the system did not enter into all the details of our *life*, *not* as I had thought of our work' (*YVP*iii. 105). 'Life', 'not . . . work'; and, significantly, 'our work', not 'mine'. The joint mediumship of the script was having a profound effect, and it is interesting to note that it is WBY who uses the plural pronoun, not necessarily the control (or the interpreter).

In poems that follow the period of the automatic script, astrological bodies of women in WBY's poems are presented as generating meaning and exerting power, in ways that variously upset stability or stasis in the beholder. In 'An Image from a Past Life', the 'sweetheart from another life' is seen not by 'He' but by 'She', not as image of an other but, she says, as 'An image of my heart', and drastically mediated, in starlight reflected in a stream. These unstable images are uncanny and threatening. She covers the eyes of her lover so that he cannot gaze on the stellar body, hair, and fingers. The celestial body of this rival is not bending but hovering, not available for capture by the power either of a lover or of a poet but wild, throwing up her arms in an unreadable gesture, perhaps aggression, perhaps freedom.

Later poems, too, show this new dynamic. In the first poem of 'A Man Young and Old', a sequence from *The Tower*, the beloved leaves the lover/speaker 'Emptier of thought/Than the heavenly circuit of its stars/When the moon sails out': woman-as-moon acts upon man-as-human and he, not she, becomes 'lunatic' (*VP* 451). Moon is pictured as woman in 'The Crazed Moon', from *The Winding Stair and Other Poems*, and again makes the humans beneath her 'moon-struck' (*VP* 487). In *Words for Music Perhaps*, the poem 'Her Dream' is spoken by a woman who imagines that, under the impress of 'night's fathomless wisdom', something translates her shorn hair into 'Berenice's burning hair' (*VP* 519), the constellation Coma Berenices, which has a particular meaning in the context of the script.[22] In the last session in which it appeared, Berenice's hair, which the Egyptian queen sacrificed to Aphrodite after her husband's safe return from war, represented 'desire & sacrifice', WBY was told. By her act, Berenice effected 'the ideal man changing into the real man', an accomplishment that was linked, intriguingly, to the myth of the 'chariot with black & white horses' that was the catalyst for the script two years before (*YVP*ii. 483, 470; iii. 399–400). The hair of a woman in the heavens, in this heavily coded reading, is associated with GY at a critical moment, when she agreed to marry WBY. By doing so, she enabled the solar and lunar horses of his chariot to pull together, providing him with doubled energy. The two gyres of a double cone could be productively yoked. Berenice's hair is an image in which love and war are linked (as they are in Sato's sword, one of WBY's favourite images because of this linkage) and drawn into a heavenly pattern. That pattern, the constellation, symbolizes

---

[22] For a summary of the references to Berenice in the script and its relation to the poems 'Her Dream' and 'Veronica's Napkin', see *MYV*ii. 343–6 and 357–8. The myth was one of four that were identified with Moments of Crisis; see, e.g., *YVP*ii. 483.

a life saved. For WBY, those horses pulling together—primary and antithetical, objective and subjective, active and passive, rational and instinctive, male and female, physical and spiritual aspects given equal rein—drive life itself. The hair, part of a woman's body that in WBY's poetry is especially sensual, is transformed into starry image by 'desire & sacrifice', under the auspices of the divinity of sexual passion, and thereby changes her husband from abstraction into a 'real man'.[23] In the sequence 'A Woman Young and Old', the poem 'A First Confession' features another example of heavenly body figured as woman, who as speaker turns the gaze of men into their weakness once again:

> Brightness that I pull back
> From the Zodiac,
> Why those questioning eyes
> That are fixed upon me?
> What can they do but shun me
> If empty night replies?

> (*VP* 533)

After 'joint mediumship' entered WBY's creative experience, we might say, the empty night began to reply. Images of women rendered as cosmic bodies show the late verse reworking gendered subjects as well as objects, and relations between subjects and objects, moving toward a tendency to represent these categories as empty until filled by interaction, but even so, remarkably unstable. Female bodies in the heavens make themselves felt as unsolvable but expressive presences, and those in their circles of influence find their illusions of separateness and singularity dissolve. Wisdom is gained through recognition of the messages that these planetary bodies represent, sexual-spiritual oppositions begetting ecstatic truths. Thus, WBY's exultant hermit Ribh, one of the most fully realized personae to emerge from this emotional and philosophical thread in the late

---

[23] 'The Myth of Berenice', the Yeatses were informed, is 'the first CM [Critical Moment] of woman' (*YVP* ii. 483). A chart on card A34 identifies the first CM of 'GHL' as having occurred in 'Sept 1917', when the Yeatses' tumultuous engagement took place.

work, sings that the 'mirror-scalèd serpent is multiplicity' (*VP* 556) and speaks of regenerating ancient truths in terms of astrological oppositions: 'If Jupiter and Saturn meet,/What a crop of mummy wheat!' (*VP* 562).

Interpenetrating Gyres

The geometries of the system—that is, the precise, measurable shapes and calculus-like movements of figures with which it is saturated—as well as its diagrammatic quality, from the most overarching concept to the smallest tetradic detail, are so alien to WBY's habits of thought as to give an almost mediumistic quality to their presentation in *A Vision*. The rhetoric, especially in the first edition of the book, adds to this sense, with frequent alterations between first-person plural and singular voice (as well as the occasional impersonal 'one' and variations within the first person that suggest that 'I' or 'we' are themselves sometimes impersonal, general subjects). Similarly, WBY refers at times to the 'documents' that are his sources and admits difficulties in understanding or in figuring out the placement of certain ideas within the exposition, as if he were faced with a task of organizing pre-written material rather than composing. He even seems to admit defeat in a few places, most often in Book II, 'The Geometrical Foundation of the Wheel'. Near the end of that book, for example, he strikes an almost pitiful note:

There is much else that I must leave to my student, if such there be, to discover as he compares symbol with symbol. His task will be easier than mine, for I had to discover all from unconnected psychological notes and from a few inadequate diagrams. These few pages have taken me many months of exhausting labour, but never once have note and diagram failed to support each other. In judging a man one should not only know his phase but his cycle, for every cycle has a different character, but into these characters I cannot go at present, for I lack information. (*AVA* 170)

The odd place of *A Vision* in Yeatsiana is due to this quality far more than any other. WBY was himself well aware of the lack of integration between the book and his work as a whole, and that, consequently, readers of WBY the belletristic writer might well find the mathematical *Vision* less than appealing. In 1937, aware of the need to address the audience of the Macmillan edition, WBY's introduction anticipates trouble: 'Some, perhaps all, of those readers I most value, those who have read me many years, will be repelled by what must seem an arbitrary, harsh, difficult symbolism' (*AV B* 23). The poet's instincts have proved accurate: of all the difficulties posed by *A Vision* in the decades since its publication, the greatest critical acrobatics have resulted from the tasks of comprehending the diagrams and accommodating their meanings to WBY's *œuvre*. Yet most serious readers of *A Vision* agree that the geometry is centrally important, even if it may not be finally understandable. Colin McDowell's work makes perhaps the strongest case for comprehensibility, and he is correct that dismissing the mathematics has negative critical consequences: 'The assumption that the geometry is irrelevant certainly makes reading *A Vision* easier, or rather it allows one to think that one is reading *A Vision*, but it is demonstrably just as much an assumption as any other. Unfortunately, it is an assumption that closes down possibilities rather than opening them up. It also allows critics to continue to believe that they are so much more intelligent than WBY, because they would not have bothered with all of that nonsense in the first place.'[24]

To browse in the *Vision* papers is to see that a diagrammatic mind other than WBY's makes the geometry possible. Although the documents are dotted with sketches by both partners, GY's are more precise, and she is more likely to solve a problem with a diagram than is her husband. Her private papers are dominated by visual representations of intellectual states, from horoscopes to Golden Dawn notebooks filled with cabbalistic drawings, tables, and diagrams copied for spiritual advancement (although WBY made similar copies in order to progress through the ranks, his drawings betray little enthusiasm for

---

[24] Colin McDowell, '"The Completed Symbol": *Daimonic* Existence and the Great Wheel in *A Vision* (1937)', in *YA* vi. 199. See also Saddlemyer, *Becoming George*, 698 n. 102.

visual and mathematical qualities), besides the numerous segmented circles, double cones, lightning flashes, and coiling spirals in the automatic script itself. There is a connection, and a strong one, between GY's precise visual imagination and the strongest meanings of *A Vision*. Her spatial thinking outstrips her husband's. This ability allows her to answer WBY's questions with visually conceived ideas or actual diagrams that present striking levels of detail.

However, although the geometry is certainly an example of elements originating with GY that influenced her husband's work, even perhaps the clearest example of this principle, the significance only begins with this observation. More crucially, WBY conceives of the geometric quality as a symbol for the joint mediumship at the heart of the automatic experience, his sense of being annulled in a series of relationships whose circles and motions describe a complex process of approaching meaning, not merely one set of such meanings. The continual process was more essential than the intellectual product. The importance of this discovery stayed with him until the end of his life. It flows into phrases from a famous letter written a few weeks before his death: 'It seems to me that I have found what I wanted. When I try to put all into a phrase I say "Man can embody [the] truth but he cannot find it".'[25]

In the coded language of the first edition of *A Vision*, WBY writes of this power as belonging not to his wife but to a mediumistic condition, which is itself generalized into a property that is available to everyone, not just mediums. The automatic faculty, he writes, along with ectoplasm, 'that plastic substance sometimes visible at séances[,] is an element of personality' (*AVA* 246). It is natural, and, significantly, it results in geometry:

[25] This passage, with its sound of final wisdom, owes much to GY not only in sentiments but also in use. When a copy, from a letter WBY had written to Elizabeth Pelham, was sent to her after his death, she made it available to biographers and critics. In this detail, as in many others, the posthumously created figure of WBY has more of her joint creation about it than is generally recognized (Saddlemyer, *Becoming George*, 559–60). Interestingly, Saddlemyer located the letter from Pelham, which has the word *find* and not *know*, as quoted in *L* 922 and elsewhere. It is interesting to speculate on who is responsible for this change.

The automatic personality is never perhaps a puppet in the hand of the spirit that created it, but has always not only its own automatic life but that reflected from the man himself. When, however, the creator's control is continuous, the thought and its expression may reveal a mind with powers of co-ordination greater and swifter than those of the embodied mind. One can most easily study these powers in their physical expression, and it has long been known that the hand of the medium can under such influences trace perfect circles or make patterns of sweeping lines with a rapidity and precision no voluntary movement can achieve. . . . One notices there and elsewhere that mathematical clarity one would expect from *Daimonic* domination. It is possible even that the first jugglers did not so much imitate the effect of magic as display a sleight of hand, the result of their obsession by an automatic personality. (*AVA* 247–8)

Diagrams confront a reader with the plane of representation as vividly as with the thematic material, foregrounding the sign as well as the level of signification, as do Pound's ideograms. The semiotic to which these particular cones and gyres draw attention is one of 'Physical expression', of 'mathematical clarity' that proves multiplex personality ('*Daimonic* domination', in the terminology of the system), and of performance, as the analogies of puppets and jugglers make clear. Indeed, these geometric figures, considered as 'masterful images' and not 'those things that they were emblems of' (*VP* 630) open into worlds of meaning only insinuated in the published book, even in the first version, with its relatively close relationship to the experience of the script and other experiments.

A trail leads backward from the passage above into a manuscript of an early version of the book. Following the twists of this trail leads ultimately to a variant of the Robartes–Aherne narratives that nearly tells a conjugal and occult secret of vital importance. The emotional energy of this secret makes necessary the fictional smokescreen of the Robartes–Aherne stories. Those strange and elaborate pieces of obvious chicanery are blown over *A Vision* at various junctures to destabilize and deflect, but also to hint broadly at directly personal (and also neither sombre nor pompous) interpretations of the philosophical prose. In the 1926 book, at the point where the automatic faculty is defined, two paragraphs signed by Owen Aherne, set off in parentheses, interrupt the disquisition (*AVA* 245–7). Both intrusions relate incidents from a tale Robartes told of a patient of 'an old Judwali doctor', a young Arab boy with an amazingly active automatic faculty. The boy 'talked in his sleep and would answer questions', allowing Robartes to carry on 'conversations upon the most profound problems of the soul with an automatic personality which seemed sometimes the boy's own spirit and sometimes an extraneous being'. Several incidents about this extraordinary boy are retellings of events featuring feathers, flowers, and smells; WBY also records them having happened to GY and himself during the period of the sleeps. Despite the air of tangential interjection, as if Aherne cannot stop himself from adding to WBY's exposition, the stories are relevant to the subject at hand, of course, in that they illustrate the automatic faculty.

Owen Aherne's parenthetical remarks are in fact distilled from longer sections of a typescript which the Yeatses filed with the numerous drafts of the book. The typescript, like many of the drafts, is a shorter version of the system as a whole. WBY composed much of the book by accretion, writing one version of a cluster of ideas and then replacing that draft with another, longer version of the same section as he came to understand the system more thoroughly. This typescript, which starts with the heading 'Book Three', Section I, 'Where Kusta-ben-Luka got his philosophy', begins with the story of the 'elderly philosopher' and his young wife, whom the caliph Harun al-Rashid bestowed on his friend Kusta.[26] The autobiographical resonances in the tale still have a level of autobiographical immediacy and potential indelicacy that would be smoothed out as WBY reworked it later:

Some say that he [Harun] bought her from a passing merchant, but others that he first thought of her on hearing that she had, to the surprise of her friends and relations fallen in love with the elderly philosopher. Kusta-ben-Luka was a christian, and had planned, one version of the story says, to

---

[26] NLI MS 36,263/24/1–2.

end his days in a Byzantine monastery, while according to another he was engaged upon a love affair which he had arranged for himself. But warned in a dream, or afraid of disobedience—both tales are told—he married this young girl. They were married but a few days when she began to talk in her sleep, and her wisdom was so great that he saw at once that the Caliph had acted under divine guidance, and that she had been brought to him that he who had sought wisdom in libraries might learn all the secrets from an ignorant mouth. When awake she was but a merry child, and he never told her of what she spoke in sleep, fearing that it would make her think his love but self-interest, and that if he praised her, or gave any sign of love, it was not for her sake but for the sake of wisdom. She taught him for a number of years, often walking to the border of the desert in her sleep, and there marking upon the sand innumerable intricate symbols.

'Book Four' of the typescript, 'Death, the Soul, and the Life after Death', begins with the story recycled for *A Vision*: 'Michael Robartes and the Judwali Doctor' (fo. 17). In this longer version, the doctor, 'an old man who returned more and more to the philosophy of his youth', is visited often by a young man, a 'turbulent and irascible' character whom the doctor had once cured of a stab wound. The doctor tells Robartes that the young man still comes round and 'spends as much of his time as I will permit' in his house, but arrives just to fall asleep. Then, the doctor continues,

"I talk a great deal, and listen a great deal for all that, and yet I do not know with whom I talk." Then he made Robartes squat down beside him, and asked some question which the sleeping boy replied to, and the question was strange and the answer profound, and for a half-hour he questioned and was answered, and Robartes noticed that if the question lacked precision or showed a misunderstanding of some previous answer, the sleeping boy seemed angry. The doctor said presently "Is it Kusta or his wife who answers?" Robartes pointed out that the arabic was modern and the answers showed just the kind of vocabulary he would expect from so turbulent a youth. (fos. 17–18)

Robartes, with his superior knowledge of occult visitations, thinks the doctor 'literal minded' in believing that the speaker is either Kusta ben Luka or his wife, but he lets the old man continue.

"It cannot be Kusta-ben-Luka's wife" the doctor said "for she is gentle and submissive, it must be Kusta-ben-Luka himself. I would ask, but when you are dead you soon cease to remember your own name, and if I were dead, and did not know who I was, I would not like to be asked for my name, even if perhaps I could find out what it was by making inquiries." Robartes noticed that the sleeper, if it was the sleeper, had strange gifts of abstraction and arrangement, as though the mind had been purged of some gross element, and at these times the range of facts upon which he could draw spread out far beyond the range of Robartes own memory or experience, and at other times both mental gifts and knowledge dwindled till anything but some simple answer seemed beyond his power. Once the doctor said as he sat squatting beside the sleeping man, who had not yet spoken, "I have come to the conclusion that it is Kusta-ben-Luka's wife who comes, for if she had been as gentle as they say, her husband would never have kept her in ignorance of her somnambulism. He was certainly afraid of her, and he could not have kept silent for so many years if he had been excitable. I think therefore that he was very placid and patient, and that she was what you call a charming little cat." (fos. 18–19)

At this point, the story takes a turn toward literal suggestibility, and moments are related in which the young man believes himself to be a cat,[27] blows as if he had a mouth full of turkey feathers, and tries to hoot like an owl he had seen recently. In a final dramatic moment, he rolls off the mat and lies 'with rigid limbs' on the floor, dreaming, the automatic voice explains, 'that men placed him between the forks of a tree, and that a woman, while musician[s] beat drums and blew horns shot him dead with an arrow'. The narrating voice of Aherne returns: 'When Robartes told me this I was able to prove that Shikkak [the young man] had dreamt an old ceremony connected with tree worship. Mr Yeats had once a similar dream or vision.'[28] Immediately preceding the dramatic moment of

---

[27] Animals occur in a number of episodes in the sleeps, and WBY seems to have been impressed, perhaps especially with the ones featuring cats. In this typescript, the sleeper 'made a sound like lapping' because, the voice says, he 'thinks that he is a cat, and I cannot keep him from lapping milk'. See also *YVP*iii. 49–50, *AV A* 245, and *AV B* 10.

[28] The ritual involving the tree alludes to the spring ceremonies of Cybele and Attis, described in Sir James George Frazer, *The Golden Bough: A Study in Magic and Religion*,

the simulated slaying of the young man, Aherne and Robartes have explicated such automatism: ' "It was", Robartes said "as if all the image-making power had been separated from the reason, and that at times the image making power took complete control of the lips, but more often it would but interrupt for a moment." ' Further, Aherne continues, 'The image making was however apparently continuous and known fully to the other half of the mind, or to the being that used that other half. Sometimes, though rarely, it seemed that the image making power acted under suggestions from the discussion, that it symbolized in some way the philosophical answers.'

The narrative of the doctor and the young man was intended to have a more integral place in the web of framing material than just that of covertly describing the automatic script, its purpose in its main published form, the poem 'The Gift of Harun Al-Rashid'. However, at this earlier point in the process of writing what would become *A Vision*, wby planned for the automatic dialogue, not the fictional book by Giraldus that is prominent in later drafts (and in the first edition of *A Vision* itself), to be the direct source for the material that followed it. The tale in this typescript ends by explaining its importance to the larger explication:

It was these conversations with a sleeping man that enabled Robartes to adapt the thought of Kusta-ben-Luka to modern necessities, and to find a European expression for the Arabian law of history. He brought his suggestions to the sleeper that they might be rejected, accepted, or modified. When the voice itself took the initiative the method of exposition was always that adopted according to legend by Kusta-ben-Luka's wife. A series of statements would be made that could not be reconciled with the system as a whole until that particular subject was exhausted. "He feared the suggestions of my thoughts" said Robartes "the reasoner is maybe as suggestible as the image maker." (fo. 20)

abridged edn. (New York: Macmillan, 1963), 403–9. wby's 'similar dream or vision' may be his 'Archer Vision' of 'a naked woman of incredible beauty, standing upon a pedestal and shooting an arrow at a star' (*Au* 280). On the importance of Frazer to wby and gy, see Warwick Gould, 'Frazer, Yeats and the Reconsecration of Folklore', in Robert Fraser (ed.), *Sir James Frazer and the Literary Imagination* (London: Macmillan, 1990), 121–53.

Several aspects of this story bear examining. The automatic process in the story resembles the one WBY recalls in the introduction to the 1937 *A Vision*, in such details as the communicators' insistence on precision in questions, the withholding of synthesizing information until a particular topic was exhausted, and that the use of vocabulary or turns of phrase be those of the sleeper. The suggestion that the wife of Kusta was not as submissive or gentle as she had been represented, or that her husband was afraid of her, do not continue into the later narrative, perhaps because the 'image maker' applied pressure on the 'reasoner' to omit potential invasions of their personal privacy. Less immediately explicable, though, as well as more potentially interesting, are the definitions and illustrations of the automatic faculty, the general principle that lies behind and explains the process. The faculty comprises mathematical figures, 'strange gifts of abstraction and arrangement, as though the mind had been purged of some gross element', and an opposite null set of utter helplessness, so that 'some simple answer seemed beyond his power'.[29] This faculty or 'image making power', we read, 'acted under suggestions from the discussion'; that is, it resulted directly from the intercourse between the young man and the doctor. Moreover, it 'symbolised in some way the philosophical answers'. The cluster of images that surround this announcement, including control of lips, rigidity of limbs, and a dream of ritual sacrifice of a man by a woman, the man inserted into the fork of a tree, join the basic characters in the story to create a highly sexualized set of symbols for that philosophy. The point is that the automatic faculty cannot be understood by figuring out if the voice is that of any of the actors on the scene, whether Kusta, his wife, the young man, the heritage of the doctor, Robartes or his mysteries, Aherne, or indeed WBY. Rather, the faculty, which symbolizes 'in some way' the philosophy

---

[29] A double meaning for this phrase may be suggested in a definition of the automatic faculty, which WBY quoted on an index card: 'The higher the cultivation the greater the automatic faculty The converse is the fixed idea. cultivation brings varience of subject' (*YVP*iii. 294; see also *YVP*ii. 3). A simple, fixed idea may well be beyond the power of someone in whom the automatic faculty is strong.

itself, arises from the relationships between the characters. Repeating geometric/sexual figures can be drawn from the positions they form: a 'turbulent' young man asleep beside an older doctor who squats beside him, both of whom may be possessed (the doctor tells Robartes at one point, 'I was always told Kusta-ben-Luka or his wife would come if we could find the right sleeper') by the 'merry' and cat-like young nameless wife and the elderly Kusta ben Luka, her unlikely husband, the multiply resonant personae Robartes and Aherne, and of course, behind them, WBY and the woman with whom he explored a many-angled and never-ceasing phantasmagoria.

Sexual desire was a major catalyst for the script, and a consistently stated purpose for the automatic sessions was to enlighten and bond the receptive partners sexually and emotionally. Any practice having to do with the script, whether meditative, intellectual, or physical, 'must be personal to yourself or it will be no use to you', the Yeatses were told in a crucial early session, on Christmas Day, 1917 (*YVP*i. 178).[30] This is the session in which the figure of the gyre was properly introduced, and a connection is made almost immediately between this most important of the geometric shapes and the human body.[31] The communicator mentions (in response to an unrecorded question) 'That which is separate and yet one now', and then gives this enigmatic visualization: 'She imagines funnell as wide part at her head [funnel] descends into herself.'[32] A diagram divides the funnel into parts labelled with cardinal directions and also Head, Heart, and

[30] This phrase follows a set of instructions in mirror writing that seem to refer to the application of spiritual exercises to love-making: after advising in mirror writing that it would be 'much better [to] ask something personal first', the communicator answers unrecorded questions with answers involving creating a 'mask of self reliance', wave-like rhythms, 'fast & then slow', and a moving figure of a funnel 'always descending to axis' (*YVP*i. 177–8).

[31] It has been suggested that WBY's reading of Tantric texts, with their geometric figures and emphases on symbolism and sexuality, influenced the development of the gyres of the system; see Foster, *Arch-Poet*, 537 and 751 n. 8, citing Naresh Guha, *W. B. Yeats: An Indian Approach* (Calcutta: Jadavpur University, 1968), 144.

[32] This body may well have belonged to Iseult Gonne, since the phrase following the one quoted above explains that 'the funnel applies only to 14', her phase, and since she had been a major topic of discussion in the previous session two days before.

Loins, the structure identified with a Blakean human body whose Loins are one of three essential components of its being.[33] It should be remembered that the system joins spatial reality to time and history by means of these geometric figures of sexualized energy. They begin outside both time and history, though. In a remarkable session many months later, as part of a long discussion of the role of daimons, the Yeatses learned the precise functions that bound the mathematical shapes with 'phisical desire', as WBY phrased it. The Third Daimon, who created the system as its presiding genius (and indeed was so closely associated with it that WBY wondered later, in summarizing the results from this evening's session on an index card, whether 'he is the system it self'), received synthetic or creative power in proportion to how well the couple satisfied each other emotionally. To the degree of their 'phisical desire', however, the daimon received a different power that Thomas called 'construction'. In an important session, WBY asked for and received clarification of what the control meant by the terms 'construction or creation'. Construction meant geometry, and it was caused by desire, as opposed to satisfaction: 'Phisical desire alone would give merely mathematical form,' he proposed, to which Thomas answered, 'Yes' (*YVP*ii. 246; *YVP*iii. 291).[34]

In the first edition of *A Vision*, this sexual energy is more occluded than in the script or early drafts, but the genetic documents help us to notice its various disguises. WBY's first explanation of the gyres, for example, attempts to show the joining of space and time, as well as historical causation (Fate and Destiny), in a phrase that adds heterosexual desire to one of his favourite ideas from Heraclitus: 'it is as though the first act of being, after creating limit, was to divide itself into male and female, each dying the other's life living the other's death' (*AV A* 130).[35] This dying and living is a metaphor for the sexual act: because 'this system conceives the world as catastrophic',

---

[33] The fourth term, Fall, had been added to the Blakean trio by the control on 22 Nov. 1917 (*YVP*i. 103).

[34] This session, from April 1919, was significant to the 'bi-sexual' gendering of the system as well as its daimonic sources. See Ch. 5 below.

[35] On the sources for this quotation, see *CVA* Notes 32.

WBY explains, people like gyres move and are moved in orgasmic motion. If a single gyre suggests male arousal, the larger double cones seem to suggest female arousal: they 'continue as before, one always narrowing, one always expanding, and yet bound for ever to one another' in a 'fourfold' form (*AVA* 132). The extensive commentary in the script on the Moments of Crisis is generalized in the published book, but what remains is another paradigm that explains human life by means of a geometric figure-cum-sexual allusion: the shape of a human life can be expressed by a series of angles called a Lightning Flash, a jagged figure whose vertices represent Moments of Crisis, precisely delineated kinds of emotional experience that define individual lives. The first two types of Moment, Initiatory and Critical, are 'the expression of the wheel in the life of sexual passion' (*YVP*iii. 111). These Lightning Flashes are not merely personal: they also trace shapes of races or movements as well as individuals.[36] They are one of many details of the system that illustrate the general principle that the rhythms of physical human connection, which are also emotional, intellectual, and spiritual, create patterns of cosmic significance.

The sexuality of the system is flexibly gendered, as we have seen. It is also flexible in terms of the object of desire: as the story of Michael Robartes and the Judwali doctor suggests, the philosophy is by no means uniformly heterosexual in orientation. The fluidity with which gender is assigned and reassigned, to people, spirits, daimons,

---

[36] Interestingly, the Lightning Flash considered as a whole is a geometric expression of non-determinism within the system. Its omission from *A Vision*, along with the Moments that comprise it, arguably tilts the balance and creates in the published version of the system an overemphasis on determinacy. 'The Lightning Flash because of its irregular & incalculable movement expresses that which is unique, that which cannot recur just as wheel & cone expres [*sic*] all that is seasonable,' WBY explains. In making symbolically present a person's 'entire emotional past' as well as his or her future, 'The Lightning Flash is therefore the man in emotional relation to his past, made present; & in intellectual relation to his future conceived as present. It is because of this that he is an individual & not merely a type of his phase. at every moment he chooses his entire past & his entire future, though he is not conscious of his choice till on the threshold of the BV' (*YVP*iii. 114–15). For diagrams of the Lightning Flashes of WBY and GY, see *YVP*i. 205–6 and iii. 330–1.

or abstractions, parallel suggestions of variabilities of desire attending some of these reversals and shifts. In the Yeatses' experience, a number of possibilities for domestic and conjugal shifts of expectations were latent in the methods of the script. The interpreter wrote the words of her authoritative and productive communicators, most of whom were male, in an activity that must have resembled male impersonation. Those male voices came for a purpose that included establishing mutually satisfying marital relations, to arouse a man's desire as well as that of the woman through whom they spoke. The questioner's identifications with patriarchal masculinity show similar swerves from the conventional in his roles of seeker or questioner as opposed to author or knower, in settings that included frequent occasions when some infirmity of his was addressed through her young strength and knowledge. Nor does the homoeroticism in the structure of the story of the old doctor and the young man disappear in WBY's parallel fictions featuring a younger figure who is female. For example, despite the gender of the mediumistic young wife in the poem 'The Gift of Harun Al-Rashid', ben Luka believes that 'the voice [that brought the mysterious wisdom] has drawn/A quality of wisdom from her love's/Particular quality' (*AV A* 126). The 'particular quality' resonates with suggestions of alternative positionings of wife and husband as 'the voice' spoke and 'A live-long hour/She seemed the learned man and I the child' (*AV A* 125).

WBY frequently represents the sexual ambiguities of the automatic experience through references to the precise diagrammatic nature of the system. His remarks often sound notes of dominance and submission, violence and nurturance, destruction and continuity. In the 1937 introduction, recalling how the communicators gave the system, WBY stresses his bafflement, especially over the geometry. '[T]hough it was plain from the first that their exposition was based upon a single geometrical conception,' he relates, 'they kept me from mastering that conception.' First it was one cone, then two. 'They shifted ground whenever my interest was at its height, whenever it seemed that the next day must reveal what, as I soon discovered, they were determined to withhold until all was on paper' (*AV B* 11). The

Scheherazade-like controls of this passage make geometric abstraction correspond, tantalizingly, to the lure of suspense for the end of the story in *The Arabian Nights*. Like the Sultan, WBY is entranced, and what we might call *textus interruptus* stands in for delayed sexual gratification as well as the erotic potential of play with roles and power. He mentions 'how completely master [the communicators] could be down to its least detail of what I could but know in outline, how confident and dominating' (*AV B* 21). Although the published introduction is more circumspect than the earlier documents, WBY's rhetoric here still retains a vestigial suggestion that he found memorable the reversals and deferrals in sexual roles that characterized the experience of receiving the automatic script. The script contains frequent admonitions, chastising the questioner with remarks such as 'just your usual lack of precision' (*YVP*ii. 278), and often commanding WBY to work out one geometric pattern or another. To give one example, on folios that have several horoscopes filed with them, he was urged to figure out relationships between himself, GY, Maud Gonne MacBride, and Iseult Gonne in terms of triangles and mathematical equations: 'state in terms of X Y Z—Z is dual'; 'X + Z − Y/ Y + Z − X'; 'No/ Frankly I am not playing/ if you are to go on to B. Vision [Beatific Vision] & script to follow certain things must be achieved'; 'Step by step the two triangles must be identified' (*YVP*ii. 384–5). It is tempting to imagine the poet enjoying and reproducing in one semi-autobiographical fiction after another the sexually resonant mathematics instructors and their willing student, hiding the pleasure beneath the shapes, stating 'in terms of X Y Z' the steps he and the interpreter took in order to achieve 'B. Vision'.

At its furthest refinement, in the 'Stories of Michael Robartes and his Friends' that frame the 1937 *A Vision*, the secret sexuality of the geometry, as well as the solution to its otherwise endless oppositions, is expressed in that most common of metonyms, the marriage-bed. John Duddon sets down 'a few passages' from 'a long discourse founded upon the philosophy of the Judwalis and of Giraldus, sometimes eloquent, often obscure':

I found myself upon the third antinomy of Immanuel Kant, thesis: freedom; antithesis: necessity; but I restate it. Every action of man declares the soul's ultimate, particular freedom, and the soul's disappearance in God; declares that reality is a congeries of beings and a single being; nor is this antinomy an appearance imposed upon us by the form of thought but life itself which turns, now here, now there, a whirling and a bitterness. . . .

Death cannot solve the antinomy: death and life are its expression. We come at birth into a multitude and after death would perish into the One did not a witch of Endor call us back, nor would she repent did we shriek with Samuel: 'Why hast thou disquieted me?' instead of slumbering upon that breast.

The marriage-bed is the symbol of the solved antinomy, and were more than symbol could a man there lose and keep his identity, but he falls asleep. That sleep is the same as the sleep of death. (*AV B* 52)

The paradox of freedom and necessity is gendered for Robartes, which is why the marriage-bed works well as a symbol for the solution of the antinomy: he puts the masculine set of principles, 'the soul's ultimate, particular freedom', the world's varied 'congeries of beings', and life itself into opposition with 'the soul's disappearance in God', apprehension of all beings as 'a single being', and death (upon whose feminine-gendered breast the masculine 'we' slumber after we die). Yet his paradigm is troubled, first by the curious mention of the witch of Endor, who, like other figures of witches (including Crazy Jane, whose witch-like qualities are part of the disturbances she represents), upsets regulatory controls on sexuality, including stable gender divisions.[37] She recalls us from the safe embrace of death, as if she were tempting us to leave our proper spouse, and her act might cause us to 'shriek' (a verb choice with feminine associations by way of misogynist resonances in WBY and other writers from the period of women's suffragism),[38] at such overturning of propriety. None the less, that symbolic resolution to the antinomy, the marriage-bed, continually offers

---

[37] The woman of Endor consulted ghosts despite a prohibition by King Saul; see 1 Sam. 28: 3–25.

[38] See Cullingford, *Gender and History*, ch. 7, for the connection between women's voices and feminist activism in Yeats.

the possibility of undoing boundaries, including sexual propriety and gender difference, even if that possibility is continually frustrated. Incidentally, Robartes's hyper-male pomposity is effectively deflated by his own metaphor for the inevitable frustration of the eternal anti-nomy not quite solved: the male lover falling asleep after coition. The world stays, as Sheba, another witch, quite rightly says in 'Solomon and the Witch' after her kingly lover's speech about what might be crowed in 'when oil and wick are burned in one' (*VP* 388).

Gender is not the stable distinction it appears to be; its two poles participate, as does every other polarity, in a dynamic that moves opposites simultaneously ever closer and ever further apart. WBY is careful, in typical fashion for the first edition of *A Vision*, to qualify that Heraclitean aphorism: 'it is *as though* the first act of being ... was to divide itself into male and female' (*AV A* 130). The marriage-bed represents the further mystery of desire fuelling the oppositions, although, given the inability of humanity to stay awake to the possibility of a reality beyond the mystery of selfhood (how to 'lose and keep ... identity'), we, like Robartes's 'man', doze off. When Judith Butler points out that matter may be conceived not as a given but rather as a 'process of materialization that stabilizes over time to produce the effect of boundary, fixity, and surface that we call matter',[39] she points to a phenomenon like that symbolized by the Yeatses' gyres. Matter itself, she and other constructivists argue, is a result of discourse as law; 'the forming, crafting, bearing, circulation, signification of the sexed body' is neither static nor the same as what we might call the real, whatever human bodies may be before or outside what they are made to be. The *Vision* manuscripts corroborate such a sense of the making of reality by construction, citation, reiteration, and performance, and they do so especially in their visual, geometric aspects.

In the published book (in both versions) WBY makes reference to the centrality of this notion in coded remarks about the Judwalis, that secret Arab tribe outside the boundaries of orderly society

---

[39] Butler, *Bodies that Matter*, 9.

('this strange sect', Owen Aherne calls them in the introduction to
the 1925 book, 'who are known among the Arabs for the violent
contrasts of character amongst them, for their licentiousness and
their sanctity' (*AVA* pp. xviii–xix)), who dance shapes on the sand
and think in geometric, concrete shapes. In the stories, the Judwalis
trace their wisdom ultimately to the voices of the wife of Kusta
ben Luka, and 'Desert Geometry or the Gift of Harun Al-Raschid',
introducing the main geometries of *A Vision* in the 1925 edition,
ends with a striking evocation of the sexual secret at the heart of the
philosophy:

> The signs and shapes;
> All those abstractions that you fancied were
> From the great Treatise of Parmenides;
> All, all those gyres and cubes and midnight things
> Are but a new expression of her body
> Drunk with the bitter-sweetness of her youth.
> And now my utmost mystery is out:
> A woman's beauty is a storm-tossed banner;
> Under it wisdom stands, and I alone—
> Of all Arabia's lovers I alone—
> Nor dazzled by the embroidery, nor lost
> In the confusion of its night-dark folds,
> Can hear the armed man speak.
>
> (*AVA* 126–7)

Wisdom, a mysterious and possibly threatening 'armed man', stands
below the enchanting and entangling embroideries and 'night-dark
folds' of 'woman's beauty'.[40] This ambiguous representation of
philosophical and sexual desire, for female body or (if not dazzled

---

[40] At the end of his study of collaborative writing between men, Koestenbaum makes
a glancing reference to WBY, who 'tapped his wife's unconscious in order to place her
visions in his own name', and who, like other modernists, 'finally wanted a symbolic
system to transcend women' (Koestenbaum, *Double Talk*, 176). Although this reading
is incorrect in its own terms, it is useful to bear in mind that receiving the system
introduced WBY to areas of sexual exploration that have considerable impact upon his
work, as they had on his life.

or lost by it) for military male one, gives additional meaning to the 'midnight things' of abstract signs and shapes, although those symbols are no more controllable than that 'storm-tossed banner', furling and unfurling violently with an unseen force.

'Two Halves of One Sixpence'

At the start of the summer of 1922, the Yeatses were living for the first time in the actual tower at Ballylee, an idyllic setting that was none the less affected by a nation whose gyre was spinning toward civil war. The Yeatses were lucky more than once not to encounter disasters. In mid-June, however, the war had not yet reached the west. WBY had recently finished *The Trembling of the Veil*, a reworked set of autobiographical reflections, and his personal past was much on his mind.[41] So was a questionable Irish national future, on the edge of a Europe changed for ever, as a number of works of verbal and visual art from the watershed year of 1922 would demonstrate. On 17 June, the day after the general election that was in effect a referendum on the Anglo-Irish Treaty, and less than a fortnight before Michael Collins gave the order to fire on the Irregulars occupying the Four Courts in Dublin, GY took dictation about a system-related conversation the Yeatses had after a sleep. The topic shows the couple working with ways to reconceptualize WBY's ageing and his place in history, by means of his psychic connection with GY and an idea of history that stresses an individual's participation even if he—and this reference is to WBY—is no longer an energetic young actor in it. They talked about the Moments of Crisis, specifically the 'interaction between individual IMs & CMs and historic IMs and CMs'. Could historical moments be 'vitalized' by individual ones, so that the personal history of a man or woman, especially the emotional life, would reflect and catalyse events on a national

---

[41] Besides writing his memoirs, WBY was grieving for his father, who had died on 3 Feb.

or world stage? It seemed so: 'if one studies the CMs of historical characters, their loves', GY wrote, 'one can find their relation with the historical events of their countries preceeding, during & after their lives.' Historical sequences—that is, large patterns affecting whole periods of time—could be formed from oppositions such as 'a sentimental poetical movement', like the one WBY had just 'described in memoirs', and the current atrocities of 'an abstract violent' time. Crucially, 'the more intense the nature of a person the more will the IMs & CMs correspond to the historical IMs & CMs'. Assuming WBY to be one of those intense people, he would be leading a life whose shape would have ramifications in the larger patterns of history. Furthermore, he noted, conjunctions between an individual and history are part of the same pattern that join two individuals: a note to the discussion adds that 'Principal part of that conversation was that the CMs which two people have in connection with one another are two halves of one sixpence' (*YVP*iii. 117).[42]

A Vision betrays in any number of ways its status as a book written from a critical moment in the life of its ageing writer, who felt himself, thanks to the revelations of the very system he was describing, a mysterious conduit for the meaning of his age. The book also speaks out of another critical moment and another connection: WBY's occult partner, the other half of his sixpence. It is important to notice this second connection, not least because that other half was related to her times in ways that are very different from her husband's. GY's historical moment, as well as his own, enter WBY's sense of history, in other words. If we remember this detail, a number of unusual qualities of *A Vision* become more intelligible, from its relationship to the cataclysmic war in Europe and its

---

[42] A cancelled start to another sentence at this point in the manuscript began to explain that the CM that WBY shared with GY (his second, her first) 'will have an importance greater than a CM which each [member of a couple] has with' someone else, like Maud Gonne, who occasioned WBY's first CM, or alone. The dates for the IMs and CMs of both Yeatses were given on occasions like the series of scripts beginning on 22 March 1919 (*YVP*ii. 207 ff.); see also *YVP*iii. 192–3.

participation in European modernism to its incessant divisions into multiplicities, each impulse requiring a split in order to function, and its characteristic rhetorical doubleness.

The sublime unity of being that is so often adverted to in Yeatsiana is in fact not peace so much as acceptance of conflict: as WBY puts it in *A Vision*, 'He who attains Unity of Being is some man, who, while struggling with his fate and his destiny until every energy of his being has been roused, is content that he should so struggle with no final conquest' (*AV A* 28). Peace, the topic of the famous missing line from the poem 'Under Ben Bulben', is also a rarity in either the generative documents or *A Vision*.[43] The turmoil of the times doubtless contributes to this stress on disunity. In Ireland, as soon as the apex of the cone of nationalism had been reached, the gyre had spun out of control again, and a new and still volatile government was forming. In England, the end of the war signalled not so much victory over an enemy as defeat for humanity in the face of the horror of twentieth-century warfare, as well as a sense of the empire's waning importance. Force was in vogue in Fascist Italy, to which WBY and GY had begun to travel, in which parts of the book were written (the dedication of *A Vision* is signed 'Capri, February, 1925', and two other sections are placed there and in Syracuse), and in whose political philosophy WBY had begun to take an active interest. Politically, as well as personally, *A Vision* is an autumnal book, which asserts plainly that it is written during one of the late phases, at 'the end of an era' (*AV A* 201). Yet it also assumes that strife is good, that unity cannot come otherwise. A passage from a sleep recorded in April 1921 makes clear that a paradoxical correlation between sexual vitality and age for WBY personally are part of a narrative of his marriage and, at the same time, symbolic substitutions for the harshness on the world stage as it whirls near the end of an era. He records complementary dreams about marriage, which came to them in answer to a question about the late phases. In

---

[43] 'The soul's perfection is from peace': see W. B. Yeats, *Last Poems: Manuscript Materials*, ed. James Pethica, The Cornell Yeats (Ithaca, NY, and London: Cornell University Press, 1997), pp. xxxvi–xli and 33.

his first dream, he 'was married to George & lost my self on coming away, found my self in some part of London instead of Coole'. Then, in another scene, 'all went well, & I invited many guests to the banquet'. Meanwhile, 'That night George dreamed of a marriage to me in a double form, on one side of altar I stood young & on the other old. The young was primary & the old antithetical & when old I was full of vitality, when young I had seeming vitality but not its reality' (*YVP*iii. 86). On a personal level, the system was to rejuvenate him by engaging him in its conflictual energy. When in the early months of script WBY was instructed, 'Do not delude yourself in the belief you have outworn everything', he asked for clarification: 'You mean that I must keep from growing old?' and was told '*Through* theory' (*YVP*i. 246).

In Ireland in the early Twenties, of course, proposing a theory of salutary violence at the end of an age could not fail to be a political statement: thus, Cullingford asserts that 'although there is little specific mention of Ireland in the text, WBY was aiming his book at the Irish'.[44] On a social level, doubtless WBY was intending *A Vision* for vetting in an Irish cultural scene, although he was neither targeting a large audience nor expecting a large public response. He did not argue with a small press run (600 copies), and added a disclaimer at the end of the volume asserting that changes in readers' imaginations do not come from even the best books of philosophy: 'the great books . . . beget new books, whole generations of books, but life goes on unchanged' (*AV A* 251). In the spring following publication, he wrote to Olivia Shakespear that the book 'reminds me of the stones I used to drop as a child into a certain very deep well. The splash is very far off and very faint.' The lack of response does not seem to have disturbed him, however, if his letter to Mrs Shakespear indicates his mood, for it ends with a note of

---

[44] Elizabeth Butler Cullingford, *Yeats, Ireland and Fascism* (London: Macmillan, 1981), 126. On Irish politics and *A Vision*, see esp. ibid. ch. 8. See also Cheryl Herr, who sees Irishness in *A Vision* in its reflection of 'the secondary codings of conflict, invasion, disaccumulation, violence, and fragmentation' of Irish history and tradition: ' "The strange reward of all that discipline": Yeats and Foucault', in Leonard Orr (ed.), *Yeats and Postmodernism* (Syracuse, NY: Syracuse University Press, 1991), 151.

equanimity: 'a few men here are reading me, so I may found an Irish heresy' (*L* 712).[45] Unlike his hopes for 'an Irish heresy' like the Celtic Mysteries, however, WBY does not hope that this philosophy will effect changes, in Ireland or elsewhere. It is worth remembering that *A Vision* was not aimed only, and certainly not immediately, at Irish eyes. Published in London, it assumes a British readership as well.

It is probably just as well that almost no one read it when it appeared: even a small audience there was unlikely to be comfortable with WBY claiming that violence is good and necessary; in the years following the Great War, such sentiments could not be more deeply problematic.[46] Yet one of the aims of *A Vision* is precisely to confront the War, albeit symbolically. As Fran Brearton notes, the war 'is a major force behind the formulation of that vision', and WBY's stance in the book is Irish not only in its dissociation from the hornet's nest of war politics but also in a suggestion of 'something alien to English attitudes toward the war—that the spectacle is ultimately, if inadvertently, productive'.[47] That productivity, a honey bee building in crumbling masonry, also

[45] His letter to his old friend complains of the lack of reviews, but he knew his Irish audience well enough to keep complimentary copies out of the hands of all reviewers except AE. Writing to Laurie the month before his letter to Shakespear, WBY foresaw trouble if others got their hands on copies. A certain bishop 'said to an acquaintance of mine the other day "We have been waiting for years to get a chance at Mr. Yeats but we are going to get it now. He is bringing out a book that will give us our chance" ', a situation, WBY notes, that 'will not help you & it will exasperate me. Their habit is to take an isolated sentence & go on repeating it for years.' W. B. Yeats Collection, Special Collections and Archives, Robert W. Woodruff Library, Emory University.

[46] The drafts of early versions of *A Vision* demonstrate that WBY had considered even bolder statements than in the published book. His imperious character Robartes dismisses the carnage in Europe as a distraction, remarking (although the passage was cancelled in the first typescript),

It is a mistake to attribute a high degree of reality to the great War. Reality is energy[.] Ben Luki has upon that matter this curious sentence "Beauty is energy in its greatest extension." The more highly articulated forms contain the most beauty and are by their nature frail soon injured, often ephemeral.... I am here because many brave Turks and Englishmen disturbed the desert by letting off their cannon, but I do not think that I have thereby been disturbed by serious life. The world is at present yawning and stretching itself; its mouth is very wide open and it [is] making a very boorish sound. (*YVP*iv. 18)

[47] Fran Brearton, *The Great War in Irish Poetry: W. B. Yeats to Michael Longley* (Oxford: Oxford University Press, 1999), 61.

bespeaks the late vitality of an ageing husband, as in his dream. In addition, it comes from a man in constructive league with the personal intensities of a second individual in her personal as well as historical gyres.

WBY had married an Englishwoman whose early adulthood had been defined by occultism and war—not only the conflagration of 1914–18 but others as well, in Persia, the Ottoman Empire, Portugal, Mexico, and China, for example (the Bolshevik Revolution ignited Russia two days after the first preserved script). Saddlemyer's biography paints a vivid picture of GHL spending the early war years in a welter of scholarly research, experiential magic, and astrological practice along with Zeppelin raids, family loss, and part-time nursing in an army hospital. By the time she and WBY married, she had spent years combining private occultism and interest in public affairs,[48] and she became 'passionately Irish in political sympathy' after her marriage, according to her cousin Grace Jaffe, an impression corroborated by her correspondence from these years.[49] Her lifelong nightmares are antinomies of her automatic sleeps, and both are expressed in the gyres of the system. It is worth remembering that WBY was writing his most compelling political poems while the first *A Vision* was being formed. Indeed, it would not be far wrong to imagine an altered version of 'The Phases of the Moon' with the old man Robartes and his friend Aherne replaced by two soldiers or weapon-carrying locals. In a silence that might be broken at any moment by the report of a gun or the setting off of dynamite, not the innocuous splash of a rat, water-hen, or otter, the two look up at the window of Ballylee lit from the nightly work not of a lone Miltonic poet seeking '[w]hat he shall never find', but two occultists

---

[48] Numerous horaries attest to this conjunction: e.g., among the Yeats occult papers is a red notebook with alphabetized tabs, whose first page is dated 1914, containing horoscopes in various states of completion for people and events in which GY was especially interested. These include a preponderance of public figures such as 'Emperor Francis Joseph of Austria', 'Nicholas II Czar of Russia', the British royal family (George V, Mary, Edward Prince of Wales, and Prince Albert), 'General Joseph Jacques Joffre', 'Kaiser', and 'Crown Prince Wilhelm Frederick of Germany'.

[49] Jaffe, *Years of Grace*, 64.

sitting across a table from each other, writing down a mysterious system that makes sense of the chaos surrounding them.

The old dichotomies, poetry and politics, love and war, swan and shadow, Art and Life, out of which WBY had written passionately for years, broaden in *A Vision*, usually into fourfold figures.[50] Increasingly, as we have seen, WBY's poems too suggest multiplicity in subject figurations flowering out of the diad of self and anti-self. We find, for example, art, the artistic living of one's life, life, and the lives of one's literal and figural children; private self, 'smiling public man' (*VP* 443), ageing or old man, and guardian or bestower of continuing value; or even young man, young woman, old man, and old woman. Put geometrically, the contrasting poles of 'the artifice of eternity' and 'that sensual music', as in 'Sailing to Byzantium' (*VP* 407–8), lengthen into axes in which time and space are reckoned in connection with the items in the equation that formerly excluded them. Art, which as a concept has been associated with a timeless spatiality of form or structure, is lengthened to include the natural, human, or social forces that both create and destroy it. Life, which is reckoned as time-ridden and linear, takes on the eternal aspect of futurity, 'those dying generations' becoming also the unending extension of life into future generations. Life as an abstraction is also embodied, in the emblematic, sacred fleshiness of late poems such as 'A Prayer for Old Age', which proclaims that 'He that sings a lasting song/Thinks in a marrow-bone' (*VP* 553), or the 'brute dolphins' and 'Intolerable music' of the disturbingly physical 'News for the Delphic Oracle' (*VP* 338). The duality of line, 'the symbol of time[,] . . . the emotional subjective mind, the self in its simplest form', and plane, which 'in combination with the moving line' symbolizes 'all that is objective', is itself doubled to form the double gyres. It is significant that the section of *A Vision* which sets forth this relation is the one

---

[50] 'Swan and shadow' are the terms used by Thomas Whitaker to clarify these contrarieties; see his *Swan and Shadow: Yeats's Dialogue with History* (Washington: Catholic University of America Press, 1989).

where that favourite phrase appears: 'It is as though the first act of being, after creating limit, was to divide itself into male and female, each dying the other's life living the other's death' (*AVA* 129–30).

On the simplest level, we might say that the doubled authorship of *A Vision*, the male and female, ageing and maturing dialogue that is its source, is manifest in the book numerically. In addition to the double cone, the Great Wheel also depends upon quaternities. The phases are divided into quarters, and the four Faculties interact among themselves in precise formation for each phase. Four Principles, four quarters of the wheel, four daimons, four books—division into four is so basic a tendency in *A Vision* that the tables in Book I of the 1925 book contain no fewer than ten sets of four characters that are associated with various phases (*AVA* 33–6). A basic point to be made about the constant division into four is that it multiplies relational possibilities among characters or principles. As in astrology, it is not only the symbols but their interaction with each other that is vital. The multiplex interaction satisfies two important requirements for any philosophical or religious system: it presents the variety necessary for a reflection of reality, and it creates sufficient complexity to bewilder the person who has not studied it with proper humility. For one who has, the Yeatsian system also makes necessary an awe at the inevitability of relationships, be they connections between parts of the psyche, between human and daimon, among present and past or future lives, or movements in history around a centre in a closed system. One level resonates constantly with others; the same interactions occur in personal life, the state between lives, history, and eternity. The moral effect of this many-layered symbolism may be seen in force in a passage that begins by describing how 'an *antithetical* philosophical inspiration' may be attained:

antithetical inspiration may demand a separation of vehicle and questioner, a relation like that between Priest and Sybil, Socrates and Diotime, wandering magician and his scryer. This relation, in its highest form, implies a constant interchange of office and such relations may so cross and re-cross that a community may grow clairvoyant. Lover and beloved, friend and friend, son and daughter, or an entire family and *coven*,[51] are brought ... into such a crisis that the *primary* oppositions and harmonies of the world are exposed in their minds and fates. There must arise in the mind of one, where the bond is between two, a need for some form of truth so intense that the *Automatic Faculty* of the other grows as it were hollow to receive that truth. Should the desire but be to impose a particular form of belief upon others or upon himself the automatic personalities may exercise their control of thought or of mechanical movement for deception; but if the man desires truth itself that which comes will be the most profound truth possible to his fate. (*AV A* 248–9)

In order for the 'most profound truth' to come, the 'highest form' of relation must be present. WBY's description of the 'constant interchange of office' that characterizes this relation, neither solitary inspiration nor each actor playing a single role, is the least veiled description of his joint mediumship in his published works. For not only must each participant 'cross and re-cross' roles, acting now Priest, now Sybil, and so on, but one role is always mediumistic: the automatic faculty must be present in order for truth on a large scale to be possible. WBY's claim here for his ability to interpret world events is very large indeed: private intensity and exchange, of the kind that he and GY were practising, illumines contemporary history within its seemingly small compass: 'the *primary* oppositions and harmonies of the world' may be 'exposed in their minds and fates'.

This large claim is staked quite obscurely, and its style is also part of this mediumistic point. The rhetoric of the passage above, and the 1925 *A Vision* generally, behaves in a curiously ambiguous fashion: on the one hand, the authorial voice is hesitant, as if reluctant to assume

---

[51] Covens are interesting conjunctions of the personal and the collective in *A Vision*. The term refers to 'the cones of each separate nation and of every school of thought and action'. They are also 'beings which have personality, though their bodies consist of a number of minds held together by a stream of thought or an event' (*AV A* 171, 228–9). WBY explains that 'I myself chose the name *Coven*' (*AV A* 171), a memory corroborated by a notebook entry from 26 Nov. 1920 that records that WBY 'asked leave to alter terminology. "COVEN" for group' (Y*VP*iii. 57). Covens do not receive as much attention in the *Vision* documents as might be expected from a writer as interested in racial theorizing as WBY. GY, however, was much less so inclined.

final responsibility for the knowledge being revealed or to be pinned down about exactly to whom it applies. Qualifying phrases like 'as it were', 'let us say', 'I think', 'it is sometimes said' (*AV A* 248, 180, 129, 160) recur, as do the passive voice, the use of 'one' as subject, and an unusually large number of conditional clauses. Throughout the book, the persona of the writer 'Yeats', friend of Owen Aherne and Michael Robartes to whom the Judwali wisdom was explained, seems intended to sound this note of uncertainty. He cites authorities and the 'documents' from which he works extensively, as if to excuse himself as authority from his material, and wanders from topic to topic, often interrupting the exposition to relate some parable or give an illustration only tangentially related to the matter at hand.[52] In structure, too, hesitancy may be felt: *A Vision* has four books, with numbered sections within each of the books, to match the precision of the philosophy, but the smaller units of organization proceed more meditatively than mathematically, anecdotally rather than analytically. The sections seem held in place by the thinnest of discursive glues, as if the writer had serious trouble figuring out how to progress from topic to topic in parts that do not have chronology or numerical sequence to guide him. Yet the authorial voice also speaks in absolutes, explaining very confusing concepts with little acknowledgement of the trouble readers must have in making sense of them, in rhetoric that is filled with logical connectives joining concepts that are not linked by logic, hierarchical use of the first-person plural, and stories or comments inserted without apology or introduction. Diagrams often add to the difficulties, especially since they often feature terms or symbols that come from parts of the script or notebooks that are not described near the points in the text where the diagrams appear. The effect is to create the subject of the book as both master and disciple, author and reader—indeed, 'vehicle and questioner', or, more concretely, 'Priest and Sybil,

---

[52] For analysis of a similar rhetorical phenomenon in the work of an earlier Irish writer, see David Lloyd, *Nationalism and Minor Literature: James Clarence Mangan and the Emergence of Irish Cultural Nationalism* (Berkeley: University of California Press, 1987), esp. ch. 4.

Socrates and Diotime, wandering magician and his scryer'. The book falls into philosophical reverie over abstract principles and displays scribe-like servitude to concrete, arbitrary geometries; it is simultaneously passionate and dispassionate at inevitable crises and equally inevitable resolutions.

At the core of these clashes and combinations of multiple positions occurring throughout the book in images, themes, rhetoric, and structures is an implied change in subjectivity, a discursive trace of the many voices of the automatic script and the dialogues between Robartes and Aherne in the early drafts of the book, but also a new prose voice to match a new vision. *A Vision* shows WBY coming to terms with new writerly possibilities in the wake of his real-life discoveries. The book was useful for him, and is to readers of his *œuvre*, not merely on the level of 'metaphors for poetry' in the sense in which his famous description of the instructors' purpose is usually taken (*AV B* 8). Quite the contrary: the significance of his presentation of the system begins with its fundamentally religious character. *A Vision* applies on a grand scale lessons learned in a private crucible, justifying that private world as well as giving levers of interpretation for the larger world. Such an act fits well with Clifford Geertz's explanation of religion's double function and circular logic:

In religious belief and practice a group's ethos is rendered intellectually reasonable by being shown to represent a way of life ideally adapted to the actual state of affairs the world view describes, while the world view is rendered emotionally convincing by being presented as an image of an actual state of affairs peculiarly well-arranged to accommodate such a way of life. . . . [In other words,] religion tunes human actions to an envisaged cosmic order and projects images of cosmic order onto the plane of human experience.[53]

A Vision is such a warrant for a way of life extended into a response to world events and an exploration of aesthetic possibility. Like the

---

[53] Clifford Geertz, *The Interpretation of Cultures: Selected Essays* (New York: Basic Books, 1973), 89–90.

poems in *The Tower*, whose energies in a curious way it makes possible, it enabled WBY to speak from a tower in the west of Ireland to a changed and changing world, to imagine mood-evoking symbols that might be adequate to the task of expressing that world. The ability of *A Vision* to envision a reality characterized by relational truth and to deny the possibility of understanding truth without submitting to shifts and multiplicities testify in good part to its silent joint author. However, WBY no less than GY is a source for such assumptions, as well as the stylistic phenomena and intellectual positions that follow from them.

The instalment of WBY's autobiographies that came to be called *The Trembling of the Veil* has a section entitled 'Hodos Camelionis', which contains memories of his intentions to found a mystical order based at a 'romantic' replica of an old castle in Roscommon that was the butt of jokes around the county.[54] He recalls that 'for ten years to come my most impassioned thought was a vain attempt to find philosophy and to create ritual for that Order'. Several important assumptions about Irishness and art that undergirded this long period of concerted effort are exposed in the next paragraphs, which describe WBY's 'unshakable conviction' that 'this philosophy would find its manuals of devotion in all imaginative literature, and set before Irishmen for special manual an Irish literature which, though made by many minds, would seem the work of a single mind, and turn our places of beauty or legendary association into holy symbols'. If its sacred texts would be creative, its rituals would not: WBY explains that they 'were not to be made deliberately, like a

---

[54] W. B. Yeats, *The Trembling of the Veil* (London: Werner Laurie, 1922), 135; *Au* 253. When *The Trembling of the Veil* was included in *Autobiographies*, the spelling of *Camelionis*, a word that WBY says vaguely that he recalls reading in 'a cabbalistic manuscript' that MacGregor Mathers showed him, was corrected to *Chameliontos*. With perhaps a touch of defensiveness at his lack of formal classical training, WBY dodges responsibility for the mistake in the later publication: 'Hodos Camelionis, not Hodos Chameliontos, were the words, a mixture of Greek and Latin typical of such documents' (*Au* 270). WBY was also hedging, using one of his favourite rhetorical strategies, a claim of memory failure that disguises a disinclination to reveal a precise source. The term came not just from some cabbalistic manuscript: it had a precise meaning in the Golden Dawn. See Ch. 1, n. 52.

poem, but all got by that method Mathers had explained to me, and with this hope I plunged without a clue into a labyrinth of images' that are warned against as 'faithless' and 'unintelligible' (*Au* 204–5). Like a good modernist, according to current critical definitions, the WBY remembered in 'Hodos Camelionis' actively colonizes the past, which is conceived as an essentially passive help to the meditations of present 'Irishmen'. He idealizes unity of culture, the making of one mind from many, but celebrates also the aestheticized individual by locating this unity in 'all imaginative literature'. Thus, although unifying values are imagined as having lost a historical position of social power, a potential restoration is envisioned for them. As David Lloyd notes, such an 'aestheticization of history and politics' is typical of Romantic nationalism, in which 'culture comes to represent the site of unity elsewhere denied by historical facts'.[55]

It is worth noting a few points of comparison between the self-portrait of the WBY evoked in *The Trembling of the Veil* and its later cousin, the WBY who wrote *A Vision* at the request of his friend Robartes. Instead of nostalgia and lamentation, which valorize the past, *A Vision* expresses a double emotion that grieves at joy and celebrates tragedy. Since 'the system constantly compels us to consider beauty an accompaniment of war, and wisdom of decay' (*AV A* 139), emotional states that might cry, 'Romantic Ireland's dead and gone' (*VP* 289) are less likely to be rewarded by being versified than the dread-transfiguring gaiety of 'Lapis Lazuli'. As Cullingford notes, recognition of otherness in time, as opposed to a state of mind which refutes or supplants the past, 'means acceptance of the validity of both the antinomies: each predominates in turn, but neither has a monopoly of truth'.[56] Temporal otherness is not only recognized; it is ritualized in the symbols that connect past and present with the soul's life. Thus the unity of culture for which the first WBY strove is shifted slightly to become a state that may only be attained through submission to disunity. History is no longer appropriated; it is an

[55] Lloyd, *Nationalism and Minor Literature*, 72.
[56] Cullingford, *Yeats, Ireland and Fascism*, 123–4.

active participant in the soul's journeys between sun and moon, as any ritual object or action changes those who use it.

Furthermore, even the primacy of aesthetic culture is subordinated to a larger pattern and separated as a concept from the autonomous subject. The first WBY is plagued continually by difficulties arising from the conflict between the individual artistic conscience and the needs of the corporate identity of the nation or culture; the author of *A Vision* sees aesthetic freedom and social reality as twin gyres. Likewise, the old argument between materialism and idealism or spiritualism is recast as the motion of a spinning gyre. Ultimately, of course, the artist and the idea still prevail, because it is he who composes and it which comprises the book. None the less, it is important to note that WBY the First, the colonizer in the name of unity of culture, was created at the same time as WBY the Second, the narrator of *A Vision*. The artist who made both (WBY the Third?) takes the measure of WBY 1 certainly, in the person of WBY 2. WBY 2 may fare better, in that he prefers the system's gyres to imposed notions of unity; but, according to Robartes, 'Mr Yeats has intellectual belief but he is entirely without moral faith, without that sense, which should come to a man with terror and joy, of a Divine Presence, and though he may seek, and may have always sought it, I am certain that he will not find it in this life' (*AV A* pp. xxi–xxii). WBY 3, the husband of GY and co-explorer with her of the system's intricacies, may look down on both, from the heights of the terror and joy he had found.

Of all of WBY's works, *A Vision* arguably carried him furthest toward the literary future. It most nearly resembles and is accessible to a postmodern sensibility, sharing a number of characteristics with later texts characterized as postmodern. For example, authentic subjects are whirled away in the dancing geometric and phasal masks, despite assertions that the individual remains. Diagrammatic surfaces draw attention away from emotive depth; indeed, charts, diagrams, and esoteric vocabulary undermine the qualities of depth suggested by language itself. Sexual desire is separated from clear gender identity, and is associated with absence or loss as well as the inadequacy of consciousness-derived subjectivity. The elaborate framing devices play with the implied epistemologies of philosophy and, more broadly, writing, at the very least casting doubt on the seriousness and reliability of the book they so carefully set up. In addition, the emphasis on disunity concomitant with a search for unity prefigures a number of Irish poets, 'postmodern' or not, from the generations after WBY, who have tended to take cultural brokenness for granted 'in a country whose most precious contribution may be precisely its insight into the anguish of disunity', as Eavan Boland commented in 1974.[57]

In *The Trembling of the Veil*, near the end of 'Hodos Camelionis', WBY digresses into a little Neoplatonic-sounding story of birds (among the most common symbols of the women in his life in the script), interlaced with an anecdote about his 2-year-old daughter, her mother, and his still unborn son. The story ends with a rhetorical question: 'When a man writes any work of genius, or invents some creative action, is it not because some knowledge or power has come into his mind from beyond his mind?' (*Au* 216). The question here proceeds from a previous answer, in the method that the Yeatses were taught to observe during the growth of the system, and the answer lies in 'the constant interchange of office' that enabled their roles to 'cross and re-cross' during their years of exploration.

---

[57] Eavan Boland, 'The Weasel's Tooth', *Irish Times*, 7 June 1974; repr. in Robert F. Garratt, *Modern Irish Poetry: Tradition and Continuity from Yeats to Heaney* (Berkeley: University of California Press, 1986), 10.

5

All the Others: Dramatis Personae

> Your system is all we think of—only that matters
>
> Thomas, automatic script, 20 March 1919 (*YVP*ii. 201)

The Yeatses' automatic sessions were an interaction between two people with a huge array of figures in the background, some speaking or yielding influence, some silent or weak in spiritual force, some with consistent presence, some fragmentary or fleeting existences. It is not easy to fix attention on this supporting crowd, not least because most of its members are not so much fully realized figures as complex symbolic elaborations of two basic ideas: first, that human beings are not single entities but complexes, on various levels and kinds of self-awareness, at various times and places; and second, that people are always connected to each other, although often the connections take place on one or other of these same levels, and so are almost infinitely complicated. A seemingly unified human being is a blend, in continually differing proportions, of such components as an Ego, a Mask, a Body of Fate, and a Creative Mind—the four Faculties—as well as the four Principles, which form a sort of reverse image of the Faculties and exist after death in a doubled temporal scheme like that of daimons: 'The Daimon is your after life both during your life & after life,' as WBY summarized it neatly in the card file (*YVP*iii. 292). At any point, a person's action or thought may come from a proper or improper relationship among any of these properties. One Faculty or Principle may interact with one or more belonging to another person. Any human being is also actually just one incarnation of many as the wheel of phases turns, and other incarnations are part of the being considered *in toto*, so that relationships from other lives may, as in the case of an overshadower, affect people unawares. Aggregate beings also exist, and they implicate individuals: marriages, families, covens, nations, or periods of historical time, all have personalities and associations. All beings, individual or aggregate, also have personal divinities or genii, their daimons, existing in an alternate anti-universe; daimons consort with each other in their mysterious mirror worlds, and the human beings on the other side of the glass are moved without knowing why. At various points, images, like eagle or unicorn, seem to describe beings.[1] Smells are signs of presences; symbols used in astrology (like Saturn or Neptune) act with some sense of personality, and various positions also seem to define something a bit like presences, such as Teacher and Victim, or primary and antithetical selves.

The power to create or communicate the system can itself seldom be rigidly assigned to one or other of the individuals, human or ghostly, who have speaking or walk-on roles in the phantasmagoria. Instead, subtle shifts in the level of control over the material occur and recur over the hundreds of sessions and later occasions on which the data was 'codified' in various ways, in notebooks and on index cards. This state of affairs is a cosmic parallel to the human affair, in which the human partners lived and worked together, had conversations and mutual experiences, formed and then wrote or spoke questions which were then recorded by one or other of them. The interpreter then prepared to answer them, writing occasionally in her own voice but most often shifting spiritual gears from being convener or scribe to being the secretary of a disembodied spirit or her own daimon, in varying states of consciousness. The writing itself is a symbol

---

[1] The unicorn is associated with GY's daimon, as WBY told his friend Sturge Moore (Ursula Bridge (ed.), *W. B. Yeats and T. Sturge Moore: Their Correspondence 1901–1937* (London: Routledge & Kegan Paul, 1953), 91). It was also equated with 'Daimon' in the script of 31 May 1919 (*YVP*ii. 294), in a cluster of questions that refer to *The Player Queen*. The play had been finished, after a long gestation, and then published while *Per Amica Silentia Lunae* and the script were also in process.

of authorial variability. The handwriting is sometimes obviously automatic, with large round loops written by a pen never lifted from the page, sometimes ordinary, sometimes in 'mirror writing' or other variations. Sometimes, especially in the later months and years, answers were typed. Sometimes she related a dream for him to write down; both kept notebooks; he made a file of index cards that usually quote a message received automatically through her hand, sometimes citing a passage incorrectly even though carefully enclosing it within quotation marks. Then came years of more hard work, with him writing sections of play-like dialogue, prose fiction, or expository prose, sometimes dictating to her, sometimes carefully avoiding dictating to her so that her creative or receptive abilities would not be interfered with, sometimes writing out a passage by hand any number of times before reading it aloud to a typist. Sometimes she corrected his typescripts, sometimes he did, and sometimes both worked on them, either relying solely on their own authority or, at times, after consulting with the communicators to make sure that the summaries and analyses were correct.

As the method infers, the dramatis personae have their primary context not in the symphony of other figures and images but in the human beings: WBY, who had long explored poetic issues of inspiration and voice, whether experimenting with the intersections of individual voice and bardic communal speech, or through concepts like the Mask or *Per Amica*'s Anima Mundi, and GY, who was able to express without descending into chaos or crisis an astounding body of philosophical and personal, creative and critical material, all the while managing varying states of conscious control. In fact, her script is usually directed toward more than one level of meaning at once. However, more than either member of the couple, the script depended upon ensemble. The ability to work out ideas jointly, questioner and medium/interpreter in effective partnership, gradually increased. This change reflected greater sympathy between husband and wife as the disastrous start to their marriage retreated into the past. The instructors made sure to note the change from productivity based on emotional distress. After about a year of the

Yeatses' married life and supernatural work, Thomas went ahead with a short session of script on genius, although he began with a refusal—'no script today'—so that summary and analysis, and the writing of poetry, could go ahead instead: 'no writing on it [the system] unless poems'.[2] After thirty questions, Thomas ended with a statement in mirror writing: 'The more you keep this medium emotionally and intellectually happy the more will script be possible now—at first it was better when she was emotionally unhappy but now the passivity is as small the opposite' (*YVP*ii. 119). The theme that satisfying his wife was necessary for the work to proceed made several appearances. In June 1919, soon after arriving alone in their well-loved Ballylee, the new control Ameritus reminded WBY again in mirror writing that 'script depends on the love of medium for you—all intensity comes from that' (*YVP*ii. 323). In the abstractions of the system, this mutuality was expressed in various ways, as the 'emotional philosophy' of phase 18, for example, or as one of four types of wisdom. The wisdom of intellect, desire, and knowledge came from other phases, but 'the wisdom of heart comes at 18' (*YVP* ii. 98).

The wisdom of heart involved more than harmony, however; tension between the two parties was also essential, as was made clear in an early and significant session. 'Is this work made possible by a certain harmony of nature', asked the new husband on New Year's Day 1918. The reply, 'harmony or rather *discord* [is] necessary', refers to the opposing gyres that would underpin the system as a whole, as

---

[2] It is rare for the instructors or GY not to encourage poetic work, although on a few occasions, like the session on 12 May 1918, after a few weeks that may have seen the composition of such poems as 'The Second Coming', system work seems to have piled up so hopelessly that WBY was told to focus on 'codifying': 'You are not to write any more poems on system for 2 or 3 weeks because I want you to finish all this work' (*YVP*i. 443). See *MYV*ii. 19. Plays were also sometimes encouraged, though less often than poetry. After a few months of script, in early January, WBY was apparently in danger of being distracted. Near the end of the session, he asked, 'Can [you] give any advice about personal spiritual training'. The answer to this, 'I dont know it', was not sufficient. He pressed: 'What further can I do'. The communicator replied, 'Simplify your life nothing else Dont look for work outside your own.' From this, WBY eventually discovered that 'The Noh plays' were 'all right', as well as 'lectures if settled & not done at random from restlessness' (*YVP*i. 208).

well as the conditions required for its arrival (the symbol had been introduced one week before, on Christmas Day). After a question about whether 'such dual work' was the kind that he and Maud Gonne attempted, to which the answer was 'It might have been but could never have been successful', WBY asked for elaboration: 'What kind of discord makes such work possible?' The answer was particularly detailed: 'Similar interests diversity of opinion sex must be alike mind different emotion alike soul different but alike—I mean in tendency not necessarily in quantity but in quality or nature' (*YVP*i. 186). WBY's 'different' and 'unlike' bride, who shared much but also asserted difference, was his necessary complement in this wisdom. Like Solomon and Sheba, the wisdom the Yeatses sought was revealed only as they went 'round and round' (*VP* 332). They strove with and against each other through the questions and answers of their method: indeed, one of the fascinations of the script, for this reader certainly and perhaps for the Yeatses as well, when they studied it afterward, is precisely the complex mixture of antagonism and alliance that its format encouraged. Although 'not a man or woman/Born under the skies/Dare match in learning' (*VP* 333) the two experimenters, they laboured long and energetically to understand the system's 'single light,/When oil and wick are burned in one' (*VP* 388). Like Blake, the couple clearly believed that contraries 'are necessary to Human existence'.[3] It did not take long for the founding oppositions of primary and antithetical to become defining principles of the system, and by the spring following the start of the script, the Blakean term had also been agreed on. 'Is life then opposition & contrast', WBY asked on 31 March 1918. Aymor answered, 'Yes it is the contact of contrasts'. WBY proposed, 'Of contraries', and GY wrote, '*Yes* that is the word' (*YVP* i. 406).[4]

Contraries were always balanced by contact, though. Complex symbols, astrological computations, and ancestral links (as well as references to a 'child') in the spring of 1918 cluster in a session

---

[3] W. Blake, *Complete Writings*, 149.

[4] This statement was important enough to be repeated in one of the notebooks that the Yeatses used for their codifying: '*Life* is the contact of contraries' (*YVP* iii. 174).

that includes this advice about intimacy between the two humans and the creation of the system: 'the closer the link the closer the reading by us of your thought & the easier it is [?sent]' (*YVP* i. 440). The Yeatses are linked, the instructors read their thought, and then, presumably, send them the philosophic information, in a convoluted chain of agency and action. In a long and productive session with Thomas, Leaf, and Fish, on the Feast of the Epiphany 1918, WBY asked whether 'soul at 15' was 'analogous to man or woman of faery', and the answer he received may reveal much about the instructors and other figures that people the script:

The difficulty is that *all descriptions* of life are in a sense only analogous—The people of fairy the souls at one & fifteen and all other legendary states are but parts of one truth—The truth is in all but in some more concealed by fable & by dream than in others—that is all I can say. (*YVP* i. 214)

'The truth is in all' the many personages of the script. This truth may be concealed by fable and dream, as the instructors say, but we may also wonder how much clearer things would be if expressed differently. Perhaps GY's determined resistance to publishing the system or even talking about it came in part from a realization that it would be very difficult to explain just what part she, or her husband, for that matter, was playing in the proceedings: no matter what the description, it would be bound to be 'only analogous'.

Daimonic Concordances

The collecting of daimons, in she & I is practically the system embodying it self by its own momentum.

WBY, index card (*YVP*iii. 291)

Of all the beings that populate the script and other *Vision* documents, daimons are perhaps both the most confusing (to the Yeatses as well as to later readers) and also the most instructive.[5] They represent

---

[5] For an instructive study of WBY and this topic, see Haswell, *Pressed Against Divinity*.

in their very nature a key instability in the system, as well as its practical twin, the process by which it was received. Daimons in Western culture have a long history of just this instability: from Socrates through Plutarch, Frederick Myers to spiritualist writers like Geraldine Cummins, to WBY's own *Per Amica*. It is never clear whether a daimon is a minor god or an emanation from someone's own interior state. The main characteristic of daimons, it would seem, is to sit squarely on an ontological fence, making a psychological phenomenon seem sacred, or domesticating the soul or divinity into mundane second selves. In the Yeatses' automatic experiments, daimons were the focus of considerable attention from the first session through late codifying,[6] but the issue of their status is never clearly resolved. This paradox makes even more sly WBY's famous equivocation about the source of the system in the introduction to the 1937 *A Vision*: 'again and again they [the communicators] have insisted that the whole system is the creation of my wife's Daimon and of mine' (*AV B* 22) could mean, as it is usually read, that the whole business came out of their own heads, even if WBY may think in terms of souls rather than just material brains.[7] This reading is corroborated by the next sentences, which contrast daimons or 'blessed spirits' to 'mere "spirits"', although WBY goes on to claim that daimons find reality in 'what they call, in commemoration of the Third Person of the Trinity, the Ghostly Self'. This Trinitarian knot not only sets up the status of the 'Ghostly Self' as distinct from the daimon,[8] but it also begs the question of the separate status of

---

[6] Daimons were an important topic as early as 10 Nov. 1917, and figure largely in the second of two copybooks containing working notes for *A Vision*. However, the first mention of a daimon occurs in the first recorded script, in a reference to '2 invisible & inaudible & immanifested but 3 who communicate' (*YVP*i. 55). This comment is quoted in one of the notebooks mentioned above and identified under the topic 'Daimons' (*YVP*iii. 174).

[7] Virginia Moore reads a change in the status of daimons as one of the most important changes in conception between the 1925 and 1937 *A Vision* (Moore, *The Unicorn*, 367–70). Colin McDowell finds an even greater significance in this topic, claiming that '*A Vision* in fact exists in order to expound Yeats's theory of daimonic existence. His mature ideas appear in *A Vision (B)*' (McDowell, 'Completed Symbol', 197).

[8] The difference between the daimon and the ghostly self was problematic not only in WBY's published prose but also in the original documents. However, notebook entries

daimons as divinities: they find reality in an analogue to one of the Persons of the Trinity, but they are not that Person. There is no safe ground on which to stand here, and this radical uncertainty—are they part of ourselves? are they beings from beyond? could they be both, in some way?—is analogous to the fundamental uncertainty in the messages of the automatic documents.

Beyond serving as handy emblems for unanswerable questions about just where the messages originated, daimons and daimonic activity bring out intriguing differences between the human participants in the experiments. Each member of the couple found powerful resonance in daimonic concepts, although, as is perhaps unsurprising, since daimons are so closely associated with the deepest sense of self, each person had her or his own preferences among these ideas. To some extent, of course, these preferences blend into each other, since all the information about the system was generated by exchange, so that neither person received anything alone. Nevertheless, it is interesting to notice variation in interests and inclinations that is revealed by their respective emphases.

In the script and notebooks, WBY's wavering ideas about daimons hover around the notions of a second or anti-self, or mask, with overtones from his own long work with poetic voice and the theatre, as well as his experiments with Leo Africanus and the 'Anima Mundi' essay in *Per Amica*. His description and rhetorical question in the correspondence with GY about *The Words upon the Window-Pane*, that 'the Daimon of a living man is a dramatist—what am I but my daimons most persistent drama', is typical of his late synthesis of the concepts that had galvanized his interest for many years.[9] The daimon often seems a more highly personified version of basic truths about the mask, demonstrating again, as is explained repeatedly with

---

about daimons made in Aug. 1920 make some attempts at distinction. In one entry, GY wrote (taking dictation from WBY), 'I forgot to state that he distinguished between the Daimon & the Ghostly self. The Daimon cannot exist apart from the 4 Faculties, whereas the Ghostly self is in a sphere. Interpreter would remember this—it has 3 circles' (*YVP*iii. 34). Another distinction was based on the idea that 'the Daimon could correct in next life a defect in experience. But Ghostly Self could not' (*YVP*iii. 39).

⁹ See Second Interlude, n. 29.

reference to various contraries in the system, 'the point is that man frees himself through his opposite' (*YVP*ii. 19). Questions about how independent a human being is from the daimon were frequently posed and answered, and on at least one occasion WBY's overemphasis was corrected, in a passage that has an edge of defensiveness. WBY should not regard the second presence as simply the reverse image of the primary actor: 'He complained of my identifying the Daimon too exclusively with the anti-self,' a notebook entry records; if the daimon and the ego were considered as mere correlatives, the daimon, which 'needed protection as much as the Ego & could not express itself where the two did not remain distinct', would lose its 'independent life', a condition known as the 'Fall of the Daimon' (*YVP*iii. 96). The daimon is indeed 'the ghostly self', the control revealed on 23 March 1919, both 'part of me' and yet also 'between lives', in the 'siftings' and 'beyond' the '13th cycle'.[10] The 1925 *A Vision* illustrates that WBY did take in some of these messages of ambiguous selfhood, neither discrete nor incorporate, in two passages: Book I, Section XI, entitled 'The Daimon, the Sexes, Unity of Being, Natural and Supernatural Unity', and Book IV, Section I, called 'Stray Thoughts' (*AV A* 26–30, 220–1). The daimon, WBY asserts, is 'another mind, or another part of our mind' (p. 27), and the highly desirable state of unity of being is in reality submission to the fundamentally disunified state between human and daimon (p. 28). The daimon is 'not phasal and yet we must speak as if she were', because she is at once 'united to man' yet 'cannot accompany man in his wanderings' (p. 220). Like a cosmic Crazy Jane, his daimon is female; he embraced the concept from the script that daimons are of opposite sex to the human beings in their charge. His own Order motto, Demon Est Deus Inversus, of course emphasizes antitheses as constitutive of identity, and his phase (17) is 'called the *Daimonic* man' with these sorts of oppositions in mind (p. 75).

[10] WBY defines 'siftings', usually spelled 'shiftings', in *AV A* 161 and 229–34. The Thirteenth Cycle (or cone), the region inhabited by daimons and human beings freed from the Great Wheel, remained more or less as vague in WBY's published works as it is unattainable in human life. See *YVP*iii. 32, 392; *AV A* 220–1; and *CVA* Notes 68.

For GY, questions of method, such as how daimons 'collect' images and where those images originate, were more compelling. It might even be said that as WBY tended to reiterate the geometric symbols as signs of sexual mutualities and oppositions, she leaned toward interest in the daimonic for symbols of the energies that drove the script, which tend to be expressed as sexual, emotional, and intellectual collaborations. A notebook reports that 'Woman is nearer to the daimonic' (*YVP*iii. 112), and the aspects of the daimonic that this statement gestures toward are relational, not positional, the daimon as an entity in a dynamic alliance rather than in its status as mask or other self. Given her vocation as wife and mother, it is not remarkable that such qualities predominate. The daimonic contexts of the Moments of Crisis, for example, are part of this complex of ideas. A long discursive passage from the notebooks contains comments that link resonant moments of a person's life with daimonic explanation for the intensities: 'The Daimons who produce the IM of a man, are his own Daimon & the daimon of that woman with whom he will attain, if attain he do[es], the Beatific Vision (BV).' The passage goes on to explore the 'certain emotions & forms of thought' that 'shall prevail which are necessary for the birth of certain children' and much about human love. Daimons play important roles with regard to 'expiatory images or symbols' and the daimonic quality of 'real' human love, for instance: '*in so far as [a man] loves the real woman, on whom the symbol is imposed, he is in relation with that womans daimon*' (emphasis original). Symbols in such passages are unlike Yeatsian poetic images. They do not lead to solitary intellectual or aesthetic states of mind being generated by the symbol itself; instead, they are themselves created by a relationship already in the world. The daimon 'chose the living woman on whom the symbols are imposed', and this act of choice, as opposed to predetermined abstraction, explains individual freedom within the seeming fixities of image and pattern in human life (*YVP*iii. 113–14). In the spring of 1919, amid a series of sessions on daimons, this crucial characteristic was stressed: WBY asked whether daimons' minds are 'automatic in any region

of thought where our minds are free' and was told emphatically,
'No *never* automatic'. Furthermore, daimonic truth results from the
heart, not the head: '*never* influenced by your *minds*—only by your
emotions & instincts—this must be remembered' (*YVP* ii. 251).

Early in the automatic sessions, in a relatively rare move, GY
raised with the control the ever present practical question of how
much the script was guided by her conscious will or her husband's
suggestiveness. '*The daimon acts in practical life?*', she asked (carefully
labelling her emphasized question with her initials, to distinguish
it from the automatic reply, also written by her hand). Like the
form of the question itself, which takes the form of daily self and
medium—this world and that—in dialogue with each other, the
answer stresses interpenetration of the two realms: 'it [the daimon]
can do so only through the man himself for the greater part'
(*YVP*i. 71). In other words, ghostly work is done through everyday
means. This revelation was the beginning of many that seldom made
their way into publication, although they explain how the system
came into being and inform the multiple levels on which it often
operates.

Daimons represent abstractly some of the subtleties and consequences
of the conjugal and intellectual partnership of WBY and GY. The weeks
and months following the birth of their daughter Anne exploded
with discussions of daimons, most of which lift emotional and
sexual mutuality into spiritual creativity. Contraries were explored,
in their 'bisexual element' as well as other conceptual levels, such
as the 'contrary of false pity' being 'true love', a state that is
'*objective*' (*YVP*ii. 286). A second term, 'correspondence', arose,
and it characterized daimonic relations more accurately than the
otherwise ubiquitous 'contraries'. After all, 'the daimon evokes no
contraries in human', but a correspondence could be awakened by a
different kind of yoking. In a session on 25 May, to a question about
whether WBY could attain a certain awareness, the communicator
elaborated on what 'state of consciousness' was necessary: 'solitary
not correspondance—dual is' (*YVP*ii. 288–9). After an interval, the

session resumed, and the sexual aspect of this new quality was made clear: 'the new' was revealed by 'equal balance—that is also why equal balance in sexual intercourse is not tiring—but it must be in both'. Sexual energy ('the greatest purity' of which occurs at 'the moment just after entering') creates it:

1. What difference does it make in the union of the daimons when ours phisically complete.

1. positive correspondance instead of negative—that is the correspondance is definite & not only apprehended.

A relationship of 'purely physical union has no correspondence' (*YVP*ii. 290–1), but when two people are closely linked (especially if they are creative, as an important session in December 1919 revealed, in which case their daimons become 'self-moving'), their experience of 'sexual union' is 'the moment of supreme activity of the daimons' (*YVP* ii. 507).

In daimonic terms, the system insists upon heterosexual union, but that union extends beyond relationships between male and female to a joining of genders, so that knowledge and power become hermaphroditic. This illumination was not achieved without snarls, though. For example, the sitting of 13 April 1919 grew increasingly confusing as the discussion attempted to clarify how daimons use the 'sexual sense' to collect imagery for the system. WBY struggled to understand how sexual desire (as well as satisfaction, but 'only if *both* people are being used by us') was bisexual and how a sexual image, which he thought of as 'single', could 'lead to your complex unity of many images'. Eventually, in an attempt to clear the air, Thomas exclaimed, 'I am sorry—I find it impossible to answer because I dont know what you are trying to find out—please stop 10 minutes & talk.' When the session resumed, GY's normal hand wrote '*not automatic*', followed by her interpretation of the gendered nature of image and thought:

Every normal sexual image is bi-sexual because there is the thinker as well as the thing thought on—It is purely emotional, but it evokes in the mind of the daimon an image that is purely intellectual: this image is not bi-sexual, the daimon having no senses it can only become bi-sexual by contact with another daimon.

Like opposing gyres, contrary positions engage with each other creatively. However, this description adds two elements to the mathematical equation: first, point of view, so that the two poles become personalized as 'thinker' and 'thing thought on'—each bringing to the marriage-bed an image of the other, as Solomon and Sheba knew. The contraries are bisexual, in that the objective 'thing thought on' is a part of each self no less than the subject position. Second, these positions are productive only if there is desire fuelling the system: the daimons of the humans must be in 'contact' with each other for the intellectual images of the system to reach their full complexity. The 'thinker and the thing thought on' are the polarities between which the 'bi-sexual' image is created, subject and object defined and dominated by a multiply directed sexual passion that simultaneously divides and unites them. 'Correct—Thomas,' she wrote in automatic handwriting beside this statement. 'Now five minutes more' (*YVP* ii. 245).

In those five minutes, an interchange occurred which established that the system depended absolutely not only upon sexual desire but also upon emotional satisfaction between husband and wife if it was to be 'created' and not merely 'constructed'. The dialogue moved toward understanding of how thought and the object of thought are gendered and which side of the subject/object division assumes the dominant position, although WBY apparently oversimplified when he assumed that 'thinker' is male and 'thought on' female (the next day, this mistake was cleared up as the communicator informed him that it worked both ways, 'she is thinker & you thought on—you are thinker & she thought on'—or at least 'this *should* be so'. The sexual and intellectual impulses which daimonic activity expresses are abstract configurations of power relations rather than entities which have a one-to-one relationship with either side of a male/female dualism. The session ended in a 'muddle' in which both WBY and the control none the less realized that the issue of sexuality leads unavoidably to questions of subjectivity and authority.

25. The greater the desire & sadisfaction the more powerful the synthesis of the daimon
25. Yes

26. Do you understand me to mean phisical desire & sadisfaction
26. Certainly

27. Does daimon receive an encreased synthetic power from our emotional sadisfaction.
27. far more

28. It is different in kind.
28. quite

29. What is the difference?
29. Construction or creation

30. If that is from the emotional what does the daimon get from the phisical.
30. Construction.

31. Phisical desire alone would give merely mathematic form.
31. Yes

32. What knowledge is collected by the female daimon as distinguished from that collected by the male
32. female daimon collects from *the thought of* never from thinker This is important

33. Is converse true of male.
33. Yes

34. medium therefore because of method of both daimons has all collected by her.[11]
34. Why

[11] GY's title had officially been changed to *interpreter* by this time, but the more familiar term continued to surface in both questions and answers. On one occasion (30 Nov. 1919), the spirits reminded WBY of the change. To his question, 'Can you suggest anything to lesscn mcdiums fatiguc', Amcritus replied, 'Can you remember I gave you the name interpreter? That was to avoid the word *medium*' (*YVP* ii. 498).

35. I mean she is thought on & the thinker
35. Why

36. If the thought on is not the woman desired by an image from AM is the thinker the man who desires or something else?
36. muddle

It was definitely time to call it an evening, as Thomas must have realized after wby superposed gendered complexity of daimonic identity (daimons being opposite gender to their human counterparts) on gendered complexity of point of view (the positions of 'thinker' and 'thought on' being located in multiple ways). 'If I think of the medium my daimon being female, collects through the faculties of the medium. If she thinks of me her male daimon, collects through her faculties also as she is the thinker,' wby asked. Thomas started to reply, then gave up: 'tomorrow on this subject please ... I say this will be a long & subtle subject & must go on tomorrow.' wby tried one more time: 'Her daimon collects from us both as thinker & mine from us both as thought on?', but the control was silent (*YVP*ii. 245–7).

Gradually, the outlines of daimonic activity became clear. Two personal daimons, of opposite gender from their human selves, gather imagery from husband and wife, male daimon collecting from man, female daimon from woman.[12] The amassing of imagery is accomplished using all the senses, but 'of all especially the sixth' or the 'sexual sense' (*YVP*ii. 243), a mysterious receptor that operates from the daimon actually 'in the body at the moments of collecting information', using 'the faculties of the body'—and altering all the other senses, 'especially touch & hearing'—but 'as different sex'

---

[12] The gendering of the daimon had a number of contemporary cultural resonances, from the Jungian *anima/animus* to the more colourful opinions of the American expatriot folklorist and writer on witchcraft and gypsies, Charles Godfrey Leland. Leyland explains a number of puzzling phenomena (including automatic planchette writing) by means of an inner opposite sex, proposing 'That what has of late years occupied much thought as the Subliminal Self, the Inner Me, the Hidden Soul, Unconscious Cerebration, and the like, may all be reduced to or fully explained by the Alternate Sex in us' (Charles Godfrey Leland, *The Alternate Sex; or The Female Intellect in Man, and the Masculine in Woman* (London: Philip Wellby, 1904), p. v.

(*YVP*ii. 248; iii. 291). The sexual sense enables daimons to 'get in touch with P.A.M. [Personal Anima Mundi] and the A.M. [Anima Mundi]', and they are thus brought in touch because the sexual sense 'makes them both male & female & that is necessary as the A.M. is bisexual'. To tap into the Personal Anima Mundi, an 'impersonal mirror reflecting all image, idea, thought, or feeling ever experienced consciously or unconsciously' (*YVP*ii. 40; iii. 244), daimons must themselves enter a state in which gender difference is most nearly dissolved. Interestingly, this dissolution is accomplished through this 'sexual sense'. One result of the system is an almost random quality to gender, when daimons, like the souls with whom their bond is not 'in this life only' but 'permanent', pass through phases 'first as man last as woman then alternating from man to woman then man then woman & so on' (*YVP*ii. 239; i. 338). Another result is a continual stress on sexuality, conceived as a mutual, shifting, and polymorphous 'sense' through which illumination can be obtained. These lessons were retained, as is clear in *A Vision*, where the oppositions between 'man and *Daimon*' contain references to the sexual partnering that is so prominent in the script:

This relation (the *Daimon* being of the opposite sex to that of man) may create a passion like that of sexual love. The relation of man and woman, in so far as it is passionate, reproduces the relation of man and *Daimon*, and becomes an element where man and *Daimon* sport, pursue one another, and do one another good or evil. . . . In so far as man and woman are swayed by their sex they interact as man and *Daimon* interact, though at other moments their phases may be side by side. . . . A man becomes passionate and this passion makes the *Daimonic* thought luminous with its peculiar light—this is the object of the *Daimon*—and she so creates a very personal form of heroism or of poetry. (*AVA* 27–8)

Two personal daimons were only the beginning of the story. In a daimon-rich session of 23 March 1919, which occurred amid conversations about Moments of Crisis that joined daimonic influence to personal fate, the question arose of the relationship between daimons and the communicators, and in turn the system the communicators brought. Thomas revealed that he did not 'speak for interpreters

310   *All the Others*

daimon' but that 'some do', although he hedged when asked 'Is this philosophy the creation or experience of that daimon?' 'This belongs elsewhere,' Thomas replied; 'It is too subtle a distinction to go into here—I do not want you to form conclusions.' But to WBY's insistent questioning, Thomas probably did encourage the humans to 'form conclusions' after all when he revealed the presence of a third daimon on whom the system depended. Was there 'a 3rd being whose experience is this philosophy'? 'Yes,' Thomas admitted. WBY wondered whether this third being was different from or related to the daimons of GY and himself. 'Distinct from daimon?', he asked. 'Speaking through both.' 'What both?' 'Two daimons.' Pressing further to know the cycle of this Third Daimon, WBY was told 'Now stop' for the evening (*YVP*ii. 211–12).

The third daimon was indeed distinct and crucial. It 'is dual', as the Yeatses had guessed; 'Yes—two in one.' It used 'ordinary sex relations' in addition to Critical Moments to collect, 'always in accordance with the unity & harmony of the moment—the greater the harmony the collection & the more vitality given to 3rd Daimon' (*YVP*ii. 249). Further, this mysterious collective, collecting daimon was attached to another joint effort, the infant Anne. Asked on 26 March if the third daimon was 'Annes', Thomas replied, 'Yes'. On 6 April Thomas reiterated that this daimon was 'born from two other daimons' and was in fact 'the daimon of the child'. A week later, in a particularly revealing session, he was even more specific: as 'two people produce the boy child—with us two daimons produce a third' (*YVP*ii. 213, 236, 244). Much discussion of daimons and their activities at Moments of Crisis yielded the information that 'the system is created by third Daimon' from 'the imagery . . . collected by First & Second Daimon' (*YVP*ii. 243). The third daimon was born on the Yeatses' wedding day, was completed not 'with birth of Anne', as WBY proposed, but 'April 17 last', the probable date of her conception,[13] and was linked with the moment in their lives 'when sympathy is complete' (*YVP*ii. 250). As WBY summarized

---

[13] See Saddlemyer, *Becoming George*, 173–4.

in an entry in his card file, ' "All communication" said in August 1919 to be "through 3rd Daimon" ', a being that 'requires passion'. Most critically, the third daimon was the symbolic link between the system and Anne. The August sessions from which the card quoted reveal that the Yeatses' '*ills* whether physical moral or emotional tend to affect not only 3rd Daimon but Anne'. WBY supposed correctly that 'The 3rd Daimon unconnected with us then connects with us', a condition that analogizes the system, with its blend of seeming independence from and dependence on the partners receiving it, and parenthood, which especially for believers in reincarnation is the arrival of a soul 'unconnected with us' into a new relation. Fundamentally, for the system as well as for the conjugal and familial relationships it echoes, 'There is always a child' (*YVP*iii. 278; ii. 380–2).

The series of conversations in the summer of 1919 about over-shadowing and ideal lovers also featured third daimons, in another context in which a presence 'unconnected with us then connects with us'. In cases where there was an ideal lover in a previous incarnation, a set of living lovers will experience the effects of a third daimon, the Yeatses discovered on 12 September (*YVP*ii. 417). When WBY asked, 'Have I a third daimon apart from medium', he was told that 'Each had but after marriage only one between two'. Two third daimons seemed to have melded into one: 'Have 2 beings become one', WBY asked, and was told, 'Yes' though 'not *inseparably* one yet'. He wanted to make sure that he had understood correctly that third daimons could actually undergo such radical joining: 'Can 2 distinct beings become one being?' he countered, and was told, '3rd daimons yes'. This revelation, coming as it did in the midst of conversations about intensities in the previous lives of both the Yeatses, implies layers of emotion underlying WBY's poem 'An Image from a Past Life' that go well beyond the narrative of the poem, in which a simple correspondence seems to exist between lover and overshadower. If unresolved passion from love affairs in other lives could blend into one daimonic presence overshadowing a marriage, causing '2 distinct beings [to] become one' in a doubled sense to the vocabulary of

Christian marriage vows, the psychic intensity of shared lives might itself multiply. For moments of intensity or luminosity, as the Yeatses knew, were signs of the work of daimons, as a notebook entry from a sleep in 1921 makes clear: 'We then spoke of the Daimon & he [the communicator] said that the Daimon can only directly affect the person in his charge at moments of exaltation' (*YVP* iii. 38).

As might be expected in a family with two children, the third daimon was not the last word on the subject. A fourth daimon, identified with their son Michael, entered the script as the couple celebrated the 'first birthday' of the third daimon in April 1919 (*YVP*ii. 253). In July 1919, they received an enigmatic suggestion of further spiritual possibility from yet another addition to the daimonic family: 'The Beatific in the mind of the fourth Daimon' (*YVP*ii. 328).[14] On 23 July, perhaps appropriately on a day when something 'makes concentration impossible' for the interpreter, who needed to do something outlandish like 'a course of metaphysics & algebra or botany' because she 'is making things very difficult', the Fourth Daimon surfaced again. As the third daimon had brought forth the system of oppositions, this daimon 'brings unlikes together' (*YVP*ii. 332). The fourth daimon was associated with the birds that emblematize WBY's emotional entanglements—WBY was told to 'notice *all* Birds that you may study all' but not to question on the topic of birds—and indeed came to be called first the 'Black Bird' and then, later, 'Black Eagle'. The historical dimension of this daimon would link it with a promised heir, an avatar, or even masters of certain ages (*YVP*iii. 65). 'The next civilization will be brought about by third daimons but it will be *achieved* by 4th,' the Yeatses learned. WBY asked about the distinction between 'brought about' and 'achieved' in this statement, and heard that a third daimon would initiate the coming age, which would be 'brought about by

---

[14] Thankfully, there were not 'an indefinite number of daimons—5th—6th etc'; four was the maximum number (*YVP*ii. 509). The existence of only four daimons parallels the injunction, given by Ameritus in the first session after the birth of Anne, to have '*only* one more' child after this one, as any more would 'destroy system/*too domestic*' (*YVP*ii. 201).

creating a need', but that a fourth would be attached to 'those that bring it to reality' (*YVP*ii. 334–5).

Perhaps appropriately for a daimon associated with Beatific Vision, the accomplishment of the coming age, a child not even conceived when many of the conversations took place, and a quality in the relationship between husband and wife that the Yeatses were not certain they had achieved, the fourth daimon remains somewhat obscure. In December 1919, a series of sessions near the effective end of the script, featuring much talk of daimons, is backlit by some emotional intensity and, it seems, sexual difficulty. GY was tired, and her husband was told that 'the cause of fatigue is that the link between her & her daimon is strengthening', as his did in 'the winter of 1916' (*YVP*ii. 504). He was instructed in mirror writing to join sleeps to sexual activity: 'let her sleep naturally—then when she is asleep put her into the mesmeric sleep'; 'make love and I will see that *she suggests a sleep* to come first'; 'I think perhaps it would be more efficacious if she did *not wake up*', he was told. The next day, Ameritus said that something was 'my fault', that whatever it was came from 'repression of manifestation of physical desire for *you* but that can be got over/Yes it will die out but a slight recurrence is bound to follow' (this in mirror writing), and that the medium felt 'an irritation against 3rd daimon' because of 'failure of last night' (*YVP*ii. 507–8). Two days later the advice about mesmeric sleep was corrected (and Ameritus was removed from his post). Dionertes warned WBY, who may have been tempted to use a gift for hypnosis to solve some problem: 'you must *never* use hypnotism without our permission' (*YVP*ii. 510). In the midst of all this difficulty, bits of information about daimons were also gleaned. The third 'represents a spiritual birth' connected to 'the soul of a possible child', although 'the spiritual being is not the child but its representative'. The fourth '*should*' arrive with the second child, 'but generally nothing operates'. To a question about the specific change in 'quality of desire', the 'psychological effect on 2 persons' associated with the mysterious Fourth Daimon, WBY was informed, 'That I certainly cannot say until the influence of the 3rd *on* you changes to that of the 4th' (*YVP*ii. 509). However, the couple did receive a formula to explain the daimonic correspondences with themselves and their two children:

First daimon   love
Second   wisdom
3rd daimon   Beauty
4th daimon   Truth[15] (*YVP*ii. 510)

In August 1920, a sequence of sleeps elaborated on this and other quaternities, stressing again that the Fourth Daimon was different in quality from the Third, and that 'it is of course the 4th Daimon which brings the man & woman together' (*YVP*iii. 32). 'The 3rd & 4th Daimons are not *new* Daimons but transformations', the Yeatses learned, the third struggling and the fourth 'free from frustration', the third expending great intergenerational effort to unravel personal wrongs, the fourth 'not the Daimon of an individual but of an idea & . . . connected with a group. It associates itself with an individual but it can leave that individual again permanently or for a time. . . . Though much of this philosophy comes through 3rd Daimon it is ultimately through the Fourth' (*YVP*iii. 33–5). When this information has been sorted through the years of work into *A Vision*, WBY sounds vaguely hopeful about the likelihood of these four mysterious beings, neither selves nor non-selves, accomplishing their complex transformations. By means of oppositional sexual desire, suffering on behalf of others across generations, contraries of 'thinker' and 'thought on', and a relationship between self and other that moves beyond its very duality, daimonic life may be able to lead human beings and their children to a scarcely imaginable freedom: 'When the conflict is sexual and the man and woman each *Victim* for the Dead and for the *Ghostly Self*—each miracle working idol and an object of desire, they give one another a treble love, that for the dead, that for the living, that for the never living.

---

[15] At some points, fourth daimons are associated with human beings who have attained great wisdom. A notebook entry from the cluster of sleeps in Aug. 1920 records that WBY 'asked if we knew any person who was a 4th Daimon & he said Tagore' (*YVP*iii. 33).

And if those two for whom the victimage had been undertaken be born of the man and of the woman then there is created, both before and after the birth, the position known as that of the *Four Daimons*, and each of the four has been set free from fate' (*AV A* 249).

Instruction and Frustration

> The spirit communicating takes on the exact mental condition of the person he is communicating with. . .
> automatic writing is two
> one definite spirit thought
> two subliminal
> both are written by an automatic mechanical velocity purely nervous which is set in motion by a spirit
>
> Leaf and Fish, 10 January 1918 (*YVP*i. 237)

Compared to the shadowy daimons, the controls and guides who were the Yeatses' familiar attendants and teachers are reassuringly domestic. The controls especially are the chatty voices of the script, the often strong personalities that give the documents the feel of transcribed telephone interviews, or even, at times, of a screenplay featuring a crowded roomful of people, sometimes all talking at once. Guides have a subordinate function, arriving to help controls, fill in gaps when the others are not available, or add their presences to a line of discussion to indicate its importance. The guides do add to the plenitude of voices, though, most of which have distinct tones, emanating from seeming characters. The words from GY's hand shift constantly in stance, mood, and intention, although the vocabulary and level of diction remain constant (and high: these spirits speak George Yeatsese in this regard). The questioner's role is tame by comparison. WBY plays the eager student, curious, provoking, insistent, often sceptical but always engaged, probing the communicators to define, clarify, or corroborate his guesses. Her segments are by turns dominating, annoyed, helpful, impatient, condescending, confused, conciliatory, pompous, or even (though rarely) meek or apologetic. At times the discourse of the script flows in and out of the third person or the plural voice as if now nearer and now further away from some indefinable self. It employs single words or phrases, full statements, questions, extended exposition, symbols, ideographs, and geometrical drawings. It speaks with new words, echoes the phrasing of the question, and alludes to other texts. At least once it throws at WBY his own voice, quoting from a recently completed essay in the course of upbraiding him for sloppy thinking.[16]

The appearance of personalities as controls or guides, a relatively common phenomenon, is a commentary on periods or aspects of the Yeatses' lives as well as varying themes in the script or sleeps. As the months and years passed, the personalities of the various instructors became increasingly distinct, and it is obvious that they embodied abstract qualities that had the potential of defining one or both of the sitters in some way, as well as (and simultaneously with) being appropriate emissaries for particular topics being discussed. New controls reflected changes in states of mind, degrees of active participation, and locations or positions, whether in domestic, social, or geographical space, of either WBY or GY, but especially the latter. As Leaf and Fish put it, the 'automatic writing is two/one definite spirit thought/two subliminal'; in other words, the system had both supernatural and natural (subconscious) sources. Page after page stresses that the relationship between worlds is the source of revelation. Spirits depend upon humans; daily selves depend upon antithetical selves; Faculties, aspects of the living person, work in concert with Principles, corresponding aspects in the state between lives; daimons collect from their mortal counterparts; and so on. And indeed, the Yeatses tended to engage in the conversations as if

---

[16] On 24 Nov. 1919, Ameritus instructs WBY to 'Hammer your thoughts into unity' (*YVP*ii. 492), using a phrase from the opening of 'If I Were Four-and-Twenty' (*Ex* 263), first published in *The Irish Statesman* on 23 and 30 Aug. 1919. WBY was probably writing a lecture for the American tour of 13 Jan.–29 May 1920 at the time, and he needed to hammer because 'your lecture must be more precise—more detailed in the main parts'.

explanations and ramifications might be found at any moment in either, or indeed both, spheres.

Even a sample of the array of communicators shows some of the links among the human beings, the philosophy, and the spirits. Thomas of Dorlowicz, the most faithful and hard-working control, was the first to appear and the main communicator for the first eighteen months of script. The first recorded script reveals that he was 'here for a purpose & must go when that is done' and 'here for her only' (*YVP*i. 55). He was consistently helpful and organized, giving personal advice as well as useful leadings as the newly wedded couple pursued mind-blurringly abstruse topics while establishing domestic routines. Thomas often worked in concert with guides according to changes in topic or emphasis. He sometimes disappeared for a time and returned when his presence was again possible or productive.

As early as the evening of Thomas's first appearance, a conflict was obvious between him and Leo Africanus, a presence that seems to have returned from the spiritual exercises in which WBY had engaged, in varying settings, until the spring of 1917. Nor was Thomas the only communicator who had trouble with Leo. In the script, as George Harper and Steve Adams note, from this first reintroduction Leo

appears as a malignant and untrustworthy spirit, and he remains 'dishonest' when he reappears occasionally (twenty-five times or more) throughout the script. He becomes, in fact, the most difficult of a category of spirits called Frustrators (that is, those who deliberately impeded or hindered the psychic investigations).[17]

Leo, WBY was told a few months into the script, was 'an evil genius but who has attached himself to you', who 'hates medium wants to displace your mind no—sheer malevolence'. However, this news may not have been as bad as it sounded, since this Leo was not the one whom WBY had entertained as his anti-self in the 'Leo Africanus' letters. 'Not really Leo', came a clarification: this being 'is a guide

---

[17] 'Leo', 15. Adams and Harper summarize the history of the Yeatses' Leo in their editorial introduction.

& therefore Leo Africanus nothing to do with him' (Y*VP*i. 277). Significantly, the script was not to carry on a practice that relied on WBY's personality as heavily as the earlier experiments with Leo as his anti-self had done. And yet the connection with WBY's past remained, for which Leo is a sign.[18] Thomas, with Fish to strengthen the force, gave WBY specific guidance on 24 January 1918, on rest to 'help against attack', 'digestion', and why he should so guard his health: '[Apple] thinks that is bad to write automatically more than two hours a day and affects you—Both but you more because you are more open to ill influence of frustrators' (*YVP* i. 286).

Frustration became part of the public story told in the introduction to the revised *Vision*:

Because they [the communicators] must, as they explained, soon finish, others whom they named Frustrators attempted to confuse us or waste time. Who these Frustrators were or why they acted so was never adequately explained, nor will be unless I can finish 'The Soul in Judgment' (Book III of this work), but they were always ingenious and sometimes cruel. The automatic script would deteriorate, grow sentimental or confused, and when I pointed this out the communicator would say, 'From such and such an hour, on such and such a day, all is frustration'. I would spread out the script and he would cross all out back to the answer that began it, but had I not divined frustration he would have said nothing. (*AV B* 13)

Frustration, as WBY notes later in this passage, is performative, raising again the question of the relationship between the communicators' asserted truths and any reality outside the 'drama' or 'dream' (*AV B* 13) of the proceedings. 'One [frustrator] said, as though it rested with me to decide what part I should play in their dream, "Remember we will deceive you if we can"' (*AV B* 13).

Even though WBY did finish 'The Soul in Judgment', of course, frustrators are still inadequately explained. They are designed to remain so. Like confusing messages from any spirit medium, frustration adds to a sense of validity: if the messages are indeed from

---

[18] Leo is quite literally a sign: his presence in the script is often indicated by the astrological symbol ♌.

other realms, it makes perfect sense that they would be at times unclear or even downright wrong. The phenomenon is of course also to some degree convenient, as it would be for other mediums, allowing a posteriori exoneration for unproductive lines of questioning. Nor are they unique to the Yeatses. As might be expected, they are well known in spiritualist literature. Frustrators constitute a topic explored by many, including the most illustrious personages in the spiritualist community. As early as 1894, W. T. Stead wrote of 'lying controls', finding remarkable 'the extraordinary glibness with which some controls will answer questions about which they know nothing'. In general, Stead advises, 'The best working plan is always to regard every automatic writing as if it were an anonymous letter, and never accept any statement which it contains, unless it is capable of independent verification, until you have received a sufficient number of communications that have been verified to justify you in placing confidence in messages from that source.'[19] Stainton Moses calls frustrators 'adversaries' and discusses them in *Spirit Teachings* as 'the antagonistic spirits who range themselves against our mission'.[20] One anonymous 'Member of the Society for Psychical Research' asserted in 1901 that frustrators were linked with the passivity required by automatic writing, recalling a case of 'obsession' in which the personality of the writer was split. 'The "control", as I now propose to call the "other one", had clearly and distinctly disclosed its true character—evidently one of diabolical malice and cunning.' The cause was clear: 'it was the frequently induced *passive attitude* of the mind and of the will which had been aimed at.'[21] 'Rita', the author of *The Truth of Spiritualism*, discusses mischievous 'elementals', who exist on a lower plane than other spirits (and are less intelligent), who enjoy tricking automatic writers.[22] 'Miss X' avers:

[19] William T. Stead, 'More About Automatic Writing: The Experiences of Three Other Writers', *Borderland*, 1 (1894): 169, 166.

[20] [Moses], *Spirit Teachings*, 12.   [21] [Raupert], *Dangers of Spiritualism*, 86.

[22] [Humphreys], *Truth of Spiritualism*, 63.

Among all the correspondence which has reached me through my connection with *Borderland*, I am bound to say that none has ever made me doubt
the expedience of so-called psychic experiment as have those letters which
deal with automatic writing. Given a clear head, a capacity for weighing of
evidence, a conscientious desire for truth, automatic writing is probably as
good or even better, than other forms of automatism; but I can only repeat
that I know of none which so readily lends itself to Fraud or, at best, to
self-deception.[23]

   In the Yeatses' scripts, frustrators are not merely figures that explain
error or indicate self-deception. They exemplify the tendency of the
script to personalize and also to valorize its own chaotic qualities.
When the waters of the spirit were muddied, the reasons for the
fluctuations no less than the clear lines of communication were
sometimes active, and were either named or sensed as personalities.
In this regard as in others, the script is saturated with issues of naming,
but with a twist: the operations, failures, and avoided relationships
participate in the cacophony of named agency as well as those it
develops. In other words, even what is wrong or missing is an author
or an actor in the improvised scene. For GY, I suspect, frustrators
were messages from her husband's past and her attitudes toward
it, but also, more importantly, various antagonisms of her own,
served up as separate beings, allowing personal distance as well as
ambivalences in the 'emotional philosophy'. The fact that frustration
is more common in the later periods, including whole sections
of sleep notebooks, indicates a correlation between malevolent or
mischievous presences and the growth in authority of the interpreter
as well as the increasing complexities of the information being
received. For her husband, frustration became integrated into the
system as flamboyant antinomies: the truths of the philosophy
were countered by opposing falsehoods that were as integral to
the larger picture. Unlike most writers about mediumship, who
decried fraudulent practices and discussed ruefully the possibilities
that messages from beyond might not have much value as truth,

----

[23] [Freer], 'Note', 368.

WBY embraces unverifiable and uncontrollable communications as necessary antitheses to established and reliable voices.

Eventually, as the energy that Thomas represented shifted and the script needed to alter direction, his identity changed as well. Such an event was not unique to the Yeatses: changes of control were common in spiritualist circles. Stainton Moses suggests that spirit guides may change as their mission advances or 'as the soul [of the sitter] progresses'.[24] The souls of the Yeatses had doubtless progressed by May 1919, as they took their first trip to England after the birth of Anne, for the task of moving from WBY's old rooms in London to a house in Oxford. The first session of script, still in Woburn Buildings, was presided over by Eurectha, whose ambiguously gendered name meant 'the builder', and who was Thomas 'in new state', the 'before life state' or shiftings, readying himself for rebirth. He or she (WBY used the masculine pronoun, but the sign of Thomas as Eurectha had the astrological symbol for Venus at its base) appeared to guide 'A year of change—a year of difficult script—too minute to be easy—too emotional to be understood rationally—too abstract to be understood rationally—no synthesis for some time—you must just go on noting & be content to wait for synthesis' (*YVP*ii. 284). The 'new sign' for Thomas appeared after the English excursion was finished, in the first session at Ballylee in June, on the day that GY gave up 'automatic' handwriting and also began recording both the questions and the answers of the sessions.[25] As was perhaps appropriate, given the resemblance of the name Eurectha to the Erechtheion, the Athenian temple dismantled by Lord Elgin (whose famous caryatids are reproduced on the porch of the new St Pancras church on Upper Woburn Place, just behind the Yeatses' soon-to-be-vacated apartment), Eurectha's first assignment for the Yeatses had been a trip to the British Museum to 'look up Annes letters' (*YVP*ii. 284).

[24] [Moses], *Spirit Teachings*, 12.
[25] Although three sittings had been conducted at Ballylee the previous year (21–3 Sept.), it was scarcely habitable; 1919 was the Yeatses' first summer there. See Saddlemyer, *Becoming George*, 218.

Anne Hyde, an ancestor and oblique *alter ego* for GY, was part of a cluster of presences that did indeed open up 'new ground' in the next month, but even Eurectha could not shepherd the Yeatses through the next stage of script. After they had returned to Ireland, Thomas/Eurectha introduced a new entity: Ameritus (*YVP* ii. 300).

Ameritus, whose name may mean 'unworthy' as well as '*that* which is *sweet in bitterness*', as the Yeatses were informed (perhaps derived from the French *amertume*, 'bitterness', or perhaps related to the Latin *mellitus*, 'honeyed' (from *mel*, 'honey'), or *amarus*, 'bitter'), reflects an increasingly direct role for the interpreter. Ameritus was the 'interpreters daimon' or, more precisely, 'a guide giving expression to interpreters Daimon' (*YVP*ii. 301). The intensity of the relationship that the interpreter felt between her soul and her husband's may be indicated in a message from 1 July 1920 when Ameritus explained that difficulties in communication were arising 'because she associated him [that is, Ameritus] with me [WBY]' (*YVP*iii. 28). 'I have wonderful things to tell you,' Ameritus informed the couple on 20 June 1919, but at the same time he warned WBY firmly against 'the kind of thing you did this morning in writing about personal script'. WBY would receive new levels of revelation, but only if he remembered that 'You cannot have your cake and eat it', by which the control meant that the very personal messages to come were not to be subjected to public scrutiny or attempts at objective proof: it is 'useless to smash one pitcher to mend the other', he said, illustrating his point with a sketch of two pitchers (*YVP*ii. 304). He was also firm about the sort of information he would be giving them: they were to expect revelatory principles, but he sometimes shied away from specific data. On 9 August, he replied testily to a question about a date, 'I do not come to you as a dictionnary' (*YVP*ii. 367). Ameritus ushered the Yeatses into months of discussions that featured deeply personal issues involving Moments of Crisis, Anne Hyde and other figures from various of their other incarnations, recurring images, the soul-defining roles of Victim and Teacher, and (couched in daimonic terms) the conception of the Yeatses' second child. A few interruptions occurred, such as a period in August when Ameritus announced, 'I leave you now—my work is done I have finished'; but Ontelos, who replaced him and orchestrated a number of specific remarks about the Yeatses in certain incarnations, was unmasked after a few days, admitting 'I was only sent as a deceiver' (*YVP*ii. 366, 372). Ameritus reappeared; GY wrote his name at the start of the next session, and then the comment 'to give interpreter confidence & security' (*YVP* ii. 373).

By September, when Ameritus announced, 'Well as you are bored with us we will go', the script had approached something like intellectual closure. Furthermore (and probably more significant for the parties involved), many of the personal issues which had troubled both bridegroom and bride two years earlier had been resolved. For example, the figures of Maud and Iseult Gonne (as well as Mabel Dickinson and Olivia Shakespear) had been distanced and fixed into psychological principles: they no longer presented immediate problems to the marriage or either partner's peace of mind. Although there was much work yet to do, Thomas returned on 10 September (joining Ameritus and the gentle guides Leaf and Rose) to pronounce something like a benediction on WBY, telling him that the controls and guides had come in chorus 'To show we do not always come to blame & scold—for aprobation of you also to herald your new rhymes'.[26] Answering the question put to him (and initialled) by G. H. L., 'Why do you praise him tonight', Thomas replied, 'Good husband—good lover'.

There is some indication that the interpreter may have underestimated her husband's interest in the project even as the proceedings neared completion. Ameritus had been expressing dissatisfaction and some impatience, in transmissions such as this answer to an unrecorded question on 13 September 1919, in the middle of an exposition

[26] A comment of 22 Nov. 1919 suggests that the sittings might have been expected to continue longer than they in fact did. On that evening Ameritus remarked about a proposed lecture tour, 'I want to remind you that you ought not to go to Japan next summer as there are certain scripts to be finished & if all goes well brilliantly finished' (*YVP*ii. 491).

about victimage for the dead and the ghostly self: 'I want you to get to understand this part of system as is easiest to you—medium would dislike this part of personal so you had better get it as you can. I mean she dislikes this case to go into on personal grounds as much as one or two others but if you cant grasp it without personal then you must have it.' Nor was WBY the only target of the spirits' disapproval: later the same evening a drawing of bowling pins being knocked down was labelled 'Idiot' and symbolized 'certain physics *we* have been administering to your bad flighty wife' (*YVP* ii. 423–4).

It took a change to another control, the raucous Dionertes, to bully WBY out of the nightly sessions. Ameritus had been plagued by lack of energy, complaining on 20 November, for example, that 'I cannot get enough force'. His own deficiency in 'creative force', appropriately enough for a daimonic control, mirrored sexual difficulty on the human plane. Some element that resulted from sexual relations between the Yeatses was missing, he explained: 'Mediumship in this case arises because of certain sexual emotions—When those lack there is no mediumship.' To WBY's question about foreplay, 'Is a long excited preliminary important in the present case', Ameritus replied in the heightened form of mirror writing: 'What is important is that both the desire of the medium and her desire for your desire should be satisfied.' Physical desire made all the truths of their philosophy possible: 'In *this* case there cannot be intellectual *desire* (not intellectual interests) without *sexual & emotional* satisfaction—therefore without intellectual desire there is no force *or* truth especially *truth* because truth is intensity' (*YVP*ii. 486–7). Again on 2 December, excusing his inability to answer the first question of the sitting, Ameritus reported that 'There is absolutely no force It would really be better to go through old script for a whole week. I will answer any question on it you like to ask but no *new* script.' He then commented more specifically on the condition of the interpreter: 'Used up—nothing else—intellectually tired ... That she has got but the existing state of exhausted faculty prevents anything being perceived Simply too much script'

(*YVP*ii. 499). By 9 December, after the session in which Ameritus informed the couple that 'The cause of fatigue is that the link between her & her daimon is strengthening', it was obvious that spiritual changes in the interpreter required a different representative (*YVP* ii. 504).

Such a personality entered on 13 December, identifying himself as Dionertes and answering several unrecorded questions, presumably about Ameritus's disappearance: 'Because he made a psychological mistake Yes but we cannot be allowed to.' A series of commands follows, including the admonition against hypnosis:

For half an hour & then stop for half an hour & go on for half an hour
But there must be no script two nights a week *regular* & one night of these 2
she ought to go to bed very early—you must *never* use hypnotism without
our permission as if you use it without you entangle your personalities
but with our permission we give the force & you merely the symbol.
(*YVP* ii. 510)

Dionertes, whose name may be related to the Greek *dia*, 'through', and either *oneiros*, 'a dream', or *nerteros*, 'the dead' or 'the gods in the underworld', was direct and abrupt. On occasion he resorted to insult, retorting thus to a complicated question about the placement of qualities among the four Faculties:

upset by muddle
better read out
Why anywhere
I cannot see why is not obvious
did Ameritus do all your thinking. (*YVP* ii. 512)

Dionertes would soon prod the Yeatses into a more potentially linear method of reception than their Socratic lines of inquiry. He was insistent from the beginning that 'We cannot waste time now—time is so short—' (*YVP*ii. 513), and was an important control throughout the sleeps and well beyond. The Yeatses got information through this no-nonsense personality regularly until the

1930s. An entry in the diary begun at Rapallo gives a rare physical description of a communicator:

Yesterday a change of controls, Dionertes came first, more anxious to speak than I to listen—for I am not yet ready—he confirmed the account I am [?shortly] to give of the state after *Beatitude*—at least in principle—but was vague & uncertain. Even said of a statement of mine that it was 'very interesting' as though he heard it for the first time. I asked him to describe him self but when the description came it was soon observed that another control was speaking. Dionertes was sallow of face & dressed in black—'of course'—baggy about the knees, bald & beardless with small eyes & head bigger behind than in front & he had a sword that he had never used. The new speaker said that he was to take his place, he himself young & fair haired & had, though he did not remember it any more than Dionertes did, been Dionertes friend in life. Dionertes, he said, wished to stay or to wait until I was ready. But it had been decided to change him.[27]

In late 1919, however, no change in control was foreseeable, although the script was shortly to change dramatically. On 23 December, Dionertes ordered, 'You must always now *refuse* any script which refers to your past present or future relations', and wby tried to obey (*YVP*ii. 522). The aggressiveness of the new control suggests a new level of resolve, one project successfully accomplished and another ready to begin. On Christmas Day, Dionertes explained the symbolic value of a gift to GY: 'Because a bracelet is a symbol [of] Daimonic concordance between two people.' He also commented on another symbolic piece of jewelry, responding to an unrecorded question, 'Yes I should like you to do a marriage invocation over one of the interpreters rings No You know why No to break link with a lost ring which is being indiscreatly worn' (*YVP*ii. 523). Perhaps the energy released by the breaking of a mysterious link with another person and the celebration of 'Daimonic concordance' between husband and wife was the signal for Dionertes to order

---

[27] The diary was eventually published: W. B. Yeats, *Pages from a Diary Written in Nineteen Hundred and Thirty* (Dublin: Cuala Press, 1944), and *Ex* 287–340. See also Matthew Gibson, *Yeats, Coleridge and the Romantic Sage* (New York: St Martin's, 2000) for examination of drafts against the latter edition.

the end of the script. By the end of the Christmas sitting he had announced that he would not allow the experiments to continue as they had for more than two years. 'Not this way anyway—I *wont write*,' he swore, adding, 'No—you must learn other methods' (*YVP* ii. 524).

Resistance to Dionertes was unsuccessful. On 26 December, Apple told the Yeatses, 'You need another communicator as well as Dionertes—He is raucus', and promised to 'bring Melodulce', presumably a sweet guide to offset the other control. However, within the hour Dionertes reassumed command, announcing that his sitting would be 'Short & precise & brisk'. It was, ending abruptly when wby asked a question which did not please: 'Off the topic goodnight *Goodnight*' (*YVP*ii. 525–7). Apple appeared for a few sittings, but was apparently unable to bring Melodulce. Dionertes returned on 4 January 1920, for an uninformative sitting which ended with a contemptuous comment: 'Wait and see What I was waiting for Ha Ha.' wby may have strayed too close to the personal in the next sitting, on 6 January, for the response to an unrecorded question (perhaps about the Beatific Vision) was a curt 'Buzz off B.V.' (*YVP*ii. 530). Nearly a month went by, and the next and final sittings were in the USA, where the Yeatses had gone for a lecture tour. By 29 March, Dionertes had his way, and the automatic writing gave way to the 'other methods—sleeps' which he advised (*YVP* ii. 539).

The new method facilitated Dionertes' injunctions to wby that there should be both 'physical & philosophical' conception (specifically of Michael Yeats, the Fourth Daimon and Avatar), that 'you have got to begin to write soon', and that 'life should be a ritual' (*YVP*ii. 535). Sleeps were much more efficient than automatic writing, and they also made possible implications and links between ideas that were necessary to make from the script both a literary and a practical whole. A change was occurring in the relationship of the system to the lives of the investigators; the psychic explorations deepened from an information-gathering project and a search for personal clarity and peace to an experiment in living. The genre of the *Vision* papers shifts from catechism to daily journal or personal essay, as the writers moved from newly wedded adventurers to householders and parents, from excited recipients of individual messages to organizers and writers of a coherent system. The Yeatses not only recorded dreams, but also set themselves meditations and the 'positive means' (*YVP*iii. 109) of staged discussions to replace the questions and answers of the early years of script.

For all their distinct qualities (even down to baggy-kneed trousers), controls and guides never cross a line into utter theatricality. They remain inextricably linked to the minds of the Yeatses, other and yet the same, according to their own intricate ontological formula. The Yeatses clearly were both fascinated by and also comfortable with beings whose identities were always both separate from and also reliant upon their own. The communicators shared their human collaborators' pasts, needing to 'gather up your memories when we come'; they depended upon the Yeatses' 'emotion and feeling' (*YVP*i. 404) as well as their intellectual and creative lives to create the philosophy that reflected this equation. Guides used 'that portion of the mind of which we are not conscious' (*YVP*ii. 323), even though they never allowed themselves to be seen as only reflections of those minds as long as they came.

Family Matters

> Why does love despair?
> because it is always unsatisfied
>
> > WBY, question; Thomas and Fish, answer; written by GY
> > (*YVP* i. 269)

One final kind of authorial presence arrived by way of reincarnation. The Yeatses were sure that they had lived other lives, and their system of course requires the idea that human beings reincarnate as a basic prop to its structures. The Great Wheel, like a carousel, keeps turning, and human souls must ride it for more than a single spin. In fact, as many commentators on *A Vision* lament, it is not easy to get off, in either version of the book. Generally speaking, reincarnation occurs in two contexts in the script and other papers: first, people circumnavigate the Wheel through the phases one incarnation at a time, although it can take more lives than one to complete progress through a phase. The Yeatses learned relatively early, in early February 1918, that GY was on her third or fourth time through phase 18, for example (*YVP*i. 332; iii. 420). WBY, by contrast, was passing through his phasal life for the first time, and Maud Gonne had been through hers once before (*YVP*i. 330). This formulation was refined later in the course of the extensive discussions in the summer and fall of 1919, where a second cluster of themes emerged, on topics like Moments of Crisis, victimage, overshadowing, and others. These topics all set forth particular ways in which emotions or events in one life recur in changed form to influence subsequent lives, often without the affected party's knowledge. Much of this material informs *A Vision* silently, since it was far too personal for the philosophical exposition, although it erupts in various guises on to the surface in some of WBY's other work, from 'An Image from a Past Life' to *Purgatory*.

In the script, the Yeatses' own lives illustrate the general principles. In several sittings in early August 1919, for example, just before the first temporary departure of Ameritus, they learned that the interpreter's third incarnation had come about so that she could work through excess emotion from two previous lives. In 1754, she had been married to a man much older than she, as she was in her current life: 'He depended on her absolutely being old & she young—very young—& that intensified love,' the couple learnt. In the eighteenth-century incarnation or the next (the Yeatses seemed to understand the sequence of events which the script intimates, but the questions and answers alone do not provide complete information), she was in love with 'but not married to' another man, and she also 'thought her husband was in love with' another woman. Her husband was apparently sent 'to madness', and she had 'an earthly child by her lover'. She even committed suicide at some point in the messy business, 'Because she thought her husband was intreeging with another woman'. All of these various complexities caused overshadowing, victimage, a Third Daimon, and need for 'purgation of the ghostly self', in a complicated blend of trauma and residual emotional excess. Her task in this life was to free herself: 'In *one* she pities herself only/In two she pities her husband *and* her lover & herself/Consequently she reincarnates as 3 in order that she may cease all self pity' (*YVP*ii. 354–66). As a true daughter of phase 18, she must 'always *desire* the unchanging' although it will never come, and she will lean in two directions, toward systematic abstraction on the one hand and creative imagination on the other. She married WBY because 'Janus looks towards 17' (his phase) but also with an eye in the other direction: '18 looks towards philosophy to 19—towards the image to 17' (*YVP*ii. 365). In other words, only because of her 'varied experience' over the course of several lives, and her success at working through its difficulties, would she now be able to express her phase to completion. A sign of that finished expression was the system now taking shape.

When Ameritus disappeared just after this exchange, Ontelos elaborated various details about WBY in other incarnations—that he was a French Revolutionist, betrayed by his mother, dying of consumption, among other details. Much of this information proved to be a false trail. When Ontelos admitted on 12 August that he was 'a deceiver', however, the name 'Eliorus' and a 'password' arrived in the next lines, 'to prevent a deceiver like the last', and then to WBY's question about whether 'the statements made about Interpreter's past lives' were true, the control replied in the affirmative: 'Yes *all*' (*YVP*ii. 372). The enthusiastic WBY was not to continue the line of personal questioning (to his next inquiry, the answer was one firmly underscored word: '*System*'). The script had become too literal and too personal for comfort, but the pieces to be retained concerned a personage who was a necessary counterpart to the Yeatses in illustrating the deeper structural meanings of their system.

Anne Hyde, a historical figure who plays a critical role in the script in terms of the couple's reincarnative histories and futures, was related to GY in at least three incarnations, the collaborators learned. First, in the eighteenth century, GY had been the 'Sister of great grandfather Hyde', and 'after her passionate pf [Persona of Fate]' in that generation, she had 'to return to Hyde family' in the next 'to exhaust it' (*YVP*ii. 357). In this third incarnation, GY was learning about her vitally important ancestor. Anne Hyde had been Countess of Ossory in the late seventeenth century, and was the mythical ancestor and namesake of Anne Butler Yeats.[28] This intense figure is the most dramatic example of the literalism of the Yeatses' beliefs, as well as the best teacher in the *Vision* papers of several of the system's more important lessons. She attests to their conviction that human lives are blended together in complex ways, passionately and fatally, and that eternal truths may be perceived from observing the patterns their interactions make. Her various appearances join immediate conjugal and familial circumstances with spiritual continuity over generations, providing a (supposed) common lineage for WBY and GY through the Butler and Hyde families and also linking them in the future through their daughter. Anne Hyde illustrates the method by which the personal becomes the philosophical, how passionate memories are revived through 'continuation of human life' (*YVP*iii. 79). She seems to have attracted GY primarily in these terms, and in the theme of troubled womanhood becoming a source of enduring philosophical and spiritual meaning. For her husband, Anne Hyde became a precursor to obsessions with blood kinship and race that would

---

[28] For more details about Anne Hyde see Saddlemyer, *Becoming George*, 152–5 and *passim; MYV* i. 209–11 and *passim*. With regard to the naming of Anne Butler Yeats, the Yeatses were told in mirror writing on 4 March 1918, in the session saturated with Anne Hyde, to keep 'family tradition name' (*YVP*i. 372). GY was not the only member of the couple excited by the possibilities raised by Anne Hyde; in a letter to a typist who had helped them discover historical details, WBY calls the Anne Hyde case 'the most important piece of psychic research I have ever done' (letter dated 30 July 1919; reproduced in Saddlemyer, *Becoming George*, 227).

characterize his reactions to the troubled politics of the late 1920s and early 1930s.

Anne is the communicator who was the most troubling for GY. Her often cloaked appearances are frequently surrounded by details that suggest difficulties with love, marriage, and the bearing of children. She communicates through a spirit whose name means Love, but she died in childbirth after her own 'passionate pf' (*YVP*ii. 355) brought repetitions of unhappy marriages and failed motherhood through generations of her family. Her arrivals are accompanied by signals of GY's discomfort such as injunctions to secrecy, displacement into other controls, mirror writing, and frustration, appropriately enough for a spirit who mirrored the interpreter's own tendency to attract 'always tragedy violent emotion' (*YVP*iii. 374). Anne speaks in her own voice in some sessions, but it took some time for her to uncloak herself. Until then, and at times afterwards, she is a presence with less-than-clear connections with other spirits, such as Aymor, spelled Amor in one script (*YVP*i. 384; iii. 78).[29] Aymor was joined by Arnault for one period and sometimes assisted by Apple; the letters A A appear in a few sessions. All the names and initials suggest (as does her surname) that Anne wanted to stay hidden, and the Yeatses were told so specifically on one occasion. Anne was identified at the top of the page, as if she were the control for the session, but mirror writing soon follows with a plan for mis-identification: 'I do not wish medium to know and if you say name familiar she will know at once Anne Hyde is writing' (*YVP*i. 379). This statement is followed by Aymor's name as well as signs of Apple as well.

The first mention of Anne Hyde occurs very early in the script, in a long series of responses to unrecorded questions from 23 December 1917. It looks as though the Yeatses had already begun planning to start a family: the enigmatic comment 'Choice had to be made from Anne' concerns reincarnation, as is made clear a few lines further down, in the phrase that presumably refers to the point in a pregnancy when Anne's choice would be made: 'at quickening'. After

---

[29] Amor was identified by another name as well, on 6 Feb. 1918 (*YVP*i. 335).

urging WBY to keep 'the pledge of secrecy', Aymor is mentioned for the first time, and then the date of Anne's marriage, '1681 I think' (*YVP*i. 174). Anne Hyde's first direct speech (not those of Aymor or AR, with their ambiguous relationship to her) occurs soon after the death of Major Robert Gregory in early 1918, while the Yeatses were living in Oxford. The death of Gregory may have influenced Anne's unmasking in the midst of prophetic statements about the war. AR intended to 'take 1914 to 1919', but interrupted him- or herself to announce that

first I must give a message from a spirit who has been very persistent for some time—I do not know anything about her—She calls herself Anne Hyde Duchess of Ormonde and gives you both her dear love.
AR
1681 married James—now I will try and send her away
yes
now give me 1914
died in childbirth (*YVP*i. 362)

Further questioning uncovered details that the Yeatses looked up several days later in the Bodleian, confirming many of the facts after a false start or two, although many of them also remained fuzzy. Incidentally, a few of the factual wild goose chases were either caused by, or were not cleared up by, the spiritual controls, who by no means possessed accurate truths beyond the knowledge of the humans through whom they communicated. The Yeatses also got further data through sleep: in one of several notebook entries devoted to this important topic, WBY recorded that two days after Anne's message, GY 'dreamed of her & that her child had lived three days & that she died very young' (*YVP*iii. 165). Through all their researches, conventional and unconventional, the Yeatses finally arrived at a fairly consistent story. Anne Hyde, the daughter of Lawrence Hyde, Earl of Rochester, was married in 1682 to James Butler, the second Duke of Ormonde. She had died suddenly, of miscarriage or in childbirth. A swirl of other data, some contradictory, came at other times throughout the upcoming months and years: Anne was not the Duchess of Ormonde, since that title was bestowed upon her husband after her death, but the Countess of Ossory. She had black hair and a lively personality. No, she had red hair with the same fiery personality. She had foreseen her death in a prophetic dream. Somewhere in Ireland there was a bundle of letters regarding her or written by her, and the Yeatses were to look for them and for her burial place in Kilkenny. She ceased to love her husband on the day he married her because of his 'brutality of nerve' (*YVP*ii. 366). Her second child was not his. Her dead child was a boy.

This last item is the most significant, because Anne's purpose in coming was not only to give the Yeatses her dear love in the abstract: she wanted to give them her son, and herself. On 4 and 5 March 1918, in the final scripts before the Yeatses' important first trip to Ireland together, WBY received stunning news, much of it given in mirror writing so that it could be kept from the medium.[30] Anne 'came for a purpose' which was ' "wain"/*old word*—wain means heir or son'. She was inclined toward the Yeatses because 'She would like to reincarnate—and the dead child that never lived—a boy—reincarnate'. The control continued to explain, although the 'medium rather nervous', with the most sensitive passages in mirror writing:

Ann wishes her boy to reincarnate because she cannot leave him till he is—she will not want you to reincarnate herself only her boy because she looks on you as on her husband and on medium as on herself

because it is the nearest in reality she can attain to in her dream memory

no a real possibility

NO

NO—in kin she hopes to renew in you the same love her son would have had through her in herself and her husband

. . .

---

[30] The importance and privacy of this script is underscored by the fact that six pages of the conversation were torn out of the notebook recording the sittings (*YVP*i. 370 n. 65).

she is most anxious for what I said & would like what I [?mentioned] but that would have to depend on mediums willingness—she wants the boy to reincarnate first

This last message seems to refer to a second child, a girl, if the medium is willing to have more than one. Aymor's sign reappears, and the session ends with another admonition, perhaps to placate the nervous medium: 'Remember warning—also personal secrecy *Always*' (*YVP*i. 376–8). WBY summarized the events of these two days' sittings in a long passage, dictated to GY, in a notebook entry dated 8 October 1921. He notes particularly the intensity of the conversation about having a child:

On *March 4* came a long script with the essential part in mirror writing the point of which was that we were to have a child; we had hitherto taken precautions against this; but that we were to continue our precautions for at least 3 months longer. The reason of the mirror writing was that I was not to allow George to know that the subject had been discussed at all. We were not to have a child at all unless I was quite sure I wanted it because (in mirror writing) 'the child would only give her happiness in being your child—she does not want a child for its own sake'. Some of the script is obscure as we did not keep the questions but I remember that the words 'apart from her' meant that I must want the child for its own sake & not for sake of her happiness. I must make my decision without telling her. . . . Much insistence on honesty of my decision & doubtless to help that honesty, a statement that she will be equally happy which ever way that decision went. (*YVP* iii. 78)

The 'passionate pf' of Anne Hyde added a particular form of intensity to the Yeatses' relationship. She would be present behind GY; WBY would be a spiritual reincarnation of Anne's lover; the love between the Yeatses would re-create the love that Anne's 'son would have had through her in herself and her husband'; and the son's second chance at life would give peace to his dead mother; all in a complex of relationships that would require an unusually perceptive family systems therapist to untangle. Moreover, as one of the cards in WBY's file indicates, this is not taking overshadowing into account.

For WBY, 'Anne over shadowed the women I have loved', although, happily enough for their genealogical efforts, 'He who over shadows me in Georges eyes not yet born though withdrawn for meditation before birth' (*YVP*iii. 348). In August 1919, after the birth of Anne Yeats had altered the gender of the reincarnated child, Ontelos added further wrinkles: 'I want you to fully grasp the meaning of your having been Anne's lover & now her father and the husband of her child who is now her mother' (*YVP*ii. 367). Her 'child is now her mother', Ontelos went on, 'because Anne did not love her child'; 'the relation of all 3', parent to child to child's child, was necessary to the spiritual advancement of the chosen family.

Ontelos may have been a deceiver, but such swirls of occult psychoanalysis only carry to absurdity a structural support that upholds every joint of the system. WBY was confident enough in the information from the August sessions led by Ontelos to condense details about Anne Hyde on another card, noting that 'a long story crossed out in details as false ... [was] said to be true in psychology' (*YVP*iii. 237). This psychological truth was copied into the notebook entry summarizing the important personal script of 4 March 1918. At the end of the session, WBY dictated: 'Then comes a statement several times repeated that the great thing was not to "break the link"' (*YVP*iii. 78). The Yeatses kept in their minds links that do not appear in the published versions of the system, or in the various creative works of his that use it: between voices in this world and the next, between human souls and daimonic others, and, most intensely, between generations. Without the context of all the participants in the discussions, and the sometimes highly emotional implications of their relationships with each other, all the documents and printed material lack intellectual and creative linkages as well. The Great Wheel becomes a prison rather than an opportunity for second chances for fullness in life; communicators deteriorate into ventriloquist's dummies; daimons become images in mirrors rather than passionate lovers who explain the attractions between philosophical abstractions and concrete images. The system itself becomes not only disjointed but sterile.

Conclusion: 'this other Aquinas'

In that day the system of ~~the~~ Aquinas will be weighed and
that ~~of this other Aquinas~~ ben Luka who thinks not more
inaccurately because he thinks in pictures

The Discoveries of Michael Robartes (*YVP*iv. 20)

The late poem 'Fragments' describes in its first stanza the gyres of one
historical age succeeding another, when 'Locke sank into a swoon'
and 'God took the spinning-jenny/Out of his side' (*VP* 439). The
second stanza switches gears abruptly to pose a question and then
answer it:

> Where got I that truth?
> Out of a medium's mouth,
> Out of nothing it came,
> Out of the forest loam,
> Out of dark night where lay
> The crowns of Nineveh.
>
> (*VP* 439)

Nemo, a medium and no one/nothing, is covertly acknowledged
in a welter of female imagery worthy of Freud or Kristeva—a
mouth full of emptiness, lush earth, and blackness, with repetitions
enforcing equivalences between them all. Yet in 1931, when this
poem was first published, WBY was at work on a second *Vision* that
is a true product of his last decade in having more of swooning

Locke than 'forest loam' about it.[1] GY's mediumistic interpretation, waking conversations, collaborative sleeps, organizational codifying, typing, correcting, and editing had gradually subsided. By 1930, as Saddlemyer notes, WBY even 'avoided dictating the major part of the system to George' as he revised *A Vision*, fearing the physical and emotional consequences to her of mediumship,[2] although the occasional automatic session was still necessary to make sure that he got details right.

GY had other reasons to avoid work on the book as well. Her interests in the system remained more personal than political, or, rather, more a blend of the two; for her, the historical cones remained somewhat psychological and mystical, with a whiff of astrological holism or a Hermetic belief in 'as above, so below' about them. Her work shows continuing interest in the multilayered quality of the system, the ways in which specific revelations duplicate larger geo-metric patterns and larger patterns exist microcosmically in smaller units. To some degree, of course, this aspect of the system became her stock-in-trade: both partners associated her with the informa-tion she continued to receive from the communicators—'George's ghosts', in WBY's phrase (*L* 781)—though with lessening frequency and a different quality than in the early years. By the mid-1920s, as they pieced the messages together into organized clusters of ideas, they had begun to use automatism merely to plug holes in their knowledge rather than continuing to explore with the intensity of the first years of script.

WBY, meanwhile, worked to fit the system intellectually into the philosophers and political thinkers he had begun to read in earnest after the first version of the book was finished. The communicators encouraged the course in reading, but evidence suggests that neither they nor the interpreter had much faith in WBY's political leanings or

---

[1] Croft is correct in noting that 'the 1937 *Vision* as a whole is focused less on the sexual, personal, or individual . . . and more upon the larger implications of the system in regard to society and history' (Croft, *Stylistic Arrangements*, 67).

[2] Saddlemyer, *Becoming George*, 435, documented from a letter to Olivia Shakespear. See also Foster, *Arch-Poet*, 412.

abstract pronouncements. Automatic warnings against 'propaganda' and 'political schemes' occurred during the years of script (*YVP*i. 152; ii. 320), and although GY was keenly interested in politics in her everyday life, she shied away from the heady mix of politics with occultism.[3] Nor was she favourably disposed toward her husband mixing right-leaning politics and poetry, as she complained in 1931 to her friend Tom MacGreevy: 'I have been reading nothing but poetry just lately *not* his!! and it has made me realise how damnably national he is becoming. Nationality throws out personality and there's nothing in his verse worth preserving but the personal.'[4] The first version of *A Vision* seems to announce itself as apolitical: 'I do not want to concern myself, except where I must, with political events' (*AV A* 194). However, 'Dove or Swan', the discussion of historical cones, with its prophecies of a 'new era [that] comes bringing its stream of irrational force', belies its author's vague disclaimer. By 1937, in the new section on 'The Great Year', correspondences with the historical systems of Gerald Heard, Adams, Petrie, Spengler, Vico, Marx, Sorel, and Croce dot the page (*AV B* 261–2), although the book's enthusiasms for 1920s Italian fascism have been modified to sound like weary confusion: 'Perhaps I am too old. Surely something would have come when I meditated under the direction of the Cabalists. What discords will drive Europe to that artificial unity—only dry or drying sticks can be tied into a bundle—which is the decadence of every civilisation?' (*AV B* 301–2).

WBY's politics have inspired vehement debate, of course, especially the politics of the early 1930s and their relation to his art. Conor Cruise O'Brien's gauntlet, that '[WBY's] greatest poetry was written

---

[3] In part, this hesitation may again reflect her distaste for popular spiritualism, which often spoke of a new age, although the coming dispensation was more often democratic than autocratic. See, e.g., William Stainton Moses' automatically received *More Spirit Teachings*: 'We were told that in such a democratic age it would not do (as in the case of the Christ) for only one prophet to be raised up. Now the truth was coming to many in many different ways' ([William Stainton Moses], *More Spirit Teachings* (London: Spiritualist Press, 1952), 27).

[4] Letter to Tom MacGreevy, 31 Dec. 1925, quoted in Ann Saddlemyer, 'George Hyde Lees: More than a Poet's Wife', in A. Norman Jeffares (ed.) *Yeats the European*, iii. (Gerrards Cross: Colin Smythe, 1989), 192. See also Saddlemyer, *Becoming George*, 322.

near the end of his life when his ideas were at their most sinister', can still seem to lie where he threw it down.[5] Interestingly, however, even in its 1937 incarnation, *A Vision* remains a somewhat recalcitrant piece of supporting evidence for most political as well as other analyses that use it as evidence for a general thesis. Every position has its counter-position, and both authors, the artful occultist of 1925 and the aged mythographer of 1937, argue from both sides of their mouths. It can be argued that the book is the most modern, perhaps even postmodern, of WBY's works, in its playful meta-narratives, its theoretical fragmentation of human personality, its global pretensions, its hard-edged geometrics and images. The book can seem typically Irish in its ironies and contrarieties, English in its drawing-room occultism, Romantic in its Neoplatonic idealism, Victorian in its ornate rhetoric. It can be read as deterministic and despairing; or, on the other hand, it can convey a curious sense of release, its continually moving structures and melodious style refusing to allow one meaning to take absolute precedence over another.

This recalcitrance to categorization, as I have been arguing, results from qualities such as stylistic and structural multiplication of authorial perspective, inscribing of mutual desire in various deep structures, thoroughly unstable positions on questions of faith and the sources of knowledge, and performative and improvisational tone in dynamic counterpart to the book's assertions of unchanging truth. These phenomena in turn are signs of the collaboration that made the book, and the collaboration is itself a sign of the degree to which the Yeatses were inclined to delve into issues of textuality, subjectivity, interconnection, and uncertainty that are both spiritual and literary as they are both personal and conceptual. Rather than giving readers an excuse to avoid *A Vision* and its numerous effects in WBY's other work (as more than a few would probably admit

---

[5] Conor Cruise O'Brien, 'Passion and Cunning: An Essay on the Politics of W. B. Yeats', in A. Norman Jeffares and K. G. W. Cross (eds.), *In Excited Reverie: A Centenary Tribute to W. B. Yeats, 1865–1939* (London: Macmillan, 1965), 224.

to doing), all of these signs point to a need for different modes of analysis. I hope that my study can open an avenue or two to *A Vision*, WBY's poems and plays that depend upon it, and the people who worked to create them. If it could stir up a little trouble for the idea that reading and writing are solitary activities characterized by firm self-possession, that would suit me, too.

When WBY began to compose the first drafts of what would become *A Vision*, in the form of dialogues in which 'Robartes & Ahearne discuss philosophy' (*YVP*ii. 485–6), the issue had already arisen of how to indicate the presence of a second author of the system, other authorial presences beyond that, and the emotional, poetic, and mystical quality of its hard-edged geometries and philosophical propositions. This issue, which gave rise to the various phantasmagoria with which both versions of the book are festooned, as well as the *mises en scène* for poems and sections of prose published in various forms, is discussed by the two old friends. One passage in particular from the much corrected manuscript is worth reading carefully, including the many cancelled passages that attempt to find an appropriate fictional situation to explain how 'Yeats' came by his esoteric knowledge. Robartes is surprised to find that WBY has spoken in a voice 'at once [?light] and dogmatic' about 'things of which he can know nothing'. WBY tells us, Robartes continues,

> ~~exactly~~ & on the whole without great inacuracy what befals the soul after death. He a man living ~~almost~~ almost a public life—
>
> Ahearne
>
> Yes & with all the small vanities of an author
>
> Robartes
>
> ~~He does not seem to~~ He cannot know these things of his own knowledge. ~~He~~ And endeed he is ~~endeed~~ always quoting—~~and he has made an amusing point with~~ & I think his quotations very appropriate & then certainty. It is [?] Some of the authorities he gives & others I know but there is one authority he quotes without acknowledgment. I admit that he has the endeed the memory [of] a few broken dreams dreamed twenty years ago & may be half forgotten~~ no doubt to[o] he has been helped by certain dreams

A hearne

    ~~and dreams~~ Half forgotten or half invented dreams put in for effect—to empress the reader, as much as to say 'I also have been upon Patmos.'

Robartes

    But there is something that the ~~memories~~ dreams & the quotations do not account for. I cannot make out how he came upon the doctrine of the Antithetical self. At first I thought ~~of it~~ it a [?~~mere~~] coincidence—[?~~guess~~] ~~but~~ no that is impossible—there are many little hints & half statements that show that [he] knows he is giving but a part. Yet it does not seem that he himself knows more than he has written for there are mistakes, ~~& a general lack of precision.~~ a vagueness very natural in a man of his position. (*YVP*iv. 63–4)

The picture of WBY, the bumbling public author who cannot be expected to produce texts that are other than vague, imprecise, and wrong on some counts, is created to be inadequate to all that he speaks, even though he is 'always quoting' (and, surprisingly, makes a point that is even 'amusing'). WBY may have gleaned his knowledge in memory, dream, or coincidence, from cited authorities or even a Leo-like performance of 'half invented dreams put in for effect', but the most mysterious comment is the much revised mention of the 'one authority he quotes without acknowledgement', whom even Robartes does not seem to know. This authority has given WBY more than the exposition that this passage introduces, but all that is left to indicate the complete wisdom, of which 'little hints & half statements' remain and of whose entirety WBY himself seems ignorant, is 'the doctrine of the Antithetical self'. That antithetical self, robed in swathes of ambiguity, not the least of which is the system that purports to explain it, is of course a symbolic parallel for GY and the 'incredible experience' that she embodied. She brought the unimaginable whole, images, diagrams, voices, dreams, desires, daily life, children, emotional intensity, conceptual challenges, that could only inadequately be described with the phases, tinctures, cones, spheres, Faculties and Principles, after-death experiences, Great Year, daimons, and other ideas that crowd the thousands of pages of documents, unpublished and published, that came from the occult work.

In *The Discoveries of Michael Robartes*, Robartes claims that the system will usher in a new era of faith, a new awareness in the world of 'the souls immortality'. With his characteristic heaviness of tone, he pronounces a seismic change: 'In a few years for it is already established to the student, they will believe once more. When that time comes it will be understood that just as a man can investigate the laws by which the ocean moves in a cup of water we can investigate by studying our own minds the final destination of the soul' (*YVP*iv. 20). The new dispensation, in which study of 'our own minds' will illuminate our final end, will come by way of the wisdom that ben Luka received through his wife: 'In that day the system of ~~the~~ Aquinas will be weighed and that ~~of this other Aquinas~~ ben Luka who thinks not more inaccurately because he thinks in pictures.' Aquinas, that great doctor of the Church, as well as the Arab philosopher ben Luka, Robartes, wby, and all the other men into whose keeping the great system is placed, speak and write and live out of its teachings. Meanwhile, gy keeps her secrets to herself. One other passage from 'The Discoveries of Michael Robartes' also illustrates her brand of wisdom. She participated to an unusually active degree in the writing and revision of the description of phase 18, which of course describes her own soul, in the various drafts of the Great Wheel, the section of *A Vision* that contains a small essay on each of the phases. The Body of Fate, the Faculty that describes the course of destiny, is 'enforced disillusion': in other words, souls at this phase do not have the lives they envisioned. However, with their Creative Mind of 'emotional philosophy', they make the best of their circumstances. Like Goethe, a man of the phase whose work gy knew well, 'a poet who became to him self a subject of knowledge', souls at 18 can know themselves, body and mind, and make of that awareness a seemingly separate 'subject of knowledge' through which they attain much. Phase 18, we recall, is 'the only phase where the most profound form of wisdom is possible, a wisdom as emotional as that of the Centaur Chiron'—an arresting evocation of a figure ambiguously situated between mortal and immortal worlds, a teacher and prophet, beloved of Apollo and mentor to kings, but also wounded beyond healing and finally left alone (*YVP*iv. 200).

Bibliography

Adams, Hazard. *Blake and Yeats: The Contrary Vision*. Ithaca, NY: Cornell University Press, 1955.

——— 'Symbolism and Yeats's *A Vision*'. *Journal of Aesthetics and Art Criticism*, 22 (1964): 425–36.

——— *The Book of Yeats's Poems*. Tallahassee, Fla.: Florida State University Press, 1990.

——— *The Book of Yeats's Vision: Romantic Modernism and Antithetical Tradition*. Ann Arbor: University of Michigan Press, 1995.

Adams, Steve L., and Harper, George Mills. 'The Manuscript of "Leo Africanus"'. In Richard J. Finneran (ed.), *Yeats Annual*, i (London: Macmillan, 1982), 3–47.

Alldritt, Keith. *W. B. Yeats: The Man and the Milieu*. New York: Clarkson Potter, 1997.

Allen, James Lovic. 'Belief versus Faith in the Credo of Yeats'. *Journal of Modern Literature*, 4 (1975): 692–716.

——— 'Yeats, Belief, and ESP: New Critical Attitudes'. *Éire-Ireland*, 24 (1989): 109–19.

Arnold, Matthew. *Essays in Criticism, Second Series*, ed. Noel Annan. London: Oxford University Press, 1964.

Auden, W. H. 'Yeats as an Example'. In J. Hall and M. Steinmann (eds.), *The Permanence of Yeats: Selected Criticism* (New York: Macmillan, 1950), 344–51.

Austin, J. L. *How to Do Things with Words*, 2nd edn. Oxford: Clarendon Press, 1975.

Bachchan, Harbans Rai. *W. B. Yeats and Occultism: A Study of his Works in Relation to Indian Lore, the Cabbala, Swedenborg, Boehme and Theosophy*. Delhi, Varanasi, Patna: Motilal Banarsidass, 1965.

Baggley, John. *Doors of Perception—Icons and their Spiritual Significance*. London and Oxford: Mowbray, 1987.

Barker, Elsa. *Letters from a Living Dead Man*. London: William Rider and Son, 1914.

_____ *War Letters from the Living Dead Man*. London: William Rider and Son, 1915.

_____ *Last Letters from the Living Dead Man*. London: William Rider and Son, 1919.

Barrow, Logie. *Independent Spirits: Spiritualism and English Plebeians 1850–1910*. London: Routledge & Kegan Paul, 1986.

Barthes, Roland. 'The Death of the Author'. In *Image, Music, Text: Essays Selected and Translated* (Glasgow: Fontana, 1977), 142–8.

Bashan, Diana. *The Trial of Woman: Feminism and the Occult Sciences in Victorian Literature and Society*. New York: New York University Press, 1992.

Bazett, L. Margery. *Some Thoughts on Mediumship*. London: Rider, [1926].

Benjamin, Walter. *Illuminations*, trans. Harry Zohn. New York: Schocken, 1969.

Bennett, Edward T. *Automatic Speaking and Writing: A Study*, iii: *The Shilling Library of Psychical Literature and Enquiry*. London and Edinburgh: Brimley Johnson and Ince, 1905.

Berry, Philippa, and Wernick, Andrew (eds.). *Shadow of Spirit: Postmodernism and Religion*. London: Routledge, 1992.

Blake, Christopher. 'The Supreme Enchanter: W. B. Yeats and the Soul of the World' (Ph.D. diss., Georgia State University, 1997).

_____ 'Ghosts in the Machine: Yeats and the Metallic Homunculus, with Transcripts of Reports by W. B. Yeats and Edmund Dulac'. In Warwick Gould (ed.), *Yeats Annual*, xv (London: Palgrave, 2002), 69–101.

Blake, William. *The Works of William Blake*, ed. William Butler Yeats and Edwin Ellis, 3 vols. London: Bernard Quaritch, 1893.

_____ *Complete Writings*, ed. Geoffrey Keynes. Oxford: Oxford University Press, 1966.

Bloom, Harold. *Yeats*. New York: Oxford University Press, 1970.

_____ *Genius*. London: Fourth Estate, 2002.

Boland, Eavan. 'The Weasel's Tooth'. *Irish Times*, 7 June 1974; repr. in Robert F. Garratt (ed.), *Modern Irish Poetry: Tradition and Continuity from Yeats to Heaney* (Berkeley: University of California Press, 1986), 10.

_____ 'When the Spirit Moves'. *The New York Review of Books*, 12 January 1995, 27.

Bourdieu, Pierre. *Language and Symbolic Power*. Cambridge, Mass.: Harvard University Press, 1991.

Bourke, Angela. *The Burning of Bridget Cleary*. London: Pimlico, 1999.

Bradford, Curtis. 'George Yeats: Poet's Wife'. *Sewanee Review*, 77 (1969): 385–404.

Brandon, Ruth. *The Spiritualists: The Passion for the Occult in the Nineteenth and Twentieth Centuries*. New York: Knopf, 1983.

Braude, Ann. *Radical Spirits: Spiritualism and Women's Rights in Nineteenth-Century America*. Boston: Beacon Press, 1989.

Brearton, Fran. *The Great War in Irish Poetry: W. B. Yeats to Michael Longley*. Oxford: Oxford University Press, 1999.

Bridge, Ursula, ed. *W. B. Yeats and T. Sturge Moore: Their Correspondence 1901–1937*. London: Routledge & Kegan Paul, 1953.

Brooks, Jr., Cleanth. *Modern Poetry and the Tradition*. Chapel Hill, N.C.: University of North Carolina Press, 1939.

Brown, Terence. *The Life of W. B. Yeats: A Critical Biography*. Oxford: Blackwell, 1999.

Burke, Kenneth. *A Rhetoric of Motives*. Berkeley: University of California Press, 1969.

Butcher, Arthur. 'Welcome News for Astrologers'. *Light*, 15 (1895): 517.

Butler, Judith. *Bodies that Matter: On the Discursive Limits of "Sex"*. New York: Routledge, 1993.

—— 'Burning Acts: Injurious Speech'. In Andrew Parker and Eve Kosofsky Sedgwick (eds.) *Performativity and Performance* (New York: Routledge, 1995), 197–227.

Cadava, Eduardo. *Words of Light: Theses on the Photography of History*. Princeton: Princeton University Press, 1997.

Campbell, John L., and Hall, Trevor H. *Strange Things: The Story of Fr Allan McDonald, Ada Goodrich Freer, and the Society for Psychical Research's Enquiry into Highland Second Sight*. London: Routledge & Kegan Paul, 1968.

Caputo, John D. *The Prayers and Tears of Jacques Derrida: Religion without Religion*. Bloomington, Ind.: Indiana University Press, 1997.

Carpenter, Edward. *The Drama of Love and Death: A Study of Human Evolution and Transfiguration*. London: George Allen, 1907.

Castle, Terry. *The Female Thermometer: Eighteenth-Century Culture and the Invention of the Uncanny*. Oxford: Oxford University Press, 1995.

Chadwick, N. Kershaw. *Poetry and Prophecy*. Cambridge: Cambridge University Press, 1952.

Chadwick, Whitney, and Courtivron, Isabelle de (eds.) *Significant Others: Creativity and Intimate Partnership*. London: Thames & Hudson, 1993.

Chartier, Roger. *The Order of Books: Readers, Authors, and Libraries between the Fourteenth and Eighteenth Centuries*, trans. Lydia G. Cochrane. Stanford, Calif.: Stanford University Press, 1994.

Chaudhry, Yug Mohit. *Yeats, the Irish Literary Revival and the Politics of Print*. Cork: Cork University Press, 2001.

Clark, David R. ' "The Poet and the Actress": An Unpublished Dialogue by W. B. Yeats'. In Warwick Gould (ed.), *Yeats Annual*, viii (London: Macmillan, 1991), 123–43.

Clodd, Edward. *The Question: "If a man die, shall he live again?" Job xiv.14: A Brief History and Examination of Modern Spiritualism*. London: Grant Richards, 1917.

Collins, Gregory, OSB. *The Glenstal Book of Icons*. Blackrock, Co. Dublin: Columba Press, 2002.

Colum, Mary M. 'Life and Literature: The Individual vs. Society. Rev. of *A Vision*'. *Forum and Century*, 99 (1938): 212–16.

Cottom, Daniel. *Abyss of Reason: Cultural Movements, Revelations, and Betrayals*. New York and Oxford: Oxford University Press, 1991.

Covino, William A. *Magic, Rhetoric, and Literacy: An Eccentric History of the Composing Imagination*. Albany, NY: State University of New York Press, 1994.

Coward, Harold, and Foshay, Toby (eds.) *Derrida and Negative Theology*. Albany, NY: State University of New York Press, 1992.

Croft, Barbara L. *Stylistic Arrangements: A Study of William Butler Yeats's* A Vision. Lewisburg, Pa.: Bucknell University Press, 1987.

Cullingford, Elizabeth Butler. *Yeats, Ireland and Fascism*. London: Macmillan, 1981.

—— *Gender and History in Yeats's Love Poetry*. Cambridge: Cambridge University Press, 1993.

Culpin, Millais. *Spiritualism and the New Psychology: An Explanation of Spiritualist Phenomena and Beliefs in Terms of Modern Knowledge*. London: Edward Arnold, 1920.

Cummins, Geraldine. *Unseen Adventures*. London: Rider, 1951.

Danius, Sara. *The Senses of Modernism: Technology, Perception, and Æsthetics.* Ithaca, NY, and London: Cornell University Press, 2002.

Davies, Margery W. *Woman's Place is at the Typewriter: Office Work and Office Workers, 1870–1930.* Philadelphia: Temple University Press, 1982.

de Man, Paul. *The Rhetoric of Romanticism.* New York: Columbia University Press, 1984.

de Molinos, Miguel. *Guida Spirituale*, trans. Kathleen Lyttelton. [London]: Methuen, [1911].

Deane, Seamus. 'Heroic Styles: The Tradition of an Idea'. In *Ireland's Field Day* (London: Hutchinson, 1985), 45–58.

_____ 'Yeats and the Idea of Revolution'. In *Celtic Revivals: Essays in Modern Irish Literature 1880–1980* (London: Faber, 1985), 38–50.

Dearmer, Percy. ' "Nomenclature": Letters to the Editor'. *Journal of the Society for Psychical Research*, 19 (1919), 104–5, 180.

Deleuze, Gillee, and Guattari, Félix. *Anti-Oedipus: Capitalism and Schizophrenia*, trans. Robert Hurley, Mark Seem, and Helen R. Lane. Minneapolis: University of Minnesota Press, 1983.

Derrida, Jacques. *Of Grammatology*, trans. Gayatri Chakravorty Spivak. Baltimore: Johns Hopkins University Press, 1976.

_____ 'Différance'. In *Margins of Philosophy* (Chicago: University of Chicago Press, 1982), 1–27.

_____ 'Signature Event Context'. In *Margins of Philosophy* (Chicago: University of Chicago Press, 1982), 307–30.

_____ 'How to Avoid Speaking: Denials'. In Sanford Budick and Wolfgang Iser (eds.), *Languages of the Unsayable: The Play of Negativity in Literature and Literary Theory* (New York: Columbia University Press, 1989); repr. in Harold Coward and Toby Foshay (eds.), *Derrida and Negative Theology* (Albany, NY: State University of New York Press, 1992), 73–142.

_____ *Specters of Marx: The State of the Debt, The Work of Mourning, and the New International*, trans. Peggy Kamuf. London: Routledge, 1994.

_____ *The Gift of Death*, trans. David Wills. Chicago: University of Chicago Press, 1995.

Dixon, Joy. 'Gender, Politics, and Culture in the New Age: Theosophy in England, 1880–1935' (Ph.D. diss., Rutgers, 1993).

Dobra, Susan Martha. 'Collaboration and Consensus: Constructing a Rhetoric of Abnormal Discourse for Composition from the Esoteric

Prose of William Butler Yeats and Annie Wood Besant' (Ph.D. diss., University of California, 1993).

Donoghue, Denis. 'The Fabulous Yeats Boys'. *The New York Review of Books*, 11 May 2000, 32–6.

_____ 'Ireland: Race, Nation, State: The Charles Stewart Parnell Lecture, 1998'. In Warwick Gould (ed.), *Yeats and the Nineties: Yeats Annual, A Special Number*, xiv (London: Palgrave, 2001), 3–32.

Doyle, Arthur Conan. *The History of Spiritualism*, 2 vols. New York: George H. Doran, 1926.

_____ *Pheneas Speaks: Direct Spirit Communications in the Family Circle, Reported by Arthur Conan Doyle*. [London]: Psychic Press and Bookshop, [1927].

Eagleton, Terry. *Literary Theory: An Introduction*. Minneapolis: University of Minnesota Press, 1983.

_____ *Heathcliff and the Great Hunger: Studies in Irish Culture*. London and New York: Verso, 1995.

Ede, Lisa, and Lunsford, Andrea. *Singular Texts/Plural Authors: Perspectives on Collaborative Writing*. Carbondale, Ill.: Southern Illinois University Press, 1990.

Ellmann, Richard. *The Identity of Yeats*. New York: Macmillan, 1954.

_____ *Yeats: The Man and the Masks*. New York: Norton, 1978.

_____ *James Joyce*, rev. edn. Oxford: Oxford University Press, 1982.

Ennemoser, Joseph. *The History of Magic: To which is added an Appendix of the Most Remarkable and Best Authenticated Stories of Apparitions, Dreams, Second Sight, Somnambulism, Predictions, Divination, Witchcraft, Vampires, Fairies, Table-turning, and Spirit-rapping*, trans. William Howitt, ed. Mary Howitt, 2 vols. London: Henry G. Bohn, 1854.

Finneran, Richard J. 'On Editing Yeats: The Text of *A Vision* (1937)'. *Texas Studies in Literature and Language*, 19 (1977): 119–34.

_____ *Editing Yeats's Poems*. London: Macmillan, 1983.

Finneran, Richard J., Harper, George Mills, and Murphy, William M. (eds.). *Letters to W. B. Yeats*, 2 vols. London: Macmillan, 1977.

Flannery, Mary Catherine. *Yeats and Magic: The Earlier Works*. Gerrards Cross: Colin Smythe, 1977.

Flournoy, Theodore. *Spiritism and Psychology*, trans. Hereward Carrington. New York and London: Harper & Brothers, 1911.

Fodor, Nandor. *Encyclopædia of Psychic Science*. Secaucus, NJ: Citadel Press, 1966.

Foshay, Toby. 'Resentment and Apophasis: The Trace of the Other in Levinas, Derrida and Gans'. In Philippa Berry and Andrew Wernick (eds.), *Shadow of Spirit: Postmodernism and Religion* (London: Routledge, 1992), 81–92.

Foster, R. F. 'Protestant Magic: W. B. Yeats and the Spell of Irish History'. In *Paddy and Mr Punch: Connections in Irish and English History* (London: Allen Lane–Penguin Press, 1993), 212–32.

—— *W. B. Yeats: A Life, i: The Apprentice Mage 1865–1914*. Oxford: Oxford University Press, 1997.

—— *W. B. Yeats: A Life, ii: The Arch-Poet 1915–1939*. Oxford: Oxford University Press, 2003.

Foucault, Michel. 'What Is an Author?' In Josué V. Harari (ed.), *Textual Strategies: Perspectives in Post-Structuralist Criticism* (Ithaca, NY: Cornell University Press, 1977), 141–60.

Frazer, Sir James George. *The Golden Bough: A Study in Magic and Religion*, abridged edn. New York: Macmillan, 1963.

—— 'Note'. *Borderland*, 4 (1897): 304.

[Freer, Ada Goodrich] Miss X. 'Note'. *Borderland*, 4 (1897): 368.

Freud, Sigmund. 'The "Uncanny" '. In *The Standard Edition of the Complete Works*, xvii, ed. James Strachey (London: Hogarth Press, 1959), 219–52.

Friel, Brian. *Faith Healer*. In *Selected Plays* (Washington: Catholic University of America Press, 1984), 327–76.

Frieling, Barbara J. 'A Critical Edition of W. B. Yeats's Automatic Script 11 March–30 December 1918' (Ph.D. diss., Florida State University, 1987).

—— 'The "Moments of Crisis" in Yeats's *Vision* Papers'. In Richard J. Finneran (ed.), *Yeats: An Annual of Critical and Textual Studies*, x (Ann Arbor: University of Michigan Press, 1992), 281–95.

—— Harper, Margaret Mills, and Sprayberry, Sandra L. 'Our Lives with Yeats's Ghosts: The Writing and the Editing of the Automatic Script'. In Richard J. Finneran (ed.), *Yeats: An Annual of Critical and Textual Studies*, xvii (Ann Arbor: UMI Research Press, 2003), 19–34.

Frye, Northrop. 'Yeats and the Language of Symbolism'. In *Fables of Identity: Studies in Poetic Mythology* (New York: Harcourt Brace and World, 1963), 218–37.

—— 'The Rising of the Moon'. In *Spiritus Mundi: Essays on Literature, Myth and Society* (Bloomington, Ind.: Indiana University Press, 1976), 245–74.

Garber, Marjorie. *Vice Versa: Bisexuality and the Eroticism of Everyday Life*. New York: Simon & Schuster, 1995.

Garratt, Robert F. *Modern Irish Poetry: Tradition and Continuity from Yeats to Heaney*. Berkeley: University of California Press, 1986.

Gauld, Alan. *The Founders of Psychical Research*. London: Routledge & Kegan Paul, 1968.

Geertz, Clifford. *The Interpretation of Cultures: Selected Essays*. New York: Basic Books, 1973.

Gibson, Matthew. *Yeats, Coleridge and the Romantic Sage*. New York: St Martin's, 2000.

Gilbert, R. A. *Golden Dawn: Twilight of the Magicians*. Wellingborough, Northamptonshire: Aquarian Press, 1983.

_____ *The Golden Dawn Companion: A Guide to the History, Structure, and Workings of the Hermetic Order of the Golden Dawn*. Wellingborough, Northamptonshire: Aquarian Press, 1986.

_____ 'Seeking that which was Lost: New Light on the Origins and Development of the Golden Dawn'. In Warwick Gould (ed.), *Yeats and the Nineties: Yeats Annual, A Special Number*, xiv (London: Palgrave, 2001), 33–49.

Goldman, Arnold. 'Yeats, Spiritualism, and Psychical Research'. In George Mills Harper (ed.), *Yeats and the Occult* ([Toronto]: Macmillan of Canada, 1975), 108–29.

Gorski, William T. *Yeats and Alchemy*. Albany, NY: State University of New York Press, 1996.

Gould, Warwick. 'Frazer, Yeats and the Reconsecration of Folklore'. In Robert Fraser (ed.), *Sir James Frazer and the Literary Imagination* (London: Macmillan, 1990), 121–53.

Greer, Mary. *Women of the Golden Dawn: Rebels and Priestesses*. Rochester, Vt.: Park Street Press, 1995.

Grossman, Allen R. *Poetic Knowledge in the Early Yeats: A Study of* 'The Wind Among the Reeds'. Charlottesville, Va.: University of Virginia Press, 1969.

Guha, Naresh. *W. B. Yeats: An Indian Approach*. Calcutta: Jadavpur University, 1968.

Handelman, Susan A. (ed.). *The Slayers of Moses: The Emergence of Rabbinic Interpretation in Modern Literary Theory*. Albany, NY: State University of New York Press, 1982.

Haraway, Donna. *Simians, Cyborgs, and Women: The Reinvention of Nature.* New York: Routledge, 1991.

Harper, George Mills. *Yeats's Golden Dawn: The Influence of the Hermetic Order of the Golden Dawn on the Life and Art of W. B. Yeats.* London: Macmillan, 1974.

―――― ' "A Subject of Investigation": Miracle at Mirebeau'. In George Mills Harper, *Yeats and the Occult* ([Toronto]: Macmillan of Canada, 1975), 172–89.

―――― *The Making of Yeats's* A Vision: *A Study of the Automatic Script*, 2 vols. London: Macmillan, 1987.

―――― (ed.). *Yeats and the Occult.* [Toronto]: Macmillan of Canada, 1975.

―――― and Kelly, John S. 'Preliminary Examination of the Script of E[lizabeth] R[adcliffe]'. In George Mills Harper (ed.), *Yeats and the Occult* ([Toronto]: Macmillan of Canada, 1975), 130–71.

―――― and Sprayberry, Sandra L. 'Complementary Creation: Notes on "Another Song of a Fool" and "Towards Break of Day" '. In Richard J. Finneran (ed.), *Yeats: An Annual of Critical and Textual Studies*, iv (Ann Arbor: UMI Research Press, 1986), 69–85.

Harper, Margaret Mills. 'The Medium as Creator: George Yeats's Role in the Automatic Script'. In Richard J. Finneran (ed.), *Yeats: An Annual of Critical and Textual Studies*, vi (Ann Arbor: UMI Research Press, 1988), 49–71.

―――― 'The Message is the Medium: Identity in the Automatic Script'. In Richard J. Finneran (ed.), *Yeats: An Annual of Critical and Textual Studies*, ix (Ann Arbor: UMI Research Press, 1991), 35–54.

―――― 'Yeats's Religion'. In Richard J. Finneran (ed.), *Yeats: An Annual of Critical and Textual Studies*, xiii (Ann Arbor: UMI Research Press, 1997), 48–71.

―――― 'Celestial Bodies: Sexual Cosmologies in a Collaborative Vision'. In Warwick Gould (ed.), *Yeats Annual*, xv (London: Palgrave, 2002), 102–19.

―――― 'Nemo: George Yeats and her Automatic Script'. *New Literary History*, 33 (2002): 291–314.

―――― 'Yeats and the Occult'. In John S. Kelly and Marjorie Howes (eds.), *The Cambridge Companion to W. B. Yeats* (Cambridge: Cambridge University Press, 2006), 144–66.

Hart, Kevin. *The Trespass of the Sign: Deconstruction, Theology and Philosophy*. Cambridge: Cambridge University Press, 1989.

Harwood, John. *Olivia Shakespeare and W. B. Yeats: After Long Silence*. London: Macmillan, 1989.

Haswell, Janis Tedesco. *Pressed Against Divinity: W. B. Yeats's Feminine Masks*. DeKalb, Ill.: Northern Illinois University Press, 1997.

Heidegger, Martin. *Kant and the Problem of Metaphysics*, trans. James S. Churchill. Bloomington, Ind.: Indiana University Press, 1962.

—— *The Principle of Reason*, trans. Reginald Lilly. Bloomington, Ind., and Indianapolis: Indiana University Press, 1991.

Heine, Elizabeth. 'W. B. Yeats' Map in his Own Hand'. *Biography: An Interdisciplinary Quarterly*, 1 (1978): 37–50.

—— 'Yeats and Maud Gonne: Marriage and the Astrological Record, 1908–1911'. In Warwick Gould (ed.), *Yeats Annual*, xiii (London: Macmillan, 1998), 3–33.

Helmling, Steven. *The Esoteric Comedies of Carlyle, Newman, and Yeats*. Cambridge: Cambridge University Press, 1988.

Herr, Cheryl. '"The strange reward of all that discipline": Yeats and Foucault'. In Leonard Orr (ed.), *Yeats and Postmodernism* (Syracuse, NY: Syracuse University Press, 1991), 146–66.

Hey, Hanson E. *The Seven Principles of Spiritualism; with a Brief History of the Spiritualists' National Union*. Halifax, The Spiritualists' National Union, 1910.

Hollywood, Amy. *Mysticism, Sexual Difference, and the Demands of History*. Chicago: University of Chicago Press, 2001.

Hood, Connie Kelly. 'The Remaking of *A Vision*'. In Richard J. Finneran (ed.), *Yeats: An Annual of Critical and Textual Studies*, i (Ithaca, N.Y., and London: Cornell University Press, 1983), 33–67.

—— 'A Search for Authority: Prolegomena to a Definitive Critical Edition of W. B. Yeats's *A Vision* (1937)' (Ph.D. diss., University of Tennessee, 1983).

Hough, Graham. *The Mystery Religion of W. B. Yeats*. Brighton: Harvester Press, 1984.

Howe, Ellic. *The Magicians of the Golden Dawn: A Documentary History of a Magical Order 1887–1923*. London: Routledge & Kegan Paul, 1972.

Howes, Marjorie. *Yeats's Nations: Gender, Class, and Irishness*. Cambridge: Cambridge University Press, 1996.

[Hughes, May]. *From Heavenly Spheres: A Book Written by Inspiration from William Morris; Poet, Socialist and Idealist Who Passed on—October 3rd, 1896*. London: Rider, [n.d.].

[Humphreys, Mrs Desmond] Rita. *The Truth of Spiritualism*. London: T. Werner Laurie, 1919.

Israel, Paul. *Edison: A Life of Invention*. New York: Wiley & Sons, 1998.

Jaffe, Grace M. *Years of Grace*. Sunspot, N. Mex.: Iroquois House, 1979.

James, William. *William James on Psychical Research*, ed. Gardner Murphy and Robert O. Ballou. New York: Viking, 1960.

Jeffares, A. Norman. *W. B. Yeats: Man and Poet*. London: Routledge & Kegan Paul, 1949.

—— *A New Commentary on the Poems of W. B. Yeats*. London: Macmillan, 1984.

—— MacBride White, Anna, and Bridgewater, Christina (eds.). *Letters to W. B. Yeats and Ezra Pound from Iseult Gonne: A Girl That Knew All Dante Once*. London: Palgrave, 2004.

Jervis, John. *Transgressing the Modern*. Oxford: Blackwell, 1999.

Joyce, James. *Ulysses*, ed. Hans Walter Gabler. New York: Vintage, 1986.

Jung, C. G. *Psychiatric Studies*, trans. R. F. C. Hull, ed. Sir Herbert Read, Michael Fordham, and Gerhard Adler. In *The Collected Works of C. G. Jung*, 17 vols. (London: Routledge & Kegan Paul, 1957), i.

Kalogera, Lucy Shepard. 'Yeats's Celtic Mysteries' (Ph.D. diss., Florida State University, 1977).

Kearney, Richard. 'Myth and Motherland'. In *Ireland's Field Day* (London: Hutchinson, 1985), 61–80.

—— *Transitions: Narratives in Modern Irish Culture*. Manchester: Manchester University Press, 1988.

Keep, Christopher. 'The Cultural Work of the Type-Writer Girl'. *Victorian Studies*, 40 (1997): 401–26.

Kenner, Hugh. 'The Sacred Book of the Arts'. In John Unterecker (ed.), *Yeats* (Englewood Cliffs, NJ: Prentice-Hall, 1963), 10–22.

Kermode, Frank. *The Sense of an Ending: Studies in the Theory of Fiction*. New York: Oxford University Press, 1965.

Kern, Stephen. *The Culture of Time and Space, 1880–1918*. Cambridge, Mass.: Harvard University Press, 1983.

Kittler, Friedrich A. *Discourse Networks 1800/1900*, trans. Michael Metteer with Chris Cullens. Stanford, Calif.: Stanford University Press, 1990.

_____ *Gramophone, Film, Typewriter*, trans. Geoffrey Winthrop-Young and Michael Wutz. Stanford, Calif.: Stanford University Press, 1999.

Koestenbaum, Wayne. *Double Talk: The Erotics of Male Literary Collaboration*. New York: Routledge, 1989.

Kristeller, Paul Oskar. 'Giovanni Pico della Mirandola and his Sources'. In *L'Opera e il pensiero di Giovanni Pico della Mirandola nella storia dell'umanesimo: Convegno internazionale, Mirandola: 15–18 settembre 1963*, i (Florence: Istituto Nazionale di Studi sul Rinascimento, 1965), 35–133.

_____ *Renaissance Concepts of Man and Other Essays*. New York: Harper & Row, 1972.

Laird, Holly A. 'Forum: On Collaborations I'. *Tulsa Studies in Women's Literature*, 13 (1994): 235–91.

_____ 'Forum: On Collaborations II'. *Tulsa Studies in Women's Literature*, 14 (1995): 11–75.

_____ *Women Coauthors*. Urbana, Ill., and Chicago: University of Illinois Press, 2000.

Latour, Bruno. *Science in Action: How to Follow Scientists and Engineers through Society*. Cambridge, Mass.: Harvard University Press, 1987.

Leland, Charles Godfrey. *The Alternate Sex; or The Female Intellect in Man, and the Masculine in Woman*. London: Philip Wellby, 1904.

Levin, David Michael. *The Opening of Vision: Nihilism and Postmodernism*. London: Routledge, 1988.

Levine, Herbert J. *Yeats's Daimonic Renewal*. Ann Arbor: UMI Research Press, 1983.

Lipking, Lawrence. *The Life of the Poet: Beginning and Ending Poetic Careers*. Chicago and London: University of Chicago Press, 1981.

Lloyd, David. *Nationalism and Minor Literature: James Clarence Mangan and the Emergence of Irish Cultural Nationalism*. Berkeley: University of California Press, 1987.

_____ *Anomalous States: Irish Writing and the Post-Colonial Moment*. Dublin: Lilliput, 1993.

Lodge, Sir Oliver J. *Raymond, or Life and Death*. London: Methuen, 1916.

Loizeaux, Elizabeth Bergmann. *Yeats and the Visual Arts*. New Brunswick, NJ: Rutgers University Press, 1986.

London, Bette. *Writing Double: Women's Literary Partnerships*. Ithaca, NY: Cornell University Press, 1999.

Longenbach, James. *Stone Cottage: Pound, Yeats, and Modernism*. Oxford: Oxford University Press, 1988.

MacDowall, James. 'A Collection of Newspaper Cuttings Relating to Spiritualism'. In BL, 1881–92.

McDowell, Colin. ' "The Completed Symbol": *Daimonic* Existence and the Great Wheel in *A Vision* (1937)'. In Warwick Gould (ed.), *Yeats Annual*, vi (London: Macmillan, 1988), 193–208.

McGann, Jerome J. *A Critique of Modern Textual Criticism*. Chicago: University of Chicago Press, 1983.

——— *The Textual Condition*. Princeton: Princeton University Press, 1991.

Maddox, Brenda. *George's Ghosts: A New Life of W. B. Yeats*. London: Picador–Macmillan, 1999.

Magliola, Robert. *Derrida on the Mend*. West Lafayette, Ind.: Purdue University Press, 1984.

Mann, Neil. *The System of W. B. Yeats's A Vision*. 17 October 2004. <http://www.yeatsvision.com>.

Marzilli, Alan S. 'Masking of Truth in W. B. Yeats's *A Vision*: A Comparison of the Two Editions in Relation to the Original Automatic Experience' (M.A. thesis, Emory University, 1993).

Melchior. *The Teaching of Melchior*. London: Herbert Joseph, 1933.

Melchiori, Georgio. *The Whole Mystery of Art*. London: Routledge & Kegan Paul, 1960.

[Moberly, Charlotte Anne, and Jourdain, Eleanor] Morison, Elizabeth, and Lamont, Frances. *An Adventure*. Glasgow: The University Press, 1911.

Moore, Virginia. *The Unicorn: William Butler Yeats' Search for Reality*. New York: Macmillan, 1954.

[Moses, William Stainton]. 'Our Principles and Purposes'. *Light*, 1 (1881): 1.

——— *Spirit Teachings*. London: Psychological Press Association, 1883.

——— *More Spirit Teachings*. London: Spiritualist Press, 1952.

Nouwen, Henri J. M. *Behold the Beauty of the Lord: Praying with Icons*. Notre Dame, Ind.: Ave Maria Press, 1987.

O'Brien, Conor Cruise. 'Passion and Cunning: An Essay on the Politics of W. B. Yeats'. In A. Norman Jeffares and K. G. W. Cross (eds.), *In Excited Reverie: A Centenary Tribute to W. B. Yeats, 1865–1939* (London: Macmillan, 1965), 207–78.

O'Shea, Edward. *A Descriptive Catalog of W. B. Yeats's Library*. New York and London: Garland, 1985.

Oppenheim, Janet. *The Other World: Spiritualism and Psychical Research in England, 1850–1914*. Cambridge: Cambridge University Press, 1985.

Ouspensky, Leonid. *Theology of the Icon*, trans. Anthony Gythiel, 2 vols. Crestwood, NY: St Vladimir's Seminary Press, 1992.

_____ and Lossky, Vladimir. *The Meaning of Icons*, trans. G. E. H. Palmer and E. Kadloubovsky. Crestwood, N.Y.: St Vladimir's Seminary Press, 1983.

Owen, Alex. *The Darkened Room: Women, Power and Spiritualism in Late Victorian England*. Philadelphia: University of Pennsylvania Press, 1990.

_____ 'The Sorcerer and his Apprentice: Aleister Crowley and the Magical Exploration of Edwardian Subjectivity'. *Journal of British Studies*, 36 (1997): 99–133.

_____ *British Occultism and the Culture of the Modern*. Chicago: University of Chicago Press, 2004.

Paracelsus. *His Archidoxes: Comprised in Ten Books, Disclosing the Genuine Way of Making Quintessences, Arcanums, Magisteries, Elixers, &c.*, trans. J. H. [?James Howell], 2 vols. London: printed for W. S., 1661.

Parker, Andrew, and Sedgwick, Eve Kosofsky (eds.). *Performativity and Performance*. New York and London: Routledge, 1995.

Parkes, Graham (ed.). *Heidegger and Asian Thought*. Honolulu: University of Hawaii Press, 1987.

Patrick, David, and Groome, Francis Hindes. *Chambers's Biographical Dictionary*. London: W. & R. Chambers, 1911.

Pearce, Donald. 'Hours with the Domestic Sibyl: Remembering George Yeats'. *Southern Review*, 28 (1992): 485–501.

Perry, Ralph Barton (ed.). *The Thought and Character of William James*, 2 vols. Boston: Little, Brown, 1935.

Pethica, James. ' "Our Kathleen": Yeats's Collaboration with Lady Gregory in the Writing of *Cathleen ni Houlihan*'. In Warwick Gould (ed.), *Yeats Annual*, vi (London: Macmillan, 1988), 3–31.

Pierce, David. *Yeats's Worlds: Ireland, England, and the Poetic Imagination*. New Haven and London: Yale University Press, 1995.

Pound, Omar, and Litz, A. Walton (eds.). *Ezra Pound and Dorothy Shakespear: Their Letters 1909–1914*. New York: New Directions, 1984.

Price, Harry. *Short-Title Catalogue of Works on Psychical Research, Spiritualism, Magic, Psychology, Legerdemain and Other Methods of Deception,*

Charlatanism, Witchcraft, and Technical Works for the Scientific Investigation of Alleged Abnormal Phenomena from circa 1450 A.D. to 1929 A.D. London: The National Laboratory of Psychical Research, 1929.

Rabaté, Jean-Michel. *The Ghosts of Modernity.* Gainesville, Fla.: University Press of Florida, 1996.

Raine, Kathleen. *Blake and Tradition*, 2 vols. London: Routledge & Kegan Paul, 1969.

——— *Yeats the Initiate: Essays on Certain Themes in the Writings of W. B. Yeats.* Mountrath, Ireland: Dolmen Press, 1986.

Rajan, Balachandra. *W. B. Yeats: A Critical Introduction.* London: Hutchinson, 1965.

Ramayandas, Swami S. D. *Mediumship: Its Laws and Phenomena.* London: L. N. Fowler, [?1927].

[Raupert, John G. F.] A Member of the Society for Psychical Research. *The Dangers of Spiritualism: Being Records of Personal Experiences, with Notes and Comments and Five Illustrations.* London: Sands, 1901.

Regardie, Israel. *The Tree of Life: A Study in Magic.* York Beach, Me.: Samuel Weiser, 1972.

——— *What You Should Know about the Golden Dawn.* Phoenix, Ariz.: Falcon Press, 1985.

——— *The Golden Dawn: A Complete Course in Practical Ceremonial Magic. Four Volumes in One. The Original Account of the Teachings, Rites and Ceremonies of the Hermetic Order of the Golden Dawn (Stella Matutina)*, 6th edn., 2 vols. St Paul, Minn.: Llewellyn Publications, 1989.

Reid, B. L. *The Man from New York: John Quinn and his Friends.* New York: Oxford University Press, 1968.

Rich, Viola Gertrude. *Thought Radio and Thought Transference.* New York: Elizabeth Towne, 1927.

Richards, Ivor Armstrong. *Science and Poetry.* London: Kegan Paul, 1926.

Riquelme, John Paul. 'The Female Collaborator: Issues of Property and Authorship in Bram Stoker's *Dracula* and the Yeatses' *A Vision*' (Paper presented at the Modern Language Association, Chicago, 2000).

Roach, Joseph. *Cities of the Dead: Circum-Atlantic Performance.* New York: Columbia University Press, 1996.

——— 'History, Memory, Necrophilia'. In Peggy Phelan and Jill Lane (eds.), *The Ends of Performance* (New York and London: New York University Press, 1998), 23–30.

Ryle, Gilbert. *The Concept of Mind*. London: Hutchinson's University Library, 1949.

Saddlemyer, Ann. 'George Hyde Lees: More than a Poet's Wife'. In A. Norman Jeffares (ed.), *Yeats the European*, (Gerrards Cross: Colin Smythe, 1989), 191–200.

_____ 'George, Ezra, Dorothy and Friends: Twenty-Six Letters, 1918–59'. In Warwick Gould (ed.), *Yeats Annual*, vii (London: Macmillan, 1990), 4–28.

_____ 'Looking for Georgie: Research Still in Progress' (Paper presented at the Annual Meeting of the Modern Language Association, Chicago, 28 December 1990).

_____ 'Reading Yeats's "A Prayer for My Daughter"—Yet Again' (Paper presented at the International Association for the Study of Anglo-Irish Literature, Otani, Japan, 1990).

_____ *Becoming George: The Life of Mrs W. B. Yeats*. Oxford: Oxford University Press, 2002.

Said, Edward. 'Yeats and Decolonization'. In Seamus Deane (ed.), *Nationalism, Colonialism and Literature* (Minneapolis: University of Minnesota Press, 1990), 69–95.

Sartre, Jean-Paul. *Being and Nothingness: An Essay on Phenomenological Ontology*, trans. Hazel Barnes. New York: Philosophical Library, 1956.

Saunders, David. *Authorship and Copyright*. London: Routledge, 1992.

Savran, David. 'The Haunted Houses of Modernity'. *Modern Drama*, 43 (2000): 583–94.

Schechner, Richard. *Between Theater and Anthropology*. Philadelphia: University of Pennsylvania Press, 1985.

Schleifer, Ronald. *Analogical Thinking: Post-Enlightenment Understanding in Language, Collaboration, and Interpretation*. Ann Arbor: University of Michigan Press, 2000.

_____ *Modernism and Time: The Logic of Abundance in Literature, Science, and Culture, 1880–1930*. Cambridge: Cambridge University Press, 2000.

Schuchard, Ronald. 'Hawk and Butterfly: The Double Vision of *The Wild Swans at Coole*'. In Warwick Gould (ed.) *Yeats Annual*, x (London: Macmillan, 1993), 111–34.

Scott, Walter. *Letters on Demonology and Witchcraft, Addressed to J. G. Lockhart, Esq.* London: John Murray, 1830.

Scott, Walter. (ed. with trans. and notes). *Hermetica: The Ancient Greek and Latin Writings which Contain Religious or Philosophic Teachings Ascribed to Hermes Trismegistus*, 2 vols. Oxford: Clarendon Press, 1925.

Seiden, M. I. *William Butler Yeats: The Poet as a Mythmaker*. East Lansing, Mich.: Michigan State University Press, 1962.

Shillingsburg, Peter. *Resisting Texts: Authority and Submission in Constructions of Meaning*. Ann Arbor: University of Michigan Press, 1997.

Sidnell, Michael J. *Yeats's Poetry and Poetics*. London: Macmillan, 1996.

Simonton, Deborah. *A History of European Women's Work, 1700 to the Present*. London and New York: Routledge, 1998.

Smith, Hester Travers. *Voices from the Void: Six Years' Experience in Automatic Communications*. London: W. Rider, 1919.

_____ *Psychic Messages from Oscar Wilde*. London: T. Werner Laurie, 1923.

Spender, Stephen. Review of *A Vision*. *The Criterion*, 17 (1938): 536–7.

Spivak, Gayatri Chakravorty. 'Can the Subaltern Speak?' In Cary Nelson and Lawrence Grossberg (eds.), *Marxism and the Interpretation of Culture* (Urbana, Ill.: University of Illinois Press, 1988), 271–313.

Stairs Project. *The Heavenly Doctrines*. Academy of the New Church, 2004. <http://www.theheavenlydoctrines.org>.

Stead, William T. 'My Experience in Automatic Writing: The Story of "Julia", and Others'. *Borderland*, 1 (1893): 39–49.

_____ 'More about Automatic Writing: The Experiences of Three Other Writers'. *Borderland*, 1 (1894): 166–9.

_____ *Letters from Julia, or Light from the Borderland: A Series of Messages as to the Life beyond the Grave Received by Automatic Writing from One who has Gone Before*. London: Grant Richards, 1898.

Sterne, Jonathan. *The Audible Past: Cultural Origins of Sound Reproduction*. Durham, N.C., and London: Duke University Press, 2003.

Stillinger, Jack. *Multiple Authorship and the Myth of Solitary Genius*. New York: Oxford University Press, 1991.

Stoddard, Roger E. *Marks in Books, Illustrated and Explained*. Cambridge, Mass.: Houghton Library, Harvard University, 1985.

Stoker, Bram. *Dracula*, ed. John Paul Riquelme. Case Studies in Contemporary Criticism. New York: Palgrave, 2002.

Suárez, Juan A. 'T. S. Eliot's *The Waste Land*, the Gramophone, and the Modernist Discourse Network'. *New Literary History*, 32 (2000): 747–68.

Surette, Leon. *The Birth of Modernism: Ezra Pound, T. S. Eliot, W. B. Yeats, and the Occult*. Montreal: McGill–Queen's University Press, 1993.

Sword, Helen. *Ghostwriting Modernism*. Ithaca, NY: Cornell University Press, 2002.

Tambiah, Stanley Jeyaraja. *Magic, Science, Religion, and the Scope of Rationality*. Cambridge: Cambridge University Press, 1990.

Taylor, Mark C. *nOts*. Chicago and London: University of Chicago Press, 1993.

Taylor, Richard (ed.). *Frank Pearce Sturm: His Life, Letters, and Collected Work*. Urbana, Ill., and London: University of Illinois Press, 1969.

Torgovnick, Marianna. *Gone Primitive: Savage Intellects, Modern Lives*. Chicago and London: University of Chicago Press, 1990.

Tweedale, Rev. Charles L. 'Electrical Conditions and Psychic Phenomena: A Suggestion'. *Light*, 37 (1917): 10.

Vendler, Helen Hennessy. *Yeats's* Vision *and the Later Plays*. Cambridge, Mass.: Harvard University Press, 1963.

Wade, Allan. *A Bibliography of the Writings of W. B. Yeats*, 2nd edn. London: Rupert Hart-Davis, 1958.

Waite, Arthur Edward. *Lives of Alchemystical Philosophers*. London: W. Foulsham, [1888].

Wallace, Alfred Russel. *On Miracles and Modern Spiritualism: Three Essays*. London: James Burns, 1875.

Wallis, E. W., and Wallis, M. H. *A Guide to Mediumship, and Psychical Unfoldment*. London: Friars Printing Association, [1903].

Washington, Peter. *Madame Blavatsky's Baboon: Theosophy and the Emergence of the Western Guru*. London: Secker & Warburg, 1993.

Whitaker, Thomas R. *Swan and Shadow: Yeats's Dialogue with History*. Washington: Catholic University of America Press, 1989.

Wicke, Jennifer. 'Vampiric Typewriting: Dracula and its Media'. In John Paul Riquelme (ed.), *Dracula* (New York: Palgrave, 2002), 577–99.

Williams, C. *Spiritualism and Insanity: An Essay Describing the Disastrous Consequences to the Mental Health which are Apt to Result from a Pursuit of the Study of Spiritualism*. London: Ambrose, [1910].

Williams, John Peregrine. 'The Making of Victorian Psychical Research: An Intellectual Élite's Approach to the Spiritual World' (Ph.D. diss., University of Cambridge, 1984).

Williams, Raymond. *Marxism and Literature*. Oxford: Oxford University Press, 1977.

Wilson, Frances. *Literary Seductions: Compulsive Writers and Diverted Readers*. London: Faber, 1999.

Wolfreys, Julian. *Victorian Hauntings: Spectrality, Gothic, the Uncanny and Literature*. London: Palgrave, 2002.

Woodmansee, Martha. 'The Genius and the Copyright: Economic and Legal Conditions of the Emergence of the "Author"'. *Eighteenth-Century Studies*, 17 (1984): 425–48.

—— and Jaszi, Peter (eds.). *The Construction of Authorship: Textual Appropriation in Law and Literature*. Durham, NC: Duke University Press, 1994.

Yeats, W. B. *The Green Helmet and Other Poems*. Dundrum: Cuala Press, 1910.

—— *Reveries over Childhood and Youth*. Dundrum: Cuala Press, 1915.

—— *Michael Robartes and the Dancer*. Dublin: Cuala Press, 1921.

—— *The Trembling of the Veil*. London: Werner Laurie, 1922.

—— *A Vision*. London: T. Werner Laurie, 1926.

—— *A Packet for Ezra Pound*. Dublin: Cuala Press, 1929.

—— *The King of the Great Clock Tower*. Dublin: Cuala Press, 1934.

—— *A Vision*. London: Macmillan, 1937.

—— *Letters on Poetry from W. B. Yeats to Dorothy Wellesley*, ed. Dorothy Wellesley. London: Oxford University Press, 1940.

—— *Pages from a Diary Written in Nineteen Hundred and Thirty*. Dublin: Cuala Press, 1944.

—— *The Letters of W. B. Yeats*, ed. Allan Wade. New York: Macmillan, 1955.

—— *The Variorum Edition of the Poems of W. B. Yeats*, ed. Peter Allt and Russell K. Alspach. New York: Macmillan, 1957.

—— *Mythologies*. London: Macmillan, 1959.

—— *Essays and Introductions*. London: Macmillan, 1961.

—— *Explorations*. London: Macmillan, 1962.

—— *The Variorum Edition of the Plays of W. B. Yeats*, ed. Russel K. Alspach. New York: Macmillan, 1966.

—— *Memoirs: Autobiography—First Draft, Journal*, ed. Denis Donoghue. London: Macmillan, 1972.

—— *A Critical Edition of Yeats's* A Vision *(1925)*, ed. George Mills Harper and Walter K. Hood. London: Macmillan, 1978.

—— *Collected Letters*, i: 1865–1895, ed. John Kelly and Eric Domville, gen. ed. John Kelly. Oxford: Clarendon Press, 1986.

_____ *Collected Letters*, ii: 1896–1900, ed. Warwick Gould, John Kelly, and Deirdre Toomey, gen. ed. John Kelly. Oxford: Clarendon Press, 1997.

_____ *Collected Letters*, iii: 1901–1904, ed. John Kelly and Ronald Schuchard, gen. ed. John Kelly. Oxford: Clarendon Press, 1994.

_____ *Collected Letters*, iv: 1905–1907, ed. John Kelly and Ronald Schuchard, gen. ed. John Kelly. Oxford: Oxford University Press, 2005.

_____ *Yeats's* Vision *Papers*, i, ed. Steve L. Adams, Barbara J. Frieling, and Sandra L. Sprayberry, gen. ed. George Mills Harper, London: Macmillan, 1992.

_____ *Yeats's* Vision *Papers*, ii, ed. Steve L. Adams, Barbara J. Frieling, and Sandra L. Sprayberry, gen. ed. George Mills Harper, London: Macmillan, 1992.

_____ *Yeats's* Vision *Papers*, iii, ed. Robert Anthony Martinich and Margaret Mills Harper, gen. ed. George Mills Harper, London: Macmillan, 1992.

_____ *Yeats's* Vision *Papers*, iv, ed. George Mills Harper and Margaret Mills Harper, gen. ed. George Mills Harper, London: Macmillan, 2001.

_____ *Michael Robartes and the Dancer: Manuscript Materials*, ed. Thomas Parkinson. The Cornell Yeats. Ithaca, N.Y., and London: Cornell University Press, 1994.

_____ *Last Poems: Manuscript Materials*, ed. James Pethica. The Cornell Yeats. Ithaca, N.Y., and London: Cornell University Press, 1997.

_____ *Autobiographies*, ed. William H. O'Donnell and Douglas N. Archibald. In *Collected Works of W. B. Yeats*, gen. eds. Richard J. Finneran and George Mills Harper. New York: Scribner, 1999.

_____ *The Speckled Bird: An Autobiographical Novel, with Variant Versions*, ed. William H. O'Donnell. London: Palgrave Macmillan, 2003.

York, Lorraine Mary. *Rethinking Women's Collaborative Writing: Power, Difference, Property*. Toronto: University of Toronto Press, 2002.

Young, George P. *The Soul's Deepest Questions: An Introduction to Spiritual Philosophy*. Halifax: The Spiritualists' National Union, 1909.

_____ 'The Attitude of Science Toward Psychic Phenomena'. In *Essays on Spiritualism* (Halifax: The Spiritualists' National Union, 1910), 21–36.

Zimmeck, Meta. 'Jobs for the Girls: The Expansion of Clerical Work for Women, 1850–1914'. In Angela V. John (ed.), *Unequal Opportunities: Women's Employment in England 1800–1918* (Oxford: Basil Blackwell, 1986), 153–77.

Žižck, Slavoj. 'Introduction: The Spectre of Ideology'. In *idem* (ed.), *Mapping Ideology* (London: Verso, 1994), 1–33.

Index